MW01057132

NUTRITION COUNSELING IN THE TREATMENT OF EATING DISORDERS

Marcia Herrin and Maria Larkin have collaborated on the second edition of *Nutrition Counseling in the Treatment of Eating Disorders,* infusing research-based approaches and their own clinically-refined tools for managing food and weight-related issues. New to this edition is a section on nutrition counseling interventions derived from cognitive-behavioral therapy-enhanced dialectical behavioral therapy, family-based treatment, and motivational interviewing techniques. Readers will appreciate the state of the art nutrition and weight assessment guidelines, the practical clinical techniques for managing bingeing, purging, excessive exercise, and weight restoration, as well as the unique food planning approach developed by the authors. As a comprehensive overview of food- and weight-related treatments, this book is an indispensible resource for nutrition counselors, psychotherapists, psychiatrists, physicians, and primary care providers.

Marcia Herrin, EdD, MPH, RD, LD, is the founder of Dartmouth College's eating disorders program. She has worked in the area of eating disorders since 1987 and is co-author of *The Parent's Guide to Eating Disorders.* Dr Herrin is a frequent presenter at conferences and offers supervision for other professionals. She has a private practice in Lebanon, New Hampshire.

Maria Larkin, MEd, RD, LD, is head of nutrition counseling at the University of New Hampshire and also has a private practice in Durham, New Hampshire. Larkin has a master's degree in counseling with a specialization in eating disorders. As a writer and workshop presenter, she has worked in the field of nutrition for over 30 years and specialized in eating disorders for over 10 years.

NUTRITION COUNSELING IN THE TREATMENT OF EATING DISORDERS

Second Edition

MARCIA HERRIN AND MARIA LARKIN

Routledge
Taylor & Francis Group
NEW YORK AND LONDON

First published 2013
by Routledge
711 Third Avenue, New York, NY 10017

Simultaneously published in the UK
by Routledge
27 Church Road, Hove, East Sussex BN3 2FA

Routledge is an imprint of the Taylor & Francis Group, an informa business

Library of Congress Cataloging in Publication Data
    Herrin, Marcia. Nutrition counseling in the treatment of eating disorders /
    Marcia Herrin & Maria Larkin.–2nd ed.p. cm.
    Includes bibliographical references and index.
    1. Eating disorders–Patients–Counseling of.
    2. Eating disorders–Treatment. 3. Eating disorders–Diet therapy.
    4. Nutrition. I. Larkin, Maria. II. Title.
    RC552.E18H47 2012616.85'2606–dc23
    2012020237

ISBN: 978–0–415–87103–7 (hbk)
ISBN: 978-0-415-64257-6 (pbk)
ISBN: 978-0-203-87060-0 (ebk)

Typeset in Bembo
by Swales & Willis Ltd, Exeter, Devon

To my grandmother, Catherine Giudici Burke, in loving memory.
  Marcia Herrin

To my father, Giovanni Salvatore Miccio, for believing in me.
  Maria Larkin

CONTENTS

PREFACE

We recognize the world is a changing place. Indeed, there are few constants in life. This truth has permeated our experience over the last two and a half years as we have laboriously researched and written this book. As our book underwent a transformation from the first edition to this new second edition, as new references replaced the old, and as chapters were renamed, reorganized and updated, we simultaneously observed many developments in the field of nutrition and eating disorders. In the last few months, the American Dietetic Association (ADA) changed its name to the Academy of Nutrition and Dietetics (AND) and produced its first position statement on and standards of practice for the treatment of eating disorders. Recently, the American Psychiatric Association (APA) proposed the DSM-5, new revisions to the DSM-IV diagnostic criteria for eating disorders.

We even hesitate to say our book is finished, as research in the field of eating disorders is emerging by leaps and bounds. Two days before our book deadline, while opening her mail, Larkin found in the *Journal of the Academy of Nutrition and Dietetics* (formerly the *Journal of the American Dietetic Association*), a new research study and shared it with Herrin over the phone. The next day Herrin applied the research information in a counseling session with a patient. This example of applied research is just one of many that occurred during the course of our researching and writing of this book. In fact, we feel the strength of our book lies in our research-based recommendations and in our successful application of information that has, time after time, improved outcomes for our patients. As a result of writing this book, we have become more skilled and knowledgeable about nutrition counseling in the treatment of eating disorders. Yet, we still consider ourselves students—less "green" than before (Larkin's masters program used the first edition as a text)—and still learning from our patients, colleagues, and researchers in the field.

Waterhous and Jacob remind us in their excellently written practice paper, *Nutrition Intervention in the Treatment of Eating Disorders*, "There is no professional consensus on how to restore weight and health in AN or stop binge and purge behaviors in BN or halt the eating disorder thoughts common to both" (Waterhous & Jacob, 2011, p. 1). And so, in this second edition, we offer not only our knowledge, skills, and insights but also pertinent techniques from cognitive-behavioral therapy-enhanced dialectical behavioral therapy, family-based treatment, and motivational interviewing techniques. Although we are not credentialed psychotherapists, we are skilled nutrition counselors and registered dietitians who garner from the evidence-based field of psychotherapy as well as from the field of nutrition that which is instructive to our patients. We have provided here detailed, clinically-oriented guidelines for assessing and monitoring weights and for weight restoration in the eating-disordered patient. We added to this edition a chapter on family-based treatment and levels of care for eating disorder treatment.

We hope the reader (nutrition counselors, psychotherapists, cognitive behaviorists, psychiatrists, physicians, and primary care providers, or whoever you may be) will benefit from the techniques, literature reviews, and clinical accounts we present in this book. We highlight these clinical accounts as case examples throughout the book. One remarkable account is the story of Annie. Annie marked each month of abstinence from bulimic behaviors with a piece of artwork. One month, she brought in a dramatic drawing of an eagle landing on a dinner plate, a fork and knife in its talons (Figure 0.1). For Annie the eagle represented aspects of her recovery. Initially, eating was frighteningly like a fierce eagle, but as she progressed, eating became a powerful eagle-like force for recovery. Her transformation and the hard work, bravery, and dedication of all our patients who struggle to recover from eating disorders are the inspiration behind the writing of this book.

Marcia Herrin, EdD, MPH, RD, LD
Maria Larkin, MEd, RD, LD

FIGURE 0.1   A Reproduction of Annie's Drawing of an Eagle Landing on a Dinner plate.

PART I
Nutrition Counseling

1

CLINICAL FEATURES OF EATING DISORDERS

Introduction

Eating disorders (EDs) are biologically-based mental disorders classified and defined in the American Psychiatric Association's *Diagnostic and Statistical Manual of Mental Disorders* (DSM-IV; American Psychiatric Association, 2000). This chapter relies on the DSM-IV and the soon to be published next edition of the *Diagnostic and Statistical Manual of Mental Disorders* (DSM-5). We conclude this chapter with a discussion of the most significant of the proposed DSM-5 criteria for EDs.

The diagnostic criteria for anorexia nervosa (AN), bulimia nervosa (BN), binge-eating disorder (BED), and eating disorder not otherwise specified (EDNOS) are based on psychological, behavioral, and physiological characteristics with the same core features: overvaluation of shape and weight and serious disturbances in eating behaviors. The severity of EDs increases over time, and individuals with EDs have significantly elevated mortality rates, especially those with AN due to associated medical complications or suicide (Arcelus, Mitchell, Wales, & Nielsen, 2011). Like other psychiatric illnesses, EDs have a strong heritability factor, as emerging studies identify chromosomal regions and genes for AN. Twin studies confirm that approximately 50–70% of risk factors for ED are heritable. A family history of an ED, obesity, or anxiety, and depression increases risk. Individuals with a diagnosis of anxiety, depression, post-traumatic stress disorder (PTSD), obsessive–compulsive disorder (OCD), and attention deficit/hyperactivity disorder (ADHD) also have an increased risk (Mehler & Andersen, 2010). (See Chapter 3: The Process of Counseling for more information on these disorders, pp. 59–78.)

The highest onset of AN and BN is during adolescence in westernized societies which value thinness. BED occurs into adulthood, with a growing trend among overweight and obese middle-aged women (Ozier & Henry, 2011; Walsh, 2011).

A recent study by Marques et al. (2011) compared the prevalence of EDs across all major ethnic minority groups in the United States. The study confirmed that the lifetime prevalence of AN and BED is similar for all major ethnicities (American African, Asian, Hispanic, and non-Hispanic Whites). BN, however, has higher prevalence rates among Latinos and African Americans. A number of studies indicate that bisexual and gay men are at a higher risk for EDs than heterosexual men. One population-based study (Feldman & Meyer, 2007) found that 15% of gay or bisexual men had at some time suffered from disordered eating, AN, BN or BED compared to less than 5% of heterosexual men. These researchers reported no differences in rates of ED between lesbian, bisexual women, and heterosexual women. Nevertheless, studies of the prevalence of EDs show them to be relatively uncommon, as illustrated in Table 1.1, in part because they are frequently underreported and undertreated.

In both AN and BN, alterations in brain structure and function as well endocrine abnormalities contribute to many of the clinical features of EDs we describe in this chapter. These clinical features are not only disabling but come with significant medical and social costs. For example, women with AN have higher rates of pregnancy complications than women without an ED, and have higher healthcare utilization than those with other forms of mental illness (Klump, Bulik, Kaye, Treasure, & Tyson, 2009). It is important to recognize the unique eating-disordered characteristics of special populations such as pregnant women. Table 1.2 describes these populations and clinical features. In addition two tables are included to define the classic clinical features of AN, BN, and BED. We further elaborate on the major complications of EDs we find useful for the assessment and treatment (including making medical referrals) as well as for the purposes of psycho-education. We end this chapter by introducing the proposed DSM-5 criteria for EDs and comparing it to the DSM-IV.

Features of Anorexia Nervosa

In western societies, AN afflicts from one-third to 3% of women and is the third most prevalent chronic disease afflicting adolescent girls. Males and older women are affected, but at lower rates. There are two subtypes of AN: restricting and binge/purge. The binge/purge subtype is distinguished from BN by low weight.

TABLE 1.1 Lifetime Prevalence of Eating Disorders in the United States

	Men	Women
AN	.3%	.9%
BN	.5%	1.5%
BED	2%	3.5%

Note. Adapted from "Position of the American Dietetic Association: Nutrition Intervention in the Treatment of Eating Disorders," by Amy D. Ozier and Beverly W. Henry, 2011, *Journal of the American Dietetic Association*, 111, p. 1237. Copyright 2011 by American Dietetic Association. Adapted with permission.

TABLE 1.2 Characteristics of Special Populations at Risk for Eating Disorders

Risk factor	Medical or lay term★	Characteristics
Type I diabetes mellitus (DM)	Diabulemia★ Diabetic EDO patients: (Mathieu, 2008)	Intentionally omit insulin in an attempt to lose weight or compensate for a binge. Higher rates of premature diabetic complications and hemoglobin A1c levels. Hyperglycemia results from omission of insulin or binge eating. Most common in BN.
Type II DM		Most common in EDNOS and BED. ED often is undetected because symptoms of DM and ED show similar features.
Athletics	Female athlete triad (FAT)	FAT: Low energy availability, menstrual irregularities, and low bone density.
	Anorexia athletica★ (AA)	AA: Female athletes who exercise beyond what is necessary for good health, with extreme focus on weight and diet. Exercise becomes a burden, does not satisfy performance goals, and takes up too much time.
Pregnancy	Pregorexia★	Fear of normal expected weight gain during pregnancy results in reducing calories and increasing exercise.
Food allergies or intolerances	Gluten-free or lactose-free diets	Food avoidance, food fears.
Middle age and menopause		Normative age-related changes and biological shifts may increase body dissatisfaction and disordered eating. Evidence is unclear whether body mass index (BMI), age, or menopause are responsible (Slevec & Tiggeman, 2011).
College students	Drunkorexia★, beer bulimia★	Calorie restriction prior to consumption of alcohol to avoid weight gain. Purging after drinking to get rid of calories.
Vegetarian and vegans		High prevalence of veganism and vegetarianism in disordered-eating and ED populations (Sullivan & Damani, 2000).
Interest in health and nutrition	Orthorexia★	Obsession with healthy eating versus the desire to be thin. Anxiety with eating that impacts quality of life.
Obesity		BED leads to obesity; BED is associated with dieting in the obese; 30% BED in obese patients (Freitas, Lopes, Appolinario, & Coutinho, 2006); 30–60% of BED patients are obese (de Zwann, 2010; Dingemans & van Furth, 2012).
Hypoglycemia		Hypoglycemia can indicate undereating or overexercise.

TABLE 1.2 (continued)

Risk factor	Medical or lay term★	Characteristics
Ematophobia		Avoids certain foods due to fear of choking or vomiting
Picky eating	Food avoidance emotional disorder (FAED) (Bravender et al., 2007).	Avoidance of food to a marked degree in the absence of the characteristic psychopathology of eating disorders.

Many individuals with the restricting subtype develop purging or binge-eating symptoms, with more than 50% developing bulimic behaviors (Mehler & Andersen, 2010).

A markedly low weight is a unique feature of AN and sets the stage for the clinical complications we discuss below. Individuals with AN characteristically restrict food intake due to an intense fear of weight gain, resulting in an extremely low body weight and symptoms of starvation. They may count calories, weigh themselves obsessively, have body distortion, and see their bodies as bigger than they actually are. Individuals with AN typically tend to be sensitive, perfectionist, and self-critical. We have a number of AN patients who are writers and poets; those who are students do well academically, but feel socially isolated.

Factors that increase an individual's risk for developing AN consist of teasing or criticism about body size and shape, especially from peers, parents, significant others, or coaches. Other risk factors include: unintentional weight loss, military or sport weight standards, obesity at menarche, trauma or abuse, and a desire to improve athletic performance. The "female athlete triad" is characterized by disordered eating, menstrual irregularity, and loss of bone density, and is seen in competitive female athletes in sports such as running, ballet dancing, cycling and swimming (Ozier & Henry, 2011). (See Chapter 12: Managing Exercise, pp. 260–276.)

Clinical Complications of Anorexia Nervosa

Cardiac Function

Underweight AN patients are at risk for cardiovascular and neurological repercussions. The most serious of these are the electrocardiographic abnormalities that can signal the risk of sudden death. AN patients may experience chest pain indicative of mitral value prolapse as the heart reduces in size. Mitral value prolapse occurs in 30–50% of patients with severe AN (Mehler & Andersen, 2010, pp. 131–132). This condition is not usually medically dangerous, but as a precaution, patients should be medically assessed for signs of heart failure.

When caloric intake is extremely inadequate, the body adapts by losing cardiac muscle in an attempt to preserve other muscle. As a result, blood pressure drops and the likelihood of cardiac failure increases. Patients with heart rates below 40 beats/minute should be under close medical supervision. The following symptoms indicate cardiac impairment: weakness, dizziness, cognitive impairment, overall fatigue, and light-headedness on standing or changing positions (e.g., moving from lying down to sitting; Mehler & Andersen, 2010, pp. 131–132). If our patients complain of these symptoms, we express concern and inform the patient's medical practitioner immediately. If the patient also has low blood pressure and feels light-headed, he or she might need hospitalization. With refeeding and weight restoration, cardiac structure and function as well as exercise capacity return to normal without long-term consequences (Mont et al., 2003; Mehler & Andersen, 2010, p. 133).

Hormonal Changes

Many of the physical signs and symptoms in AN are the result of endocrine dysfunction (i.e., hypothalamic–pituitary dysregulation, hypothalamic amenorrhea, and hypothalamic–pituitary adrenal axis dysregulation). For example, sensitivity to cold, hypotension, and low heart rate indicate hypothyroidism. These symptoms are ameliorated with weight restoration and without the need for thyroid medications (Mehler & Andersen, 2010). Diminished libido may be the result of reduced androgen levels and, in men, low testosterone.

In AN, amenorrhea, also called hypothalamic or functional amenorrhea, occurs in some but not all patients, as there is a highly variable "individual susceptibility of the gonadal axis to undernutrition" (Miller, 2011, p. 2939). Further, amenorrhea may be masked by the use of prescription medications used for birth control. Hypothalamic amenorrhea reflects a state of estrogen deficiency, which can occur with dieting, with excess exercise, and with or without significant weight loss (Mehler, Cleary, & Gaudiani, 2011). Although no longer recommended as a diagnostic test, estrogen deficiency is sometimes assessed by a progestin challenge test. Withdrawal bleeding within 10 days of the challenge indicates that amenorrhea is caused by an estrogen deficiency. A lack of withdrawal bleeding, on the other hand, demonstrates a more profound estrogen deficiency or possibly an unrelated medical problem. It is now well accepted that the prescription of estrogen–progesterone medications do not result in clinical improvements in bone mineral density (BMD; Mehler & Andersen, 2010, p. 143). Of note, a person with amenorrhea can become pregnant, but with active AN, ovulation is unlikely. We refer the reader to as an excellent general reference, Mehler and Andersen's (2010) book, *Eating Disorders: A Guide to Medical Care and Complications,* for detailed guidelines for testing and treatment of hormone abnormalities secondary to EDs. Table 1.3 outlines the general endocrine changes seen in AN (Mehler & Andersen, 2010, p. 163; Miller, 2011, pp. 2939–2949, Table 3).

TABLE 1.3 Changes in Hormone Levels in Anorexia Nervosa

Hormone	Change in hormone levels
Gonadal hormones	Decrease in estrogen (females) and testosterone (males). Decrease in luteinizing hormone (LH) pulsatility.
Adrenal	Increase in plasma cortisol.
Growth hormones	Decrease in insulin-like growth factor-1 (IGF-1). Increased or normal fasting growth hormone (GH). Decrease in serum growth-hormone-binding protein (GHBP).
Appetite-regulating hormones	Decrease in leptin. Increase in grehlin. Increase in peptide YY (PYY).
Cholesterol	May be increased.
Glucose	Decrease in fasting blood sugar.
Thyroid hormones	Low or low normal thyroxine (T4) and triiodothyronine (T3). Normal thyroid stimulating hormone (TSH). Increase in reverse T3.

Bone Health

The endocrine alterations described above contribute to low BMD in AN (Miller, 2011). As a result, osteoporosis, characterized by loss of bone density and deterioration of the structure of bone, is common. Although the research is mixed, it appears possible that some individuals may recover from osteoporosis, while others will have only partial improvement in BMD despite resumption of hormone levels and weight restoration (Olmos et al., 2010). In both osteopenia and osteoporosis, bones become less dense and more fragile, but rarely is there any pain.

Achieving peak bone mass is important for preventing osteoporosis. On average, 90% of peak bone mass is acquired by the age of 19 years (Bogunovic, Doyle, & Vogiatzi, 2009). As a consequence, adolescence marks a critical period on which a lifetime of bone health is dependent. Failure to achieve peak bone mass is associated with an increased risk of osteoporosis and fracture in adulthood (Bogunovic et al., 2009). Adolescent girls with AN do not experience the usual linear increase in bone mass during puberty (Miller, 2011).

In addition, loss of BMD is thought to occur quickly and early in the course of AN. Significant losses occur in as little as six months of amenorrhea-associated with AN (Mehler & MacKenzie, 2009). But, conventional dual energy x-ray (DEXA) scans do not detect early loss of bone volume and trabecular thickness in adolescents (Miller, 2011). Both duration of amenorrhea and body mass index (BMI) predict bone density. Mehler et al. (2011) predict that BMI less than 15 and six months of amenorrhea are prognostic of significant loss of BMD.

Osteopenia occurs in 92% and osteoporosis in 40% of women with AN (Mehler, 2011). More than 50% of AN patients present with osteopenia at the time of diagnosis (Munoz & Argente, 2002). In normal populations, osteopenia is infrequently diagnosed before the age 50, at which point most people begin to lose

0.5% of BMD every year. The type of bone loss associated with AN is unique and is considered more damaging than that induced by menopause (Mehler et al., 2011). Males with AN often have more severe bone loss than females with a similar course of illness (Mehler, Sabel, Watson, & Andersen, 2008).

Individuals with osteoporosis are at greater risk for fracture even with a small trauma and have a higher lifetime risk for future fractures. The bones most affected are the hip, spine, and wrist. Advanced osteoporosis can lead to loss of height, stooped posture, humpback, and severe pain if fractures occur. Bone fractures occur in more than 40% of individuals with long-term AN. Biller's classic study found AN lasting 5 years leads to an annual fracture rate seven times greater than that of healthy women (Biller, Saxe, Herzog, Rosenthal, Holzman, & Klibanski, 1989).

The etiology of bone loss in AN is multifactorial. Low body weight, depleted fat cell mass (less than 10%), and the deficiency of estrogen and progesterone that occurs with amenorrhea all increase bone resorption and decrease bone formation. Young women with estrogen deficiency may lose bone mass at a rate of 3–5%/year. Other hormonal disturbances involved in bone formation are affected in AN, namely, low testosterone levels, low insulin-like growth factor-1 (IGF-1) levels and excess cortisol secretion (Mehler et al., 2011). Increased levels of ghrelin and Y peptide along with changes in leptin and endocannabinoid levels also affect bone formation and resorption (Horst-Sikorska & Ignaszak-Szczepaniak, 2011; Mehler et al., 2011). Although both recovery of menses and normalized weight improve BMD, the strongest indicator is normalization of menses (Miller, 2011).

There are currently no evidenced-based research studies for the treatment of osteoporosis in AN. The results of trials with hormonal therapies (estrogen and contraceptives) and bisphosphonates have been either unclear or the therapies have been found to be ineffective these patients. Most studies use adult subjects, but data from adult studies cannot easily be applied to adolescents, who are at greatest risk of osteoporosis. Individuals, who take contraceptive hormones or have had withdrawal bleeding with a progestin challenge, often have a false sense of recovery and strengthened denial of their illness.

Gastrointestinal Problems

Gastrointestinal symptoms are very common in individuals with AN and are often misdiagnosed as irritable bowel syndrome rather than recognized as symptomatic of an ED. Some gastrointestinal disturbances may cause permanent damage to the gut even after the ED has resolved. Gastrointestinal complications in AN patients are known to impede treatment and recovery by perpetuating and reinforcing disordered eating behaviors.

Gastrointestinal symptoms in both AN and BN individuals are considered by most medical experts to be a direct result of the hypometabolic state of chronic starvation in addition to the gastrointestinal disturbances caused by binging and purging. For instance, delayed gastric emptying is well documented in AN. Researchers speculate starvation and protein malnutrition causes smooth muscle atrophy in the gastrointestinal tract, affecting gastric emptying and intestinal transit time. Others hypothesize that gastric dysrhythmias occur because of AN, contributing to delays in gastric emptying. Symptoms of delayed gastric emptying include: early satiety, bloating, and abdominal distention. These symptoms may make patients "feel fat" and curtail food intake further, or trigger purging or laxative abuse. Bloating is often the most severe for AN individuals who consume vegetarian diets high in fiber.

Constipation is another distressing gastrointestinal complication in which the underlying pathophysiological mechanisms remain unclear. Constipation that results from restrictive eating may stimulate rectal distention followed by a reflex mechanism that inhibits gastric emptying. What is certain is that AN slows gut transit time by approximately 50%. BN patients have significant delays as well (Benini, Todesco, Dalle Grave, Deiorio, Salandini, & Vantini, 2004). Tricylic antidepressants, in particular, and other medications used to treat co-morbid diseases may also contribute to constipation.

Malnutrition or purging leads to hypokalemia (low potassium) and hypomagnesemia (low magnesium). These deficiencies slow colonic transit time by interfering with nerve function in the bowel wall. Laxatives used as a solution for bloating and constipation cause electrolyte imbalances, pancreatic damage, interstitial nephropathy, and delayed intestinal motility. Salivary gland hypertrophy, typical of BN, has also been known to occur in malnourished anorexics who do not binge or purge. It may take several months for glands to normalize after weight restoration. Salivary gland hypertrophy, bloating, abdominal distention, and constipation contribute to the "I feel fat" lament we often hear from our underweight patients.

AN patients are at risk for developing yet another gastrointestinal complication known as superior mesenteric artery syndrome (SMA). Loss of normal intra-abdominal fat allows compression of the third portion of the duodenum by the overlying superior mesenteric artery. Abdominal pain made worse by eating is a major symptom of SMA. SMA resolves with weight gain. Although relatively rare in eating-disordered patients, pancreatitis can and does occur when weight loss is sudden or patients are rapidly refed. To further add to the risk, pancreatitis can be masked by the elevated serum amylase levels found in approximately 10–20% of patients who binge and vomit frequently (Mehler & Andersen, 2010).

Brain Health

Cerebral atrophy has been described in patients with AN and in some patients with BN. Patients with a history of adolescent AN show significant deficits in cognitive, emotional, and social function compared to healthy controls. These deficits resemble those of mood and anxiety disorders and interfere with decision-making abilities. Patients with absent or irregular menses despite weight recovery also show cognitive impairments (Addolorato, Taranto, Capristo, & Gasbarrini, 1998; Chui et al., 2008; Krieg, Backmund, & Pirke, 1987). The impairments in social cognition affect interpersonal relationships, especially during the acute phases of AN, but can remain after recovery (Klump et al., 2009). It is postulated that the body is not able to protect the brain at low weights as the brain requires approximately 20% of the body's total energy expenditure to function (Treasure, Wack, & Roberts, 2008).

There is no debate that AN is associated with significant loss of cerebral gray and white matter, cerebral atrophy, and enlarged ventricles. Gray matter is a type of neural tissue associated with intelligence, concentration, emotions, personality, and creativity. White matter consists of the nerve fibers that connect various parts of the brain and determines how fast the brain can process information. The precuneus is an area of gray matter essential in self-processing, reflections upon self, and other aspects of consciousness and memory retrieval. Changes in the precuneus of AN patients is currently under study since it is the brain tissue most affected by weight loss. Recent research shows that loss of volume in the precuneus region is associated with distorted body image and it appears not to respond to weight recovery (Sachdev, Mondraty, Wen, & Gulliford, 2008). The severity of cerebral changes appears to be directly related to the amount of weight loss. Similar but less pronounced structural brain abnormalities have been found in BN.

With weight restoration, partial restoration of brain tissue has been documented. A number of studies show brain restoration during active weight gain (Joos et al., 2011). In a series of German studies, brain-tissue volume increased in weight-recovered patients by 25% compared to the brain volume measured at patients' lowest weights (Schlegel & Kretzschmar, 1997). Yet, brain-tissue deficits, especially of gray matter, have been documented 5 years after recovery (Mühlau et al., 2007). Early consensus is that lowest lifetime BMI is the critical variable that predicts irreversible brain changes. There is ongoing debate about whether these brain changes associated with eating disorders are the cause or the consequence of restricted eating and malnutrition (Kaye, 2008).

We recently updated our knowledge about seizures after several patients experienced mild to serious convulsions. We learned that seizures in ED patients occur for the same reasons as they do in individuals without EDs, and that is as a reaction to a triggering or stress factor. In general, everyone has a threshold that, if breached, leads to a seizure. Seizure thresholds are lowered by low blood sugar, restrictive eating, purging, excessive exercise, elevated cortisol levels, decreased blood flow to the brain, and lack of sleep. In epilepsy, the unremittingly low seizure threshold is due to the brain abnormalities associated with the epilepsy itself. Angela, a low-weight high-school-aged patient, was diagnosed with epilepsy after several severe seizures led to ambulance trips to the emergency room. Even treated with epilepsy medications, Angela continued to have seizures. Angela's doctors explained that her low weight and restricted eating lowered the blood glucose levels in her brain, leaving her at high risk for another seizure. Angela was told that, once she gained weight, her anti-seizure medication would keep her from having seizures and she could expect to safely go off to college in the fall.

Protein Deficiency

The semi-starvation of AN leads to protein depletion and loss of lean body mass. Adequate protein is necessary for maintenance of the immune system, bones, tendons, connective tissues, oxygen transport, and other essential functions. Low electrolyte levels, particularly, hyponatremia (low sodium) and hypokalemia, can occur as a result of protein malnutrition, which lowers blood urea nutrition and, in turn, alters renal glomerular filtration pressure, impairing sodium reabsorption (Bahia, Chu, & Mehler, 2011). Loss of lean body mass is associated with reduced overall metabolism, low body temperature, and depletion of brain, heart, and other organ tissues. Lean body mass losses of up to 40% have been documented in men in the well-known Keys Minnesota starvation studies (Keys, Brozek, Henschel, Mickelson, & Taylor, 1950). (See Box 1.1 for a summary of the Keys starvation studies.) More recent studies in both male and female adolescents, found 10–15% less lean body mass in adolescents with AN compared to healthy controls; male patients had greater losses than females (Haas et al., 2009; Misra et al., 2008). Haas' study (Haas et al., 2009) of an AN patient population found that one-third were severely protein depleted. Protein-depleted adolescents have linear growth retardation and chronic morbidity (Hass et al., 2009). Haas et al. (2009) conclude that a BMI less than 16.5 in female adolescents indicates protein depletion. In adults with AN, low protein status is associated with chronic morbidity.

BOX 1.1 KEYS' STUDY ON STARVATION

Familiarity with the Keys' classic study of starved, young, male conscientious objectors during World War II provides ample data on the effect of starvation on physical and mental functioning and food behavior (Keys et al., 1950). The Keys' study is often used to illustrate that most symptoms associated with AN and BN are the result of starvation. Keys' subjects entered the study in good physical and psychological health. After 6 months of consuming one-half of their normal food intake, the subjects developed labile mood, cognitive dysfunction, poor concentration, social withdrawal, obsessive, ritualized eating behaviors, insatiable appetites, binge eating, food cravings, apathy, anxiety, depression, irritability, and frequent outbursts of anger. These young men became negative, argumentative, withdrawn, and exhibited low self-esteem and relationship problems. Physical changes included: hair loss, gastrointestinal discomfort, edema, dizziness, headaches, increased fatigue, cold intolerance, lowered body temperature, decreased heart and metabolic rates, and decreased need for sleep. Cognitive changes included: impaired concentration, comprehension, and alertness. Food became the principal topic of conversation, reading, and daydreams. Food behaviors changed. Of note were an increased interest in cooking, inordinate amount of time spent meal planning, food hoarding, increased gum chewing, increased consumption of liquids, and eventual bingeing. A very readable summary of Keys' study is given in Garner and Garfinkel's *Handbook of Treatment for Eating Disorders* (2nd ed.; Garner, 1997, pp. 153–161).

Total body nitrogen (the standard indicator of body protein) improves with weight gain. Patients restore protein levels and regain lean body mass during the early stages of recovery, and regain fat mass during the later stages of recovery. Body temperature normalizes with gains in muscle mass. Distribution of lean body mass and adipose tissue match controls after a year of maintaining a normal weight (Mayer et al., 2009). During the acute phase of weight restoration, adipose tissue is preferentially deposited centrally in the abdomen and trunk.

Hair, Nails, and Skin

Patients often complain of bad nails and of hair loss. The most vocal complaint is for the noticeable loss of hair. Telogen effluvium, common in AN, is the name for temporary shedding of dead hair that occurs when the body suffers a shock such as weight loss or a high fever (Strumia, 2009). Paradoxically, dramatic hair loss usually does not occur until, in recovery, hair regrowth pushes out the dead hair. When this happens, we point out the sign of recovery that we call "recovery bangs," the fine fringe of new hair that can be seen along the forehead hairline. Weakened nails and fragile, dry hair are generally related to general malnutrition, particularly of calories, protein and zinc (Kim et al., 2010).

Hypercarotenemia (high carotene levels associated with yellow-orange skin) is seen frequently in AN. Carotene processing is slowed down in AN, especially in children, adolescents, and young adults, who already metabolize carotene more slowly than adults ("Hypercarotenemia," 2002). Overconsumption of fruits and vegetables contributes to hypercarotenemia. The unique yellow hue of hypercarotenemia is most obvious on the palms, cuticles and soles of the feet (Tung, Drage, & Ghosh, 2006). Birmingham (2012) recommends that counselors compare the color of their own palms to those of the patients to help them more fully grasp that they have a medically serious condition. Hypercarotenemia, in and of itself, is not dangerous, but it does indicate slowed metabolic processes and an unbalanced diet. Birmingham also uses this opportunity to emphasize that, in addition, AN has robbed patients of the ability to maintain a healthy body temperature, as he predicts patients' hands will be either markedly cold or warm (Birmingham, 2012).

Metabolism

Metabolism is the sum of all cellular activities necessary to sustain life. The calories needed to maintain metabolism plus the calories expended in physical activity account for a patient's total caloric needs. The caloric cost of metabolism is affected by height (taller people use more energy to maintain body temperature than do shorter people), age (younger people have faster metabolisms than older people), and muscle mass (muscles require more energy to maintain than fat tissues). Undereating, fasting, starvation, and malnutrition lower an individual's metabolic needs as the body tries to compensate for the potentially life-threatening consequences of a low caloric intake. Normally, exercise increases metabolic rate. But when caloric intake is inadequate, the body lowers metabolic rate to conserve energy despite regular exercise. Depressed metabolic rates have been measured in AN and BN. In AN, this is no doubt due to the cumulative effect of loss of muscle mass and decreased caloric intake. Signs of lowered metabolic rate in anorexic patients are bradycardia (slow heart rate), dry skin, brittle hair, constipation, cold intolerance, and fatigue. Over time, improved calorie intake and weight gain normalize metabolic rate. It is not clear why metabolic rates measure low in BN, besides the fact that BN patients also restrict caloric intake.

Blood Chemistry

We feel it is important for nutrition counselors to be aware of signs and blood chemistry findings that indicate problems (Box 1.2). The Academy of Eating Disorders' Critical Points for Early Recognition and Medical Risk Management in the Care of Individuals with Eating Disorders (2011, pp. 9–11) provides guidance for interpreting laboratory values in ED patients.

BOX 1.2 THE EFFECT OF EATING DISORDERED BEHAVIORS ON LABORATORY VALUES

- Glucose: ↓(poor nutrition), ↑(insulin omission).
- Sodium: ↓(water loading or laxatives).
- Potassium: ↓(vomiting, laxatives, diuretics, refeeding).
- Chloride: ↓(vomiting), ↑(laxatives).
- Blood bicarbonate: ↑(vomiting), ↓(laxatives).

- Blood urea nitrogen: ↑(dehydration).
- Creatinine: ↑(dehydration, renal dysfunction), ↓(poor muscle mass). "Normal" may be "relatively elevated" given low muscle mass.
- Calcium: slightly ↓(poor nutrition at the expense of bone).
- Phosphate: ↓(poor nutrition or refeeding).
- Magnesium: ↓(poor nutrition, laxatives, refeeding).
- Total protein and albumin: ↑(in early malnutrition at the expense of muscle mass), ↓(in later malnutrition).
- Total bilirubin: ↑(liver dysfunction), ↓(poor red blood cell (RBC) mass).
- Aspartate aminotransaminase (AST), alanine aminotransaminase (AST): ↑(liver dysfunction).
- Amylase: ↑(vomiting, pancreatitis).
- Lipase: ↑(pancreatitis).

Note. Comprehensive serum metabolic profile and important electrolytes and enzymes. Reprinted from *Eating Disorders Guide to Medical Management. Critical Points for Early Recognition and Medical Risk Management in the Care of Individuals with Eating Disorders*, by The Medical Care Standards Task Force of the Academy of Eating Disorders, co-chaired by O. Bermudez and M. Warren. Academy of Eating Disorders. Copyright 2011 by Academy of Eating Disorders. Reprinted with permission.

Emotional and Cognitive Changes

AN patients present with a variety of psychological concerns, such as fear of maturation, anxiety, depression, low self-esteem, trauma, and interpersonal problems. AN provides an identity that is the embodiment of the value of will-power and self-control, which once well-established has a self-reinforcing life of its own (Andersen, 2006; Fairburn, 2008). The limiting of the type and amount of food that is characteristic of AN becomes an effective coping mechanism.

ED patients without a primary history of OCD commonly have OCD-like tendencies (Box 1.3). The difference in these ED patients is that their obsessions and compulsions are limited to food, weight, or body image, and these behaviors decrease with adequate food intake and weight restoration. These patients believe their obsessions and compulsions to be rational and necessary, and not obtrusive or senseless. Patients often engage in compulsive behaviors such as cutting food into small pieces, eating only cold foods, using strong non-caloric condiments such as mustard, pepper, and vinegar, or drinking large amounts of non-caloric liquids. They may acknowledge a new interest in cooking, recipes, and food shopping, though they rarely eat what they purchase or prepare. It is not unusual for ED patients to be employed in food-related jobs or even to feel compelled to "shoplift" food. A surprising number remain perplexed about why they engage in these behaviors and are not able to relate them to their ED. They may express relief to know that their behaviors are characteristic of an ED, and that the behaviors usually resolve as their ED resolves. Besides EDs, OCD-like tendencies also occur with other DSM diagnoses such as psychosis, substance abuse, and obsessive–compulsive personality disorder. True OCD cannot be diagnosed in a patient with ED until weight is normalized.

BOX 1.3 OBSESSIONS AND COMPULSIONS ASSOCIATED WITH EATING DISORDERS

A. Rituals before, during, and after meals.
B. Rigid schedules and plans for meals or exercise.
C. Researching food and nutrition facts.
D. Excessive calorie counting.
E. Compulsive exercise or other behaviors to burn calories.
F. Perfectionism:

- striving for the perfect body, shape or weight
- exclusively eating "good" foods
- exercising until it feels "just right"
- criticizing lazy behaviors
- concern over changes in routines or meals
- striving for perfection in school, work, and relationships.

Note. Reprinted from "Managing OCD in severe eating disorders ," paper presented at the annual meeting of MultiService Eating Disorders Association (MEDA), Needham, MA, by S. D. Tsao, May 2009. Reprinted with permission.

As of this writing, the typical ED patient avoids red meat, foods with fat and sugar, and carbohydrate-containing foods. Which foods are viewed as either "good" or "bad" or "healthy" or "unhealthy" depends on the latest popular diet or nutrition theory. ED patients tend to believe, "Maybe others can eat fat or meat and not get fat, but not me; my metabolism is just different." Generally, patients progressively limit their intake of food over the duration of their eating disorder. First, snacks are eliminated, then breakfast, followed by lunch. Patients who live with others may continue to eat near-normal dinners to avoid concerning family members. Some patients "justify" eating in the evening by limiting caloric intake during the day.

Anxiety and depression are two major co-morbid psychiatric disorders in AN. In women with AN, overnight blood cortisol levels are positively associated with severity of depression and anxiety symptoms. Depression is observed in 50–75% of AN patients (Klump et al., 2009). Treatment can be complicated by personality changes caused by chronic undernutrition, such as irritability, sullenness, dependency, obsessiveness, compulsivity, and passive–aggressive behaviors. Although these changes can persist after recovery, the majority improve with weight restoration or cessation of binging and purging (Klump et al., 2009). Certain personality traits, including perfectionism and neuroticism, are also apparent before and during the course of the illness (Miller, 2011). Suicide and other self-harming behaviors are highly prevalent in patients with EDs. Twenty to 40% of deaths in AN are attributed to increased rates of suicide (Guillaume, 2011). Suicide rates are 40-fold higher in AN than in the general population (Preti, Rocchi, Sisti, Camboni, & Miotto, 2011). The research is less clear about rates of suicide in BN, but a 2009 longitudinal assessment of mortality over 8–25 years found nearly similar rates for BN and AN (Crow et al., 2009). Overall there has been a decline in suicide rates in ED in recent years. There is some evidence that this decline could be attributed to improved quality of and access to ED treatment (Preti et al., 2011). Tables 1.4 and 1.5 summarize the physiological characteristics, medical complications, and behavioral, emotional, and cognitive characteristics of AN.

TABLE 1.4 Physiological Characteristics and Medical Complications of Anorexia Nervosa

Body weight	Significantly low body weight. Intense fear of gaining weight or becoming fat, or persistent behavior that interferes with weight gain. Disturbance in the way in which one's body weight or shape is experienced, undue influence of body weight or shape on self-evaluation, or persistent lack of recognition of the seriousness of the current low body weight.
Brain and neurological problems	Decreased gray-matter volume. Increased fluid in brain. Dizziness, faintness, headaches, seizures. Disordered thinking. Numbness or odd nerve sensations in the hands or feet (peripheral neuropathy).
Heart problems	Dangerous heart rhythms (arrhythmias). Slowed heart rate below 60 beats/minute (bradycardia). Fatigue. Low blood pressure, electrolyte imbalances, dehydration. Weakened heart muscle, reduced size of heart, heart attack, heart failure. Death.
Blood problems	Low blood iron (anemia). Low vitamin B12 (pernicious anemia). Potentially fatal bone marrow problems (pancytopenia). Increased risk of infection due to low white blood cells (leucopenia).
Kidney problems	Increased urination.
Liver problems	High blood levels of liver enzymes causing liver damage.
Bone problems	Low bone mineral density (osteopenia and osteoporosis). Increased risk of stress fractures.
Digestive problems	Bloating, abdominal pain, constipation. Uncomfortable fullness.
Hormonal problems	Decreased reproductive hormones, including estrogen and dehydroepiandrosterone (DHEA, a male hormone). Increased stress hormones. Decreased thyroid and growth hormones. Retarded height growth in children and adolescents. Irregular or absent menstruation (amenorrhea).
Reproductive problems	Infertility. Higher risk for complications, miscarriage, cesarean section, low birth weight, birth defects, post-partum depression. Poor success with fertility treatments.

TABLE 1.4 (continued)

Immune problems	Lowered resistance to infection.
Muscular problems	Muscular weakness. Loss of muscle tissue.
Emotional problems	Difficulty concentrating. Increase in "bad moods."
Sleeping problems	Insomnia and early morning awakening. Sleep disturbances.
Hair and skin problems	Brittle, thinning hair on scalp. Thinning of hair or hair loss on scalp. Increased downy hair growth (lanugo) on face, neck, arms, back, legs. Dry skin. Blotchy or yellowed skin, especially on palms (hypercarotenemia). Brittle nails.
Body organ failure	Organs simply fail in long-term AN. Death.

TABLE 1.5 Behavioral, emotional, and cognitive characteristics of anorexia nervosa

Restrictive behaviors	Excessive dieting, food control, fasting. Avoidance of water or excessive water intake. Extreme interest in nutrition. Collects recipes. Likes to cook or bake; usually doesn't eat what cooks or bakes. Refuses to eat in front of others. Tension at mealtime. Fear of food. Vegan or vegetarian. Frequent weighing (multiple times a day).
Exercise behaviors	Compulsive exercising or excessive physical activity. Participation in a sport that requires thinness, e.g., gymnastics, wrestling, swimming, distance running, ballet, cross-country skiing, figure skating.
Bingeing behaviors	May eat food in secret. May binge on occasion.
Purging behaviors	May self-induce vomiting or abuse diuretics, laxatives.
Eating behavior	Calorie counting, rigid rules and schedules, unusual use of condiments, low calorie foods. Odd food rituals. Eats alone. Fear of eating in front of others. Plays games with food (e.g. cutting it into tiny pieces).
Dressing behaviors	Layering of clothes. Wearing large pants and sweaters to mask thinness.
Social behavior	Social withdrawal, physically and emotionally. Extreme focus on job or school work.
Self-destructive behavior	Slow suicide progression. Self-hatred and feeling of unworthiness. Substance abuse.
Body image problems	Intense fear of becoming fat. Distorted body image.
Perfectionist behavior	Perfectionist: thinnest, smartest, neatest. Dichotomous thinking: all or nothing, black or white.
Self-esteem	Depression and low sense of self-worth and self-esteem.
Sexuality	Decreased interest in sex.
Social behavior	Self-centered and non-social, isolation from others, irritable.
Cognitive symptoms	Difficulty thinking clearly, potential severe cognitive deficits due to malnourishment.

Features of Bulimia Nervosa

BN differs from BED in the use of a compensatory behavior following a binge such as self-induced vomiting (SIV), restricting food intake, excessive exercising, or laxative or diuretic abuse. SIV is by far the most dominant purging method. One variant of SIV is rumination, self-induced regurgitation from the stomach to the mouth of recently ingested food that is chewed and then re-swallowed. Chewing and spitting out of food is considered yet another means of purging. No purging method is effective in eliminating consumed calories. After SIV, the body retains 1,200 calories (Kaye, Weltzin, Hsu, McConaha, & Bolton, 1993). It appears that, if the binge is less than 1,200 calories, the body retains all of the consumed calories (See Chapter 11: Managing Purging for more information, pp. 246–259.) Most individuals who binge and purge eventually gain weight, though weight may stay within normal parameters.

SIV is usually accomplished by inserting fingers into the throat (Mehler, 2011). Eventually, abrasions, sores, and calluses form on several knuckles (Russell's sign) as they scrape against teeth. Several of our patients explained that this is why they always wear gloves or very long sleeves, embarrassed that someone would notice the telltale knuckles. Over time, SIV leads to a diminished gag reflex; then, feeling desperate, patients experiment with increasingly vigorous efforts to induce vomiting, often using elongated objects, such as spoons. One of Herrin's patients swallowed a toothbrush that subsequently had to be surgically removed.

The strain and force of vomiting can cause hemorrhages on the cornea (appearing as very bloodshot eyes) and petechial hemorrhages (appearing as small red dots caused by minute amounts of blood that are pushed through the skin around the eyes). While unsightly, neither are of medical significance. One of our patients suffered a more serious consequence from forcible vomiting: a retinal detachment which required laser surgery to repair.

Emotional and Cognitive Changes

Patients with BN tend to exhibit impulsivity, emotional intensity, and fluctuations in mood, but usually appear healthy and manage to maintain weight within a normal range. This, coupled with secretive behaviors, makes it relative easy to conceal BN. Some individuals suffer for years before seeking help. In BN, the cycle of binge followed by a purge is thought to demonstrate an inability to self-regulate negative emotions. Emotional states which may precipitate bingeing include: boredom, depression, disappointment, loneliness, procrastination, stress, anxiety, and anger. Bingeing may also serve as a vehicle for acting out, for disassociating, for expressing impulses, for self-soothing, and to inflict self-punishment. Psychological factors related to binge eating include low self-esteem, feelings of ineffectiveness, and extreme concerns about shape and weight. Co-morbid illnesses common to BN include anxiety disorders, depression, substance-use disorders, and personality disorders.

Clinical Complications of Self-Induced Vomiting

Oral/dental problems become evident as early as 6 months after the onset of SIV. These include dental erosion, dental caries, periodontal disease, and cheilosis (fissuring and dry scaling along the angels of the mouth; Mehler, 2011). The erosion of the enamel that occurs on the lingual surface of maxillary teeth (perimyolysis) will look smooth and unnaturally glossy (Mehler, 2011). After several years of vomiting several times a week, most patients suffer from serious dental erosion, decalcification of tooth enamel, and, eventually, erosion of the dentin. Chronic purgers will inevitably have painful, yellow-colored, dull, jagged-edged, and obviously eroded teeth, and costly dental bills. Some bulimic patients are bothered by painful sensitivity to hot and cold foods and beverages.

Parotid and salivary gland enlargement is a common in BN, occurring in up to 50% of patients (Mehler & Andersen, 2010). Patients complain of a swollen face and puffy cheeks that may exacerbate their fear of weight gain. Because the swelling is most evident 3–6 days after a binge–purge episode, patients may not always attribute it to BN (Mehler, 2011). Although the swelling is painless and harmless, it may take several months after abstinence from purging for glands to return to normal size. Parotid hypertrophy elevates serum amylase, which can be misdiagnosed as pancreatitis unless patients self-disclose SIV.

Multiple gastrointestinal complaints (i.e., bloating, heartburn, flatulence, constipation, and stomach pain) are common among purging patients. A rare but serious complication is pneumonia when food is aspirated into the lungs during SIV. Esophagitis, erosion of the esophagus, ulcerations, and strictures are consequences of recurring vomiting. SIV may also result in hoarseness, sore throat, odynophagia (painful swallowing), dysphagia (difficulty swallowing), dyspepsia (indigestion), and hematemesis (vomiting bright red blood). Nutrition counselors should insist on a medical evaluation for patients who report blood in their vomitus as it could indicate serious esophageal or gastric tearing. It is more likely, though, that the blood originates from minute lacerations in the esophageal or gastric walls that are not medically serious. Stomach acids can burn sensitive tissues in the tongue, mouth, and throat, leaving these tissues chronically sore. Hoarseness and sore throats are the most common complaints of patients who regularly vomit. Repeated SIV causes laxity of the lower esophageal sphincter and loss of the gag reflex, resulting in spontaneous gastro-esophageal reflux (Mehler, 2011). Abdominal tenderness can result from the strain of vomiting. Recurrent strenuous vomiting can lead to Mallory–Weiss syndrome, tears in the gastro-esophageal junction, leading to bleeding or hematemesis. In Barrett's esophagus, the esophageal mucosa becomes inflamed by constant exposure to stomach acids, leading to precancerous lesions and a significant risk of adenocarcinoma. Most patients with Barrett's esophagus have acid reflux-like symptoms, but some do not. Screening by an upper endoscopy procedure is recommended for patients with long-standing BN (Mehler, 2011). SIV may cause a serious esophageal rupture, known as Boerhaave's syndrome, a rare but life-threatening condition (overall mortality is 20%). The most significant symptom is severe chest pain.

Clinical Complications of Laxatives and Diuretics

Purging (via SIV, or laxative or diuretic abuse) that occurs twice a week or more may result in fluid or electrolyte imbalances. Undereating adds to the risk of fluid and electrolyte imbalances, as does maintaining a low body weight. We remind ourselves not to be complacent about normal electrolyte lab results in a patient who purges frequently because electrolyte levels fluctuate and recover quickly. We have seen patients have normal electrolyte results despite very frequent purging behaviors. Table 1.6 shows how various methods of purging affect specific electrolytes.

ED behaviors often cause a cycle of dehydration followed by excessive water retention. Patients with dehydration present with increased thirst, decreased urinary output, and feelings of weakness, dizziness, or lightheadedness. Dehydration stimulates the renin–angiotensin–aldosterone system to retain fluid, causing "puffiness," edema, and temporarily increasing body weight. Patients, who interpret fluid retention as weight gain, feel compelled to restrict or purge, or both, and the cycle begins again. Hypokalemia (low blood potassium) is the most common electrolyte concern in BN (normal range 3.6–5.2 mmol/L). It occurs in about 5% of patients and is a good diagnostic indicator of BN in an otherwise healthy-appearing patient. Patients with hypokalemia present with muscle weakness, fatigue, constipation, and heart palpitations (Mehler & Andersen, 2010). Hypokalemia (less than 2.5 mmol/L) can cause life-threatening cardiac arrhythmias and death in patients, regardless of their body weight (Mehler, 2011). Of note, AN patients may also be hypokalemic without engaging in SIV, due to malnutrition.

Metabolic alkalosis, an increase in serum bicarbonate, is observed in patients who self-induce vomiting or take diuretics on a regular basis. Bicarbonate levels are used to diagnose SIV. Serum levels greater than 40 mmol/L generally indicate vomiting (Mehler, 2011). Metabolic alkalosis usually is not an immediate concern, but it can progress into loss of consciousness and coma. Early symptoms include lightheadedness, nausea confusion, and muscle twitches. Hypomagnesemia can exacerbate cardiac arrhythmias. Patients with magnesium and other electrolyte losses can be asymptomatic or experience muscle weakness, cardiomyopathy, seizures, acute renal failure, convulsions, and coma. Electrolyte levels of low-weight patients and patients who purge frequently should be monitored by frequent blood and urine tests.

TABLE 1.6 Electrolyte Levels Associated with Purging

Method of purging	Serum levels					Urine levels		
	Sodium	Potassium	Chloride	Bicarbonate	pH	Sodium	Potassium	Chloride
Vomiting	Increased, decreased or normal	Decreased	Decreased	Increased	Increased	Decreased	Decreased	Decreased
Laxatives	Increased or normal	Decreased	Increased or decreased	Decreased or increased	Decreased or increased	Decreased	Decreased	Normal or decreased
Diuretics	Decreased or normal	Decreased	Decreased	Increased	Increased	Increased	Increased	Increased

Note. Reprinted from "Medical complications of bulimia nervosa and their treatments," by P. S. Mehler, 2011, *International Journal of Eating Disorders*, 44, p. 99. Copyright 2011 by Wiley Periodicals, Inc. Reprinted with permission.

Laxative Abuse

Both AN and BN patients may purge by abusing laxatives, despite the fact that calorie absorption takes place in the small intestine and laxatives act on the large intestine. Only an estimated 10–12% of ingested calories are lost as a result of laxative use (Bo-Linn, Santa Ana, Morawski, & Fordtran, 1983). Complications of laxative abuse include the electrolyte and fluid imbalances mentioned above and gastrointestinal problems such as, nausea, vomiting, and diarrhea. Serious consequences of chronic use of laxatives to purge are: confusion, convulsions, skeletal muscle weakness, urinary tract infections, osteomalacia, osteoporosis, rectal bleeding, finger clubbing (swelling), increased pigmentation of the skin, pancreatic damage, malabsorption, and cathartic (flaccid and dilated) colon. Acute diarrhea associated with laxative abuse can cause hyperchloremic metabolic acidosis.

Laxative abuse produces a benign, reversible brown-black discoloration of the colonic mucosa and submucosa, called melanosis coli, and a low-grade inflammation of the colon (Mehler, 2011). It is seen in approximately half of patients who take anthraquinone-based laxatives (such as those containing cascara, buckthorn, senna, senokot, or aloe vera) but does not have significant medical consequences (Mehler, 2011).

Because chronic use of laxatives disrupts intestinal peristalsis, patients often complain of alternating diarrhea and constipation that may resemble irritable bowel syndrome. Tolerances build up to the effects of stimulant laxatives, necessitating larger and larger doses for stool evacuation (Mehler, 2011). As a result, patients are at risk for laxative dependence, diarrhea, rebound constipation, fluid retention, and cathartic colon. A cathartic colon, having suffered damage to neurological innervation, becomes permanently flaccid, dilated and atonic. The loss of normal colonic peristalsis leads to problems transporting fecal material, possibly requiring partial colonic resection, colectomy, or ostomy.

When laxatives are withdrawn, the ensuing constipation and rebound peripheral edema (especially in the legs) called, pseudo-Bartter's syndrome, presents a challenge for patients. Although the edema usually resolves in 10 days or less, patients are likely to be convinced that they are gaining weight. Salt restriction and leg elevation can help, but diuretics do not (Mehler & Andersen, 2010).

Diuretic Abuse

In our practices, we rarely see patients who use prescription or over-the-counter (OTC) diuretics. Neither cause calorie malabsorption; OTC products are not even effective for water retention. Patients who abuse diuretics are usually older and have access to prescription diuretics. Abuse of prescription diuretics increases risk of dehydration, weakness, nausea, palpitations, polyuria, hematuria (blood in urine), pyuria (pus in urine), constipation, hypokalemia, cardiac conduction defects, nephropathy, and abdominal pain. Continued abuse of prescription diuretics leads to eventual renal impairment from direct toxicity to the kidneys or from the effects of severe dehydration. When prescription diuretics are discontinued, most experience transitory "reflex" water retention. As with laxatives, salt restriction and leg elevation is the treatment of choice when weaning off diuretics.

OTC diuretics rarely cause serious medical complications, but many of them contain substantial amounts of caffeine. High doses of such diuretics, if misused, can cause headaches, trembling, and rapid heart rate, among other caffeine-related symptoms. Despite the fact that non-prescription diuretics have few side-effects, even if abused, their use should be discouraged for several reasons: first, the use of OTC diuretics may evolve into abuse of more dangerous prescription diuretics; and, second, taking diuretics of any kind perpetuates the binge–purge cycle and an unhealthy approach to weight control.

The physiological characteristics and medical complications of BN and BED are summarized in Table 1.7, and the behavioral, emotional, and cognitive characteristics of BN and BED are summarized in Table 1.8.

Features of Binge-Eating Disorder

Binge-eating disorder (BED) is classified under "eating disorder not otherwise specified" (EDNOS) in the DSM-IV but is expected to be a discrete diagnosis in DSM-5. BED has nearly two times the lifetime prevalence rate of AN and BN. Bariatric surgery patients have a 27% lifetime prevalence of BED (Kalarchian et al., 2007).

One variant of BED is a grazing pattern of bingeing. Grazers may eat relatively small amounts of food throughout the day or most of the evening, never feeling hungry or full. Though grazers may not consume a large amount of food in a discrete period of time, they do feel out of control and may end up consuming a significant amount of calories over the course of a day (Anderson, Lavender, & De Young, 2010). We have had patients ask us about the differences between compulsive eating and BED. In clinical practice, compulsive overeating is similar to grazing in that eating may continue for hours. Compulsive eaters tend to repeatedly reach for food and to feel overfull and out of control. Like other patients with BED, patients with compulsive overeating become preoccupied with eating and worry about weight, contributing to feelings of low self-esteem, guilt, and depression (Matz & Frankel, 2004).

Individuals presenting with BED may actually be suffering from night eating syndrome (NES), currently proposed as an addition to EDNOS in DSM-5. Keel Brown, Holland, and Bodell. (2012) predict that NES will likely become a provisional, and then an independent, diagnosis in a future edition of the DSM. In NES, the individual undereats or does not experience hunger during the day. Consumption of at least 25% of daily caloric intake occurs after the evening meal or after awakening to eat during the night. Individuals with NES often believe that they must eat in order to get to sleep.

TABLE 1.7 Physiological Characteristics and Medical Complications of Bulimia Nervosa and Binge-Eating Disorder

Body weight*	Weight fluctuations with body weight below, at, or above normal range due to alternating bingeing and fasting.
Slowed heart rate	Potential heart arrhythmia; irregularities related to electrolyte imbalance.
Body fluid regulation	Swollen glands, "chipmunk cheeks," puffiness around the face (burst blood vessels in eyes). Edema (swelling due to retention of body fluids). Possible impaired renal function.
Blood pressure	Normal or fluctuating blood pressure.
Body temperature	No change.
Menstrual period	Menstrual irregularities.
Body hair and skin	Finger or hand calluses. Small red dots around the eyes (petechiae) after forceful vomiting episode due to increased facial pressure.
Movement and functioning	Chemical imbalance caused by low potassium and sodium, producing dehydration, muscular fatigue, cardiac rhythm irregularities, cardiac arrest.
Imbalances	Fluid and electrolyte imbalance. Edema accompanying refeeding. Swelling of hands and feet.
Heart problems	Possible heart arrhythmias and irregularities.
Muscular symptoms	Overall muscular weakness.
Gastrointestinal disorders*	Abdominal pain, esophageal burning, heartburn or gastric dilation or rupture, non-responsive bowel. Constipation, diarrhea, stomach distress, bloating, hiatal hernia, gastrointestinal bleeding, dry mouth, nausea. Symptoms may mimic irritable bowel syndrome.
Nutritional problems	Vitamin deficiencies, hypoglycemia, diabetes mellitus.
Bone and dental	Tooth decay, gum erosion from regurgitated stomach acids. Periodontal disease. Dental caries. Mouth ulcers. Enlarged salivary glands.
Other symptoms	Headaches, tiredness, fatigue, weakness. Damage to esophagus (sore throat, horse voice, difficulty swallowing).
Disease states	Increased incidence of BN in Type 1 diabetes mellitus (especially in young women).

* Characteristic of BED as well as BN.

Features of Bingeing

BN and BED are both defined by recurrent and uncontrollable episodes of binge eating. Most ED patients, including those with AN, will engage in binge eating at some time over the course of their disorder. Binge eating is one sign that AN patients are migrating along the ED continuum from AN to BN (Meh-

TABLE 1.8 Behavioral, Emotional, and Cognitive Characteristics of Bulimia Nervosa and Binge-Eating Disorder

Bingeing★	Eating, in a discrete period of time (within any 2-hour period), an amount of food that is definitely larger than most people would eat during a similar period of time and under similar circumstances. A sense of lack of control over eating during the episode (a feeling that one cannot stop eating or control what or how much one is eating).
Purging	Recurrent inappropriate compensatory behavior in order to prevent weight gain: self-induced vomiting; misuse of laxatives, diuretics, or other medications (diuretic, thyroid or diet pills, or use of other emetics such as syrup of ipecac); fasting; or excessive exercise.
Frequency of bingeing★ and purging	At least once a week for 3 months.
Eating behavior★	Secret food foraging and hoarding, especially at night. Shoplifting or petty stealing of money to buy binge food.
Sleeping behavior★	Sleep disturbances. Often binge eating occurs at night.
Clothing and dress rituals	Obsessive–compulsive patterns such as trying on clothes multiple times a day.
Social behavior	Social irregularities: alternating withdrawal with erratic need for social contact and approval. Chaotic relationships and interactions.
Abusive behavior	Drug or alcohol abuse. Suicidal gestures or attempts. Self-hatred and self-mutilation. Feelings of self-disgust.
Body image problems★	Preoccupation with appearance and "image." Overly concerned about body weight and size.
Perfectionist behavior	Perfectionist: high performance and achievement expectations. Perfectionist inside, but sometimes chaotic outside. Façade of normalcy. Seemingly "has it together."
Self-esteem★	Low self-esteem: self-loathing, self-disgust, depression.
Sexuality	May be promiscuous or confused about sexuality—a mask for a desire to be accepted or respected.
Social behavior	Constant feeling of being out of control; vacillates between isolation and extreme need for external validation.
Cognitive symptoms	Inability to accurately identify and express feelings. Out of touch with one's feelings (e.g., anger, affection, humor). Obsessive thoughts focused on the eating-disorder cycle.

★ Characteristic of BED as well as BN.

ler & Andersen, 2010). Binge eating is a distinctive behavioral pattern in which attempts to restrict eating (which may or may not result in actual dietary restriction) are interrupted by repeated episodes of binge eating. This pattern is set in motion when self-evaluation is based almost exclusively on achieving a thin body, and it is maintained by mood intolerance, sensitivity to external events, negative moods, perfectionism, low self-esteem, and major interpersonal difficulties (Fairburn, 2008). ED patients tend to overreact to even minor dietary blunders and use them as evidence of their lack of self-control. Because binge-eating behaviors are indefensible and antithetical to ED core values, patients internalize a sense of being unable to control eating or weight. It is self-fulfilling to binge and then, in an effort to regain control, return to restriction. Restricted eating is difficult to maintain in the face of life's challenges and negative moods. Binge eating, on the other hand, may temporarily improve a negative mood or serve as a distraction from difficult circumstances.

Also central to the problem of binge eating is the difficulty patients have assessing and responding appropriately to hunger and satiety signals. The alterations in levels of brain serotonin, neuropeptide systems, and brain neurocircuitry found in AN and BN contribute to lack of appetite, mood and impulse control in both disorders (Waterhous & Jacob, 2011).

In a binge-eating episode, one feels unable to stop eating and consumes an amount of food that is definitely larger than most people would eat under similar circumstances (American Psychiatric Association, 2010). Many of our patients report bingeing and purging just out of habit, which Mehler and Andersen (2010, p. 23) describe as "an almost automatic conditioned reflex based on autonomic conditioning for a certain time of day." Binges typically consist of carbohydrate-containing foods, and may create a financial drain on food budgets.

In the aftermath of a binge, one feels guilty, uncomfortably full, and fearful about weight gain. A binge often ends with a vow to restrict caloric intake in the future. Researchers have described "subjective binges." In these eating episodes, which may be as insignificant as several hundred calories, one feels out of control or eats more than intended, but does not consume more than a normal eater would. Subjective binges, like objective binges, are associated with shame and guilt and can lead to restriction or purging or both. We agree with other clinicians who conclude that loss of control over food intake is clinically more significant than the amount of food consumed (Wildes & Marcus, 2010). Furthermore, there is evidence that individuals engaged in subjective binging experience the equivalent levels of both eating-disorder psychopathology and general psychopathology as do those who objectively binge (Anderson et al., 2010).

Clinical Complications of Binge Eating

Patients frequently ask, "Does the stomach stretch?" Gastric capacity does increase in BN. Repeated large-volume binge-eating episodes can overstimulate the enteric vagal afferent fibers within the stomach, causing an autonomic dysregulation that contributes to decreased stomach-wall tone and enlarged gastric capacity. Normalization of gastric tone occurs with a decrease in binge/vomiting frequency.

Enhanced gastric capacity in BN patients increases the risk for gastric dilatation (extreme enlargement of the stomach), with the potential for gastric rupture. Acute gastric dilatation may go unrecognized in patients who continue to eat or binge and SIV. Symptoms of gastric rupture include: nausea, spontaneous vomiting, distention, and pain. While gastric rupture requires surgical repair, gastric dilatation usually is diagnosed with a barium meal and treated with nasogastric suction. One of our patients, after bingeing on a batch of cookie dough, had to go through nasogastric suction to prevent rupture. Very underweight patients are also at risk for acute gastric dilatation. As mentioned above, superior mesenteric artery syndrome, which compresses the duodenum, can cause acute gastric dilatation, as can rapid refeeding in fasting patients.

The physiological characteristics and medical complications of BN and BED are summarized in Table 1.7, and the behavioral, emotional, and cognitive characteristics of BN and BED are summarized in Table 1.8.

Features of Males With Eating Disorders

The diagnosis and treatment of an ED in males is less likely to be recognized than in females. Men are less forthcoming than women with their problem due to social stigma, and treatment programs do not always accept male patients. Medically, anorexic men have low levels of plasma testosterone, luteinizing hormone (LH), and follicle-stimulating hormone (FSH). Because men have more lean muscle mass than women, weight loss and muscle breakdown may be slower at the onset of AN. Men may have more vitamin and mineral deficiencies than women, as they tend to be less inclined to take a supplement.

Males with ED have high probability of substance abuse, obsessive–compulsive disorder (OCD), and depression. Like women, rates of EDs are higher in men who participate in activities such as sports that require thinness (wrestling, gymnastics, and track). Men who participate in football or body-building sports may suffer from a type of body dysmorphia called, "reverse anorexia," believing they are not big enough or muscular enough. These men may exercise excessively in a "drive for bigness" (Mehler & Andersen, 2010, p. 216). Body dissatisfaction among men is usually targeted at the upper body (stomach, chest, shoulders, and arms) and women from the waist down.

Features of the New Diagnostic Criteria for Eating Disorders: DSM-IV and DSM-5

Publication of the fifth edition of Diagnostic and Statistical Manual of Mental Disorders (DSM-5) is scheduled for May 2013. In the meantime, the proposed revisions to the current diagnostic criteria for ED diagnoses are available at the APA DSM-5 Development website (http://www.dsm5.org/Pages/Default.aspx). Box 1.4 highlights the differences between DSM-IV and DSM-5.

BOX 1.4 DSM-IV COMPARED TO PROPOSED DSM-5 DIAGNOSTIC CRITERIA FOR EATING DISORDERS

Anorexia nervosa. Types: Restriction or binge-eating/purging

Diagnostic and Statitical Manual of Mental Disorders (DSM) IV
- Exaggerated drive for thinness
- Refusal to maintain a body weight above the standard minimum (e.g., <85% of expected weight)
- Intense fear of becoming fat with self-worth based on weight or shape
- Amenorrhea (absence of three consecutive periods)

Proposed for DSM-5
- Restricted energy intake relative to requirements leading to a markedly low body weight
- Intense fear of gaining weight or becoming fat or persistent behavior to avoid weight gain, even though at a markedly low weight
- Disturbance in the way in which one's body weight or shape is experienced

Bulimia nervosa

DSM-IV
- Overwhelming urges to overeat and inappropriate compensatory bahaviors or purging that follow the binge episodes (e.g., vomiting, excessive exercise, alternating periods of starvation, and abuse of laxatives or drugs)
- Similar to anorexia nervosa, individuals with bulimia nervosa also display psychopathology, including a fear of being overweight

Proposed for DSM-5
- Recurrent episodes of binge eating with a sense of a lack of control with inappropriate compensatory bahavior
- Self-evaluation is unduly influenced by body shape and weight
- The disturbance does not occur exclusively during episodes of anorexia nervosa

Binge eating disorder

DSM-IV
- Classified under eating disorders not otherwise specified

Proposed for DSM-5
- Repeated episodes of overconsumption of food with a sense of a lack of control with a list of possible descriptors such as how much is eaten and distress about the episode
- Frequency described as at least once a week for 3 months

BOX 1.4 (continued)

Eating disorders not otherwise specified

DSM-IV
- Considered to be partial syndromes with frequency of symptoms that vary from above diagnostic criteria
- Distinguishing feature of binge eating disorder is binge eating, with a lack of self-control, without inappropriate compensatory behaviors

Proposed for DSM-5
- Diagnostic criteria to be established for binge eating disorder
- Possible descriptions of eating problems such as purging disorder and night eating syndrome

Note. DSM-IV compared to proposed DSM-5 diagnostic criteria for eating disorders. Adapted from "Position of the American Dietetic Association: Nutrition Intervention in the Treatment of Eating Disorders," by American Dietetic Association, 2011, *Journal of the American Dietetic Association*, 111, p. 1237. Copyright 2011 by American Dietetic Association. Adapted with permission.

Anorexia Nervosa

In contrast to the DSM-IV, the DSM-5 proposes to remove the words "refusal" and "denial" from the language of the AN criteria, as these words infer the patient is an adversarial role to the counselor. "Weight gain phobia" may also be dropped. The proposed revision will likely improve the cross-cultural representation of AN, because weight phobia is less often endorsed by non-western patients and has not been associated with course or outcome in non-western settings. Another change from DSM-IV to DSM-5 is eliminating amenorrhea as a diagnostic criterion. Arguments supporting this proposal contend that the amenorrhea criterion lacks any relevance to men, women using hormonal medications, girls who are pre-menarche and postmenopausal women. Furthermore, most evidence suggests that amenorrhea represents a consequence of starvation in AN rather than a defining feature.

The DSM-5 has redefined the weight criterion for AN. The DSM-IV weight criterion has been widely criticized for being arbitrary: below "a minimally normal weight", e.g., "a body weight less than 85% of than expected" (Thomas, Roberto, & Brownell, 2009). DSM-5 will use instead a "markedly low body weight." The text of DSM-5 will recommend several weight guidelines, including a BMI less than 18.5kg/m^2 for adults and a BMI below the 10th percentile for children and adolescents. On the other hand, DSM-IV in its text cites the weight criteria of BMI $< 17.5 \text{kg/m}^2$ from the International Statistical Classification of Diseases and Related Health Problems, 10th Revision (ICD-10). Of note, most AN research has been based on the weight criteria of BMI $< 17.5 \text{kg/m}^2$.

Bulimia Nervosa

The proposed criteria for BN have changed very little from the DSM-IV, except for the reduction of the minimum frequency criterion for binge eating and inappropriate compensatory behaviors from twice per week to once per week over the prior 3 months.

Binge-Eating Disorder

The most significant proposed revision to the eating disorders category in the DSM-5 is the inclusion of BED as a formal diagnosis. Criteria for this new disorder are nearly identical to those included as research diagnostic criteria listed in an appendix in DSM-IV; except that DSM-5 recommends the minimum frequency and duration of binge episodes in BED match those proposed for BN.

Eating Disorder Not Otherwise Specified

Where the DSM-IV provided an enumerated list of unnamed examples for EDNOS, the DSM-5 proposal includes subthreshold AN, BN, and BED, purging disorder, and NES (Keel et al., 2012).

Summary Points

- Patients with AN characteristically restrict food intake due to an intense fear of weight gain, resulting in extremely low body weight and symptoms of starvation.
- Underweight AN patients are at risk for cardiovascular and neurological repercussions; gastrointestinal problems; brain tissue losses and cognitive impairments; protein depletion; and depressed metabolism.
- BN and BED are both defined by recurrent and uncontrollable episodes of binge eating. Most ED patients will engage in binge eating at some time over the course of their disorder.
- Oral and dental problems are a major complication of SIV.
- Clinical complications of diuretics and laxatives include dehydration and electrolyte imbalances. Laxative abuse also results in disturbances to the colon.
- Proposed changes in the DSM-5 include specific criteria for BED and revised diagnostic thresholds.

2
COURSE OF TREATMENT

Introduction

In Chapter 1: Clinical Features of Eating Disorders, we provide the reader with a diagnostic and medical perspective of the patient with an eating disorder (ED). In this chapter, we offer a broader perspective of the patient from our seat in the nutrition counselor's chair. We outline the structure of an initial nutrition counseling session from the beginning, through the middle, and the end. This chapter includes advice on appointment frequency, scheduling follow-up sessions, and making referrals. Finally, we discuss when and how to end nutrition counseling sessions.

The Eating Disordered Patient

Who do we treat for an ED? In our practices we counsel diverse populations for EDs: people of different sexual orientations, the young and old, students, athletes, professionals and non-professionals, and people of various ethnic and cultural backgrounds. We also treat patients who present from various points in the recovery process. Some patients may not have considered the possibility that they have an ED, while others may be too entrenched in their ED behaviors to work on recovery. Patients may also seek nutrition counseling for the first time, while others have been in treatment before and wish to resume working. Others are referred from residential treatment centers for maintenance, to prevent relapse, or to continue working toward recovery.

For the purpose of nutrition counseling, it is important to understand not only who the patient is, but where the patient is in his or her stage of recovery, including any prior treatment he or she has or has not received. Two models help clarify stages of ED recovery. Reiff and Reiff (1999) use a model of recovery that shows the learning, changing, and maintenance stages, and points out the patient's current state (e.g., denial, needing the behaviors, changing; Figure 2.1). We use this model to illustrate that recovery is a process that occurs over time and not in one fell swoop. Our patients are often relieved to know they can gradually progress toward recovery without immediately having to give up their ED behaviors. Patients are assuaged by the expectation that they will at times take two steps forward and one step back in recovery.

Prochaska's stages-of-change model (Greene Rossi, Rossi, Velicer, Fava, & Prochaska, 1999) outlines in detail five stages of treatment based on the patient's readiness to change for each stage. (See Chapter 4: Counseling Interventions, pp. 79–104, for more on the use of Prochaska's five stages of change and suggested approaches for each stage.)

In our practices, we frequently see patients with chronic histories of EDs. By the time they seek nutrition counseling, they or their loved ones or both are experiencing great pain, fear, or frustration as a result of the ED. Yet there are other patients who hesitate to seek professional help because of the expected commitment of time and money, the embarrassment that they need help, the fear of deeply exploring their problems and giving up their ED identity, and the commonly held negative stereotypes about people who need counseling. It goes without saying that almost all patients have an abject fear of gaining weight, and many think that they can recover on their own.

Frequently, patients are apprehensive about nutrition treatment because they fear being misunderstood or because they expect to be castigated for thoughts, feelings, and behaviors related to their ED. Others are distrustful of professionals and resistant to the idea of entering into a therapeutic relationship that may foster dependency. Some feel ambivalent about giving up the sense of control and identity their ED provides. Acknowledging, appreciating, and respecting these feelings helps patients engage in treatment.

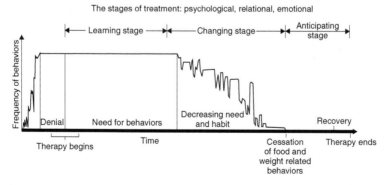

FIGURE 2.1   The recovery model. Reprinted from *Eating disorders: Nutrition therapy in the recovery process*, (p. 19) by D. W Reiff and K. K. L. Reiff, 1999, Gaithersburg, MD: Aspen. Copyright 1999 by Wolters Kluwer Law & Business. Reprinted with permission.

Session Structure

No matter who patients are or at which stage of recovery they may be, the overall course of treatment involves a pre-session, followed by an initial session, a series of follow-up sessions, and, finally, termination of treatment. Each nutrition counseling session has three parts: The first part is the beginning of the session, consisting of greeting the patient and ascertaining the reason for the visit. The middle part of the session includes assessing the nature of the problem and what advice or behavior changes would benefit the patient. The ending, or summary, of the session includes a review of homework assignments and a plan for future visits.

Presession

Before we see the patient for the first time, we work to obtain as much background information as possible. Our initial contact may be the patient or a referral source such as a family member, practitioner, or ED treatment program. A common example is an email or phone call directly from the patient (Case Example 2.1). Another typical example is a mother who calls to make the appointment for her child and provides detailed information at length. Practitioners or ED programs may fax or mail information on the medical and nutritional status of the patient. A psychiatrist or therapist may provide background information on the individual's social and behavioral history and current status. Knowing the concerns of these sources before the first meeting helps the nutrition counselor provide consistent and appropriate care.

CASE EXAMPLE 2.1: GEORGIA

Dr. Herrin,
In my Google search to find a treatment center, I found your website, which just might be a stroke of fate. Seeing your picture and your web page made me feel hopeful. Maybe I don't have go to rehab to start living my life, and that I can do it on my own with the help of a specialist. I'm a 24-year-old, lesbian newlywed, mother of a soon to be 5 year old, and I have been struggling with ED issues for about 10 years now. I am bulimic. I have spent a good deal of time educating myself on nutrition- -I know what my body requires and what I should be eating.
  If you think we would be an appropriate match for treatment, please contact me as soon as possible. I am just looking to expedite the process in getting help at this point.

Georgia

Georgia, I can confirm 1/24 @ 4 pm. The appt with be about 50 minutes. We should have no problem with your insurance as I am a preferred provider. I take care of the billing and I think I have everything I need from you but if you feel comfortable you could tell me in a return email a little more about the specifics of your ED.

Marcia

Initial Session: Beginning

Kellogg (2010, Tip No. 102) writes, "What we do and say in the first moments of an initial session have a profound impact on the whole treatment." We greet the individual warmly and maintain good eye contact throughout the session. Consider offering a handshake at the first meeting. Herrin offers tea or spring water. Larkin positions her chair to be at the same height as and facing the patient's chair. The counselor should sit at a conversational distance from the patient. Speech should be moderate in tone and rate, yet include variations to convey warmth and interest.

To put the patient at ease, we begin an initial session with a bit of small talk that directly pertains to the patient, such as the weather or his or her ability to find parking. This can be followed with the counselor providing a brief personal introduction, along with credentials as well as the time allotted for the session, what the session typical entails, fees, including insurance co-payments, and the Health Insurance Portability and Accountability Act of 1996 (HIPAA) confidentiality policies (Case Example 2.2).

CASE EXAMPLE 2.2: INTRODUCTION

"Thank you for coming today. We have about 50 minutes for this session. I like to start by introducing myself and learning a little bit about you. But first, I should tell you about the regulations governing confidentiality. Would that be ok?"

We prefer, if possible, to separate the business component of the initial session (e.g., fees, policies, insurance) from the counseling part of the session. We give our new patients a registration packet of forms and a clipboard, and ask the patient to complete the forms in the first few minutes of the session. Additional options are to email the forms to new patients or to include the forms on your website and direct patients to print and fill them out in advance of the first session. Our packets include: privacy practices, insurance information, personal information (social security number, email and home addresses, phone numbers), and other contact information (parents and other providers), as well as authorizations for release of confidential information, as needed (see Appendix A).

We then offer the patient the opportunity to introduce him or herself and to explain his or her reason for coming. If we have obtained details about the patient's ED history prior to the appointment from other than the patient, we inform the patient about this. It is important that the nutrition counselor demonstrate familiarity with the patient's reported history if he or she has had prior access.

Confidentiality: Adults

HIPAA outlines the regulations for sharing of medical information between practitioners and others. HIPPA requires that patients sign forms acknowledging they have been informed about HIPPA by the practitioner. HIPPA forms and guidelines can be provided to the individual prior to the initial session via the practitioner's website or during the first session. More information about HIPPA can be found at: http://www.hhs.gov/ocr/privacy. In addition, adults must sign a release form before information can be divulged to another party. (See Appendix A for sample release of information and HIPPA forms.)

Confidentiality: Children

In initial sessions with minors, counselors should share information they have received prior to the patient's visit and reiterate that their primary relationship is with the patient and not with the concerned others. Underscoring the confidential nature of counseling and explaining under what circumstances information may be shared with others is important to developing a therapeutic relationship. Patients who are minors should be told they will be apprised before information is disclosed to parents or other professionals. In addition, parents or guardians must sign a release form before information about patients under the age of 18 years can be divulged to another party.

Young patients and their parents should be told that the nutrition counselor's practice is to inform the patient to relevant conversations with parents and concerned others. This practice reassures patients that the nutrition counselor will not "collude" with parents. Neither is collusion with young patients productive. We let our patients know that important information will not be kept from parents. Likewise, it is important that patients know their reports will be confirmed with parents. We explain confidentiality to our young patients by saying, "We will discuss together what your parents need to know." Patients should be consulted before information is passed on to parents: "Do you mind if I share this information with your parents?" If the patient does "mind," we must ascertain whether it is in the patient's best interest for the information to be shared with parents. If that is the case, we may say something like, "I understand how you feel, but I am convinced your parents have to know."

After introductions and review of confidentiality policies, the initial session is focused on setting the stage for the formation of a collaborative relationship, to assess the nature of the problem, to delineate the individual's expectations and goals, and to provide hope for recovery.

Establishing a Collaborative Relationship

It is well known that a collaborative relationship between counselor and patient is fundamental to any counseling endeavor, including nutrition counseling. An empathetic counseling style combined with respectful listening validates the patient's perspective without judgment or criticism and accepts that ambivalence about change is normative. Counseling environments should feel safe, secure, and free from threat and judgment, where the patient is a true collaborator and the tone is friendly and warm. An individual whose body language appears relaxed, who has good eye contact, and who is disclosing pertinent information is engaged in counseling.

We seek to exude a confident and relaxed expertise that is kind, wise, and firm. The ideal counselor is an empathetic listener and a collaborator who provides supportive helpfulness and non-intrusive concern. Establishing a collaborative relationship requires the counselor to be active and direct, to develop rapport, and to establish credibility, while being sympathetic, honest, and maintaining a sense of humor. Improving basic counseling skills such as active listening can develop these attributes. (For more on active listening see Chapter 3: The Process of Counseling, pp. 59–78.) Overall, collaboration is built from establishing a partnership with the patient in which exploration and support, rather than persuasion or argument, is communicated. By respecting the individual's autonomy and supporting the individual's self-efficacy, the counselor attempts to elicit and evoke intrinsic motivations for change (Miller & Rollnick, 2002).

A productive collaborative bond requires empathy and an obvious interest in patients and their food-related problems. Interactions should convey genuine caring, deep respect, and an unbiased, non-judgmental attitude. "You must have felt …" or, "It sounds like you …" are examples of empathetic responses. Reference one's own experiences or the experiences of others by saying, for example, "I feel like … when that happens" or "Other patients have told me …" or, "Lots of people do just that …" Responding in this way lets patients know they have been understood and that their experiences are not out of the ordinary. Normalizing patients' experiences helps them feel more competent and more capable of making behavior changes. Verbally acknowledging the individual's strengths and accomplishments helps him or her feel valued and competent. For example, the counselor can comment on the personal strength necessary to recognize the need for and to engage in treatment.

An active collaborative approach is signaled by asking, "How can I be of help?" or "What do you need help with?" If the patient doesn't know the answer to this question—which is likely if the patient hasn't voluntarily sought help—then ask, "What brings you here?" This type of questioning helps the professional grasp the patient's goals. Our aim is to strike a balance between being advisor, facilitator, and teacher. When patients ask questions, it is generally best to answer directly and honestly. When patients ask for advice, answer in a way that encourages dialog: "What have you tried?" or, "What do you think would help?" If counselors never give advice, patients will experience them as withholding and resistant. If they always give advice and direction, then they will seem overbearing and intrusive.

We remind ourselves that our role is to provide information, advice, direction, and encouragement, but it is up to the patient ultimately to take responsibility to change his or her behaviors. We are cognizant that a "laissez-faire attitude," that allows patients to engage in nutrition counseling at their own pace, will lead to stagnation, and, in the case of an anorexic patient, may result in a stable or declining weight. Not only does this style of nutrition counseling impede behavioral progress, it can inhibit the patient's concurrent psychotherapy as well.

Open-ended questions help the nutrition counselor gather information. Use of "encouragers," such as "uh, huh," "tell me more," "so …" help patients continue to explore. Restatements and direct repetitions of the patient's story let the patient know that the counselor is listening. Hearing their thoughts restated helps patients better understand their situation. Reflecting back the patient's feelings, paraphrasing, and summarization are also effective in establishing a collaborative relationship.

Collaborative relationships are difficult when the counselor and the patient have conflicting goals. This is the dilemma that we face when we focus on helping patients gain weight, stop dieting, and reduce eating-disordered behaviors. The challenge is to remain calm and philosophical while addressing entrenched food beliefs, attitudes, and behaviors. Our job is made even more difficult by the fact that the ED patient often thinks he or she is completely self-sufficient. Regardless of any distress or difficulties the individual may be having, he or she feels obliged to take care of his or her problems without accepting help from others. The AN patient may respond to the opening question by saying, "I am fine, I am only here because my mother (or my doctor) is worried about me." One possible response might be, "Oh, so you need help reassuring your mother and your doctor. What are they worried about?" Dialogue like this helps patients find tangible reasons to participate in treatment.

Oftentimes, reluctant patients are unable to identify any problems attributable to their ED behaviors. These patients may benefit from hearing about symptoms of other ED patients. Noting that "many of my patients who have lost as much weight as you, have trouble keeping their hands warm" is likely to lead to further conversation. Disclosure of minor but pertinent details about the counselor and his or her practice can spark interest in an unenthusiastic patient. An example of a self-disclosing statement is "I am partial to working with ED patients because it gives me an opportunity to work with such great people."

Rolling with Resistance

Motivational interviewing has coined the phrase to "roll with resistance," that is to say, the counselor should respond to resistance with nonresistance. (For more on motivational interviewing see Chapter 3: The Process of Counseling, pp. 59–78.) Miller and Rollnick further (2002) note that "resistance is usually used to describe the behavior of only one person, the patient," but they go on to suggest that it is a "meaningful signal" that something is not working in the counselor–patient relationship, whether it be different goals or agendas, anger or frustration, or a misunderstanding about roles. In any case, it is the responsibility of the counselor to detect and dissolve resistance; how the counselor responds to resistance will determine in which direction the counseling will go. Arguing, interrupting, negating, and ignoring are indicative of patient resistance behavior (Miller and Rollnick, 2002). See Box 2.1 for how to respond to resistance.

BOX 2.1 EXAMPLES OF HOW TO RESPOND TO RESISTANCE

- Simple reflection to identify resistance

    - **Patient:** I don't want to be here. My mother is making me come.
    - **Counselor:** This was not your idea.

- Amplified reflection to exaggerate resistance without being sarcastic

    - **Patient:** My mother is always forcing me to do things.
    - **Counselor:** Life would be better without your mother always telling you what to do.

- Double-sided reflection to show ambivalence

    - **Patient:** I am so sick of thinking about food and weight all the time, but I know if I eat I will gain weight.
    - **Counselor:** Part of you wants to give up eating restrictively but another part is afraid if you eat you will gain weight.

- Shifting focus to redirect attention

    - **Patient:** There is no way I am going to keep a food journal.
    - **Counselor:** Let's not worry about that for now. Tell me more about
        ...

BOX 2.1 (continued)

- Reframing to validate and reinterpret

  - **Patient:** I like not having a period; it doesn't bother me.
  - **Counselor:** Yes, it's nice not to have to deal with it. What concerns me is the dangerous effects not menstruating has on your bones.

- Promoting patient control to offer choices

  - **Patient:** I'll never follow a food plan.
  - **Counselor:** That's OK. What would work for you instead?

Patients who are in treatment at the behest of another may be particularly resistant to giving up their ED behaviors. We acknowledge the fact that he or she may not be coming to sessions on his or her own accord. A look at the "bigger picture" of their ED and likely short- and long-term consequences may also help such patients engage in nutrition treatment. "What are your parents worried about?" "Can you imagine engaging in these eating behaviors at age 30?" Asking, "What would you suggest to someone else with a similar problem?" can help the resistant patient engage in goal setting. These explorations help patients see a discrepancy between their present behaviors and their goals and aspirations so that they are able to convey reasons why they want to change (Miller & Rollnick, 2002).

Others may dismiss nutrition interventions by saying, "I know everything there is to know about nutrition and EDs." We may agree that it is not unusual for patients to be well informed about nutrition and even EDs, and to make it clear that working with knowledgeable patients is rewarding. We add that our role includes providing "direction and support" as well as nutrition information. Knowledgeable patients can be asked, "What prevents you from making changes in your food behaviors?" Or, even more specifically, "If you could manage food the way you want to, what would you do about dinner?"

We suggest counselors avoid engaging in power struggles with patients. If an impasse develops, return to discussion of the patient's situation and difficulties, or their feelings about nutrition treatment. Ask, "How are you feeling about our sessions, since it seems like none of my suggestions have been helpful?" Resistant patients often respond to suggested behavior changes, "Yes, that is a good idea, but …" and then list all the reasons they cannot comply. This usually indicates the patient has not accepted the professional's direction. An appropriate response might be, "I see that you feel that my suggestion is not helpful. What might be more useful to you?" In this situation, we may advise an even smaller step. Paradoxically, when such patients are not challenged, they can feel more open to making behavior changes.

Another obstacle is the patient who is dishonest. Patients lie for various reasons: they may not feel safe telling the truth, or even believe that the lie is the truth.

Falsehoods may help them deny the seriousness of the ED or protect them or their family from the shame of the ED. We tend to take everything our patients say at face value, giving the patient the benefit of the doubt. After all, we are not lie detectors. But if we know a patient is lying, we do not get angry or take it personally. Instead we might casually tell a dishonest patient, "EDs make liars out of really honest people." If we suspect a lie, we may attempt to draw a distinction between the patient's reports and objective data. For example, we may express curiosity about a significant weight loss that is inconsistent with the patient's report of eating 100% of his or her food plan. Patients often "fess up" when we advise adding to their food plan. If the patient lies consistently, it may be worthwhile for the counselor to have a conversation with the patient's therapist and for the counselor to bring up the topic during supervision. (For more on supervision see Chapter 3: The Process of Counseling, pp. 59–78.) Chronic dishonesty also can indicate consideration of a higher level of care (see Chapter 7: Levels of Care, pp. 150–166).

Focusing on the establishment of a supportive rather than a confrontational relationship can help the nutrition counselor refrain from participating in the all too common power struggles these patients engender. A patient's motivation to recover is enhanced when the counselor acknowledges the difficulty of changing ED behaviors and empathize with the patient's distress at the prospect of changing. This approach helps to start the change process, and may lead the patient to identify reasons for change, as illustrated in the case of Courtney in Case Example 2.3. The budding collaboration between Courtney and her nutrition counselor shows how a patient can begin addressing his or her weight-related fears. In subsequent sessions, Courtney was able to experiment with healthier behaviors that led to slow steady weight gain.

CASE EXAMPLE 2.3: COURTNEY

The following dialog illustrates how the nutrition counselor began to forge a collaborative working relationship with a 17-year-old patient with anorexia nervosa.

Nutrition counselor: Courtney I am so glad to meet you. I'd like to be of help, but before we talk about that I'd love to hear about your previous treatment experiences, especially what you liked and what you didn't. Then maybe you and I can figure out how I can be of the most help to you.

Courtney talked for a few minutes about how she hated doing the required self-monitoring records and that she found the nutrition sessions boring because "all we talked about was what I ate and what I was going to eat."

> **Nutrition counselor:** It is good to know that food journals didn't work for you. They are a basic technique and sometimes are helpful, but if you didn't like doing them, there is no reason we should start with them. Is there anything you would like my help with?
>
> **Courtney:** Well, I always dreamed that in my senior year I would spend spring break in France with the French Club, but my parents say that I can't go because of my ED.
>
> **Nutrition counselor:** I can certainly see why your parents would feel this way. But, on the other hand, we would have about 7 months to turn around your ED. The trip doesn't sound totally out of the question, but it would be lots of hard work to get you ready to go. I know from talking to your doctor that you have to gain some weight before you can go back to school in the fall. I can find out what your doctor would think about this plan, and of course your parents would have to be agreeable.
>
> **Courtney:** How much weight would I have to gain to go to France?

Establishing Rapport

Rapport is built on the belief that patients are courageous when they recognize and secure the help they need. Like collaboration, rapport is also established when the counselor shows genuine interest in the patient's experiences, anxieties, obsessions, and misconceptions. Most ED patients will approach nutrition counseling with some ambivalence so that creating a sense of rapport and trust between the patient and the counselor may be complicated.

Patients with AN may feel they will be forced to relinquish behaviors that allows them to feel special and in control. Bulimic patients, though often eager for treatment, may not feel ready to give up the sense of independence or even rebellion that their behaviors provide. A curious, interested, empathetic approach helps ambivalent patients feel understood. We make it clear that the patient's own attempts to correct their problems are appreciated. Directly affirming the individual by giving compliments and statements of appreciation help to build rapport (Miller & Rollnick, 2002). Some other examples of affirming include: "Thank you for coming today." "It takes a lot of courage to seek out help." "I enjoyed talking with you today."

If the patient is a child, the counselor must be attuned to the possibility that the child may believe the professional is "on the parents' side." Having sessions alone with young patients can help foster a therapeutic relationship. We avoid using complicated words and concepts and strive to use the patient's syntax and language, such as "you make yourself sick" if the patient describes purging in this manner.

Counselors should indicate that the patient, regardless of age, and her or his experiences are taken seriously. Patients' opinions, thoughts, struggles, and feelings should be responded to in ways that indicate that they are legitimate and of interest and value. For example, Larkin's patient, Rose, a college student, believed that talking to her father on the phone caused her to binge. Larkin acknowledged that the stress of a difficult phone conversation could easily trigger a binge, particularly if one had not eaten all day.

It is wise for counselors to remember that, though they may be quite experienced in treating EDs, they should not assume they understand a particular patient's ED. Many patients relish opportunities to tell their story and explore their own thoughts and feelings about their ED. The patient's story provides an opportunity to learn more about the patient's perspective. Reflecting back to patients that their viewpoint "makes sense" in the context of their ED communicates empathy and respect. Some patients will need to spend time telling their story before they can accept specific guidance from a counselor. Otherwise, these patients are likely to feel they are receiving "canned" treatment or advice. Others, however, will want to focus on changing their problematic behaviors from the first few moments of the initial session rather than spend time recounting their past experiences. A caring approach helps the patient to feel hopeful, nurtured, and valued. Working with ED patients' misconceptions and maladaptive behaviors can be exasperating. Counselors should scrutinize their own attitudes if they find themselves arguing or becoming frustrated with patients.

Initial Session: Middle

Assessing the Nature of the Problem

The middle of the counseling session consists of assessing the nature of the patient's ED. For the counselor, the assessment process provides data necessary for making an accurate diagnosis and providing effective treatment. For the patient, the assessment process may increase self-awareness and motivation. For both the counselor and the patient, the assessment process facilitates the establishment of a collaborative relationship. We think of assessment as a dialogue between patient and counselor. During this dialogue, we take notes, which allow us to find our way back to a topic that might need further discussion or to jot down something in the margin as a reminder. At times we allow patients to vent, or we follow their direction. If they get off track or talk too much about an issue that may better be served by their therapist, we gently redirect them back to the food and weight part of their story.

We have virtually memorized the information templates for nutrition assessments (see Appendix B: Checklist for Nutrition Assessment of Eating Disorders) and the Academy of Nutrition and Dietetics *Nutrition Care Manual* for ED, which outlines information required to make an assessment (http://nutritioncareman-ual.org). Consequently, we are able to move through the assessment process with fluidity, gathering and prioritizing pertinent information as topics arise. We may decide to weigh the patient or not, we may obtain a 24-hour recall (see Chapter 6: Self-Monitoring, pp. 140–149) and diet history or not. We may decide to use the decision-to-change matrix (see Chapter 4: Counseling Interventions, pp. 79–104) to obtain information about the patient. Our readers may use the Checklist for Nutrition Assessment of Eating Disorders (see Appendix B) over the course of several sessions as a guide to ensure their evaluation is comprehensive.

Essentially, we strive to balance the process of data collection (which continues throughout treatment) with listening to the patient's story. Peterson (2009) writes that it is challenging to obtain all the assessment data in one interview. To ease the pace of assessment interviewing, background information can also be collected during pre-session contact or via questionnaires completed by the patient prior to the initial session.

Furthermore, when initial sessions are devoted solely to history taking, a collaborative relationship may not develop. The counselor should focus initial sessions on piquing the patient's interest and curiosity about treatment and about the counselor rather than devoting the entire session to gathering clinical data. Focus subsequent sessions on the problems and history the patient presents. Although the counselor is necessarily quite interested in the patient's food-related history, some patients will be bored and frustrated by extended history-gathering sessions. They may feel ready, almost immediately, to begin working on solutions to their current eating problems. Others need to be "known" before they can accept direct guidance or feedback. A style of questioning in which the counselor asks permission before proceeding is less threatening. "What do you think is important for me to know about your eating problems?" "Would you be willing to tell me about yourself, especially in reference to coming to see me today?" This style of questioning encourages patients to tell their story at their own pace. Nevertheless, over the course of treatment, the patient's history should be fully explored in regard to eating behaviors, body weight, knowledge, and attitudes about food. We find that one advantage to obtaining personal and dietary histories over time is that it allows for more in-depth exploration and education. Peterson (2009) also notes that it is important to consider ourselves as part of the assessment process and not focus solely on data collection. Our own emotions and reactions during the interview process can inform us about the patient's experience and status, as well as allow us to be more effective, empathetic counselors. Furthermore, the patient may display non-verbal behaviors such as body position, eye contact, body movements, and facial expression, that are, more often than not, reliable indicators of the patient's affect or underlying feelings. These non-verbal affective messages help the counselor determine how to respond to and communicate with the patient (Okun, 2002).

Determining the Diagnosis

We are not too concerned—except for the purposes of using insurance coding—about labeling our patients with a specific ED diagnosis using the American Psychiatric Association's *Diagnostic and Statistical Manual of Mental Disorders* (DSM), since treatment approaches are similar for all ED diagnoses. We prefer instead to address the immediate, day-to-day problems our patients are enduring and to have them leave each session with something to work on (see discussion on problem solving, below). However, that being said, we are responsible for assessing whether the individual is medically stable and safe from suicide or self-harm, especially if we are the individual's first point of contact. It is our job to refer the patient to the appropriate medical and psychological care and communicate our concerns to the patient's physician or therapist. It is also of utmost importance to diagnose and treat the ED as early as possible to improve prognosis and recovery.

Peterson (2009) notes the difficulties counselors have assigning DSM criteria for EDs. The counselor may be too rigid with assigning the diagnosis of anorexia nervosa (AN) or bulimia nervosa (BN) if the patient does not meet the exact criteria, and instead use the eating disorder not otherwise specified (EDNOS) criteria. We have seen in our practices practitioners using different diagnostic codes for the same patient, which is not surprising since patients with AN and BN share many clinical features and may "migrate across diagnostic categories" (Reiter & Graves, 2010, p. 122). On the other hand, insufficient probing about the patient's ED behaviors may also result in misguided treatment strategies, such as with the patient who defines overeating as "binge eating." Mehler and Andersen (2010, p. 204) emphasize the need to make the ED diagnosis "simply and accurately," using a brief set of questions (such as the SCOFF questionnaire, see Box 2.2) rather than using more extensive assessments for clinical levels of psychopathology. Two or more positive answers on the five questions of the SCOFF questionnaire have been proven to be clinically accurate in diagnosis (Hill, Reid, Morgan, & Lacey, 2010).

BOX 2.2 THE 'SCOFF' QUESTIONS

S Do you make yourself SICK (vomit) because you feel uncomfortably full?
C Do you worry that you have lost CONTROL over how much you eat?
O Have you recently lost more than ONE stone (15 pounds) in a 3-month period?
F Do you believe yourself to be FAT when others say you are thin?
F Would you say that FOOD dominates your life?

Note. SCOFF Questionnaire. Reprinted from "SCOFF, the development of an eating disorder screening questionnaire," by L. S. Hill, F. Reid, J. F. Morgan, and J. H. Lacey, 2010. *International Journal of Eating Disorders, 43*, p. 345. Copyright 2010 by John Wiley and Sons. Reprinted with permission.

We also use the widely used and accepted Eating Attitudes Test (EAT-26) with its 26 questions as an initial assessment and during treatment to assess progress (Garner, Olmstead, Bohr, & Garfinkel, 1982). The EAT-26 with instructions for scoring and interpretation can be downloaded from http://www.eat-26.com. The same assessments can be used to diagnose EDs in males as are used in females.

A synopsis of an initial session with an individual with new-onset AN and a patient with a chronic history of BN are given in Boxes 2.3 and 2.4, respectively.

BOX 2.3 INITIAL SESSION SYNOPSIS: INDIVIDUAL WITH NEW-ONSET ANOREXIA NERVOSA

Presession information

Father: Charlotte is a 19-year-old new-onset patient referred by her father after the college physician noted a 10-pound weight loss in 3 weeks. Charlotte is a college athlete recruited to play soccer at college.

Physician: Physician notes indicate unexplained weight loss, amenorrhea and fatigue. Lab values are unremarkable.

Counselor's questions/ comments	Charlotte's responses	Counselor's assessment/plan
What are you hoping to accomplish with nutrition counseling? Tell me about yourself?	I want to know what I need to do to get back to playing soccer. I'm most happy playing soccer. I work out after soccer practice to keep in shape.	Soccer is important. Patient may be overexercising. Additional data regarding duration and intensity of exercise is obtained.
What else do you like to do besides soccer?	Not much. I usually go home on weekends. I don't hang out much with anybody.	Patient may be isolating and disconnected with peers, teary and not easily engaging in conversation. Counselor considers need for referral to therapist.
What concerns you most?	I feel like I am hitting the wall. I can't keep up during soccer practices.	Patient is most likely restricting food intake, resulting in low energy availability, which is affecting the activity she likes most.
Tell me how you eat?	I'm a picky eater. I eat breakfast and dinner but I usually don't have time for lunch. I don't like to eat lunch before soccer practice. I never snack.	24-hour recall shows inadequate caloric intake. Counselor reviews patient's food likes/dislikes/ feared foods.
What other physical concerns do you have?	I get headaches and I can't sleep at night.	Further substantiates low food intake and long periods between

		food events. Counselor suspects patient needs between-meal snacks, including a bedtime snack.
I am excited about helping you.	What I care most about is my soccer.	Good. That's what we will work on. I am excited to help you improve your playing.
To reach your goal, we will have to add to what you are eating. Where would like to add?	I could eat an apple for lunch.	Counselor assumes the add needs to be at least 300 calories.
Gee, how about some protein with that apple?	I like cheese sticks.	Sounds good.
It might be good to eat a little at bedtime to help you sleep.	Would a greek yogurt be OK?	Counselor summarizes and writes out plan for patient. Tells patient, "This is a good start to getting you back to playing soccer."

BOX 2.4 INITIAL SESSION SYNOPSIS OF A PATIENT WITH A CHRONIC HISTORY OF BULIMIA NERVOSA

Marta is a 52-year-old referred by her therapist for chronic (30 years) BN. She is a sexual-abuse survivor and has a history of alcohol and drug abuse. Marta is a single parent of a difficult 10-year-old boy; she works full time as an occupational therapist. Pre-session history reveals that Marta uses laxatives and self-induces vomiting at least three times weekly.

Counselor's questions	Marta's responses	Counselors' assessment/plan
What are you most worried about?	I'm really worried about the purging. I feel exhausted and my throat hurts.	Patient's purging is an effective place to start. Counselor obtains details about purging.
How does bingeing fit in?	I don't know if it's a binge, but I basically eat all night.	Counselor obtains details about bingeing and suspects patient is restricting.
Would you mind telling me what you ate yesterday?	Patient recounts skipping breakfast and lunch yesterday. She usually skips lunch every day.	Patient eats less than 1500 calories daily, skips lunch. Counselor provides psychoeducation re: connection between restriction, bingeing/purging.
When was the last time you saw your doctor?	Not for over a year.	Counselor expresses concern for medical safety. Counselor encourages patient to make an appointment with her physician for medical assessment.
Do you like to read?	Yes, very much.	Counselor lends patient the book, *Life Without Ed* (Schaefer, 2003).

Delineating Expectations

Another important objective of initial sessions is exploration of the individual's motivations for and expectations about nutrition treatment. "What do you hope to accomplish with nutrition counseling?" "If you had a magic wand, what would you wish for in relationship to your eating behaviors?" "What's worked in the past?" "What's not worked?" These questions allow the counselor to understand what is important to the patient and what the patient values, and reinforces the establishment of a collaborative relationship. Addressing these core concerns allows the patient to feel validated and less anxious about treatment. Including the patient in the process for setting the agenda of each session is yet another means of collaboration. This also allows the counselor to individualize interventions according to the individual's readiness to change.

Once the individual's concerns are identified, counselors should articulate their conviction that solutions exist and that they have the necessary expertise and experience to help the patient overcome these problems. These first sessions are aimed at reassuring, and even inspiring, the patient about the potential for progress as the result of engaging in treatment. Yahne (2004, p. 5) writes "inspiring hope in our patients" is "our first duty as clinicians." Throughout each session, the counselor should remain optimistic about the likelihood of the patient's eventual success in overcoming the ED and confident in his or her ability to guide and assist the patient is this endeavor.

We enhance the patient's confidence by noting and praising all progress, however modest. Restored hopefulness, in and of itself, has been shown to have a significant positive impact on ED behaviors. Some patients, especially those who have suffered from an ED in spite of years of treatment, will have difficulty making progress because they are resigned to their behaviors and cynical about the effectiveness of treatment. These patients will need regular "pep-talks," gentle feedback, encouragement, and support routinely at the end of each session throughout treatment. Patients can be told that even a long history of an ED does not predict a poor outcome.

Along with hope, an effective counselor gives the patient confidence in the nutrition counseling process and fosters the belief that recovery is possible. Counselors who are confident, knowledgeable, firm, authoritative, and experienced are likely to have credibility with patients. The counselor can enhance his or her own credibility by explaining how EDs usually develop and describing likely symptoms. Bulimic and binge-eating patients are likely to be eager for assistance and in dire need of hope. Such patients can be galvanized by references to positive research findings on the efficacy of various treatments, as well as success stories from the counselor's practice. Adult bulimic patients are usually quite willing to work with a professional who offers to help them control their eating behaviors. Role modeling healthy viewpoints on dieting, nutrition, health, and physical attractiveness has a positive impact on patients' beliefs and values about these issues. When giving such information, however, it is important to acknowledge that the individual may be quite well informed. Knowledge of a professional's long-term availability is also associated with a positive prognosis.

Patients find it inspiring to hear that recovery is possible, that the counselor is capable, and that the counselor is responsible for pacing and managing the treatment. "I don't want you to worry about how treatment is going to go or what to do next." "I don't want you to worry if things aren't going well, that's my job." "You can't fail treatment if you are in it." These adages are reassuring when patients are young, frightened, intimidated, overwhelmed, or not confident in their ability to recover.

Goal Setting

For most individuals, to engage in goal setting they need to feel confident in the nutrition counselor's expertise. Devoting time in initial sessions to assure patients that you have the skills, experience, and, yes, the patience necessary to guide the individual's recovery is vital. We always keep in mind that ED individuals are often severely malnourished and, consequently, may not be able to think clearly. Patience and compassion are required, as these patients may need to have behavioral goals and plans repeatedly clarified.

We encourage patients to concentrate on goals that are in their best interest and relevant to their recovery. Patients will become more enthusiastic about experimenting with behavioral goals if every effort has been made to offer solutions that are uniquely tailored to their situation. We elaborate on how each behavioral goal benefits the patient and addresses her or his particular concerns.

Patients should be directed to choose as goals behaviors that are under their own control. Instead of weight-change goals, for example, we encourage our patients to select food- or exercise-related assignments, as these behaviors are under an individual's direct control. We are active, but also gentle, in helping patients choose sequential behavioral goals that match their problems and level of insight and understanding. "What do you want to change about your eating?" Making routine the question, "What do you want to work on this week?" can prompt productive discussions about possible goals. Occasionally, a patient will require very little, if any, direct guidance. Such patients make behavioral progress with just support for and appreciation of their efforts, and the knowledge that specific assistance is available if needed. Other patients have definite ideas of what they could do to improve their situation. Being inquisitive about the patient's own sense of where to begin can be productive: "What do you feel ready to work on?" or, "Where should we begin?" Asking, "What bothers you the most?" helps the nutrition counselor suggest relevant behavioral goals. Behavioral goals proposed by patients should be enthusiastically endorsed, though it may be necessary to suggest modifications. Establishing appropriate behavioral goals, which are specific and detailed, requires familiarity with the behaviors that perpetuate the patient's ED and her or his goals for treatment. Patients should be queried about their recent and historical food-related problems and attempts at solutions. Throughout the course of treatment they need to be provided with germane information and given help in correcting misconceptions and changing cognitions.

Goal setting makes most patients either anxious about giving up control over eating, or body weight, or both. Patients should be assured that these concerns, and any others, are taken seriously and will be addressed in treatment. Larkin allays patient's anxieties and fears by comparing an ED to a coat. If an individual's coat (or ED) is taken away without offering a replacement (healthy coping skills) then the person will feel cold and unprotected against the elements (confused and vulnerable). The metaphorical loss of only a button or a thread from a coat (i.e., a small decrease in ED behaviors) is less uncomfortable (i.e., less threatening) than loss of a whole coat. As an old coat gradually disintegrates, the individual considers getting a new coat (i.e., learns a new concept or skill to help with his or her recovery).

An important principle of goal setting with ED patients is to aim small and low. Small, feasible goals are more likely to be attained than more ambitious ones. It is not uncommon for professionals, or patients for that matter, to initially propose behavioral goals that are too difficult for the patient to achieve. "Downgrading" behavioral goals and reminding patients they are not required to change or to make rapid progress can, paradoxically, free reluctant patients to be less oppositional (Hill & O'Brien, 1999, p. 313).

If the patient is not at least enthusiastic about the likelihood of success of a behavioral plan, we revise the goals or return to further discussion about the patient's readiness to engage in goal setting. We often ask, "What would you like to do differently?" Before goals are agreed upon, both patient and professional should be "90%" sure the patient can be successful. As "success breeds success," mastering smaller goals increases the patient's confidence to tackle more difficult goals. Using a confidence rating scale (see Chapter 4: Counseling Interventions, p. 98) can help elicit potential obstacles or concerns. Still another tactic is for the counselor to encourage patients to speculate about possible obstacles by asking:

- "What would make this assignment difficult to achieve?"
- "What problems will you have following through on this goal?"
- "How could you resolve these problems?"
- "Can you see yourself doing 'x'?"

The counselor needs to be willing to adjust plans and modify approaches if the patient is not making expected progress. Behavioral goals (including food plans) should be continually modified based on the patient's report of "what worked" and "what didn't work." On the other hand, patients often need help recognizing unproductive behavioral patterns. It can be helpful to reflect cause and effect as in, "I noticed that you didn't binge the evenings you ate a better dinner."

When patients are not making progress, the fault may lie with the counselor who inadvertently has become too invested in whether and how patients change. If patients have had a hand in formulating behavioral goals, they are more likely to take responsibility for their own progress than if the nutrition counselor simply tells them what to do. Conversely, some patients may be hindered because the professional is not focused on the fundamental goal of nutrition counseling–behavior change. Professionals who have a sensitive and perceptive style of nutrition counseling, in particular, need to guard against being diverted from focusing on behavior-change goals by patients' psychological issues. Patients who choose to focus on such issues in nutrition sessions should be referred to conjoint psychotherapy. Always bear in mind that the primary goal of nutrition counseling is behavior change.

Problem solving should be applied when patients are not making progress correcting food behaviors or body weight, or when they continue to have problems completing homework assignments or keeping appointments. Problem solving involves analyzing what happened and what went wrong, and then helping patients revise their approach based on this analysis. We advise that patients adopt a common-sense problem-solving approach, namely, that they identify the problem and its antecedents, consider a variety of potential solutions, evaluate the effectiveness and feasibility of possible solutions, define the steps required to carry out the chosen solution, implement the chosen solution, then evaluate the results.

Each nutrition session should end with the patient committed to a plan that includes several behavioral goals. Appropriate behavioral goals or assignments (e.g., eat breakfast, add a protein serving to dinner, completing food journals, or take a vitamin and mineral supplement) will become apparent over the course of the session. Further along in treatment, behavioral goals might include following a food or exercise plan, or assignments to go food or clothes shopping. Although underweight patients may have weekly weight goals, these goals should be "operationalized" so the patient agrees to food and exercise assignments that contribute to achieving the necessary weight gain.

Writing out food plans or assignments is helpful for many patients, but discuss semantics with patients first. Some will prefer calling the plan or list of assignments "homework" so that they can think of treatment much like a class. Others may feel demeaned by this terminology. As previously mentioned, assigned tasks should be manageable and designed to provide the patient with a sense of success and provide the professional with the opportunity to give positive feedback. The patient's progress, however modest, in achieving these assignments should be acknowledged and praised.

Initial Session: End

We often use the "15-minute rule" to inform patients that the session will end shortly and to direct them to what is to follow. What follows in the last few minutes of the session is time devoted to answering patients' questions, to summarizing what has transpired in the session, and to giving patients positive feedback for their efforts. This time can also be spent discussing the possibility of doing homework. Summarization at the end of the session highlights what the patient has said during the session. Summarization also can be tactfully used throughout the session to link and transition between various topics or themes. Both the patient and the counselor can participate in summarizing, as well as decide to agree on the summary. Summarization gives the patient the opportunity to elaborate and reflect on his or her situation or feelings. Besides giving the counselor the opportunity to reinforce and validate what the patient has said, summarizing may also reveal what the counselor may have missed (Box 2.5). Agreeing on a summary at the end of the session strengthens the collaborative relationship between patient and counselor.

BOX 2.5 QUESTIONS FOR ENDING SESSIONS

- "How was this for you today?"
- "Do you have any questions you would like to ask me?"
- "Today we've talked about ..."
- "Is there anything I've missed?"
- "What do you want to do between now and the next session?"
- "Where do you want to go from here?"
- "I appreciate the courage it takes to come to sessions."
- "You have given me a lot to think about."

Homework

Homework is likely to consist of food or exercise behavioral agreements or instructions for self-monitoring behaviors. Since patients rarely make progress without doing homework, most nutrition counseling sessions should end with assignments to be completed before the next scheduled session. The regular assignment of "homework" assures patients that they are actively engaged in treatment. Effective homework assignments are derived from the patient's previous successes and modified to address current difficulties.

It may encourage compliance to write out homework assignments. The counselor can introduce this approach by saying, "I'll write out the assignment for you, or would you rather do it?" There are situations, however, when we are circumspect about giving homework assignments. If the patient is emotional, exhausted, or overwhelmed, it may be more productive for the counselor to affirm, support, and encourage rather than to give an assignment.

Common homework conundrums are assignments that are too difficult or too vague. Consider asking patients how confident they are that they can complete the assignment. If they are not 90% sure they can be successful, break down the desired behavior change into smaller increments which then can be assigned instead. In some cases the patient may not have fully grasped the rationale behind the assignment and would benefit from further clarification of relevant educational themes. Specificity helps. For example, "Can you abstain from purging on Thursday evenings?" or, "Can you add a slice of bread to your lunch?"

Typically, ED patients have trouble completing assignments that involve increasing planned food intake due to fear of weight gain. If a patient's weight is not currently monitored, and she or he is struggling, weigh-ins should be seriously considered, as patients often imagine that their weight has increased when it has not.

This may be the time to assign self-monitoring records (for details on self-monitoring see Chapter 6: Self-Monitoring). Food monitoring provides increased awareness about behavioral problems. Increased awareness can make it easier for patients to change behaviors. Agras and Apple (1997) recommend using data from the patient's self-monitoring forms or self-reports to illustrate how homework assignments address particular problems. Food journals can also show how a patient's present behavior is unproductive: "Isn't this interesting," Herrin remarked to Dan, a purging anorexic. "I see from your food journals that when you drink two cups of water with meals you almost always purge."

It must be underscored that, if homework is assigned, it *must* be reviewed at the subsequent session to be effective. When homework assignments are ignored by nutrition counselors, patients are likely to infer that the tasks are not important and cease to do them. Another negative outcome is that patients can conclude the nutrition counselor is not truly invested in their treatment.

In assigning homework, we point out that progress usually does not occur unless there is a willingness to take some risks and experiment with new behaviors. Nevertheless, some patients improve from the paradoxical reminder that if they are not pleased with the results of behavior changes, they can revert to old behaviors. For example, the normal-weight patient, who is hesitant to agree to the assignment to add a serving of protein to dinner for fear of weight gain, can be assured that if she actually gains weight, she can always choose to return to her more restrictive meal pattern. There is no advantage to engaging in power struggles with patients around homework assignments or other issues. Remain empathetic and reflective while expressing the conviction that progress, and eventually recovery, will result from modest but sustained behavior changes.

Follow-Up Sessions

We find that encouraging patients to reflect on the previous session is a good place to start a follow-up session. "How did you feel about our last session?" Other helpful questions are, "What would you like to talk about today?" "How are you doing?" "Where should we start?" "Since our last session, I've wondered about ..." "How did you do with your homework?" During follow up sessions, the counselor should review any homework that was assigned previously. Significant time should be devoted to food planning and problem solving, with special attention to identification of food behaviors that interfere with progress. The counselor should encourage patients to discuss apprehensions they may have about nutrition sessions, body weight, food planning, and any physical complaints. If the patient's weight must be monitored, this should be done early in the session to allow plenty of time to process the patient's reaction to the weigh-in and to draw reasonable conclusions about the connection between the patient's behaviors and body weight.

Appointment Frequency

Nutrition counseling is most effectively provided on a weekly basis for new-onset patients as well as for those patients with chronic ED diagnoses. Patients tend to not make behavioral progress with less frequent appointments unless they are highly motivated. Our experience has shown that more frequent visits at the beginning of treatment are more beneficial than meeting once monthly for a longer period of time. Bi-weekly and then monthly sessions are indicated as patients successfully meet and maintain treatment goals.

Anorexic patients who require weight restoration may benefit from more frequent than once-weekly sessions, especially if the patient is an adolescent or child. Meeting with the nutrition counselor up to three times weekly allows the counselor to closely monitor weight changes and to adjust the caloric content of the meal plan accordingly. Frequent monitoring of this type also helps to manage the commonly held fear about gaining weight too fast.

From time to time patients inquire about the amount of time or the number of nutrition counseling sessions required for recovery. Although this seems like a fair question, it is difficult to predict a time frame for recovery. Much will depend on the patient's background, support system, and level of motivation. What we can tell the patient is that, ideally, the first three sessions are necessary to obtain background information, to gain an understanding of his or her situation, and to establish treatment goals. Additional sessions are required for implementation and monitoring of treatment goals. A patient may have financial constraints or a limited number of visits covered by insurance; in this regard, the nutrition counselor needs to be flexible with scheduling sessions and to outline with the patient a realistic plan for providing treatment.

The Eating Disorder Treatment Team

Nutrition counselors are sometimes the first point of contact for a patient seeking help for an ED, and, therefore, become responsible for helping the patient establish a treatment team. It is important for the nutrition counselor to convey that a team approach is the standard of care for treating EDs. Sloan (2009) said that, if it takes a village to raise a child, surely it takes a team to treat an ED. Halmi (2009), in an excellent review of treatment approaches, reinforces this view: "Experienced ED clinicians have come to the conclusion that a multidisciplinary team approach provides the most effective treatment."

In our over 40 years of combined experience, we have found it rare for patients to successfully recover from an ED without the help, guidance, and support of a team of knowledgeable collaborating professionals. Both the Academy of Nutrition and Dietetics and the American Psychiatric Association position statements support team treatment as an essential component of ED recovery, and with nutrition counselors as integral members of such teams (American Dietetic Association, 2006; American Psychiatric Association, 2006).

We are willing to create ED treatment teams with any professionals who are willing and able to provide support and appropriate services to our patient. The typical traditional team-treatment model consists of a medical provider (pediatrician, family doctor, internist, nurse practitioner, or physician assistant), psychiatrist or psychiatric nurse practitioner, psychotherapist, and nutrition counselor. Who is on the team, however, may differ from case to case. The type of professional support and direction required may vary as the challenges and obstacles of recovery evolve.

A medical provider must be part of the team whether other professionals are involved or not. Outpatient treatment requires that the patient's health be assessed and monitored regularly to ensure the patient's safety. Both nutrition counselors and psychotherapists are almost always essential, but for varying lengths of time. In the treatment of children and adolescents, parents or other family members are also part of the treatment team. Mature patients, themselves, may have a role on the team. Early in recovery, the psychotherapist may play a supporting role to patients as they struggle with compliance with the food plan. Once the patient is better nourished, the psychotherapist can take a more major role focusing on emotional needs, feelings, beliefs, and pre-morbid problems.

The nutrition counselor and the medical provider collaborate on weight issues; the psychotherapist, psychiatrist, and the medical provider collaborate on medications; the nutrition counselor and the family collaborate on food planning; and the psychotherapist and family members collaborate on family issues. The nutrition counselor focuses on restoring healthy body weight, normalizing food habits, expanding food choices, changing attitudes and beliefs, and correcting misguided notions about eating, food, and body size and shape. With physical stability, medical monitoring shifts from one to two times per week to less frequent visits focused more on preventive primary care. As the young patient progresses, family members become less involved in treatment.

In a genuine team treatment, each member thinks of the patient as his or her patient. In other words, the team functions collaboratively, without a designated leader and with each member's contribution being of equal importance. On effective teams, team members share a treatment philosophy and consistently challenge patients' assumptions, beliefs, and attitudes. On such teams, members deliver similar messages on the need for adequate food intake, the importance of restoration of menses, the effects of starvation on the body and brain, and so forth. Team members appreciate that patients may have good reasons, for example, low self-esteem or societal pressures, for engaging in ED behaviors and thinking. They are committed to helping patients develop more effective ways of handling food and emotions and to develop new definitions of self that do not revolve around weight, size, and shape.

Outside of full-spectrum treatment facilities, assembling a skilled team takes effort. With regular communication and direction from the more experienced members, clinicians with basic knowledge and skills can function effectively on *ad hoc* treatment teams. Ideally, team members are not only experienced and competent, but kind, empathetic, confident, no-nonsense, and firm. Such professionals expect progress and are confident that their approaches are effective and lead to full recovery. They take EDs seriously, recognizing that an ED is a grave, potentially life-threatening disorder that must be treated with determination and effort.

The "adding one professional at a time" method of assembling a team is what is known as "stepped care." In this model, treatment is "stepped up" until the patient begins to make progress, beginning first with the lowest intensity intervention and progressing, as needed, to gradually more intensive interventions (Wilson, Vitousek, & Loeb, 2000). For example, patients may first be offered a trial of a nutrition therapy or psychotherapy. Antidepressant medication may be considered as an alternative or additional first step. If these simpler treatments elicit no response, the patient is advised to work both with a nutrition counselor and a psychotherapist, and to consider a trial of medication if not already prescribed (Williams, Goodie, & Motsinger, 2008).

How to Make a Referral

Kellogg (2010, Tip No. 98) suggests a "format for referring" which includes the following: reflect what you hear about the patient's needs and concerns, such as increased anxiety; inform the patient of one or two truths, such as seeing a therapist for anxiety helps with eating concerns; ask permission to provide referrals and then wait for a response before giving the referral. We have ready a list of ED practitioners in our local areas.

Some nutrition counselors require patients to engage simultaneously in treatment with a psychotherapist. On the other hand, patients who are hesitant about seeking any treatment at all may feel exasperated by the prerequisite that they arrange for conjoint psychotherapy. If nutrition counselors are experienced in treating ED patients and are willing and ready to make mental health referrals, then it is acceptable practice *to begin* treatment as the sole counselor. Referrals to a psychotherapist, however, must be made if and when patients' psychological issues become apparent or begin to dominate nutrition sessions or when patients do not make expected progress.

Kellogg (2010, Tip No. 98) writes, "There are always a few patients who will be best served by someone else." If you feel your patient may be better served by a different nutrition counselor who is more experienced with this particular patient's concerns or who is able to see the patient more frequently, then a referral is warranted. Referrals should also be made if you have a dual relationship with a patient, such as he or she is also your hairdresser or your neighbor. Use your professional opinion about what is in the best interest for your patient.

Termination

Kellogg (2008, Tip No. 75) maintains, "Taking time and respect with endings reinforces the value of your work," and rightly so, as termination of treatment is associated with increased risk for relapse (Beumont, Beumont, Touyz, & Williams, 1997, p. 183). As long-term availability of treatment (2–3 years) is associated with positive prognosis in cases of severe EDs, we are cautious about terminating treatment earlier. One approach is to suggest that a reduction in the frequency of sessions is warranted when the patient has made significant progress. When termination is gradually approached, patients are less likely to experience it as a cessation of support, nor are they liable to develop an unhealthy dependency on professionals. Less frequent sessions allow patients to practice relapse-prevention and problem-solving strategies while still receiving professional support. It is not uncommon for patients to need a month's worth of additional sessions within a year of ceasing regular visits. Some patients, especially those with additional psychological diagnoses, may need to continue regularly scheduled appointments indefinitely to keep ED symptoms at bay.

Because it is common for ED patients, particularly anorexic patients, to experience termination of treatment as a rejection, any planned reduction in appointment frequency should be sensitively discussed. It is essential that patients do not feel abandoned once eating-disordered behaviors subside. Planning a last session or termination session may be helpful to reinforce and summarize the patient's progress and behavior changes, and to bring closure to the treatment process. We make it clear that patients are always welcome back for a "tune-up."

We recommend that counselors consider terminating the treatment of patients who have not made significant improvements in ED behaviors in 8 weeks of treatment. Typical indicators of ineffective treatment include bingeing episodes occurring more frequently than once per day or continued weight loss in anorexic patients. It may be that the patient is not following his or her treatment recommendations or has not followed through with establishing a treatment team. However, it may be that other members of the treatment team themselves, including family members and other practitioners, are not adequately attending to the patient's treatment so that a collaborative and supportive treatment team is lacking, rendering the nutrition counselor's efforts ineffective. Making continued sessions contingent on some signs of progress sometimes is an effective motivator. We also terminate treatment for patients who do not pay the agreed fee or who do not show for appointments.

The decision to terminate treatment should only be made after consultation with other members of the treatment team or with a supervisor. We recognize that there are always exceptions to such guidelines and have, on occasion, made exceptions.

Summary Points

- For the purpose of nutrition counseling, it is important to understand not only who the patient is, but where the patient is in his or her stage of recovery, including any prior treatment he or she has or has received.
- Each individual nutrition counseling session has three parts: the beginning, middle and end. The beginning of the session, consists of greeting the patient and ascertaining the reason for the visit. The middle part of the session includes assessing the nature of the problem and what advice or changes the patient requires. The ending, or summary part, of the session includes a review of homework assignments and a plan for future visits.
- A collaborative relationship between counselor and patient is fundamental to any counseling endeavor, including nutrition counseling.
- Instead of weight-change goals, for example, patients should be encouraged to select food- or exercise-related assignments, as these behaviors are under the patient's direct control.
- Since patients rarely make progress without doing homework, most nutrition counseling sessions end with giving assignments to be completed before the next scheduled session.
- Patients need the guidance and support of an ED treatment team consisting of knowledgeable collaborating professionals if they are to successfully recover.

3

THE PROCESS OF COUNSELING

Introduction

Nutrition counselors who treat patients with eating disorders (EDs) benefit from understanding the dynamics of counseling this complex population. As an overview, we have included the Academy of Nutrition and Dietetics position statement's outline of the clinical responsibilities of nutrition counselors who treat patients with EDs (see Box 3.1; Ozier & Henry, 2011). The rest of this chapter

---

BOX 3.1 CODE OF ETHICS FOR NUTRITION COUNSELORS

1. The dietetics practitioner conducts himself/herself with honesty, integrity, and fairness.
2. The dietetics practitioner supports and promotes high standards of professional practice.
3. The dietetics practitioner accepts the obligation to protect patients, the public, and the profession by upholding the Code of Ethics for the Profession of Dietetics and by reporting perceived violations of the Code through the processes established by ADA and its credentialing agency, CDR.

Note: Fundamental principles of the code of ethics for nutrition counselors. Reprinted from "American Dietetic Association/Commission on Dietetic Registration Code of Ethics for the Profession of Dietetics and Process for Consideration of Ethics Issues," by American Dietetic Association, 2009, *Journal of the American Dietetic Association, 109,* p. 1461. Copyright 2009 by American Dietetic Association. Reprinted with permission.

delves deeply into the counseling process, highlighting the ethics of counseling and the management of psychotherapeutic issues that often arise during the nutrition counseling process. We offer guidelines about co-morbid illnesses that frequently affect patients with EDs and how these illnesses impact nutrition counseling. Finally, we include a section on body-image disturbance, as this feature is a diagnostic criterion of EDs and is intertwined with the food, weight, and shape issues that are in the scope of practice for the nutrition counselor.

Counseling Ethics

The Role of the Counselor

First and foremost, nutrition counselors should do no harm, which includes being able to effectively recognize, assess, and appropriately plan treatment for a patient with an ED. Except in the case of minors, the process of counseling is based on the premise that patients are allowed the right to make their own decisions if they do not do harm to themselves or to others. (For more on working with children, see Chapter 2: Course of Treatment, section on: Confidentiality: Children, p. 36.) Counselors should aim to support the growth and development of patients by being sincere, dependable, and trustworthy. Giving honest feedback, keeping confidences, being on time for appointments, and being direct about one's availability outside of sessions all help foster a counseling relationship. In initial sessions, we inform patients of our policies regarding phone calls and e-mails between sessions. In general, dual relationships (providing counseling to friends or other family members of current patients) should be avoided. In some circumstances (e.g., when only one experienced nutrition counselor is available) such relationships may be unavoidable. If so, counselors should first obtain approval from the original patient, and take pains to keep treatment sessions devoted to each patient's individual treatment issues. In addition, counselors should be prepared for times they may encounter patients in social settings. If this is likely to occur, a behavior plan should be discussed with patients in advance. When unexpected meetings occur, it is best to let patients take the initiative. We respond with courtesy, without engaging the patient. Finally, those who work with ED patients should aim to personally eat and exercise in a responsible manner. Adequate self-care ensures that counselors can competently care for others.

The Academy of Nutrition and Dietetics recommends that registered dietitians (RDs) working with EDs have advanced-level training via self-study, continuing-education programs, and supervision by another experienced RD or an ED therapist (Ozier & Henry, 2011). Professional support and supervision and continuing education are particularly important when the nutrition counselor works with complicated patients. Specialized trainings are offered through practice groups of the Academy of Nutrition and Dietetics, including:

Dietetics in Developmental and Psychiatric Disorders; Pediatric Nutrition; and Sports, Cardiovascular, and Wellness Nutritionists. A number of international, as well as state-level, organizations offer high-quality continuing education. Some of these include: the Academy of Eating Disorders, the National Eating Disorders Association, and the International Association of Eating Disorders Professionals.

Nutrition counselors, especially those who treat difficult patients, are advised to arrange for formal supervision sessions with an experienced psychotherapist. Supervision helps nutrition counselors improve their work with patients; understand and manage feelings of countertransference (i.e., the counselor's feelings about the patient; see below for more information, p. 66–67); and deal with any personal food and body issues. Another way to access professional tutelage is to join a team of mutually supportive professionals who meet regularly for case conferences. Still another worthwhile experience is that of co-leading an ED group with a psychotherapist. Leading a therapy group together gives both professionals exposure to the other's style and areas of expertise. Enrolling in counseling courses, attending appropriate conferences, and the counselor's own self-study of counseling and ED treatment texts and research journals also improves counseling skills.

Handling Unrelated Issues

Until recently, it was commonly understood that the territory of nutrition counselors included any issue related to food, weight, eating patterns, and body image but excluded clearly psychological issues such as relationships, fantasies, flashbacks of childhood sexual or physical abuse, memories, hearing dangerous voices, and suicidality. Now, however, it is recognized that patients in the therapeutic milieu of nutrition counselor's office may well be inclined to discuss such psychological issues. Patients who experience nutrition counselors as being as concerned with their psychological issues along with their food issues are less likely to be resistant or to respond negatively to nutrition counseling. Some patients will need to devote time to describing the "non-food" aspects of their lives and other dilemmas to feel understood. It is not unusual for eating-disordered patients to reveal emotions and feelings to their nutrition counselor that they have not shared elsewhere.

We believe that psychological digressions in nutrition counseling should be permitted within appropriate professional boundaries. The Academy of Nutrition and Dietetics' position statement (American Dietetic Association, 2011) asserts:

> The RD working with ED patients relies on a good understanding of professional boundaries, nutrition intervention, and the psychodynamics of eating disorders. Understanding of boundaries refers to recognizing and appreciating the specific tasks of each member of the team. Specifically, the

RD addresses food-related problems relative to the patient's thought processes, behaviors, and physical status.

(p. 1236)

When there is overlap between nutrition counseling and psychotherapy, such as with body-image issues, the nutrition counselor might ask the patient, "What does your psychotherapist say about that?" When patients ask nutrition-related questions of mental health providers, they in turn should respond, "What does your nutrition counselor say about that?" When significant "non-nutrition issues" are revealed, nutrition counselors should ask, "May I let your psychotherapist know about this?" After listening reflectively to our patients' concerns, we redirect them back to food-related issues. Tolerating the patient's persistent use of nutrition counseling sessions to meet psychotherapy needs will dilute the nutrition treatment as well as intrude on the patient's psychotherapy relationship. Communicating regularly with psychotherapists (and other team members) who treat mutual patients is good practice. If significant psychological issues surface for patients not currently in therapy, the benefits of conjunctive psychotherapy needs to be discussed. Nutrition counselors should be ready to provide these patients with names and phone numbers of local psychotherapists who specialize in EDs.

The nutrition counselor's task is to understand what the patient does, thinks, and feels about food, weight, and body-image issues. Gaining insight into why the patient's food problems developed is not the main focus of nutrition counseling. When nutrition counselors delve into psychological areas, they may not give appropriate attention or time to nutrition issues. Resistant patients have been known to bring psychological issues into nutrition sessions for exactly this purpose. In the same way, in-depth discussions of food and weight issues may overwhelm or distract psychotherapists.

The responsibilities of the nutrition counselor in the treatment of eating disorders are delineated by the Academy of Nutrition and Dietetics in "Position of the American Dietetic Association: Nutrition Intervention in the Treatment of Eating Disorders" (Osier & Henry, 2011, p. 1238) and summarized in Box 3.2.

BOX 3.2 RESPONSIBILITIES OF THE NUTRITION COUNSELOR IN THE TREATMENT OF EATING DISORDERS

Nutrition assessment: Identify nutrition problems that relate to medical or physical condition, including eating disorder symptoms and behaviors.

- Perform anthropometric measurements: height and weight history, complete growth chart, assess growth patterns and maturation in younger patients (ages 20 years and younger)
- Interpret biochemical data: especially to assess risk of refeeding syndrome

- Evaluate dietary assessment: eating pattern, core attitudes regarding weight, shape, eating
- Assess behavioral-environmental symptoms: food restriction, bingeing, preoccupation, rituals secretive eating, affect and impulse control, vomiting or other purging, excessive exercise
- Apply nutrition diagnosis; create a plan to resolve nutrition problems; coordinate plan with team members

Nutrition intervention: Calculate and monitor energy and macronutrient intake to establish expected rates of weight change and to meet body composition and health goals. Guide goal setting to normalize eating patterns for nutrition rehabilitation and weight restoration or maintenance as appropriate.

- Ensure diet quality and regular eating pattern, increased amount and variety of foods consumed, normal perceptions of hunger and satiety, suggestions about supplement use
- Provide psychosocial support and positive reinforcement; structured refeeding plan
- Counsel individuals and other caregivers on food selection considering individual preferences, health history, physical, psychological factors, resources

Nutrition monitoring and evaluation: Monitor nutrient intake and adjust as necessary.

- Monitor rate of weight gain; once weight restored, adjust food intake to maintain weight
- Communicate individual's progress with team; make adjustments to plan accordingly

Care coordination: Provide counsel to team about protocols to maximize tolerance of feeding regimen or nutrition recommendations, guidance about supplements to ensure maximum absorption, minimize drug nutrient interactions, and referral for continuation of care as needed.

- Work collaboratively with treatment team, delineate specific roles and tasks, communicate nutrition needs across the continuum of settings (e.g., inpatient, day treatment, outpatient)
- Act as a resource to other health care professionals and the family, provide education
- Advocate for evidenced-based treatment and access to care

BOX 3.2 (continued)

Advanced training: Seek specialized training in other counseling techniques, such as cognitive behavioral therapy, dialectical behavior therapy, and motivational interviewing.

- Use advanced knowledge and skills relating to nutrition, such as refeeding syndrome, maintaining appropriate weight and eating behaviors, body image, and relapse prevention
- Seek supervision and case consultation from a licensed mental health professional to gain and maintain proficiency in eating disorders treatments

Note: Roles and responsibilities of registered dietitians caring for individuals with eating disorders. Reprinted from "Position of the American Dietetic Association: Nutrition Intervention in the Treatment of Eating Disorders," by A. Ozier and B. Henry, 2011, *Journal of the American Dietetic Association*, 111, p. 1238. Copyright 2011 by American Dietetic Association. Reprinted with permission.

Counseling Issues

Self-Disclosure

Self-disclosure is the sharing of personal feelings, thoughts, and experiences with patients by counselors. It is generally believed that brief self-disclosures on the part of counselors help create a genuine therapeutic bond with the patient. Such disclosures free patients to make their own disclosures and prevent them from developing misconceptions or idealizations about counselors. Self-disclosures can instill an open, honest atmosphere that patients find reassuring, as when we say something like "I felt too full after lunch today." Self-disclosures about the experiences of the nutrition counselor or of other patients in similar circumstances can be useful ways to express direct guidance and normalize what the patient is feeling. We sometimes use self-disclosure to elicit information from the patient or to give the patient a different perspective. When talking about how the patient will handle food at the movie theater, Herrin disclosed that she loves the popcorn with a big diet coke. This patient had previously thought of movie popcorn as off limits. Kellogg (2006) suggests using self-disclosure as a way of modeling healthy behaviors in her example of modeling self-forgiveness with patients who struggle due to perfectionism.

Nevertheless, self-disclosure should be used sparingly, especially early in treatment, as it is a very powerful tool that can diminish a professional counseling relationship. Patients expect to talk about themselves when they come to a session and may be confused about the about the nature of counseling if the counselor talks too much about him- or herself. Nutrition counselors should examine their motivation for self-disclosure; it must always be for the patient's benefit. Disclosures should be brief and immediately followed by an inquiry into the patient's response to the disclosure, and then back to the patient's issues. For instance, after a self-disclosure, the nutrition counselor might say, "I wonder if something similar might work for you?" or "How was it for me to share this with you?"

Counselors should be prepared for questions from patients concerning personal information: professional credentials, age, marital status, and children. Kellogg (2006) notes personal questions are "not about you (the counselor) but about the patient" (p. 127). Patients typically have a motive or concern behind the personal question and it is up to the counselor to figure out what that is. We ask the patient how knowing our personal information might help him or her, then focus our response on what best serves the patient. For example, ED patients often ask counselors whether they have had an ED. We advise that counselors provide information to the degree that feels comfortable but, more importantly, explore why the patient is curious about these details. One might encourage patients to say more by inquiring, "I am curious about why you would want to know about my background." For some professionals, a policy of refusing to disclose any personal information beyond professional credentials is the most comfortable. For others, brief disclosures in response to patients' inquiries feel appropriate. In any case, always be truthful, as patients are good at detecting less-than-honest responses.

Idealization

Self-disclose of the counselor's everyday gaffes can minimize the issue of idealization. Nutrition counselors who are compassionate and supportive are likely to become idealized by their patients. Initially, idealization may be therapeutic, especially for patients who have been denied the experience of a responsive caregiver on whom they could depend. The power and influence of idealization, however, often is disconcerting to counselors who may become "overstimulated" by the level of esteem in which patients hold them and lose perspective about their own abilities or appropriate spheres of influence. In this context, nutrition counselors must guard against tendencies to offer too much advice in areas outside of their professional expertise or to initiate social contact with patients. It is important to acknowledge the idealization but not dwell on it. When idealization occurs patients may try to overly please, or withhold, or lie about any difficulties. They may decline to work with other professionals or want to socialize with the counselor outside of scheduled appointment times. In these situations, we advise nutrition counselors to consult with the patient's mental health provider or the counselor's professional supervisor or both. Casual self-disclosures of our minor blunders helps patients develop realistic views of their nutrition counselor and injects some much needed humor into sessions.

Splitting

Idealization may be evidence of splitting, that is, the patient may comment that the nutrition counselor is better than the mental health provider, or vice versa. Splitting, which is often defined as pitting one professional against another, is most likely to occur when multiple providers are involved in the treatment of the same patient. An early sign of splitting are attempts by patients to engage more fully with one team member over the others. They may share information with only certain providers or imply that only one provider truly understands. When splitting, the patient may report that team members have different views from each other. Splitting may also may be evidence the tendency to resist treatment with a divide and conquer strategy or it may indicate an underlying psychological disorder that leads to all-or-nothing thinking.

Splitting can be minimized by ample communication between team members who are clear about each other's roles and consistent in their articulation of this understanding to patients. Joint sessions or team meetings in which treatment team members have the opportunity to present a "united front" to patients can reduce splitting. Team consultation is important before a team member suggests significant changes in tactics to a patient. We suggest that nutrition counselors talk directly with other team members and avoid making any deprecating comments about fellow team members. One way of managing splitting is to say, "I am sure your physician or psychotherapist or parent must have a reason for suggesting this; I'll talk to him or her so I can understand, too." Another strategy is to remind patients that we will not keep secrets from other members of the treatment team. Of note, splitting can challenge providers' sense of their own self-worth if they become labeled as the "bad provider." It should not be taken personally.

Transference

Transference is a counseling term that refers to the natural, mostly unconscious, process where the attitudes, feelings, and emotions of the patient's early significant relationships get *transferred* onto the counselor. Herrin's patient, Lindsey, experienced transference when she broke down into sobs while talking about the need to add to her food plan. Hearing that she had lost weight, when she thought she had gained weight, triggered Lindsey's old feelings of inadequacy and loneliness which she often felt in relation to her mother, hence a transferring of feelings about her mother onto Herrin. Herrin gave Lindsey a moment before asking in a quiet voice if something else was bothering her. Lindsey sobbed again as she explained that her mother always found fault with her, even when she was trying her best. Herrin listened sympathetically and asked when Lindsey was next seeing her therapist. Relieved to hear that the appointment was the next day, Herrin said, "Lindsey I am so impressed with the connection you are making between your childhood and your current difficulties. And I am glad you are seeing your therapist soon to further work through these important issues. You and I will keep working away at figuring out how to make adds to your food plan that don't make you feel so vulnerable and ashamed."

In this example, Herrin avoided the countertransference that might have occurred had she been unaware of its possibility. Countertransference is similar to transference, but it refers to a counselor's emotional reaction to a patient. Countertransference happens when the counselor unconsciously identifies with a patient's situation, feelings, and emotions in such a way that it affects the counseling process. Herrin could have assumed she had been too harsh in her response to Lindsey and could have focused on trying to make amends instead of wondering why Lindsey was so upset.

Difficult patients are likely to generate within counselors two types of countertransference. The first type, called subjective countertransference, consists of feelings, drive, attitudes, and defenses that the counselor transfers from other parts of his or her life onto the patient (Kellog, 2006, p. 114). Positive or negative feelings may arise, such as anger, jealousy, fear, or a feeling of nurturing. The second type of countertransference consists of reality-based reactions to the patient's behaviors, such as resentment, boredom, or confusion (Kellog, 2006, p. 114). These feelings can lead to overinvolvement in a patient's recovery, or even in her or his life, ultimately hindering treatment progress. Common countertransference-generated mistakes include making decisions for patients, becoming the patient's friend, scolding the patient, or colluding with the patient by sharing an attitude of hopelessness regarding the possibility of recovery.

Counselors should seek professional supervision if countertransference issues arise. In advance of working with ED patients, nutrition counselors should work through any problems they may have with their own eating, weight, or exercise behaviors, or prejudices based on body size. The difficulty understanding and managing countertransference is one reason we recommend that nutrition counselors who work in ED be engaged in their own psychotherapy. Strong countertransferential feelings may suggest that work with ED patients is not advisable.

Caring Behaviors

Well-defined boundaries that minimize touch and expressions of affection maintain a professional relationship. Inexperienced counselors should be particularly cautious in these areas since patients easily misinterpret caring behaviors and may conclude the counselor desires a social relationship. For example, when patients become teary-eyed or cry, have tissues handy, rather than offer a hug or consolation; we then give the patient a few moments before gently exploring what the patient is feeling. We often say something like, "Can you tell me what your tears are about?" We agree that compliments and similar expressions of fondness can help promote recovery, and we err in the direction of being honest and compassionate with our patients, knowing that withdrawing support or availability is more disruptive than to not offer it in the first place. Male counselors should be especially cautious about touching female patients. If we do feel a hug is appropriate, we ask the patient's permission first, e.g., "How would you feel about a hug from me?" Beginning and ending sessions on time contributes to the sense of care counselors demonstrate for their patients.

Co-morbid Psychological Disorders

Nutrition counselors working with a broad population of patients should understand the characteristics of co-morbid psychiatric disorders and their impact on the course of treatment. To this end, we provide in Box 3.3 an abbreviated chart outlining the common features of co-morbid disorders. Co-morbid illnesses typically amplify ED severity and complicate treatment strategies. It is important, therefore, to recognize the symptoms of co-morbid illness and ensure that patients are receiving appropriate treatment. For example, attention-deficit/hyperactivity disorder (ADHD) is common enough in bulimia nervosa (BN), binge-eating disorder (BED), and obesity that some researchers recommend screening for ADHD in these patients (Cortese et al., 2007; Davis et al., 2009; Dukarm, 2005). Nutrition counselors should ask for permission to speak to the patient's doctor or mental health provider if they suspect a patient is showing signs and symptoms ADHD or other psychological disorders. We also recommend the latest revision of the American Psychiatric Association's *Diagnostic and Statistical Manual of Mental Disorders* (American Psychiatric Association, 2000, 2010) which provides an excellent overview of the characteristics of patients with specific mental diagnoses. Nutrition counselors may also wish to pursue continuing education about psychiatric illnesses as a fulfillment of a cultural competency learning activity.

BOX 3.3 CLINICAL FEATURES OF CO-MORBID ILLNESSES

Major depressive disorder

- Depressed mood (such as feelings of sadness or emptiness).
- Reduced interest in activities that used to be enjoyed, sleep disturbances (either not being able to sleep well or sleeping too much).
- Loss of energy or a significant reduction in energy level.
- Difficulty concentrating, holding a conversation, paying attention, or making decisions that used to be made fairly easily.
- Suicidal thoughts or intentions.

Generalized anxiety disorder

- Mild heart palpitations.
- Dizziness.
- Excessive worry.

Substance use and addictive disorders

- Use of substance impairs functioning at home, work, school.
- Drives while intoxicated.
- Continued use despite legal, social, interpersonal problems.

Borderline personality disorder (BPD)

- Unstable relationships.
- Poor or negative sense of self and self-destructive behaviors.
- Inconsistent moods and intense anger.
- Significant impulsivity.
- Fear of abandonment and rejection.
- Patients feel needy, helpless, clingy.

Bipolar disorder

- Extreme intense high (euphoric) followed by depression.
- Elevated self-esteem.
- Talkative.
- Reduced need for sleep.
- Easily distracted.
- Excessive spending, rash decisions.
- Dangerous sexual behavior or use of drugs or alcohol.

Post-traumatic stress disorder (PTSD)

- Re-experiencing the trauma through nightmares, obsessive thoughts, and flashbacks.
- Avoids situations, people, or objects which remind him or her about the traumatic event.
- Increased anxiety, startles easily.

Attention-deficit/hyperactivity disorder (ADHD)
- Inattention: difficulty organizing activities, easily distracted, and forgetful.
- Hyperactivity: fidgets, restless, talks excessively, "on the go."
- Impulsivity: interrupts, has trouble waiting.

Obsessive–compulsive disorder (OCD)

- Persistent, irrational obsessions that cause anxiety.
- Uncontrollable thoughts disruptive to everyday functioning.
- Repetitive behaviors performed to reduce anxiety.

Note: Adapted from AllPsych Online. Available at http://www.allpsych.com. Copyright 1993–2003 by Heffner Media Group.

Co-morbid illnesses, such as anxiety, depression, obsessive–compulsive disorder (OCD), body dysmorphic disorder (BDD), substance use and addictive disorders, borderline personality disorder (BPD), ADHD, post-traumatic stress disorder (PTSD), bipolar disorder (manic depression), and multiple personality disorder coexist with EDs with some frequency. Patients with a coexisting psychiatric diagnosis often make slower than expected improvements in eating behaviors. Patients with depression, for example, may have difficulty undertaking behavioral change. Depression also may increase or decrease a patient's appetite or lead to the use of food to "self-medicate."

A diagnosis of primary or "true" OCD has been considered to increase clinical severity among patients with EDs (Sallet et al., 2010). Approximately 10–35% of patients with EDs actually have primary or "true" OCD, which typically is diagnosed before the onset of the ED and continues after weight restoration. As mentioned in Chapter 1: Clinical Features of Eating Disorders (p. 15–16), patients without a primary history of OCD commonly have OCD-like tendencies, especially in regard to food, weight, or body image, that resolve with ED recovery.

BPD is considered to be an adaptive response to a traumatic event, and patients with BPD often have PTSD, major depression or substance abuse. Many eating-disordered patients with BPD have experienced childhood abuse or neglect. BPD patients almost always require a team approach, and respond best to structured, directive, and supportive interventions. We advise nutrition counselors to be hesitant to treat patients with co-morbid BPD unless they are working within a well-coordinated treatment team. It is not uncommon in BPD for counselors to have to manage recurring problems such as missing appointments, asking overly personal questions, or initiating inappropriate contact between sessions. Regular consults with the patient's mental health provider are imperative, as these patients can be demanding, displaying dramatic mood swings. They are inclined to split, verbally attack, and criticize practitioners. Such patients may increase self-destructive behaviors (e.g., cutting) in order to preserve their relationship with the counselor, or they may have difficulty trusting a caring counselor. Supervision for counselors is important to manage any negative countertransference reactions.

We recommend the setting of firm, matter-of-fact, well-defined, and repeatedly clarified limits around issues such as availability of clinicians outside of sessions, phone calls, payments, behavior within counseling sessions, and secret-keeping from other professionals. Written contracts outlining behavioral goals and plans for handling crises are helpful. BPD patients are often engaged in dialectical behavioral therapy (DBT)-oriented individual or group therapy and will benefit from a nutrition counselor who is familiar with that treatment approach. (For more on DBT, see Chapter 4: Counseling Interventions, pp. 79–104.)

Nutrition counselors should have a "low threshold" for insisting that patients with co-morbid illnesses seek concurrent psychotherapy. Patients who report feeling helpless or hopeless, or those that bring significant psychological issues to nutrition sessions should also be referred for psychotherapy. Consider the wisdom of insisting that patients with these diagnoses also participate in conjoint psycho-therapy with a mental health provider who is willing to engage in regular com-munication with the nutrition counselor.

Suicidal ideation, self-harming behaviors, or a history of sexual abuse are often connected with ED diagnosis and co-morbid illnesses. It is appropriate for nutri-tion counselors to assess risk of serious self-harm by directly questioning patients about their intentions, such as asking: "Have you been thinking about suicide?" "Do you have a plan for hurting yourself or attempting suicide?" "Do you have means (weapon, alcohol, or pills) to hurt yourself?" We assume when patients talk about the possibility of suicide they are asking for help, and we provide them with a referral list containing the names and phone numbers of appropriate mental health practitioners. If patients acknowledge suicidal ideation and they are not currently in psychotherapy, they should be instructed in no uncertain terms to find a skilled men-tal health provider immediately. For patients already engaged in psychotherapy, we say, "I would like your permission to share these concerns with your therapist."

Confidentiality no longer applies when patients indicate intent to harm them-selves or someone else. If the nutrition counselor has any concern about a patient's safety, the patient's psychotherapist or a significant other (if the patient is not engaged in psychotherapy) should be notified immediately.

It is good practice to request that patients promise not to hurt themselves and promise to contact their mental health provider (or the nutrition counselor if they have not engaged a psychotherapist) when they feel suicidal. Having patients sign a "contract" attesting to a "safety" plan comprising written instructions to contact a professional before inflicting harm on themself is very effective. (For an example of a safety plan see Box 3.4.)

Patients who cannot contract for their safety and who have a definite plan and means to harm themselves should not be left alone or sent home. If a mental health provider or crisis hotline is not available, the nutrition counselor should call an emergency number such as 911 for assistance. Risk for suicidality should be carefully evaluated by a mental health professional and treated aggressively, since ED patients are at higher-than-average risk.

Since sexual abuse puts individuals at special risk for developing an ED (Sanci, Coffey, Olsson, Reid, Carlin & Patton, 2008), nutrition counselors will likely treat a significant number of patients who also have a history of sexual abuse. Nutrition counselors thus should have some understanding of appropriate thera-peutic responses to patients with this type of history. First, nutrition counselors must keep in mind that delving into the patient's sexual abuse history is not their task, though patients may bring this information to sessions. Should patients dis-close a history of sexual abuse, the nutrition counselor should listen respectfully and respond with appropriate empathy. It is important to be watchful for coun-tertransference reactions that are inappropriate (e.g., a desire to comfort patients by hugging or excessive touch). Patients with a sexual-abuse history should also be working with a skilled psychotherapist.

BOX 3.4 EXAMPLE OF A SAFETY PLAN

This is an agreement between my nutrition counselor, ...
. ., and myself, ..., to help keep me safe from harm.

1. I agree that if I have thoughts about physically hurting myself or anyone else, I will call my emergency contact person, who is. . . . ., at . . . .
2. If that person is not available, I will call the 24-hour crisis line at . . . . or the 1 800 SUICIDE line.
3. If I still feel suicidal and out of control, I will go to the nearest hospital emergency department.
4. Signing my name on this paper means that I agree not to hurt myself or anyone else.

Your name . . . . Date . . . .
Witness/Nutrition Counselor . . . . Date . . . .

Body-Image Issues

One of the best definitions of body image is also one of the earliest. In 1935, Schilder defined body image in his book, *The Image and Appearance of the Human Body: Studies in the Constructive Energies of the Psyche*, as "the picture of our body which we form in our mind, that is to say the way in which our body appears to ourselves" (as cited in Garner, Garfinkel, Stancer, & Moldofsky, 1976, p. 327). Another way of defining body image is how an individual perceives and evaluates his or her body. The body-image-related DSM-IV criterion for AN is "a disturbance in the way in which one's body weight or shape is experienced" (American Psychiatric Association, 2000, p. 589). Another DSM diagnostic criterion for anorexia nervosa (AN) and BN "is an undue influence of body weight or shape on self-evaluation" (American Psychiatric Association, 2000, p. 589). Although not included in the current DSM as a criterion, in clinical practice many BED patients meet the same body-image-related DSM criteria as patients with AN and BN.

Body-image issues in EDs are multidimensional and include: body dissatisfaction; intense fear of weight gain or becoming fat even when underweight; denial of seriousness of current low body weight; disturbance in the way one's body weight or shape is experienced; negative evaluation of one's physical appearance; undue influence and overevaluation of body weight or shape on self-evaluation and self-worth; and internalization of the socio-cultural ideal of thinness. Of note, a number of terms have been applied interchangeably to

body-image issues, including body-image disturbance (BID), body-weight disturbance, body dissatisfaction, body-image disorder, body-image distortion, distorted
body image, negative body image, poor body image, unhealthy body image, and
fear of fatness. Body dysmorphic disorder (BDD) is an extreme form of body dissatisfaction in which an excessive preoccupation with an imagined or slight physical defect causes significant distress, and impairment in function that cannot be
accounted for by an eating disorder. BDD, along with hypochondriasis and other
pain disorders, is a distinct somatoform (physical complaints for which this is no
medical explanation) disorder (American Psychiatric Association, 2000).

Body dissatisfaction and body image dissatisfaction are characterized by a negative evaluation of one's physical appearance. Body-image distortions are inaccu-
rate in that patients have distorted perceptions of their body size and shape. BID
includes the internalization of the socio-cultural thin ideal, body dissatisfaction,
and body-image distortions (Garner, 2004, pp. 295–303; Stice, 2004, pp. 304–
311). Each of these can manifest in body checking (see below). In our discussion,
we have chosen to use "body-image disturbance" (BID) to refer to general body-
image issues associated with EDs.

BID related to weight, shape, or thinness serves, for many patients, as their
sole or predominant reference for assessing self-worth. Garner and Bemis (1985)
explain that body weight is appealing as a measure of worth because it is culturally sanctioned and "unambiguous, observable, and quantifiable" (p. 129). In
addition, preoccupation with body size, shape, and weight often serves as a way
to avoid and distract from uncomfortable feelings (Pearson, Heffner, & Follette,
2010). Villapiano and Goodman (2001) write that for ED patients "weight represents in physical and concrete form, the pain, anguish, terror, rage, shame, or
sorrow in their lives" and that "the will to suppress overwhelming feelings has
been perverted in the will to control the body" (p. 73).

Managing Body-Image Issues

BID is clearly one area in which the nutrition counselor's territory naturally over-
laps with the mental health provider's. Psychotherapists are trained to pursue the
origins of poor body image, such as childhood teasing, negative feedback about
one's body from significant others, or a history of physical or sexual abuse, and to
help patients adopt more functional schemas for self-evaluation and self-esteem.
Nutrition counselors, on the other hand, focus on providing accurate feedback
about body weight, education about healthy weight ranges and the genetic deter-
minants of body size, and information on the negative consequences of weight-
loss behaviors.

Because erratic eating and undernutrition cause the cognitive dysfunction
that contributes to BID, resolution of BID does not respond to direct treatment,
though it usually improves with the restoration and maintenance of a healthy
weight and the use of a food plan. In our experience, BID is the one of the last

components of an ED to resolve. We remind our patients that BIDs are hallmarks of an ED and are expected to improve as progress (namely, weight regain and normalized eating) is made in treatment. One of Herrin's patients exclaimed, "As I gain weight, I feel thinner!" Hearing anecdotes like this often reassures patients that, eventually, they too can experience themselves more accurately. In the meantime, we tell our patients, it is perfectly normal to continue to struggle with body image throughout treatment, but it is worth tackling.

Accordingly, we continue to work on the development of a healthy body image in our patients by using cognitive–behavioral therapy (CBT), dialectical behavioral therapy (DBT), motivational interviewing (MI) techniques, and acceptance and commitment therapy (ACT) as outlined below (for more on these approaches, see Chapter 4: Counseling Interventions). Using psycho-education, a component of CBT, we help patients recognize the degree to which they misperceive their body size and shape. A child or adolescent's current weight can be plotted on the body mass index (BMI) for age growth chart, or their clothing size can be compared to average to show inconsistencies. An adult can be shown that his or her BMI is within the normal range. A discussion about set point, settling point weight, hereditability as well as normal growth through the life span is instructive to the patient with BID (see Chapter 8: Assessing Weight). While educating patients about the effects of genetics on body shape and size, we inquire, "Whose body do you have?" "Who do you most resemble?" Patients may want to look through family photos to see how relatives looked when they were of a similar age.

CBT techniques, such as the creation of a formulation and self-monitoring (see Chapter 4: Counseling Interventions, pp. 79-104), help patients understand how body checking maintains BID. Body checking consists of frequent weighing, pinching or touching body parts (e.g., stomach, arms, thighs), measuring the size of body parts, repeatedly touching bones (e.g., hip, scapula, clavicle) to check for protrusions, looking down at one's stomach or thighs, assessing tightness of clothes, looking in mirrors, and comparing body size and shape with others. Of note, patients rarely disclose compulsive body checking. Fairburn (2008, pp. 96–123) maintains body checking is a behavior many patients do not recognize, nor do they understand how it maintains body dissatisfaction. Simply realizing how unhelpful body checking is can be enough for some to stop doing it (Fairburn, 2008, p. 108). Others may need to practice resisting body checking by covering up mirrors or committing to not touching certain body parts for set periods of time. Patients who obsessively check their body shape and size can be advised to temporarily avoid full-length mirrors and tighter clothes. Another strategy is to have patients record every time they body check. Once patterns are identified, we collaborate on ways to make it easier to resist body checking, such as not dressing in front of a mirror or limiting time in front of the mirror to twice daily for 2 minutes. To make the body checking less automatic, we may ask patients to say to themselves, "I'm body checking." ED patients who actively avoid situations that may reveal their body size to others or themselves may benefit from "exposure" to their shape in mirrors and by wearing more revealing clothes.

We also initiate discussions about cultural and social pressures that constantly bombard all those who live in westernized cultures. Such discussions can raise an appropriate sense of indignation that can help patients find a way to protect themselves from cultural pressures to be unnaturally thin. We acknowledge to patients that it is unfortunate that weight loss is socially acceptable and measurable, and go on to explain that it is a no-win situation—no amount of weight loss is satisfying if weight loss is the goal. Moreover, since substantial weight loss leads to metabolic compensations, subsequent weight loss is harder to achieve. The result is further erosion of self-esteem due to a sense of failure and guilt. Once patients realize they have succumbed to cultural pressures to be thin, it can be helpful to engage in a compassionate discussion about the enormous pressures we all face. In order to achieve the unrealistic sizes and shapes that emanate from society, the fashion industry, and even from family members, one can feel forced to focus on dieting and exercise. Hearing the nutrition counselor express frustration about the current definitions of attractiveness and how this promotes eating-disordered behaviors can help patients garner the strength to begin to improve their body image and overcome their ED. Box 3.5 lists activities that can help patients manage social and cultural pressures that lead to BID.

BOX 3.5 MANAGING SOCIAL AND CULTURAL PRESSURES

- Avoid magazines designed to change or sculpt your body.
- Be skeptical about magazines that show idealized body images.
- Write to magazines or advertisers that only portray thin models.
- Talk back to the TV when you see an ad or hear a message that makes you feel bad about yourself or your body by promoting only thin body ideals.
- Write a letter to an advertiser you think is sending positive, inspiring messages that recognize and celebrate the natural diversity of human body shapes and sizes. Reinforce sending positive, affirming messages.
- Tear out the pages of your magazine that contain advertisements or articles glorifying thinness or degrading people of larger sizes. Enjoy your magazine minus negative media messages about your body.
- Talk to your friends about media messages and the way they make you feel.
- Make a list of companies who consistently send negative body-image messages and make a conscious effort to avoid buying their products. Write them a letter explaining why you are using your "buying power" to protest their messages.

CBT's cognitive-restructuring techniques to reframe thoughts and self-talk from negative to positive (see Chapter 4: Counseling Interventions, pp. 80–84) can be effective. Since BID is reinforced by thoughts and self-talk critical of body size and shape, patients can be instructed to notice their tendency to engage in such self-talk and then alter their internal dialog so it is neutral on the topic. We teach patients "counterarguments" to avoid the cycle of thinking that justifies poor body image, such as: "I know that a cardinal feature of AN is misperception of my own size so I can expect to feel fat even though I am not." Patients can also learn to say, "I will experience my weight and shape more accurately and as thinner than I do now once I have recovered."

To illustrate how negative body thoughts are linked to emotional distress, Larkin uses Kratina's cartoon diagram called the "Theory of Expando Thighs" (Kratina, King, & Hayes, 2003, p. 139). In this provocatively titled cartoon, the main character's problem with her boss is causing overwhelming and uncomfortable feelings that she avoids by worrying about the size of her thighs. In the cartoon, the character has a choice of two paths: a never-ending path to change her thighs (dieting and overexercising), or the path to the real solution (talking with her boss) that ends with neutral feelings about her thighs. Another strategy is to discuss the reality that "fat is not a feeling." *Weight Wisdom* by Kingsbury and Williams (2003) is a collection of affirmations that challenge poor body image and the accompanying anxiety and depression.

We make the point to all our patients that it is difficult to care for one's body if one does not like it. To that end, we teach our patients to practice self-care activities, (DBT techniques) aimed at caring for their bodies such as personal hygiene and grooming, and investments in relaxation. Patients may choose to have a manicure, get a massage, take a nap, or meditate. Larkin reminds patients, "We are all babies in adult bodies. Babies love routine, need adequate sleep and food; babies love attention and play. It is up to us to respond to our basic self-care needs and ask for what we cannot give ourselves." Reducing physical vulnerability by responding to our bodies and physical needs for sleep, physical activity, and nutrition also makes handling uncomfortable emotions more manageable.

In a MI-influenced manner, we empathize and sympathize with our patients about their body-image concerns while providing hope for recovery. We validate body-image issues and point out that negative evaluation of the body does not indicate that the body is unacceptable in size, shape, or weight, but it does illustrate that the patient "does not feel good" about his or her body. We join with the patient's body-image distress by actively listening to their concerns. We may inquire how his or her body-image concerns interfere with his or her life. A decision-to-change matrix (see Chapter 4: Counseling Interventions, pp. 97–98) helps patients examine the pros and cons of BID and the impact it has on his or her well-being. Taking the time to address body-image issues in these ways reflects empathy on the part of the counselor towards the patient.

We have had success using acceptance and commitment therapy (ACT) to treat BID. ACT is a relatively new approach that focuses on non-judgmental living in the present and acceptance of distressing thoughts and feelings rather than trying to change them (Pearson et al., 2010). We do not agree, argue, or challenge patients, when they say, "I can't do xx until I lose weight." We respond with simple restatements like, "OK, so you don't like your body." We also use ACT-like activities, including a body-acceptance meditation, to help patients improve body image. These meditations foster self-compassion and loving kindness, allowing patients to befriend and care for their bodies. We refer the reader to Bays' book (2009), *Mindful Eating: A Guide to Rediscovering a Healthy and Joyful Relationship with Food*, which has an accompanying CD of effective mediations.

In Box 3.6 we list activities that our patients have used to improve BID.

BOX 3.6 ACTIVITIES TO IMPROVE BODY-IMAGE DISTURBANCE

- Write a letter to your body and have your body write one back to you.
- Write positive body affirmations such as "I love my body no matter the size" and "Why do I love my body so much?"
- Look at other women or men with appreciation, not criticism or envy (Goodman & Villapiano, 2001, p. 80).
- Buy clothes that fit.
- Do activities that you love.
- Make a list of positive characteristics about yourself unrelated to appearance.
- Connect with your body in positive ways, such as through yoga practice.

Summary Points

- Counselors should aim to be sincere, dependable, and trustworthy. Giving honest feedback, keeping confidences, being on time for appointments, and being direct about one's availability outside of sessions all help foster therapeutic relationships.
- Patients who experience nutrition counselors as being concerned with their psychological issues along with their food issues are less likely to be resistant or to respond negatively to nutrition counseling. However, psychological digressions should be permitted only within appropriate professional boundaries.
- Self-disclosures about the experiences of the nutrition counselor or other patients in similar circumstances can be useful ways to express direct guidance and normalize what the patient is feeling.

- It is often necessary for nutrition counselors to remind patients that they will not keep secrets from other members of the treatment team or engage in splitting.
- Nutrition counselors need to understand the characteristics of co-morbid psychiatric disorders and their impact on the course of treatment.
- BIDs include the internalization of a socio-cultural thin ideal, body dissatisfaction, and body-image distortions, and is the one of the last components of an eating disorder to resolve.

4

COUNSELING INTERVENTIONS

Introduction

The inspiration for our counseling interventions comes from an eclectic mix of five different models, namely: cognitive–behavioral therapy (CBT), dialectical behavioral therapy (DBT), family-based therapy (FBT), motivational interviewing (MI), and, most recently, acceptance and commitment therapy (ACT). We chose these models for several reasons. In the beginning of our practices, CBT was the most revered and evidenced-based model for the treatment of eating disorders (EDs), namely, bulimia nervosa (BN). The well-thumbed chapters on CBT treatment for anorexia nervosa (AN) and BN in the *Handbook of Treatment for Eating Disorders* (2nd ed.; Garner, Vitousek, & Pike, 1997; Wilson, Fairburn, & Agras, 1997) and Fairburn, Marcus, and Wilson's (1993) comprehensive CBT treatment manual for BN and binge-eating disorder (BED) helped launch our evidence-based approach to nutrition counseling in the treatment of EDs. Although CBT has since fallen somewhat out of the limelight, we believe it to be "the mother" of the newer models and the foundation of our work. This is especially evident with the new enhanced version of CBT (CBT-Enhanced), which incorporates many of the nutrition counseling techniques we have used over the years, namely: educating about weight and ED symptoms; weekly weighing; real-time monitoring of eating behaviors; reducing evaluation of shape and weight on self-value; establishing a regular eating pattern; and maintaining and preventing relapse (Fairburn et al., 2009; Karbasi, 2010; Wagner & MacCaughelty, 2011; Wonderlich, 2009).

As research on DBT, FBT, and MI progressed and the models were adopted by many professionals trained in psychology as well as by ED treatment programs, we found it helpful to adapt these techniques into our practices. These techniques give us the proficiency and confidence to handle the complex issues of even the most difficult patients. Understanding these models helps us reinforce the techniques with patients already familiar with them and facilitates team work with mental health professionals. With the lead researcher on a study of the effectiveness of ACT at Dartmouth colleague, we have been eager to experiment with these techniques as well (Berman, Boutelle, & Crow, 2009). Finally, it seems unavoidable but to adapt psychological models into our practice, as there are no evidence-based approaches specific to nutrition counseling; most research into ED treatment is aimed at studying interventions conducted by professionals trained in psychology. The CBT, DBT, MI, and ACT techniques described in this chapter are derived from the psychological literature, utilize basic counseling skills and can be appropriately applied to nutrition counseling (Spahn et al., 2010). Chapter 13: Working with Families (pp. 277–298) is dedicated to the nutrition counseling techniques of FBT. We conclude the present chapter with a discussion of how we use the stages of change model to select appropriate interventions (i.e., whether to use CBT, DBT, MI, or ACT techniques) for our patients.

What is Cognitive–Behavior Therapy?

CBT in the treatment of EDs is based on the principles that self-worth is determined by weight and shape and that stress and emotions are managed by disordered food behaviors. CBT is devoted first to the establishment of a collaborative therapeutic relationship, then to a mutually agreed upon establishment of a "formulation," or a flow chart, of the factors that maintain the patient's ED. In CBT, this formulation is regularly reviewed to highlight problems that need to be targeted and solved. Treatment in CBT consists of three components: behavioral activities, cognitive restructuring, and psycho-education. The behavioral activities are essentially nutrition counseling techniques and are a significant focus of this book. The reader will find detailed descriptions of the following CBT activities: weight checks (see Chapter 8: Assessing Weight, pp. 169–190); real-time in-the-moment self-monitoring using food journals (see Chapter 6: Self-Monitoring, pp. 140–149); homework (see Chapter 2: Course of Treatment, pp. 32–58); a food plan (see Chapter 5: Food Planning: Rule of Threes, pp. 107–139); and consumption of fear foods (see Chapter 9: Restoring Weight, pp. 191–228). As a result, our discussion in this chapter centers on the cognitive restructuring and psycho-education components of CBT.

Cognitive Restructuring

Cognitive restructuring involves identifying and correcting irrational beliefs and cognitive distortions. (See Table 4.1 for examples of cognitive restructuring of ED-related cognitive distortions.) As beliefs and distortion are challenged and corrected, their power to cause anxiety is decreased.

TABLE 4.1 Restructuring Cognitive Distortions

Cognitive distortion	Restructuring or reframing
Black or white thinking (you are either perfect or a total failure) *"I cannot eat any food with fat in it."*	*"I can eat some food with fat. Fat contains fat-soluble vitamins and essential fatty acids. Eating fat does not mean I will get fat."*
Catastrophic thinking (exaggerating the significance of one single event) *"I ate a half a bag of candy. It's hopeless. I'm always going to overeat."*	*"I usually eat a whole bag of candy. I am making progress."*
Self-fulfilling prophecy *"If I get stressed out, I know I will binge."*	*"I have tools to help me when I am stressed. I can listen to music, call a friend, write in my journal, or meditate."*
Pessimistic thinking (seeing only the negatives and assuming the worst) *"If I go out I will eat everything on the menu."*	*"I can order just enough to feel satisfied. I can stop eating at moderate fullness."*
Personalizing *"I would eat more if the food on campus was not so greasy."*	*"Not all food on campus is greasy. I can ask the food service to offer more foods prepared the way I like them."*
"Should" statements (being ruled by a rigid set of rules) *"I should eat only salad at every meal."*	*"I will be hungry if I just eat salad. I need protein and other nutrients to help feel satisfied."*
"It's not my fault" thinking (shifting responsibility for behaviors) *"I would eat more if it did not bother my stomach."*	*"Eating more will help me digest better in the long run. I can eat small frequent meals which will not feel as uncomfortable."*
Overgeneralization *"All carbohydrates are fattening."*	*"No one food makes me fat."*
Mindreading (assuming people are thinking the worst about you) *"If I eat in front of others, they will judge the type and amount of food I am eating."*	*"There is no evidence that anyone is really looking at me or what I am eating. If they do judge me it's about their issues with food, not mine."*
Discounting (can't accept positive feedback) *"People tell me I look healthy but I feel fat."*	*"I do feel healthy and have energy. Feeling fat is not about how I actually look."*
Comparing (always comparing self to others) *"I am not as thin as the other girls."*	*"I have different genetics than the other girls. Bodies come in all shapes and sizes. Comparing my body only makes me despair."*

Challenge expressions of faulty thinking about nutrition, food, and weight control by asking:

- What is the evidence for this belief?
- Does this belief look at the whole picture?

- Does it take into account both positive and negative ramifications?
- Does it promote well-being and peace of mind?
- Did you choose this belief on your own or did it develop out of your experience?

Cognitive restructuring can be applied to common food misconceptions such as "eating fat will make me fat." Evidence that casts doubt on this thought can come from regular monitoring of the patient's weight on an accurate scale, comparing the patient's weight to standards from height and weight charts, and comparing the patient's fat intake to official health recommendations. For example, a binge-eating patient may believe that eating breakfast leads to weight gain. We reflect, "It sounds like you believe that anyone who eats breakfast is destined to gain weight." The patient is likely to reply, "Of course not, my roommate eats breakfast every morning and she is thin." Another example of cognitive restructuring is illustrated in the vignette, The Oreo Cookie Story, demonstrating how the cognitive distortion of black and white thinking (labeling of food as good or bad) is challenged (Box 4.1).

BOX 4.1 THE OREO COOKIE STORY: AN EXAMPLE OF BLACK AND WHITE THINKING

We often use this story when we talk about how labeling a food as good or bad (black and white thinking) can make us think about it more and be less able to make an attuned eating choice.

My son is at a friend's house waiting in the kitchen while the friend is upstairs changing into his soccer clothes. On the kitchen table is an open bag of Oreo cookies.

In scene one, my son comes from a family where cookies are bad (processed, containing sugar, fat, etc.); in scene two, my son comes from a family where a cookie is just a cookie, neither good nor bad.

In scene one, my son eats as many cookies as he can, putting some in his pocket. He feels sneaky and guilty. His stomach does not feel good while running on the soccer field and he is thirsty.

In scene two, my son makes a conscious decision whether or not he wants to eat the cookies by first checking in with his hunger. He ultimately decides that three cookies and a glass of milk will satisfy his hunger but not upset his stomach during his soccer game.

Through gentle challenge and persuasion, as in the case example of Deidre (Case Example 4.1), we help patients shift their thinking and arrive at new con-

CASE EXAMPLE 4.1: DEIDRE

Deidre was afraid of putting salad dressing on the big salad she regularly ate for lunch.

Nutrition counselor: What is so scary about salad dressing?
Deidre: Well, it is high in fat and calories.
Nutrition counselor: (Explaining) Salad dressing is about half oil and half spices and vinegar, and spices and vinegar have no calories to speak of.
Deidre: But the oil is really a fat, isn't it?
Nutrition counselor: Oil is a very healthy fat that is a good source of essential fatty acids and fat-soluble vitamins that your diet, by the way, is quite low in.
Deidre: But fat is fattening.
Nutrition counselor: I know that most people think so, but in reality no food is fattening. We gain fat if we consistently eat more calories than we need. It doesn't matter whether those extra calories come from protein, carbohydrates, or fat.
Deidre: So I won't gain weight if I add salad dressing to my salad if I don't eat too many calories?
Nutrition counselor: That's right. How much salad dressing do you like on your salad?
Deidre: I used to use about a tablespoon, but that is too much, isn't it?
Nutrition counselor: Well, that is a normal serving and only about 75 calories. Is that too much?
Deidre: (After a moment of thought) No, I guess not since I am suppose to be eating 2,000 calories every day.
Nutrition counselor: What would you have to tell yourself to be able to add salad dressing to your salad tomorrow?
Deidre: (With some confidence) Salad dressing is good for me and as long as I don't use too much, it isn't very high in calories.
Nutrition counselor: We'll talk at your next visit about what eating a dressed salad was like for you. How many times do you want to eat a dressed salad between now and then?
Deidre: How about every other day?
Nutrition counselor: Great! Eating a dressed salad every other day will be your assignment this week.

clusions. For example, we sometimes use behavioral experiments to test faulty thinking. "While I know that eating breakfast will help keep your metabolism up and keep you from overeating later in the day, let's experiment this coming week to see if this is true for you." When cognitive skills are affected by malnutrition or when patients are overwhelmed by anxiety, however, they may not be able to use cognitive restructuring to challenge irrational thoughts. In these cases, we focus on helping patients change the way that they behave and wait to analyze the effects and implications of those changes.

CBT counseling interventions include skills to help patients deal with "self-talk," the inner dialogue that evaluates and interprets situations. Self-talk is based on one's thoughts and beliefs that may be positive, negative, neutral, rational and based on reason, or irrational and based on false information. Typically, in an ED negative self-talk could be experienced by a patient as a negative, critical inner voice that often says, "You are fat and can't control your eating or weight." Positive affirming self-talk assists patients in becoming connected to their bodies, appetites, feelings, and the present moment, and can prevent acting on impulses and cravings (Boudette, 2011).

Psycho-education

Psycho-education, defined as the education provided to individuals with a psychological diagnosis, is a standard component of CBT-Enhanced and ED treatment in general. Effective psycho-education is presented under the assumption that the patient is responsible and rational and is involved in a collaborative relationship with the counselor (Garner, 1997, p. 145). Understanding pertinent facts allows patients to feel more in control of their recovery and can help provide motivation to change. The goal of psycho-education for EDs is to make patients aware of the scientific evidence regarding the topics listed in Box 4.2 (Fairburn 2008, pp. 76–7; Garner, 1997, 145–146).

BOX 4.2 TOPICS FOR PSYCHO-EDUCATION ON EATING DISORDERS

- Multiple causes.
- Cultural context.
- Medical consequences and clinical features.
- How to determine a biological appropriate weight (BAW).
- Normal and eating-disordered eating and hunger and fullness patterns.
- The effects of starvation, semi-starvation, and restriction on metabolism.
- Benefits of regular eating patterns.
- The ineffectiveness of purging and exercise for weight control.
- Laxative and diuretic misuse.

- What happens with weight gain.
- Consequences of overexercising.
- Amenorrhea and bone health.
- Diets and diet myths.
- Relapse prevention.

Nutrition counselors should present basic nutrition facts and be familiar with the latest nutrition research and fads, as patients' erroneous beliefs about food, eating, and weight often arise from related media reports. Teaching patients about the medical consequences of EDs, for example, allows patients to make the connection between their physical, cognitive, and emotional symptoms and their ED behaviors. Denise did not know that long-term bulimics will eventually have painful, unsightly, and expensive dental problems. Anna was unaware that rapid weight loss usually leads to hair loss.

While it is important not to use scare tactics, patients deserve to be informed of the significant long-term risks EDs pose. We remind patients that most, but not all, symptoms resulting from ED behaviors can either be avoided or reversed with weight restoration or cessation of binging and purging. However, some medical complications can be serious, irreversible, and even fatal, as every organ system may be adversely affected by weight loss and malnutrition. (For more details see Chapter 1: Clinical Features of Eating Disorders, pp. 3–31.)

In some cases, patients may not be aware they have an ED. Reviewing the main characteristics of an ED diagnosis and clinical features can be clarifying. Eve sighed with relief when she realized her behaviors fit the diagnostic criteria for BED. "I finally know what's wrong with me," she said. Naomi had a similar experience after reviewing a medical complications handout on which she was asked to circle her symptoms.

In addition, it is important to educate patients about weight fluctuations (emphasizing weight trends versus a single weight) and prepare patients for regaining weight. What will it be like to regain weight? How much time will it take to restore weight? How does the body change? What thoughts and feelings will surface with weight restoration?

We offer the following advice on delivering psycho-educational messages to patients. First, find out what the patient already knows and determine what he or she needs to know. Because patients come to counseling with a range of knowledge and at various levels of readiness to receive nutrition information, we find that tailoring educational messages to each patient is most effective. Second, communicate respect for the patient's point of view. Third, deliver educational messages in a non-judgmental, compassionate, and even humorous manner.

It is important not to lecture but rather to weave educational material into interactions with the patient. We look for signs of interest and readiness on the part of the patient before embarking on an educational topic, and remain watchful of the patient's reactions. Any misinformed beliefs of the patient should be corrected with accurate and up-to-date facts. Educational messages have the most impact if presented early in treatment, but it is not unusual for patients to need facts restated in later sessions. The malnutrition and anxiety that plague most patients make it difficult for them to remember and process complex information. Limiting information to no more than three facts at a time, focusing on just what a patient needs to know, and putting important information in writing can be helpful. Bibliotherapy further educates patients. Suggested readings can come from the counselor's own lending library or ED catalogs such as the Gürze Eating Disorders Resource Catalogue of self-help books (http://www.bulimia.com/client/client_images/orig_images/2012GBEDCatalogue.pdf).

What is Dialectical Behavior Therapy?

DBT is a relatively new approach. The first treatment manual, published in 1993, was based on the assumption that patients with problematic behaviors lack skills to regulate mood, tolerate distress, and make behavior changes (Linehan, 1993). The "dialectic" of DBT is the balance between acceptance and change. DBT assumes that patients use these problematic behaviors to solve legitimate short-term issues, but in the long term these behaviors make problems worse. For many patients, eating-disordered behaviors can seem like the only way to cope with overwhelming emotions. The counselor explains to the patient that eating-disordered behaviors are ways to manage emotional reactions to internal or external events, and that DBT aims to replace eating-disordered behaviors with more skillful adaptive responses. DBT labels various skills to help patients immediately turn to a specific practical skill in difficult situations. Key DBT skills and techniques are:

- mindfulness (awareness and acceptance of the current moment in time)
- distress tolerance (development of coping skills)
- emotional regulation (modulate emotions without using destructive behaviors)
- behavior chain analysis (problem-solving strategies)

In the years since its development, DBT has been used with some success to treat a variety of difficult-to-treat disorders, such as EDs and borderline personality disorder (BPD), and behavioral problems, such as substance abuse, self-injury, suicide risk, and previous therapy failure. Because many of these behavior problems often coexist in patients with EDs, DBT outpatient treatment programs provide a concrete, cost-effective, and comprehensive treatment for both an ED and concurrent co-morbid illnesses and behavior problems.

Recent studies show promising results for using DBT in the treatment of BED and BN (Chen, Matthews, Allen, Kuo, & Linehan, 2008). DBT in AN is less effective because it is theorized that those with AN are not as distressed by disordered behaviors. They are less likely to want to stop eating-disordered behaviors than are patients with BN or BED. They may, however, express a desire to be free of the negative consequences of their chronic ED (McCabe & Marcus, 2002). In our practices, we find that the following DBT-inspired approaches are particularly effective.

As DBF instructs, we make an effort to remain a consultant and teacher rather than an authoritarian figure. We elicit from patients their own reasons to want to have success with homework assignments and other aspects of treatment. A DBT activity that we use often is to have patients make a note card to keep with them. On one side of the card they write the five most positive outcomes of abstaining from eating-disordered behaviors. On the other side they list the five worst consequences of engaging in eating-disordered behaviors. We encourage patients to look at their card when they are feeling ambivalent about treatment or recovery.

Mindfulness

Mindfulness, a DBT acceptance-based skill and a key component of ACT, has been studied as a mental health skill since the 1970s and has been around for thousands of years. Simply put, mindfulness is paying attention to the present moment with curiosity and attentiveness and without judgment or criticism. While being mindful, an individual becomes an observer or witness of his or her thoughts and feelings, allowing for more effective behavioral responses. We particularly like this definition: Mindfulness is non-judgmental living in the present.

In our practices, we often encourage patients to use meditation as a means of mindfulness. Boudette (2011, p 108) writes "… meditation is the foundation for deepening mindful responses and can help to interrupt the links in the chain of destructive patterns." Patients learn to identify emotions and how to let them pass without resorting to eating disordered behaviors. Boudette (2011, p. 108) suggests, "Through slowing down and observing—moment by moment—a space opens. Within this space, awareness is possible. Awareness, in turn, offers the possibility of choice." One of Herrin's patients says 5 minutes of mediating is helpful. "I wish I could do more, but five minutes works for me."

Another way of looking at mindfulness is that it offers a Zen-like ability for self-observation. Mindful people are able to focus on one thing at a time so that they are not inundated with overwhelming emotions. They are able to quiet overpowering emotions and diminish judgmental thoughts that exacerbate emotions and recognize negative self-talk. With practice, one can learn to name an emotion, notice the physical sensations, breathe with the emotion, observe the intensity of the emotion, and notice how urges to block the emotion or act on the emotion ebb and flow.

As of this writing, mindfulness in the treatment of EDs is not yet evidence based. A systematic review by Wanden-Berghe, Sanz-Valero, and Wanden-Berghe (2011), however, found evidence supporting the use of mindfulness-based interventions as treatment for eating-disordered patients, particularly those with BED and BN. Kristeller and Wolever's (2011) mindfulness-based eating-awareness training (MB-EAT) for the treatment of BED also has empirical support. See Box 4.3 for mindfulness practices that our patients have found helpful.

BOX 4.3 MINDFULNESS-BASED PRACTICES

Triangle of awareness. Show patients three points of the triangle: bodily sensations, thoughts, and emotions. Awareness should move along the points of the triangle without judgment or criticism, anchoring the present moment. Ask patients to use the triangle to describe what they experience during a session (Boudette, 2011).

Breathing. Teach diaphragmatic breathing to bring the patient into the present moment and be connected with his or her internal self. Count to 10 with each in and out breath, or using a word such as "calm" for each in and out breath. Demonstrate 1-minute stress reduction with mindful breathing: ask the patient to rate his or her present level of stress on a scale of 1 to 10, 10 being the most highly stressed. Then do 1 minute of mindful or diaphragmatic breathing and ask the patient to rate stress again. If the patient's stress level goes down, then suggest to the patient how much better he or she would feel if he or she did the breathing for 3 minutes or 5 minutes. Remind patients that they do not need any equipment to do this exercise; it can be done anytime and anywhere, especially before or after eating to decrease anxiety.

Rituals. Eating rituals provide meaning and intention to meals. Rituals at mealtimes give patients time to reflect and reconnect with food. Encourage patients to create mealtime rituals such as: setting the table, lighting candles, turning off the TV, saying a prayer or blessing before the meal, having a dessert and a cup of tea to end the meal.

Mindful questions. Use questions to increase mindfulness at meals and snacks: How does the food taste? What is my hunger level? Am I am approaching moderate fullness? Am I beginning to feel satisfied? How does this meal or snack make my body feel? Do I like this feeling? How do I feel when eating in this manner?

> **Eating meditation.** Mindfulness can be demonstrated during a session by having the patient eat a small piece of chocolate or a raisin, then directing the patient to notice any judgments, textures, tastes, smells, temperature of the food prior to swallowing.

Binge eaters, compulsive overeaters, patients with BN, or patients using hunger and fullness as a guide to eating, are the most appropriate candidates for applying mindfulness to eating behaviors. We are, however, careful to watch for mindfulness and mindful eating that lead to or justify undereating and dieting. We reiterate to our patients that an organized approach to food is their main medicine, and that following a food plan must occur regardless of hunger and satiety. As we observe a patient's mastery over the act of eating and maintaining a healthy weight, we usually encourage a more mindful approach to how much to eat. The practice of mindful eating is helpful in reducing the restrictive mindset of patients who have chronically dieted (Courbasson, Nishikawa, & Shapira, 2011).

As we have mentioned previously, mindfulness is of limited use to AN patients because of their need for distraction from, rather than intense awareness of, eating behaviors. Nevertheless, Merwin, Timko, Moskovich, Ingle, Bulik, and Zucker (2011) suggest that mindfulness may help to break through the AN patient's psychological inflexibility and intolerance for uncertainty. They speculate that mindfulness could help AN patients understand and respond to physical and emotional needs, redirect their limited ability to concentrate on more helpful internal and external cues, consider alternative purposeful actions rather than narrow and rigid responses to internal experience, and enhance social functioning. In AN, mindfulness may increase openness to experiences and values outside the world of weight and food restriction. Patients who are very low weight, however, are rarely candidates for mindfulness work.

Emotion Regulation Skills

Emotion regulation is a behavior-based skill that helps patients deal with emotions in healthy ways so that they can avoid engaging in destructive behaviors. ED patients generally have difficulty identifying or responding to their emotions or both and often turn to self-destructive food behaviors to cope. Box 4.4 lists the techniques we use to improve emotion regulation.

Distress Tolerance

Rather than working on finding solutions to distressing circumstances, distress tolerance is focused on accepting, finding meaning for, and tolerating distress.

BOX 4.4 EMOTION-REGULATION SKILLS

- Encourage patients to name emotions: Use a food journal that includes a column for noting emotions or suggest the patient records his or her emotions in a personal journal.
- Explain how emotions, behaviors, and thoughts all influence each other and are linked in a continuous cycle. The more overwhelming the emotion, the more rewarding the resultant behavior is (binge eating may be calming or numbing), and the more likely the patient is to continue to use ED behaviors. Patients should be told they have a choice how to react to their emotions and whether to use ED behaviors.
- Teach how physiological factors such as hunger or fatigue affect emotions. When patients ignore their bodies' hunger signals, they become more vulnerable and reactive to their emotions. When hungry or over-full, they are more likely to misinterpret others' actions and their own emotions (McKay, Wood, & Brantley, 2007, p. 136).
- Teach the acronym HALT: Take care of yourself when you start to get too (H) hungry, (A) angry, (L) lonely, or (T) tired.

Distress tolerance helps patients develop the patience to tolerate without overreacting to situations that are beyond their control. To achieve a composed response, patients learn to stay in the moment and to engage in alternative activities that soothe emotional pain and distract from ED behaviors and thoughts. Ideal alternative activities are pleasurable and incompatible with bingeing or purging. We assist our patients in creating a list of activities (see Box 4.5) they can use when they have eating-disordered urges. Effective alternative activities are calling or writing a friend, using the computer, journaling, taking a bath, or going for a walk. We caution against choosing schoolwork or housework, because few will consistently choose unappealing activities over bingeing. For example, Jasmine took on the assignment to find something fun to do that was incompatible with eating. A week later she excitedly reported that knitting was the distraction activity of her choice. Although BN and BED patients, like Jasmine, are cautioned not to pair eating with other activities, highly anxious AN patients often benefit from distractions while they are eating meals and snacks. Eating with a trusted person, playing cards or a board game, listening to music, or watching a movie while eating can help divert attention away from fears associated with eating. In Case Example 4.2, we show how Jane learns how to tolerate and manage her distress around dinner.

BOX 4.5 DISTRESS-TOLERANCE ACTIVITIES

Distraction techniques

- Observe other people (people watch), do something good for someone else, or think about people you care about.
- Fantasize, read your favorite poem or quote, or walk in nature.
- Organize your room, or redecorate or your desk, your room, garage, or house.
- Count in increments of seven, count your breaths, count the number of petals on a flower.
- Take a nap, read a book, sit in the sun, listen to music, stretch or do some yoga, draw or paint, or visit a friend.
- Safe-place visualization: sit in a quiet room and imagine a (real or imaginary) peaceful, relaxing place.
- Connect to your higher power (God, the divine universe or human goodness). Participate in religious activities, look at the stars, be with someone you admire, appreciate your body which is designed and directed by 30 to 40 thousand genes.

Soothing techniques

- Burn aromatic candles or incense, notice outdoor odors such as fresh cut grass or fresh flowers, or spray on some perfume.
- Go to a place that soothes you, such as the beach or a park. Look at pleasing magazine pictures, photos, or artwork.
- Listen to calming music, television, nature sounds, meditations, or flowing water in a fountain or a stream.
- Say aloud or read self-affirming and self-encouraging coping statements:
  - "I might have a less than perfect body, but I'm still a good person."
  - "I care about what and how much food I put into my body."
  - "It would be great to pick our body parts out of a catalog and pick our parents, but we can't."
  - "Each day I do the best I can to follow my food plan."
- Create an emergency coping plan or an emergency meal.
- Create a scrapbook or life-vision board by cutting out pictures and pasting on the board activities you value and feel are important.
- Use mindful breathing to stay calm.

CASE EXAMPLE 4.2: JANE

Jane has a problem eating dinner. She is not hungry, often gags, and has to force the food down. She does well at other meals, especially breakfast. From a behavior-chain analysis, the counselor learns that Jane has an afternoon snack one hour before dinner (which explains her lack of hunger). Jane fixes dinner the minute she arrives home from work, but she is usually tired from her hard workday and wants to rest. Jane suspects that being home alone makes her feel anxious, so she distracts herself with dinner preparations. Jane and her counselor brainstormed possible ways to allow Jane to eat dinner comfortably: rest when she first gets home, so she can prepare dinner later in the evening at which time she may feel more hungry; use affirmations to reinforce positive self-talk such as "Eating is pleasurable and relaxing" or "I enjoy eating my breakfast so I should expect to enjoy my dinner;" practice 1 minute of mindful breathing before eating; listen to music or watch television while eating for distraction; be kind and gentle with herself.

Behavior-Chain Analysis

A very useful DBT technique is behavior-chain analysis. In CBT, a similar technique is called "reviewing the formulation" (Fairburn, 2008, p. 70). A chain analysis is a detailed examination of a problematic behavior, starting with the trigger or prompting event. We use the questions in Box 4.6 to conduct a behavior-chain analysis.

BOX 4.6 BEHAVIOR-CHAIN ANALYSIS QUESTIONS

- Tell me about the problem behavior?
- What happened in your environment that triggered this behavior?
- What was your immediate reaction to the prompting event?
- What other things (links in the chain) happened between the prompting event and the behavior?
- What other things did you think? Feel? Do?
- If you had thought that you were going to do the problem behavior, what happened just before the thought?
- What happened immediately before the behavior?
- What prompted the behavior?
- What made you vulnerable?

- What are the consequences of the behavior?
- How did you feel during the behavior?
- How did you feel/what did you think immediately after the behavior?
- How did you feel/what did you think 30 minutes after the behavior?
- Can you think of anything you could have done differently to stop the behavior (break the chain)?

The counselor and patient then look for factors that increase vulnerability (e.g., feeling tired) to engage in ED behaviors, and together examine the patient's thoughts, feelings, body sensations, events, and internal and external experiences, review the consequences of the problematic behavior, identify obstacles for resolution of the problem, and brainstorm detailed solutions to the problem. DBT assumes that persistence of problematic behaviors is due to positive consequences or reinforcement that the behavior provides. For example, if patients binge because they are hungry and lonely, the negative consequence is that they will feel guilty, have indigestion, and possibly gain weight. Positive consequences include feeling satisfied, comforted, distracted, or simply having something to do on a lonely Saturday night. The goal of DBT is to guide the patient in finding a dialectical balance between tolerating being alone on a Saturday night (e.g., by engaging in a solo activity) and at the same time to enjoy the comfort of a meal or snack. As we study each link in the behavioral chain, we stop often to ask the patient, "What could you have done differently (at each link in the chain of events) to avoid the problem behavior? What coping or skillful behaviors could you have used?" These questions were asked of Alice in Case Example 4.3 and illustrated in Figure 4.1.

CASE EXAMPLE 4.3: ALICE'S BEHAVIOR-CHAIN ANALYSIS

Alice: I binged yesterday. I ate one half of a loaf of bread at the counter in secret. When my husband came into the kitchen, I hid the rest of it in the drawer.

Nutrition counselor: What was the prompting event?

Alice: There was a crisis situation with my business.

Nutrition counselor: What was your immediate reaction to this? What did you think, feel, do?

Alice: I thought the business was in ruin. We would lose everything. I went to the kitchen and started to eat bread.

Nutrition counselor: Sounds like a catastrophe. You slipped into your old pattern of dealing with crisis. How did you feel while you were eating the bread?

CASE EXAMPLE 4.3 (continued)

Alice: I was numb but felt guilty. I was afraid my husband would catch me in the kitchen eating the bread, so I ate fast.

Nutrition counselor: I want to make sure I understand what happened. Let me draw out a behavior-chain analysis.

Alice and her nutrition counselor work together to devise a behavior chain. The counselor draws circles, and then writes inside the circle the chronological events, thoughts, and behaviors that occurred. "So, what happened next?" The counselor and Alice examine the behavior chain and decide where she could break the chain in the future by considering alternative and behaviors.

Nutrition counselor: What could you have done differently at the first link in the chain?

Alice: Let's see, I could have taken a deep breath. I could have talked to my husband about my business worries. What would you do?

Nutrition counselor: Oh, I sometimes I release stress by yelling, "damn it!"

Alice: I could do that. No one would hear me at my office in the basement. I could also leave my knitting in sight so I would think of knitting to help me relax. Or I could go outside through the back door instead of through the kitchen and take a swim in my pool.

The nutrition counselor notes Alice's suggestions on the behavior chain at each link.

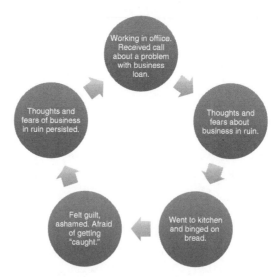

FIGURE 4.1 Alice's' behavior–chain analysis.

Motivational Interviewing

We have studied and use MI-style interactions to facilitate behavioral change in our patients. MI is a style of communicating with patients that utilizes listening, questioning, and gentle guidance. The goal of MI is to help patients resolve ambivalence about change and to strengthen motivation for and commitment to change (Rose, Rollnick, & Lane, 2004; Rollnick, Miller & Butler, 2008).

The foundation or "spirit of MI" is not a set of techniques but a counseling style. First is the assumption that the patient and the counselor are both authorities on the counseling relationship. In MI it is not assumed that the counselor is the expert or that the patient is deficient in knowledge or skills. As in the other approaches we utilize (i.e., CBT, DBT, and ACT), MI relies on the development of a collaborative rather than confrontational relationship between counselor and patient. Indeed, counselors are encouraged to avoid "the righting reflex," which is the urge to correct patients, to tell the patient what to do, or to tell them they are wrong. Another aspect of MI is the notion that ambivalence about change is a normal, natural human tendency. These MI assumptions help create a counseling atmosphere in which patients can decide if, how, and when they choose to change. Below we discuss how we use MI-style listening, questioning, and guiding in the treatment of ED patients.

Listening

In our sessions with patients, we aim to listen reflectively and with empathy, without judging or blaming. Nevertheless, patients often need to be encouraged to open up, to elaborate, and to give specific examples. Open-ended questions, like the ones below, elicit a broad range of information from the patient rather than one-word answers.

- "What brings you here today?"
- "Tell me a little about you."
- "What are you worried about?"
- "Why are others worried about you?"
- "How can I be of help?"
- "If you had a magic wand, how would you change your life?"
- "How would you like things to be different 5 years from now?"
- "What is a typical day like for you?"
- "What is mealtime like for you?"
- "What are some foods that you are afraid to eat?"
- "How are you managing to prevent purging?"

Reflective listening validates the meaning of a patient's statement and may help the patient continue to elaborate. For example, when Andy said to his counselor,

"I want to gain weight, but I make excuses not to eat." The counselor accurately reflects back what Andy said and then restates it slightly amended as a hypothesis. In this case, the counselor reflected, "Part of you wants to recover, but the other part is afraid." And then something interesting happens, says Rollnick et al. (2007, pp. 71–72). It doesn't matter whether the patient either agrees or disagrees with the counselor's hypothesis, but what is remarkable is that he or she continues to elaborate.

Summarizing what patients say indicates that the counselor has heard and understood the patient. A summary may collect themes of the conversation, link the conversation to previous conversations, or shift the conversation to either a new topic or to end a session. For example:

- "Tell me more about ..."
- "I hear you saying that ..."
- "Your bingeing and purging behaviors tend to escalate whenever you are stressed. It sounds like you often experience stress whenever you go home to visit your mother."
- "Today you talked about ..."

Change Talk

Another important feature of MI is the encouragement of patients to express their true feelings about change and to generate their own reasons to change. In MI it is believed that, when people talk about change themselves, they are more likely to change than if a counselor suggests a change. In initial sessions, in particular, the counselor does not instruct the patient to change or try to persuade the client to change, or give unsolicited advice. Rather, the counselor focuses on listening to and assessing the patient's ideas and attitudes about change. For example, Tiffany would like to cut down on bingeing. She says, "It would be very hard for me stop bingeing because it helps me unwind after classes. I'd have to start by cutting back to just bingeing after dinner." Using an MI style to reinforce a change that Tiffany says she is considering, her counselor responded, "Although it would be hard for you reduce bingeing, it seems like keeping your bingeing to just after dinner might be a place to start." Of note, hearing the patient use the word "but" often is a clear sign of ambivalence and of an interest in change. For example, Beth said, "I'd like to stop purging, but I don't want to gain weight." The following are examples of questions that promote change talk:

- "What do you want to change and why?"
- "What are the reasons you would change?"
- "Why is it important to change?"
- "Why is now the right time to change?"
- "What would it take to change?"

- "What do you think you need to do to change?"
- "What makes now feel like the right time?"
- "If you had a day without your ED, what would you do with your time?"
- "How does your ED fit into the rest of your life?"

Decision-to-Change Matrix

MI practitioners often use a decision-to-change matrix (also called a balance sheet) to reveal why patients are seeking counseling, what their core values are, and what emotional, cognitive, and medical complications they may be experiencing. Hailey's decision-to-change matrix is shown in Case Example 4.4. The upper right quadrant of the matrix is where "change talk" lives. The decision-to-change matrix activity is useful for most patients, except possibly for those who enter treatment clearly motivated to change.

CASE EXAMPLE 4.4: HAILEY'S DECISION-TO-CHANGE MATRIX

	Maintaining current behavior	*Changing current behavior ("change talk")*
Benefits of behavior	Feels safe. Helps me lose weight. Sets me apart. Gives me identify. Purging calms me. Makes me feel in control.	More time, more energy, more confidence and pleasure. Better relationship with food. Feel happy. All costs listed under maintaining behavior would go away.
Costs of behavior	Tired, lethargic, irritable, anxiety, sore throat, headaches, shame, stomach pains, constipation, bloating, chipmunk cheeks, depression, isolation, social anxiety, secrecy, preoccupation with counting calories, food and weight.	Give up comfortable habits. Risk of gaining weight. Lose sense of security. Separating from a part of myself.

Questioning

The focus of MI sessions move from listening to questioning when the patient demonstrates sufficient change talk and expresses openness to learning about options for change. An effective opening question is "What would be most helpful for us to talk about today?" Other questions that assess readiness and commitment to change are:

- "What would be a first step for you?"
- "What do you think you will do?"
- "Is xx working for you?
- "What would it be like to go one day without vomiting?
- "What would be a good thing about following your food plan?"
- "What do you want to work on this week?

Importance and confidence ratings are often used in MI. "How important is it, on a scale of 1 to 10, for you to change x?" "On a scale of 1 to 10, how confident are you that you can make this change?" These ratings reveal how important a particular change is to the patient and the extent to which he or she feels the change in behavior is possible. The most attainable changes are those that are of high importance to the patient and those in which the patient is confident he or she can execute the change.

Pros and cons, a similar activity, are used in MI to explore uncertainty about change. It is important to ask first about the "pros" of the ways things are. For example, "What do you like about purging?" To elicit "cons," Rollnick et al. (2008, p. 62) recommend, "And what is the downside of purging?" Or, "What are the not so good things about restricting?"

Guiding

In MI, counselors present a range of options to patients for their consideration. Direct guidance or information is provided only if requested by the patient. Further, it is recommended to ask permission before providing guidance or information. For example "May I suggest ...?" or "Would it be ok to tell you about ...?" We use conditional language such as "Some of my patients have tried ..." or "You might consider ..." As we have mentioned before, when we do provide information, we make no more than three points at a time to avoid information overload. We are careful to avoid saying, "I think ..." or "You should ..." After giving advice, we turn back to the patient, "What do you think? "What ideas do you have for yourself?" "What do you need or want to do differently?"

Acceptance and Commitment Therapy (ACT)

ACT is derived from CBT and emphasizes mindfulness (defined as non-judgmental living in the present). What makes ACT unique is that there is no attempt to change or correct irrational thoughts. Instead, patients are helped to *face* their thoughts, *see* them from a different perspective, and in turn *respond* in a way that is more productive. ACT is based on the premise that it is more effective to "change behavior first and let thoughts and feelings take care of themselves" (Heffner & Eifert, 2004, p. 43). ACT has only recently been applied to the treatment of EDs. The few studies that have been published show clinical improvements in AN patients (Berman et al., 2009). Two recently published professional handbooks describe the application of ACT to AN and BN (Kelly, Wilson, & DuFrene, 2011) and to the treatment of body-image problems (Pearson, Heffner, & Follette, 2010). Our patients have found Heffner and Eifert's (2004) ACT self-help workbook for AN helpful.

Paige, a twenties-something, did not want to go out with her friends until she lost enough weight to feel confident. Kater (2009) suggests that counselors not agree with patients, like Paige, when they state such conclusions. Nor should we argue or challenge them, but instead respond with simple restatements like, "Ok, so you don't like your body." With successful ACT, the patient may feel fat and unattractive, but still eats, does sports, socializes, and dates. In ACT, the counselor does not directly aim to eradicate ED behaviors. Michael, a high-school senior with purging AN, was advised to broaden his array of potential responses to feeling full. The fundamental goal in ACT is to help patients live life fully, regardless of how they feel about their shape and size.

Stages of Change

The stages of change model postulates that people pass through a series of five stages in the process of changing, including: pre-contemplation, contemplation, preparation, action, and maintenance. Using this model, counselors can identify which stage the patient is in and select appropriate interventions based on specific stages. In general, patients in early stages of change respond best to MI listening approaches, and those in the later stages respond best to MI questioning and the behavioral techniques of CBT and DBT.

Nevertheless, there has been some debate about the utility of using the stages of change in treatment. Identifying states and matching interventions can be difficult. Patients migrate between stages, and the stages of change may differ for particular behaviors. A mismatch between stage and intervention can increase patient resistance. Although there appears to be some validity to this debate, awareness of stages of change has provided helpful illumination in our work. We often review the stages of change model with patients and ask them which stage best applies overall or for a particular behavior.

In the earliest stage, pre-contemplation, patients may not want to change or even be unaware they have problem or they may be discouraged and resigned to having problems. These patients may feel forced into treatment by family members or health professionals. Many ED patients, particularly AN patients, who first enter treatment, appear to be in the pre-contemplation stage. The next stage, contemplation, is characterized by extreme ambivalence. Patients are willing to consider changing a behavior, but they can see an equal balance between the pros and cons of change. A good example of the contemplation stage is the patient who wants to eat normally but is afraid of gaining weight. In the preparation stage, patients are ready to work on strategies that support behavior change. For example, the patient can eat dessert if she eats it with her boyfriend. In the action stage, patients are experimenting with desired behavior changes, but have mixed feelings about the changes. In this stage, patients are usually partially implementing their food plan. The final stage is maintenance. In this stage, patients successfully practice behavior changes such as resisting urges to binge and purge, though periods of relapse are likely. Strategies for each stage are described below (adapted from Villapiano & Goodman, 2001).

Pre-contemplation Stage of Change

It is common for ED patients to want to please others and not to directly disagree or express anger. Instead, they display passive–aggressive forms of resistance, such as restricting, purging, and other ED behaviors. After her mother grounded her for not coming home on time, Lucy told her nutrition counselor that she would get back at mom by restricting and isolating over the weekend. In this stage the counselor should join with the patient's resistance (for more on resistance see Chapter 1: Clinical Features of Eating Disorders, pp. 3–31) by conveying empathy. We find ourselves often saying, "It is difficult to change when you are used to restricting when you are angry." "There are a lot reasons to not want to change." "No one can force you to change." Accepting, not confronting, the patient's resistance shows the patient you understand his or her problem, allowing the patient to be more open and relaxed.

Strategies for the Pre-contemplation Stage of Change

- Develop a trusting relationship.
- Evaluate the costs and benefits of current eating behaviors using a decision-to-change matrix (see p. 107 in this chapter).
- Emphasize the positives about change.
- Educate using a supportive non-confrontational style with scientific facts (give articles, lend books).
- Ask theoretical questions. ("What would it be like to be able to eat whatever you wanted?")
- Review medical complications (see Chapter 1: Clinical Features of Eating Disorders, pp. 3–31).
- Discuss the Keys study about the effects of semi-starvation (Keys, Brozek, Henschel, Mickelsen, & Taylor, 1950; see Chapter 1: Clinical Features of Eating Disorders, pp. 3–31).
- Provide information about weight, body image, genetics, and frame size.

- Explain set-point weight and metabolism (see Chapter 8: Assessing Weight, pp. 169–190).
- Present the reasons why diets fail.
- Tell stories about others with EDs.
- Affirm and encourage self-efficacy.
- Ask "What do you want to work on?"

Using simple and complex reflections as well as summarization allows patients to feel understood and heard. We rephrase or reflect statements, acknowledging the patient's current state of affairs. In order to move the patient along to the next thought and get to deeper meanings, we use double-sided reflections. Double-sided reflections reveal ambivalence. For example, if the patient is afraid of gaining weight, the counselor could say, "I see that you are terrified about gaining weight, but you are also afraid your coach won't let you back on the team if you don't gain." The counselor should avoid asking too many questions and talking too much during the session. We respond with at least one reflection, preferably two, before asking another question. A good rule is to avoid asking three questions in a row.

Examples of Simple and Complex Reflections

Simple reflection (mirrors back to the patient):

> **Patient:** *I hate self-monitoring food journals.*
> **Counselor:** *Writing food journals does not work for you.*

Complex reflection (adds meaning and emphasis):

> *Your ED lets you cope with your sexual abuse.*

Double-sided reflection (targets both sides of the issue):

> *On the one hand you are tired of dealing with your ED, but on the other hand, you are afraid to give it up.*

Summarization (helps to see if you understand what the patient is saying):

> *You are successfully tuning into your hunger and satiety cues but are not sure how to deal with cravings.*

Contemplation Stage of Change

In the contemplation stage of change, patients are aware of an equal balance of reasons for and against changing. They recognize the benefits of changing, but are fearful of giving up ED behaviors. They do not want to forego the positives of having an ED, but at the same time they recognize the negatives.

Strategies for the Contemplation Stage of Change

- Explore with patient how life would be different without an ED.
- Explore the reasons not to change.
- Explore how the patient would feel without an ED.
- Explore what the ED does for the patient.
- Explore what it might be like to live without the ED.
- Explore what the patient will need to do to survive without an ED.
- Explore what the patient will have to deal with or feel if he or she gives up a specific ED behavior:

  - What does xx (e.g., vomiting/skipping lunch) do for you?
  - How would your life be different if you stopped xx (e.g., using laxatives, running every day)?
  - How has xx (e.g., counting calories, binge eating) helped you?
  - What would it be like to feel emotions rather than use xx (e.g., avoiding carbohydrates, body checking) to cope?
  - What do you have to feel, face, and do without xx (e.g., daily weight checks, bingeing in your bedroom)?
  - What do you believe will happen if you give up xx (e.g., losing weight, buying binge food)?

- Talk about the pros and cons of preoccupation with weight and giving up the fear of weight gain.
- Teach the function of fat in food and in the body.
- Talk about ways to add fat to food.
- Challenge incorrect beliefs and myths about food.
- Discuss the pros and cons of increasing or decreasing food intake.

Preparation or Decision Making Stage of Change

In the preparation stage of change, patients intend to take action in the immediate future (within a month or two). The patient generally has a plan of action, and is actively participating in counseling.

Strategies for the Preparation Stage of Change

- Identify specific goals and develop strategies to reach those goals.
- Role play with the patient versus the ED, encouraging the patient to have the last word.
- Discuss hypothetical situations and how they might be managed.

- Change negative self-talk into positive self-talk (write positive self-talk on an index card for the patient to refer to between sessions).
- Encourage the patient to challenge the ED voice using a healthy voice.
- Remind patients to use HALT: Stop before too hungry, angry, lonely or tired.
- Involve supportive people to help with implementing goals and strategies.
- Develop skills and strategies to deal with fear of weight gain.
- Make a list of alternative behaviors in place of ED behaviors (listen to music, read, people watch).
- Journal thoughts and feelings.
- Read affirmations written on an index card before during or after eating.
- Eat with a supportive friend or family member.
- Implement the food plan.
- Forecast obstacles and problem solve strategies.

Action Stage of Change

A patient in the action stage is actively asking questions and is dynamic in sessions. Behavioral strategies can be very helpful in this stage (e.g., menu planning, rewards, and distraction techniques) and should be offered. The counselor ensures that the patient has an effective support team, namely, family and friends, in order to prevent relapse. We explain the physical symptoms the patient might experience (e.g., uncomfortable gastrointestinal bloating, early satiety, or intense hunger; see Chapter 1: Clinical Features of Eating Disorders, pp. 3–31). Emotional volatility typically arises at this stage and should be mentioned and discussed with patients and their therapists. We remind patients that it usually takes 3–6 months of consistently practicing and integrating new behaviors before one can move into the next stage—the maintenance stage.

Strategies for the Action Stage of Change

- Teach behavior strategies.
- Enhance self-confidence.
- Encourage and support.
- Participate in an EDs support group.
- Involve family for support.
- Written self-monitoring.
- Forecast obstacles.
- Practice the food plan.
- "Food is my medicine."
- Be patient.
- Remember slips do not always lead to slides (Kingsbury, & Williams, 2003).
- Learn from slips.
- Identify and satisfy physical hunger.
- Work toward lifestyle changes.

Maintenance Stage of Change

In the maintenance stage of change, patients are practicing making changes. Practice and problem-solving are key. The goal is preventing relapse and sustaining normal eating behaviors for at least 6 months. Patients may benefit from keeping a food journal to stay on track. As the patient progresses, we consider reducing the frequency of nutrition counseling sessions.

Strategies for the Maintenance Stage of Change

- Identify any triggers for relapse, such as denial.
- Talk about relapse as an integral part of the recovery process.
- Develop and review a relapse-prevention plan (see Chapter 7: Levels of Care, pp. 150–166).
- Reinforce efforts and emphasize personal strengths and coping skills.
- Affirm healthy versus ED behaviors.

Summary Points

- CBT focuses on self-monitoring, cognitive restructuring, psycho-education, and nutrition-focused behavioral activities. Cognitive restructuring involves identifying and correcting irrational beliefs.
- DBT balances acceptance-based with behavior-based skills. Mindfulness and distress tolerance are the acceptance-based skills. Emotion regulation and interpersonal effectiveness are the behavior-based skills.
- MI is a patient-centered directive style of counseling that emphasizes self-direction. It uses both listening and instruction to help the patient change. Interventions are informed by the patient's stage of change.
- ACT includes mindfulness and CBT-based strategies. It is based on the premise that it is more effective to "change behavior first and let thoughts and feelings take care of themselves."
- The stage of change model postulates that people pass through a series of five stages in the process of changing: pre-contemplation, contemplation, preparation, action, and maintenance. Using this model, counselors can identify which stage the patient is in and select appropriate interventions based on that stage of change.

PART II
Tools

5

FOOD PLANNING: RULE OF THREES

Introduction

A food plan is a key tool in the treatment of eating disorders (EDs), providing practical guidance to ED patients who need to normalize their food intake. Effective food plans achieve three ends: ensuring nutrient needs are met; providing an organized approach to food consumption; and desensitizing feared, binged, or purged foods. Experts in the field support the use of a food plan for treating EDs, describing it as "the most effective behavioral intervention;" an indispensable "prescription;" and a "medication" which "inoculates" patients against ED behaviors. Because the field lacks an evidenced-based, standardized food plan, plans based on the Diabetic Exchange List System (for exchange lists see Daly et al., 2008), or on MyPlate/MyPyramid (see United States Department of Agriculture, 2011) are usually used by residential and outpatient practitioners. In this chapter we describe and outline the use of the rule of threes (RO3s; see Box 5.1), the food plan which Herrin developed to treat EDs and which we use in our practices.

The Benefits of the Rule of Threes

The structure of three meals and three snacks provided by the RO3s gives patients a sense of self-control over eating behaviors and body weight. When patients follow this plan, they spend less time thinking about food, and counting calories or servings, and more time focusing on other aspects of recovery, including psychotherapy. We find our patients have fewer bingeing and purging episodes. The RO3s food plan teaches patients to recognize and appropriately respond to hunger and fullness signals by mimicking an appetite-based eating pattern. In our experience, eating three meals a day plus snacks of normal portion sizes is the most effective method for successful long-term weight management. When we

BOX 5.1 RULE OF THREES GUIDE TO FOOD PLANNING

Breakfast
Calcium
Complex Carbohydrates
Fruit or Vegetable
Protein (optional)
Fat (optional)
Snack
Lunch
Calcium
Complex Carbohydrates
Fruit or Vegetable
Protein
Fat
"Fun Food"
Snack
Dinner
Calcium
Complex Carbohydrates
Fruit or Vegetable
Protein
Fat
"Fun Food"
Snack

Normal serving size usually is one cup or twice the size indicated on food labels.

Calcium suggestions (one serving is about 200 to 500 mg)
Milk, yogurt, cheese, frozen yogurt, tofu, calcium supplement

Complex carbohydrate suggestions
Cereal, bagels, bread, crackers, rice, potatoes, pasta, corn

Fat suggestions
Butter, margarine, peanut butter, cheese, cream cheese, salad dressing, mayonnaise, sauces, muffins, bacon, nuts, olives, avocado, egg yolks, fried/sautéed foods, chips, ice cream, some meats

Fruit or vegetable suggestions
Any fresh, cooked, dried, canned, or juiced fruits or vegetables

"Fun food" suggestions
Any dessert, cookies, cake, ice cream, pudding, doughnuts, croissants, candy bars, chips, fries, non-diet soda, milk shakes

Protein suggestions (one serving is about 20 g of protein)
Meat, fish, poultry, eggs, cottage cheese, Greek yogurt (1 cup), cheese, dried beans, hummus, tofu, tempeh, peanut butter, other nut butters

Snack suggestions
Calcium, complex carbohydrates, fruit or vegetable, protein, fat, "fun food"

introduce the RO3s in a supportive and collaborative manner, the patient's anxiety decreases but his or her autonomy stays intact.

Patients of all ages and educational levels respond well to the instructions implied by the RO3s. The RO3s template presumes three meals and three snacks with no longer than 3 hours between eating times. This is a biologically sound guide designed to counter the common tendency of ED patients to either undereat or to overeat. The spacing of three meal and three snacks over the course of a day matches the liver's capacity to maintain blood glucose levels with glycogen, the storage form of carbohydrates. Depletion of glycogen is associated with feelings of hunger. However, ED patients unable to interpret and act on internal sensations of hunger may benefit from "eating by the clock." Patients who report bingeing between planned eating episodes should experiment with shorter intervals between meals and snacks. As patients progress, whether to have a snack or not depends on whether they are hungry and interested in a snack. At this juncture, we say, "Snacks are optional, meals are required."

In addition, the RO3s offers a flexible eating style that easily fits into family and social gatherings and work and school routines. For example, college students who have a late breakfast and an early lunch may not be hungry for a morning snack but may need two evening snacks when they stay up late studying. Some patients prefer, and seem to do well with, a breakfast that does not include protein or fat. Other patients prefer a pattern of four or five small meals over the more standard pattern of three meals and three snacks. The RO3s can be adjusted to fit this and, indeed, any pattern. "What is important is you get your food groups in over the course of the day." We help patients rearrange meals and snacks to match their lifestyle. Patients who must gain weight will likely have to eat beyond the basic RO3s template by adding additional food groups to snacks or by increasing the size of servings. For example, we designed a RO3s plan around Chloe's morning routine of a flavored latte: a small breakfast at home and a latte on the way to class.

The RO3s plan makes food planning simple. We believe that more complicated food plans are counterproductive, especially for ED patients. We also believe that most people have an intuitive sense of how to eat normally without needing the equivalent of a college course in nutrition. Hence, we generally do not discuss details about the caloric or nutrient content of the components of the RO3s or educate about various nutrient food sources—unless asked. Below, however, we do provide details on the nutritional aspects of the RO3s for the benefit of our readers.

We have many patients entering treatment who are using a plan based on the Exchange List or MyPlate/MyPyramid. When it is clear that the patient's current food plan is interfering with recovery, or when the patient finds his or her plan impractical for normal living, then, and only then, do we introduce the RO3s. Heather's story is typical. She was discharged from residential treatment with a food plan based on the Exchange List that specified the number of servings per day for each food group. Her plan consisted of: six meat proteins, three milk proteins, six fats, eight starches, three fruits, two vegetables, and desserts a minimum of four times a week (one dessert counts as one fat). Heather's parents were confused about the "eight starches," which sounded like too much food. They were reassured once they learned that, according to the Exchange List, a serving of starch is equivalent to a quarter of a bagel. Next, they worried that Heather's plan was too low in carbohydrates since, according to the Exchange List, a bagel would "cost" four carbohydrate servings. Herrin was concerned that Heather's plan, typical of residential food plans in that it limited desserts to a certain number per week, would result in a sense of deprivation on days she didn't eat dessert.

Sadie was also limited to four desserts over the course of a week. Within 2 weeks of discharge from a residential center Sadie was back to bingeing and purging. Sadie blamed her relapse in part on being overwhelmed with having to decide which day to have a dessert and which day to go without. We have had patients complain that their discharge food plan made it difficult to eat at restaurants and to have meals with family and friends. MyPlate/MyPyramid and the Diabetic Exchange have been criticized as being too numerical, precise, complicated, and inflexible for patients to rely on in the real world (Krebs-Smith & Kris-Etherton, 2007). These plans tend to confuse parents of recently discharged patients to the point that the child ends up running the show. MyPlate/MyPyramid can perpetuate ED obsessions due to emphasis on: eating more fruits, vegetables, legumes, and whole grains; eating less added sugar and saturated fat; and encouraging plant oils over animal fats. That being said, when a patient arrives in our offices with a food plan prescribed by an inpatient program or another provider that we view as inadequate, we do not change the plan. Instead, we support the food plan if it is working for the patient, and, if necessary, we help parents implement it.

Introducing the Rule of Threes

We use the RO3s for all patients. However, presenting a paper version of the RO3s can overwhelm anxious patients, especially those who begin treatment with severely restricted food intake. In these instances, it is often best to wait to introduce the concept of a formal food plan until somewhat later in treatment, if at all. We instead direct these patients, at each session, to add one or two foods to specific meals or snacks so that, over time, their intake approximates the RO3s. At first meeting, Darcy started the session with, "I don't do well with food plans." Rather than try to convince her otherwise, Herrin asked, "What do you feel ready to add to improve your food intake?"

Prior to presenting a copy of the RO3s, we take time to explore each patient's efforts to manage their eating problems as well as to learn about current beliefs about nutrition and weight. After exploring what has worked in the past and what is not currently working, we discuss specifically how the RO3s will solve the patient's specific weight and eating problems. We may tell a patient preoccupied with food, "Following the RO3s will decrease your preoccupation with food because you will know what, when, and how much you will be eating. The RO3s food plan will meet your energy and nutrient needs so that your body feels satisfied."

Another strategy that can pique interest in the RO3s (and to assess current eating patterns) is to direct patients to compare their eating to normal eating as defined by Satter (2008, p. 16) whose description of normal eating is a well accepted benchmark. See Box 5.2. We might ask, "What stands out for you as

---

BOX 5.2 WHAT IS NORMAL EATING?

Normal eating is going to the table hungry and eating until you are satisfied. It is being able to choose food you like and eat it, and truly get enough of it—not just stop eating because you think you should. Normal eating is being able to give some thought to your food selection so you get nutritious food, but not being so wary and restrictive that you miss out on enjoyable food. Normal eating is giving yourself permission to eat sometimes because you are happy, sad, or bored, or just because it feels good. Normal eating is mostly three meals a day, or four or five, or it can be choosing to munch along the way. It is leaving some cookies on the plate because you know you can have some again tomorrow, or it is eating more now because they taste so wonderful. Normal eating is overeating at times, feeling stuffed and uncomfortable. And at times it can be undereating and wishing you had more. Normal eating is trusting your body to make up for your mistakes in eating. Normal eating takes up some of your time and attention, but keeps its place as only one important area of your life.

In short, normal eating is flexible. It varies in response to your hunger, your schedule, your proximity to food and your feelings.

The essence of normal eating. *Reprinted from Secrets of Feeding a Healthy Family* (2nd ed., fig. 2, p. 16), by E. Satter, 2008, Madison, WI: Kelcy Press. Copyright 2008 by Ellyn Satter. Reprinted with permission.

you read this quote?" "Does anything here describe your eating behaviors?" For example, Nora responded that she does not eat three meals a day, she afraid to eat cookies, and does not trust her body to make up for her eating mistakes.

Yet another tactic is to show patients Craighead's Appetite Awareness Tracking (AAT) models (2006). Figure 5.1 shows the AAT for bulimia nervosa (BN)

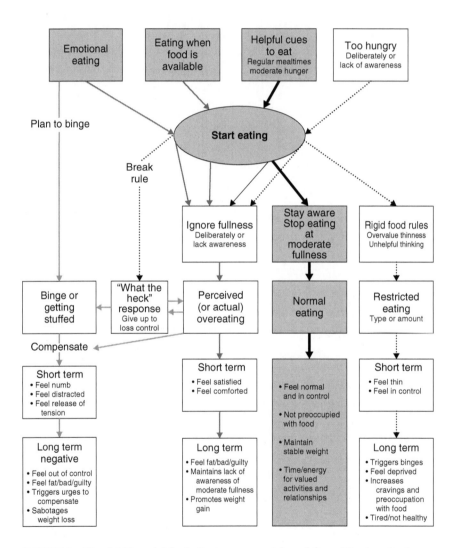

FIGURE 5.1 The AAT model for bulimia nervosa. Adapted from *The Appetite Awareness Workbook: How to Listen to Your Body & Overcome Bingeing, Overeating, & Obsession with Food* (p. 149), by L. Craighead, 2006, Oakland, CA: New Harbinger Publications. Copyright 2012 by New Harbinger Publications. Reprinted with permission.

and Figure 5.2 shows the AAT for binge-eating disorder (BED). Of note, the only difference between AAT for BN and BED is that in BN normal eating may be perceived as overeating. Asking "where do you see yourself in this model" validates a patient's struggles. AAT is particularly effective for those in the precontemplative or contemplative stage of change (see Chapter 4: Counseling Interventions, pp. 79–104). Most patients clearly grasp from AAT how restrictive eating leads to binge eating and how food rules result in a "what the heck" response.

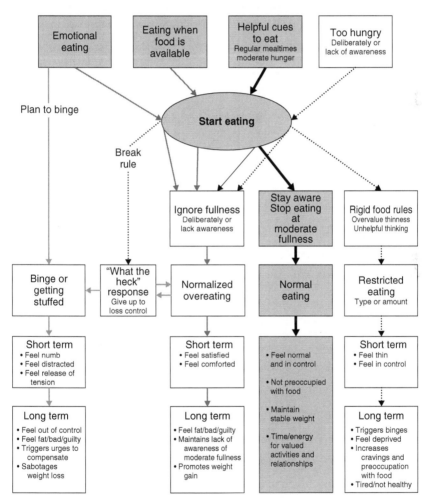

FIGURE 5.2 The AAT model for binge-eating disorder. Reprinted from *The Appetite Awareness Workbook: How to Listen to Your Body & Overcome Bingeing, Overeating, & Obsession with Food* (p. 22), by L. Craighead, 2006, Oakland, CA: New Harbinger Publications. Copyright 2012 by New Harbinger Publications. Reprinted with permission.

Implementing the Rule of Threes

Standardized food plans, even the RO3s plan, do not generate much enthusiasm unless they are individualized. One way to individualize the RO3s is to detail "sample days," incorporating foods the patient routinely eats and showing how the plan can be adapted to match his or her lifestyle. At each visit we offer to provide patients with a hand-written individualized version of their food plan. Depending on the patient's need for specificity, the written plan may incorporate foods reported in a recent dietary recall, outline several "sample" days, or simply be a reiteration of the standard RO3s format. Some patients benefit from explicit instructions about where, when, what, and how much to eat. At the very least, these written plans should include the dietary improvements agreed upon by both the nutrition counselor and the patient. At the subsequent session, it is important to ask about the patient's success in complying with his or her plan, asking, "How did it go? Were you able to do the things we agreed upon last time?" We also devote time to discussing adapting the RO3s for upcoming events that differ from usual routines (e.g., weekend days, holidays, and vacation days) and to writing out sample plans for these days. Another approach is to define snack or fun food items in calories (e.g., 300 calories) so patients can choose appealing or convenient items. We use this strategy cautiously and suggest it only to patients who already "think" in calories.

We often use a "this or that" format. An example is Sophie's breakfast plan:

Breakfast
1 cup oatmeal
1 cup yogurt
1 piece of fruit

or

1/2 cup cottage cheese
1 wasa cracker
1 piece of fruit
1 cup hot chocolate

Adrienne's lunch plan is below. Herrin explained to her parents that the "slash mark" means she could have "either this or that."

Lunch
Sandwich (2 pieces of bread and 3 oz. of protein)/2 cups of macaroni and cheese
1 cup of fruit salad/1 cup yogurt
1 cup juice/1 cup milk/1 cup sports drink
1 of mom's brownies/1 cup of ice cream

We take notice of the patient's least entrenched food behaviors as candidates for first interventions. These are often the most recently adopted behaviors. Jane, for example, had been moistening her salads with vinegar instead of her favorite Italian salad dressing, but only for the last several weeks. She was quite amenable to returning to the use of her regular salad dressing. "I really didn't like the tartness of the vinegar anyway," she confided later. Another strategy is to direct the patient's attention to one specific dietary component per session. For example, an early session might be devoted to improving the adequacy of the patient's protein intake, the next session focusing on calcium, the following week on fat intake, and so on.

We recognize the substantial time, effort, and support patients may need with food planning, but we look for ways to gradually return the responsibility for food planning to the patient. When patients ask for a sample RO3s food plan for each day of the week, we are judicious in complying. An undue dependence on the nutrition counselor may result, or the professional may become the scapegoat if the patient has difficulty with his or her plan. Furthermore, in an outpatient setting, unless the patient is seen frequently, it usually is not possible to plan any more than several "sample" days. Although initial food plans are usually quite detailed, over time, as patient gains confidence in making effective food choices, they serve more as a general guide rather than a prescription. Some patients are able to make progress simply using the RO3s plan as a checklist for what they need to be consuming on a daily basis.

Longer term goals for food planning include resolution of fears about food-related issues, restoration and maintenance of a biologically appropriate weight (BAW; see Chapter 9: Restoring Weight, pp. 191–228), and recognition of hunger and fullness. The increased sense of hopefulness, competency, and self-care that patients gain as the result of efforts to follow a food plan usually enhances progress in psychotherapy. We make mention of other patients who learned important problem-solving skills and life lessons as result of mastering a food plan. It is well known that, until at least a modicum of nutritional restoration has been achieved, most patients cannot truly profit from adjunctive psychotherapy. For all these reasons, we devote considerable time and attention to developing an individualized RO3s food plan for each patient.

During each food planning session, we encourage our patients to commit to at least *one* highly specific and relevant behavioral goal. At this juncture we ask, "What do you want to work on this week?" For example, patients who currently do not eat breakfast could choose to "add breakfast." Other patients may want to incorporate a serving of protein at lunchtime or to devise alternative plans for the evening so bingeing is less likely. As patients progress, we make it a habit to direct them to pick "one easy thing, one medium thing, and one hard thing" to work on between sessions.

For example, Andrea, who is of normal weight but gaining, and has been diagnosed as having BN, complained that she was getting too full at dinner. Herrin asked, "Tell me about last night's dinner" (see Case Example 5.1).

Case Examples 5.2 and 5.3 are individualized RO3s plans for Jenny, who is an underweight picky eater and new to treatment, and for college student Isabelle.

CASE EXAMPLE 5.1: ANDREA'S EASY, MEDIUM, AND HARD ASSIGNMENTS

Andrea: Mom served her famous meatloaf. I had two servings of mashed potatoes, and a salad, and milk to drink. And, of course, my fun food. Last night it was two cookies and half a cup of ice cream.

Herrin: How big is a serving of potatoes at your house?

Andrea: Oh, about three-quarters of a cup.

Herrin: Let's experiment. You could do one serving of mashed potatoes or make each serving about half a cup ("the hard thing"). Remember, if you are still hungry after your fun food (the "easy thing"), have the piece of fruit (the "medium thing") we talked about before.

CASE EXAMPLE 5.2: JENNY'S RULE OF THREES FOOD PLAN

Jenny is in middle school and a very picky eater. She is new to treatment and underweight. Her parents supervise all her meals.

* New additions since Jenny's last nutrition appointment are marked with an asterisk

Breakfast
2 pieces of toast
8 oz. yogurt with two sprinkles of fruit and two sprinkles of cereal
* Drink with calories

Lunch
Salad with two tablespoons of dried fruit, two tablespoons of almonds, and two tablespoons of regular dressing
Fruit
Protein – 3 instead of 2 slices of turkey
Chocolate milk
200-calorie fun food

Or

Wrap (low carbohydrate is OK) with 3 slices of turkey
One tablespoon of real mayonnaise
Sweetened iced tea
Fruit
200-calorie fun food

Afternoon snack
Yogurt smoothie
Bread/crackers

Or

8 oz. yogurt

CASE EXAMPLE 5.3: ISABELLE'S RULE OF THREES FOOD PLAN

We often use this form when writing out a sample plan. Below is Isabelle's plan. Isabelle is a college student who tries to eat healthily but found herself often bingeing in the evening.

RO3 plan	Sample plan
Breakfast	
Calcium	Milk
Complex carbohydrate	Cereal
Fruit or vegetable	Banana
Protein (optional)	
Fat (optional)	
Snack	Granola bar
Lunch	
Calcium	Cheese
Complex carbohydrate	Sandwich bread
Fruit or vegetable	Orange juice
Protein	Turkey
Fat	Mayonnaise
Fun food	Cookies
Snack	Greek yogurt, berries
Dinner	
Calcium	Milk
Complex carbohydrate	Sweet potato
Fruit or vegetable	Broccoli
Protein	Chicken
Fat	Margarine
Fun food	Pudding
Snack	Peanut butter crackers, juice

The Role of the Nutrition Counselor

To be successful in helping our patients with food planning, we take on a number of different roles in order to handle the significant issues that arise as the patient attempts to change entrenched eating behaviors. The nutrition counselor may be:

- the trusted professional who offers an alternative management system that is proven to be scientific and effective
- the knowledgeable teacher who knows even more than the patient does about nutrition and health
- the kind confidante who listens compassionately and respectfully to the shameful details of the patient's difficulties
- the wise guide who carefully supervises restoration of normal eating habits
- the enthusiastic coach who applauds each small step and who continually describes a vision of the patient's future in which food is managed independently and competently.

The patient's respect and confidence in the nutrition counselor's expertise is a crucial factor in deciding whether he or she will comply with a food plan. Ideally, patients conclude that this experienced and compassionate practitioner is capable of guiding them in the design of just the right food plan for them. We keep aware that our beliefs, values, and philosophies about food, weight, and body image can be transmitted to patients whether discussed directly or not. Nutrition counselors who have adopted a carefree, comfortable, accepting approach to food, exercise, weight, and body-image issues can be an asset to patients who struggle with these issues. For example, hearing that the professional regularly eats some of the patient's feared foods or does not exercise every day is reassuring. Herrin may disclose that she is still following the RO3s plan 40 years after her recovery. It is helpful to express the unequivocal conviction that "If we work together on a food plan, we can beat this eating disorder." Some patients are stirred to action just from the expectation that they will follow the RO3s. Acknowledgment and praise for any improvement in food, exercise, and weight-related behaviors (not matter how insignificant) can bolster continued behavioral change. Accolades should be given for attempts, whether successful or not, at following the food plan.

It is important to be non-judgmental about the food choices patients make, as long as these choices are not associated with ED behaviors. For instance, we investigate a reported binge, but do not focus on the fact that the patient ate potato chips except to "wonder out loud" if the patient needs to "legalize" potato chips so she or he can eat them in moderate amounts. Patients should be assured that their food plan can include every possible type of food, including snack foods, higher fat foods, sauces, fried foods, and desserts if consumed in normal serving sizes and at appropriate times. These foods may be demystified if nutrition counselors occasionally allude to their personal use of them. We may mention newly published research that indicates that variety in food intake improved outcomes whereas lack of variety is associated with relapse in anorexia nervosa (AN; Schebendach et al., 2011) or that fun food eaten as part of balanced meals is associated with successful weight loss (Jakubowicz, Froy, Wainstein, & Boaz, 2012). We share our research-based conclusion that there are no bad foods, only bad amounts. As we work with patients on improving food behaviors, we keep in mind the dialectical behavioral therapy (DBT) philosophy that patients are doing the best they can and that they need help to do better (for more on DBT see Chapter 4: Counseling Interventions, pp. 79–104).

Collaboration

Like other aspects of nutrition treatment, food planning should be a collaborative endeavor between nutrition counselor and patient. Patients are more likely to follow a plan that they have had a part in designing. We take into account each patient's likes and dislikes, initially excluding foods that patients fear or regularly consume during binges. Although, over time, we aim to reduce patients' fears about specific foods or nutrients, early in treatment it is more important for patients to feel that their concerns and issues are recognized and respected. One technique we sometimes use is to have patients write out a sample of a current day of eating alongside the standard RO3s template. Next, we ask them to write in, with another color of ink, foods that could fulfill the food groups they are missing. Or, on a copy of the RO3s template, we have patients highlight with a colored marker the RO3s food suggestions that they have not yet incorporated in their daily eating. Related homework assignments would be to choose one or two 'colored-ink' or highlighted food items to try over the coming week.

When patients take the lead in incorporating foods into the RO3s, we applaud them for their initiative. The counselor should encourage patients to participate in food planning to the extent of their abilities, and guard against providing too much food-related direction and advice. While some patients may be eager to turn over control of food intake to a professional, others will become increasingly resistant if they are not involved in the food-planning process. Other patients may become excessively dependent on the nutrition counselor if they sense the professional feels they are not capable enough to participate in solving their own problems. We have found that overly prescriptive advice (e.g., "I want you to eat a turkey sandwich for lunch tomorrow") diminishes the patient's ability to generate strategies or solutions. A more effective approach is to say, "What can you eat for lunch tomorrow? Remember, it needs to be high in protein." If the patient, however, cannot come up with suitable food choices, we provide the necessary guidance.

In the style of motivational interviewing (MI), we often explore the patient's confidence in his or her RO3s plan and the importance the patient places on following a food plan. (For more information on MI see Chapter 4: Counseling Interventions, pp. 79–104.) "How confident are you on a scale of 1 to 10 (10 being the most confident) that you can do the food plan you and I just designed? How important to you is following a food plan, on a scale of 1 to 10 (10 being the most important)?" When Abby, a very young 14-year-old just discharged from a residential program and losing weight, was asked these questions, she responded with "big fat zeros!" Abby said she did not feel like eating and was worried that a dress she borrowed from a friend to wear on Saturday would not fit. She admitted to "faking" that she is following her plan (dirtying dishes, pouring her supplemental "Ensure" down the sink, missing snacks, not eating breakfast). Abby was thanked for her honesty and told that, she has three obvious options: "You can follow your food plan, we can have your parents feed you (for more information on parent-assisted meals see Chapter 13: Working with Families, pp. 277–298.), or you can return to a higher level of care because your team can't let you lose weight and starve to death." And finally, in a matter-of-fact way, Abby was told that these options would be passed along to the rest of the team (i.e., her parents, therapist, and doctor) for their consideration. When Abby's mom was invited into the session, she was advised to begin checking on insurance coverage for a readmittance to the residential program "so it would be there if we need it."

Abby's response fortunately is not typical. Usually, providing directive, but open-ended, guidance (Box 5.3) helps patients gain confidence in their ability to do food planning and to follow a plan. We modify the RO3s food plan until patients can affirm with some confidence that their plan is realistic. We keep dated copies of each patient's food plan in our files.

BOX 5.3 "COLLABORATIVE" QUESTIONS FOR DESIGNING OR REVISING THE RULE OF THREES

- What do you think you could change about breakfast?"
- What do you feel ready to add to lunch?
- How do you want to get your protein for dinner?
- What will be difficult about putting the plan into practice?
- Where would you like to add something?
- Can you see yourself following this plan?

Experimenting

Many BN and BED patients will be emphatic in their belief that following a RO3s will lead to unwanted changes in body weight. Responding to such concerns, we may suggest the patient try the RO3s to see if they actually gain weight. In the spirit of scientific investigation, we tell hesitant patients: "Let's experiment! It is like I am the head researcher in the office and you are the field researcher as well as the subject of the experiment. Let's see if eating a morning snack makes you gain weight." We often add, "If you are dissatisfied with the results, you can return to your former eating style." Patients should be warned, however, not to overreact to small fluctuations in body weight.

Selling the Rule of Threes

Many ED patients come into treatment having lost confidence in their ability to eat normally and have little hope that they can regain control over their eating. It is of utmost importance, therefore, to "sell" patients on the benefits of the RO3s food plan. We start by telling patients that the RO3s food plan has been successfully used to treat patients with a variety of EDs as well as for other medical nutritional diagnoses, such as diabetes and obesity. It has effectively helped a wide range of patients, including physicians, therapists, children, parents, athletes, and people of all shapes and sizes. We also bill the RO3s plan as an antidote for many gastrointestinal complaints. For some patients it is initially of benefit to "let go" of the responsibility of deciding what, when, and how much to eat. Patients find comfort in knowing their food intake will be managed by an experienced professional until their own natural control over eating is re-established. Patients need to be reassured that their RO3s plan is designed to provide them with all the nutritional requirements for good health and weight maintenance, or weight gain or weight loss, depending on the aim of treatment. Finally, it should be emphasized that there is no more "powerful" treatment tool than the RO3s food plan. Following a food plan is hard, tedious work, but it is doable and worth the effort. We are fond of saying, "Life will be better when eating is normalized."

Many patients enter nutrition counseling disheartened about treatment in general, having concluded that their prognosis is poor. For very impaired patients who are demoralized by their ED behaviors, we treat the food plan like a prescription. "The RO3s is your medicine." Patients often describe to us a sense of relief and even hope when offered the RO3s in this manner. Reasoned enthusiasm on the part of the nutrition counselor for the effectiveness of the RO3s has an inspirational effect. In this regard we regularly extol its benefits (see Box 5.4) and often explain the biological basis for the RO3s as detailed in Box 5.5.

BOX 5.4 BENEFITS OF THE RULE OF THREES

- Decreases preoccupation with food.
- Decreases binge eating, overeating, emotional eating, and undereating.
- Reduces purging.
- Decreases negative self-talk and feelings.
- Restores hunger and fullness cues.
- Manages body weight.
- Restores metabolism otherwise lowered by undereating.
- Prevents storage of body fat otherwise caused by restrictive eating.
- Improves problem-solving abilities and concentration.

BOX 5.5 THE RULE OF THREES FOOD PLAN: THEN AND NOW

The RO3s food plan is based on human biology. Our bodies are programmed to consume enough food every day until we've managed to provide the 50 vitamins and minerals, and the protein, carbohydrates, and fat we need for health. Thanks to our large, complex brains, we humans require higher quality protein than do most primates and mammals. Humans are specifically programmed to continue to eat until we've had enough protein, even if we have enough calories and all the most nutrients we need. When we have enough protein and adequate nutrients, the body relaxes and we lose interest in eating.

Historical times

In the old days, when there wasn't an overabundance of food, this drive to overeat worked well. We'd eat as much as we could of everything that was around that was safe to eat, and if we couldn't get enough of the right nutrients, our tribe would move on to a more hospitable location.

Modern times

In these modern times, our primitive drive to eat everything we can, works against us. As much as we registered dietitians know about nutrition and are mindful of our bodies, we have yet to hear our bodies say "go eat 200 mg of potassium" or what or how much of the over 50 other nutrients we need. Our bodies just tell us to eat. When we haven't eaten the variety or the amounts, or by the pattern prescribed by the RO3s, we will experience a biological drive to keep eating, even overeat, until we get all our nutrient needs met. A supporting fact to this notion is that, as poorly as many Americans eat, they do not experience nutrient deficiencies. We have to assume people who eat poorly are getting the nutrients they need by eating so much so that the traces of nutrients in junk and fast food add up to cover nutrient needs.

The modern solution to a historical problem

The RO3s provides everything the body needs for optimal health. Furthermore, with the nutrients provided by the RO3s, feelings of hunger and satisfaction accurately reflect whether one needs to eat or to stop eating, making it easy to eat just the right amount and not a bite more. We need such a food plan in this modern world because, although we are surrounded by every kind and type of food, the body still thinks we live with the constant threat of famine. It makes sense then that the body will drive us to overeat to get the nutrients we need and then some—just in case a famine is around the corner. The body can't tell, unless we regularly eat according to the RO3s, that most of us are surrounded by a stable supply of plenty of a wide variety of foods, making getting the nutrients and protein we need without overeating "easy as pie."

Managing Resistance to the Rule of Threes Food Plan

Depending on their readiness to change, patients may initially respond with resistance to adding to the RO3s or to eating a forbidden food. Patients often remark:

- "This is too much food."
- "I don't have enough time to eat this often."
- "I'm going to be traveling."
- "I'm in class or lab during meal/snack times."
- "I'm a vegetarian."
- "I try to only eat when I feel hungry."
- "I'll feel too full and will want to binge."
- "If I eat this, I will gain weight."

We respond with both empathy for their concerns and enthusiasm for helping them figure out how to make the RO3s work for them. We "roll with their resistance," recognizing that arguing or persuading does not allow patients to make progress. Using MI, cognitive–behavior therapy (CBT), DBT, and acceptance and commitment therapy (ACT) tools outlined in Chapter 4: Counseling Interventions, we problem-solve with patients. As we have emphasized in these chapters and throughout the book, we aim to work collaboratively with patients, applying appropriate counseling skills to promote behavior change.

Kylie was underweight with AN and worked in a research laboratory where food was not permitted. After brain-storming, Kylie decided she could take a bathroom break to eat her snack as well as eat a more substantial lunch before starting her shift in the laboratory. Colleen was afraid the RO3s would cause gain weight because it seemed like too much food. Colleen was reminded that her nutrition counselor was monitoring her weight and, if necessary, her RO3s plan would be revised. Emily worried she was not getting enough protein, so a list of foods with protein was generated during a session. Morgan did not want to eat lunch everyday, so several snacks that covered her nutritional needs were worked into her RO3s instead of a lunch.

When patients cannot identify solutions to problems such as getting adequate protein, we help with, "I don't know if you like turkey, but it is high in protein, something your food plan really lacks." We also share examples of what other struggling patients have done in similar situations, "One of my other patients with similar worries added peanut butter to her afternoon snack."

Problem-solving as illustrated above is an ongoing part of each nutrition counseling session. We help patients "work backwards" to figure out "what went wrong," focusing on what they "could have done differently." Problem-solving concludes when the patient commits to a retooled plan designed to solve a particular problem. Although it is important not to be "argumentative" or slip into the "righting reflex (see Chapter 4: Counseling Interventions, pp. 79–104)," it is also important to correct any misinformation that may prevent patients from following their plan. If a patient is still unrelenting in her or his opposition to add to the food plan, we recommend crafting a plan that relies on foods she or he is currently consuming, perhaps by saying, "Let's see if I can meet your nutrient needs with foods you are comfortable with even if it means your diet will lack variety." Chantel, for example, who had agreed to eat a quarter cup of mixed nuts for snacks the week before, needed to add to her food plan. After being asked the standard questions, "What would you like to add to your food plan?" or "What do you feel you can add?" to no avail, Chantel agreed to upping her nut serving to a one-half cup. When faced again with the same dilemma several weeks later in treatment, Chantel was sensitively informed that she will need to soon need to manage to eat a more balanced food plan, even if the idea of eating certain foods is still frightening.

When patients report problems following their RO3s plan, we elicit a detailed description of how they are eating, either by reviewing self-monitoring records (see Chapter 6: Self-Monitoring, pp. 140–149) or by conducting a 24-hour recall of food intake (See Chapter 6: Self-Monitoring, pp. 140–149). Recalls are for data collection; counselors should not show approval or disapproval. When reviewing the recall, however, it is important not to embarrass the patient about his or her food intake. An example of a non-judgmental response to a recall might be, "I wonder if you noticed you did not have any protein at this dinner?"

The Details

As of this writing, there is no recommendation for macronutrient distribution or total calorie intake specific to patients with ED (Reiter & Graves, 2010). The RO3s is nutritionally well balanced and approximates the Dietary Reference Intakes recommended by the Food and Nutrition Board (2011). See Table 5.1 for the nutrient composition of the RO3s. The caloric value of the RO3s food plan is determined by food choices and serving sizes, depending on the individual patient's hunger, fullness, and body weight. (For more on calorie needs for underweight patients see Chapter 9: Restoring Weight, pp. 191–228.)

To our patients, we point out that there is a basic pattern for each meal to be composed of foods from the five major food groups: the high-calcium, the fruit or vegetable, the complex carbohydrate, the protein, and the fat groups. The plan also includes two fun foods strategically placed at the end of lunch and dinner. Any food can be incorporated in the RO3s plan: no foods are fattening, forbidden, or addictive. We support the view that "all foods fit," and, as we have said earlier, there are no "bad" foods. Too much of any food can cause problems, even too much water (i.e., water intoxication).

Calcium

We assume that each calcium serving provides approximately 200–500 mg of calcium. Despite being aware that calcium is necessary for strong bones, many ED

TABLE 5.1 Nutritional Details of the Rules of Threes Food Plan

Food group	Suggested amount for each portion	Examples	Substitutes
Calcium	200–300 mg calcium	1 cup milk or yogurt (300 mg), 1 oz of cheese (200 mg), ½ cup of beans (60 mg), ½ cup calcium-set tofu (120 mg), 24 almonds (75 mg), 5 figs (70 mg), ½ cup tempeh (90 mg), calcium-fortified functional foods: Nutrigrain bar (200 mg), breakfast cereal (55–1000 mg)	Calcium-containing mineral supplements (300–500 mg)
Complex carbohydrates	30–60 g carbohydrate	1 cup of pasta, cereal or rice, 2 slices of bread, 1 bagel, 1 English muffin	
Protein	20–30 g of protein	3–4 oz of meat, fish, poultry; 1 cup Greek yogurt, 2 oz cheese, 2 eggs, ¾ cup cottage cheese, ½ cup tofu, ½ cup nuts and seeds, 1 cup cooked beans, 2 T nut butters (8 g)	Protein powder supplements and egg substitutes
Fruits/vegetables	1 cup/1 piece of normal-sized fruit	Juice, canned, frozen or fresh	
Fat	10–15 g/serving (at least 65 g/day when assessing total fat intake)	2 T salad dressing, 1 T mayonnaise, 1 T nut butters, 1 T oil, 1 oz cheese, 15 nuts, 1 T seeds, ½ avocado (½ cup)	
Fun food	200–300 calories/serving	Dessert, cookies, ice cream, pudding, doughnuts, croissants, candy bars, chips, fries, non-diet soda	

patients do not consume adequate amounts. Younger patients may be open to drinking milk at meals, an easy way to assure calcium needs are met. The market boasts numerous functional foods that have added calcium, including non-dairy sources such as breakfast cereals, bars, juices, waffles, and margarines. Research is mixed on the effective delivery (i.e., shaking does not keep the calcium that settles to the bottom in calcium-fortified drinks in solution) and absorption of calcium from calcium-fortified beverages. We therefore encourage our patients not to rely on calcium-fortified beverages as a reliable source of calcium (Heaney, Rafferty, Dowell & Bierman, 2005; Straub, 2007; Tang, Walker, Wilcox, Strauss, Ashton, & Stojanovska, 2010).

It is important to note that, on principle, we use a simple approach on such issues so as not to complicate the patient's efforts to normalize eating. In the case of calcium, we are more likely to suggest the use of calcium supplements than to give a lecture on all the possible issues associated with calcium nutrition. However, if we have a patient who is unable, for whatever reason, to consume dairy products or use a supplement, we offer a handout that lists non-dairy sources of calcium and explain: Non-dairy foods contain calcium (e.g., nuts, seeds, beans, and low-oxalate leafy greens) but in considerably smaller amounts than do dairy products. Low-oxalate leafy greens include bok choy, broccoli, collard greens, kale, okra, and turnip greens. When calcium intake is inadequate, caffeine can have a negative effect on bone density. Therefore, moderate caffeine intake is recommended if calcium intake is nominal.

Rather than hound patients who are unable or unwilling to consume enough calcium-containing foods, we recommend calcium-containing supplements taken in doses of no more than 500 mg for maximum absorption (Straub, 2007). Despite the lack of evidence that calcium and vitamin D contribute to restoration of bone density in AN, there appears to be clinical consensus for recommending both calcium and vitamin D in the same doses prescribed for the general population (Mehler & MacKenzie, 2009). The Dietary Reference Intakes (DRIs) developed by the Food and Nutrition Board (FNB) at the Institute of Medicine of The National Academies (formerly the National Academy of Sciences) for healthy children, adolescents, and adults to maintain bone health and normal calcium metabolism is 1,000–1,300 mg of calcium and 600 IU of vitamin D. Of note, patients who use calcium-containing supplements are often less interested in consuming servings from the calcium food group in the RO3s plan. Such patients can be advised to add another serving of a high-protein food, as one serving of protein provides the energy, protein, and some of the vitamins and minerals found in a serving of dairy. Because, even with good intentions, many find it difficult to regularly take supplements, nutrition counselors should occasionally query those who have resolved to take calcium supplements about their success in this regard.

Complex Carbohydrates

A reasonable amount of complex carbohydrate per portion for the RO3s food plan contains approximately 30–60 g. The foods in this group (dubbed "carbs," "grains," or "starches") along with simple carbohydrates (sugars) are the body's preferred source of fuel. Besides energy, they provide an array of other nutrients such as protein, vitamins, minerals, and fiber. Patients should be encouraged to choose full servings as detailed in Table 5.1. Carbohydrate foods are good choices for snacks, especially if combined with a serving of fat or protein. Although carbohydrate-containing foods figure prominently among binge foods, it is common for ED patients to avoid carbohydrate-containing foods at meals, in large part because the press has vilified them as unhealthy and obesogenic.

Protein

According to the RO3s plan, lunch and dinner should contain at least 20–30 g of protein, the amount typical of a modest 3–4 oz serving of meat. Though diets of typical ED patients are often low in protein, many patients are quite agreeable to suggestions to consume high-protein foods, accepting the idea that eating protein will help restore lost muscle mass. Patients quite easily come to embrace the obvious benefits of high protein intake for appetite regulation, improved sense of well-being, and better health. In fact, most patients report they "just feel better" once they begin regularly to consume enough dietary protein. Although the research about the thermic and satiating effects of protein are mixed, we find our patients who consume meals adequate in protein feel more satisfied and are less likely to overeat or binge later on high-fat foods and sweets (Raben, Agerholm-Larsen, Flint, Holst, & Astrup, 2003). Protein-containing meals also have longer thermic effects than meals of predominantly carbohydrates or fats or both (Jönsson, Granfeldt, Erlanson-Albertsson, Ahren, & Lindeberg, 2010). This is due to the higher caloric costs of protein digestion and absorption.

As only a few foods are high in protein and most of those also contain fat, patients (particularly vegetarians) often struggle to find acceptable protein choices. Nutrition counselors can comment, "In nature, protein and fat most often occur together." Cottage cheese is an acceptable choice for patients resistant to eating fat since it is available in reduced-fat and non-fat forms. We have had fat-phobic patients initially choose non-fat protein powders or egg substitutes for a protein serving. Eventually it usually becomes obvious to patients that it is in their best interest to broaden their intake of high-protein foods. Most likely, they will tire of using supplemental forms of protein or they will want to socialize with friends over pizza or at a barbecue.

According to the RO3s plan, a serving of protein is optional at breakfast (though not at other meals). Some patients thrive when protein is added to breakfast. Others find that protein consumed at this meal leaves them feeling overly full, while still others find that time is the factor that precludes adding protein to breakfast. Patients who are at risk for bingeing at breakfast or over the course of the morning should be directed to include a serving of protein at breakfast or as part of a morning snack. Patients who binge in the afternoon or evening should experiment with a serving of protein at either afternoon or evening snacks, or both.

Fruits and Vegetables

Be on the lookout for excessive consumption of fruit and vegetables as they are well known to be nutritious, filling, and low in calories. We do not focus on consumption of adequate amounts of fruit and vegetables when patients are in need of weight restoration often to the surprise of patients and their families who expect nutrition counselors to push fruits and vegetables. When patients ask, "How many fruits and vegetables should I have?" Herrin paradoxically says "I don't really care. If you take a multiple vitamin and mineral supplement we aren't going to worry about it." On the other hand, too many servings (more than 5/day) of these foods can contribute to feelings of over-fullness and to diarrhea or constipation. Patients who must gain weight should choose fruits over vegetables, as vegetables are very low in calories, offering only about half the calories of similar amounts of fruit. Fruit juices, like other fluids, are digested quickly. Theoretically, juices are an efficient way to obtain the nutrients and calories offered by whole fruit but without contributing to feelings of over-fullness (though some patients tell us otherwise).

Fat

We are assured that our patients are consuming enough fat if they consume a source of fat at least twice a day, at lunch and dinner, and eat fat naturally found in the other food groups such as protein, carbohydrates, calcium, and fun food. We inform those patients who count fat grams that a moderate intake of fat is 65 g/day (equivalent to a 30% of a 2,000-calorie food plan). Most patients are surprised that the requirement is this high. The public perception that fat is unhealthy is a powerful force underpinning the reticence to add fat. We point out that the once-popular Atkins and South Beach diets proved that even very high fat diets can be associated with weight loss (Sacks et al., 2009). And, ironically, as the percentage of fat in the American diet has gone down, the rate of obesity has gone up (Willett, 2002). We reiterate often the important point that a moderate amount of fat in the diet effectively curbs overeating. Most patients need to hear repeatedly that, contrary to public opinion, fat is a necessary nutrient, providing essential fatty acids and fat-soluble vitamins. We also elaborate on the societal tendency to demonize a nutrient. In the 1970s and 1980s it was fat, and now it is "carbs." We joke that we are waiting to figure out which nutrient will be the next bad guy. As some ED patients do not fear fat or carbohydrates, we are careful not to presume that they do. Of note, young adolescents and children are the least likely to fear and avoid high-fat foods.

To preserve health, we say, fat must be consumed daily. For patients who severely restrict fat, we may *wait* to add fat until they are able to confidently follow the rest of their food plan. Even apprehensive patients are often able to add peanut butter or cheese to their plans because these foods can also be viewed as high in protein. Moreover, patients who must gain weight eventually come to appreciate that foods containing fat are less bulky than foods that do not contain any fat.

An oft-asked question is, "Can I count the fat in the peanut butter or cheese or dessert as fat?" We hesitate to consent to allowing a food to count in more than one category. But in the case of fat, we use our professional judgment, taking into account the patient and his or her caloric needs. If we are working with a heavy patient with BED, then we likely consider the fat in her fun food as his or her fat for the meal. If we are counseling a patient who needs to restore weight, we want both a fat and a fun food to be consumed.

Fun Food

Fun foods, as the name implies, are foods eaten for pleasure, and usually are made up of primarily simple carbohydrates and fats. They are desserts, snack foods, and "junk" food. Specialty coffee drinks such as frappés can be considered a fun food. We explain to our patients that one to two servings of fun food (the equivalent of at least 200–300 calories/serving) are recommended for recovered patients, normal eaters, and even those who need to lose weight, because several servings of fun food per day help to normalize eating and protect against overeating. Eating fun foods at the end of the meal puts a natural boundary around the eating episode, i.e., "Fun foods end the meal." Once dessert is eaten, most normal eaters stop eating, having naturally fulfilled the "I just felt like something sweet and now I am satisfied" feeling. Not surprisingly, in a controlled experiment of binge eaters, Gendall, Joyce, and Abbott (1999, p. 312) found that, after meals containing protein, subjects could stop further eating by consuming "sweet-tasting, palatable food." We say, "You're probably not going to want to eat more broccoli or mashed potatoes after you have a brownie." Fun foods can also be eaten as a snack, but patients who want to lose weight or have trouble bingeing on sweets may want keep fun foods to mealtimes.

ED patients typically reject fun foods, believing fun foods to be unhealthy and fattening. Most patients report that consuming these foods creates anxiety and guilt, and avoid these foods except as constituents of a binge or when they plan to purge. We allow and even encourage patients to voice the fears and feelings that consumption of these foods engenders. The thoughts behind these emotions can be addressed using CBT-style cognitive restructuring (see Chapter 4: Counseling Interventions, pp. 79–104). ED patients are likely to believe that fun foods have the capacity to trigger overeating episodes. We inform our patients about "food habituation," i.e., that the "more a person is exposed and allowed to eat a food, the less desirable it becomes over time" (Tribole, 2005, p. 1). Eating fun foods on a regular basis diminishes the deprivation mindset that encourages binging and overeating. We caution patients against approaching fun foods, as special treats to be consumed infrequently. Sporadic consumption of fun foods makes them seem even more enticing, and like other forbidden foods, more likely to trigger a binge when eaten. Consuming fun foods twice a day effectively destigmatizes them, making them less desirable. When fun foods are consumed every day, patients regularly report that they do not taste as good as they had imagined.

We may occasionally refer to the calories per serving of fun foods to help patients feel more confident they are not eating too much. We often suggest that patients, especially those who fear overeating, start with prepackaged single-serving fun foods. Or we compare a fun food to a safe food of the same caloric value, e.g., a cookie has the same caloric value as a small serving of cereal and milk or an apple. We reassure patients by explaining that, after fulfilling nutrient needs, everyone has unfulfilled calorie needs. These additional caloric needs can be met through choosing additional nutrient-rich foods or by adding fun foods. For instance, after eating a well-chosen meal that takes care of nutrient needs, one could choose to eat more dinner, three apples, or a bowl of ice cream to meet caloric needs.

A carefully explained rationale is necessary before most patients can understand the efficacy of consuming two fun-food servings per day. First and foremost, we explain that if fun foods were dangerous to eat they would not be "FDA approved." Another point worth making is that the healthfulness of any food plan is best assessed by looking at the total nutrient composition, not by assessing the nutritional quality of each food that is consumed. Since fun foods effectively prevent overeating and bingeing, eaten judiciously they are important components of a healthy food plan, especially for those with an ED. It is true, however, that if fun foods regularly take the place of other foods needed to meet nutrient requirements, health problems may result. But it is also true, for example, that if a patient allowed fruits and vegetables to take the place of protein foods in the diet, health problems would also arise. From a health perspective, we remind patients that if nutrient needs are met by well-chosen foods at meals, it is of no health consequence whether or not they regularly eat several moderate servings of fun foods. Patients who are hesitant about including fun foods in their food plans can be reminded that consumption of these foods is standard protocol in many hospital and residential eating-disorder treatment centers. One center calls fun foods in 200–300 calorie portions "convenience snacks." Other centers do activities in which a dessert is required to be consumed to help patients learn to tolerate the anxiety and other negative feelings these kinds of foods provoke.

Alcohol

We typically do not "count" alcohol. We prefer to treat alcohol like we do "condiments," such as cream in our coffee or ketchup with our hamburger, as something some people choose to include and others do not, but which has little nutritional consequence. We do not give advice about alcohol consumption, for several reasons. Many of our patients are not of drinking age and some of our patients are in recovery from alcohol abuse. We are not licensed or trained as alcohol counselors, so we try to limit our discussion about alcohol to the caloric composition of alcoholic beverages or to notice in a non-judgmental manner if alcohol abuse seems to be interfering with recovery. "I notice you binge when you drink a lot of alcohol. It looks like drinking is part of the mix here." In truth, we rarely can help patients who are actively abusing alcohol until their substance problem is under control. We keep a current referral list of appropriate mental health providers for such patients.

Snacks

Although patients will ask for guidance about choosing foods for snacks, we have only a few hard and fast rules about snacks. We do, however, suggest snacks can be chosen to nutritionally compensate for any "missing" food groups in meals. For example, "I didn't have my fruit at breakfast, so I'll have it for snack." If patients have fulfilled the food groups prescribed by the RO3s, they can freely choose snacks from any of the food groups. "If your meals are well balanced, choose what you like for snack. We try to be non-judgmental about snacks that patients choose, but we have noticed that binge eaters may particularly benefit by choosing relatively high protein foods and avoiding fun food at snack time. Once patients are maintaining a biologically appropriate weight (BAW) and are not bingeing, we move to a hunger-based guide for snacks. Our basic rule is "get hungry, but don't go hungry for more than 30 minutes." For example, Jacob reports getting hungry at 4:00 pm, but his college dining hall doesn't open till 5:00 pm. Herrin advised him to experiment with a snack that would calm his hunger down but leave Jacob with an appetite for dinner at 5:00 pm. After several tries, Jacob settled on having a big juicy apple. Herrin warned Jacob not to go hungry for more one-half hour, "if you get hungry at 4:30 pm and you know dinner is at 5 pm, you can decide to wait it out or have a smaller snack, but if its 4:00 pm and dinner is at 5 pm, there is no question—have the snack. The important thing is that your body learns to trust that you will take care of its basic needs within a reasonable time." Herrin added that going hungry much longer than one-half hour could lower metabolism and put one at risk for overeating or bingeing

Serving Sizes and Portions

Except for our underweight patients who require specific directions about how much, when and what to eat, we prefer to not be particularly precise or prescriptive about serving sizes in the RO3s plan. Our guidelines about portions (i.e., one cup, or twice the serving size on labeled foods) in the RO3s food plan are purposively vague and are designed to move patients to becoming attuned with their bodies. We rarely mention portion guidelines when we first introduce the RO3s.

We concentrate more on the importance of eating balanced meals, normalizing eating times, reading physical cues for hunger and fullness, and developing a healthy relationship with food. Nonetheless, many patients ask about portioning parameters. We often tell the story (true) of how the plan was first used by Dartmouth College students and it did *not* include any advice on serving sizes, but the students insisted Herrin come up with something. After a lot of consideration and research, she came up with our "one cup, or twice the serving size on labeled foods," adding that this works for almost everything except candy bars (which tend to be generally packaged in reasonable servings sizes). We stress that these are just general guidelines and are not meant to be interpreted literally. We both continue to be amazed how good this advice is for most people (especially females), for most foods, for most of the time. We are aware, however, that one cup may be too much for some people (e.g., older adults) or too little for others (e.g., athletes). For example, Herrin's patient Emma, retired, heavyset, and with BED, said "one cup was way too much;" Herrin advised Emma to start with one-half cup. Of note, we rarely advise patients to use less than one-half cup as a guide, as it is nearly impossible to meet nutrient needs on smaller servings. When patients worry that one-half cup is still too much, we suggest smaller between-meal snacks, or skipping them all together.

"Two times the label" continues to be a close approximation of a normal serving size for many foods and many people. As of this writing, food labels use portion sizes that are too small to be satisfying or nutritionally adequate (we suspect to imply that the food is low in calories). We also note that consumption of meager serving sizes of foods offers no advantage. Less-than-satisfying meals and snacks are likely to lower metabolism and to trigger bingeing, purging, and restricting, as well as eventual weight gain.

Concerning the question of portions and the effect on body weight, our motto is that the RO3s food plan supports BAWs. We inform patients who are at a BAW that the RO3s does not cause weight gain. We tell heavier patients that using RO3s will support achieving and maintaining a BAW, and we tell underweight patients that it is a framework for restoring and maintaining a BAW. Patients can be guaranteed that eating appropriate portions of foods distributed across three meals and three snacks does not cause weight gain unless the plan is designed for weight gain (Fairburn, 2008, p. 80).

We advise the following to patients who struggle with servings sizes:

- Observe eating habits of friends or relatives (if they do not have eating problems).
- School or college cafeterias usually offer normal portions.
- Restaurants usually serve generous portions, but it is normal to eat what is served at restaurants (though you may not be hungry for your next snack). At restaurants known for particularly large portion sizes, it is OK to eat at least one-half of what is served (though you probably will need your usual snack).

We do not ask patients to weigh or measure their food, though some may choose to weigh or measure for reassurance. Instead, we suggest "eye-balling" portions. Many patients can visualize cup portions, or we may offer the old standards that the size of one's fist or a baseball is equal to about a cup. A minimal serving (we usually recommend larger servings) of meat, fish, or poultry is the size of deck of cards or one's palm. Food models and measuring cups are useful in-office teaching tools but we aware that most food models tend to depict the meager food servings characteristic of the Exchange List.

When we are working with parents who portion their child's food, we focus on helping parents become confident that they offer correct portions. Unless completely off-base, we try to endorse the portion sizes parents usually serve. The benefit of having patients who trust their parents when it comes to food issues cannot be overemphasized (see Chapter 13: Working with Families).

We tell all our patients that portions sizes are less important that learning to eat balanced meals, to normalize eating times, to use physical cues of hunger and fullness, and to develop a healthy relationship with food

Hunger and Fullness

We wait to focus on hunger and fullness cues until patients are confidently and competently using the RO3s, are maintaining a stable weight, and are reporting the emergence of hunger and fullness signals. Once patients are maintaining a BAW and are not restricting or bingeing, we move toward hunger and full-ness-based advice and away from a literal interpretation of the food plan. Larkin tells patients the story of how she ate a large serving of fried clams for lunch one day and did not get hungry again for 8 hours, her body adjusting her appetite in response to a calorically dense, high-fat meal. Hunger tells normal eaters when it's time to eat, and fullness tells them when it is time to stop. Hunger makes itself known in various ways, but typically feels like emptiness in the stomach area, queasiness, light-headedness, irritability, shakiness, or a headache. Herrin likes to tell her patients, "Hunger is like love. If you are unsure, wait." She adds with a smile that, "Unlike love, you can count on hunger to show up." We tell patients:

- "Food tastes better when you are hungry."
- "Food loses its taste when you are full."
- "It is difficult to know when to stop eating when you start out not feeling hungry."

"Famine metabolism" makes fullness particularly thorny to decipher. In more ancient times, getting as full as possible was paramount to survival. Now with meals and snacks usually available, there rarely is a biological need to get over-full. These facts mean that the body is happy with a wide range of fullness levels from absence of hunger, balanced, satisfied, and overfull to stuffed, as long as the body is not forced to go hungry. With practice, one can forecast how much food it will take to reach a comfortable level of fullness, a state in which one will not feel hungry again for 3 or 4 hours or until the next planned meal or snack.

Hunger and fullness cues are problematic for low-weight patients. Once AN patients improve caloric intake, many report insatiable hunger. We explain, "Your body thinks you have just been rescued from a famine and is on overdrive to repair and restore itself." We predict that reports of sudden hunger in an AN patient foretells lack of weight gain or even weight loss. AN patients who are slowly gaining usually do not feel hungry but they complain instead of chronic fullness. See Box 5.6 for an explanation of the biology of this enigmatic loss of appetite. We also hear AN patients declare, "I would eat, but I am just not hungry." Until patients are at a BAW, we advise:

- "You can trust hunger, but not fullness."
- "Your hunger and fullness cues will recalibrate, but right now your body is confused."
- "Until you are at a BAW, rely on the RO3s, not your appetite, to tell you how much and when to eat."
- "If you feel hungry between or before meals, you need to be eating more."

BOX 5.6 LOSS OF APPETITE: AN ADAPTATION TO FAMINE?

In a famine, carbohydrate deficiencies occur first because the body is able to store only small amounts of carbohydrates. Since brain cells must have carbohydrates (glucose) to function, the body has a backup plan. When carbohydrate stores are depleted, the body switches to obtaining glucose through a complicated process that requires breaking down stored protein and fat and converting some of the by-products to glucose. As ketones, another by-product of this conversion, increase (resulting in ketosis), appetite is suppressed. Loss of appetite in response to famine is considered adaptive as hunger triggers searching for food, which wastes energy (Whitney & Rolfes, 2011, pp. 142–143). Guisinger (2003) and Gatword (2007) postulate that the major characteristics of AN (restricting food, loss of appetite, denial of starvation, and hyperactivity) all facilitate survival in nomadic foragers, who eventually must leave depleted environments to survive. These adaptations occur in animals as well. In laboratory research, rodents increase activity and refuse food when underfed.

To all patients, regardless of weight, we emphasize that hunger is trustworthy unless one is underweight, undereating, or going too long between meals and snacks. When eating is sporadic or inadequate, famine biology mutes hunger signals due to ketosis (Box 5.6). Most people have had an experience of famine metabolism. A classic example is when missing breakfast makes lunch easy to skip. Over the morning, hunger pangs will come and go, but they are usually gone by lunchtime. On the other hand, we are naturally programmed to satisfy physical needs like hunger. In our modern world, hunger is easy to avoid, but it can come to symbolize unmet psychological needs. For example, Jane, an overeater and binge eater, eventually recognized she was afraid to feel hungry because she unconsciously associated hunger with vulnerability and loneliness. Jane admitted that she had not felt the sensation of hunger for more than 40 years. After a month on the RO3s plan, Jane excitedly reported feeling hunger pangs about 10 minutes before meals.

Calories in the Rule of Threes

We are often asked by patients, "How many calories are in the RO3s?" and "How many calories should I be eating?" To these questions, we respond, "I wish I knew. Fortunately, weight checks tell us everything we need to know about the adequacy of your caloric intake." We explain that the field lacks exact methods for determining an individual's calories needs outside of hospital-based metabolic research units. The various mathematical equations (i.e., the Harris–Benedict and Mifflin-St Jeor equations) used to predict metabolic rates have, at best, a 20% error rate, making them clinically irrelevant (Frankenfield, Roth-Yousey, & Compher, 2005). Furthermore, it is very difficult for even researchers to count calories accurately (Mendez et al., 2011).

Many patients enter treatment obsessively counting calories. Presumably calorie counting provides a seemingly necessary sense of control over food intake. With food labels, restaurant postings, and smart phone apps all providing caloric values, it is no surprise that many ED patients have memorized the number calories in a vast array of foods. Initially, we find it useful to accommodate a patient's desire to manage food intake via calorie counting as long as her or she is making progress in other ways. Some patients will ask for the caloric values of specific foods added to their food plan, and we usually provide the requested information.

Calorie-counting patients should be assured that the nutrition counselor knows the "language of calories" and has access to caloric information about foods. We keep coming back to the fact that one's weight is ultimately what establishes whether one is eating an appropriate amount of calories. Although our patients may know the caloric value of countless foods, we have found that many are less well informed about their caloric needs. We provide the following information to help correct misperceptions:

- It takes at least 1,500 calories to fulfill basic nutrient requirements. Most people need substantially more calories to meet the calorie costs of the individual's metabolism and activity. Because of the hypermetabolism of AN, these patients will need even more calories to restore weight. (For more information see Chapter 9: Restoring Weight, pp. 191–228.)
- Food labels are based on a 2,000 calorie diet, so chosen by the FDA because 2,000 calories is close to the calorie requirements for postmenopausal women, the population group most prone to weight gain (Nestle & Nesheim, 2012). Caloric needs are likely to be higher than 2,000 calories for other people.
- Calorie counting is an external activity than prevents a person from learning how to self-regulate his or her food intake, and from using internal cues of hunger, fullness, and self-satisfaction.

Food Planning Versus Calorie Counting

Food planning should be encouraged over the counting of calories. Food planning is a healthy non-ED way of managing food intake; whereas, counting calories is characteristic of ED patients and dieters. Patients should be advised that the RO3s provides the calories they need to maintain a BAW. However, patients who are severely underweight will need an energy-augmented food plan to ensure they consume the calories necessary to support weight gain (see Chapter 9: Restoring Weight, pp. 191–228).

We have concluded that only rarely is there a clinical reason for either nutrition counselors or patients to count the calories patients consume. First, counting calories is time consuming and difficult to do with any accuracy. Second, determining the calorie needs of specific patients is even more inexact. Third, there is little benefit in acquainting patients (particularly children) with calorie counting, a potentially compulsive behavior. Fourth, as long as patients are following a reasonable food plan, satisfying their hunger without becoming overly full, and maintaining a reasonable body weight, caloric intake can be realistically assumed to be adequate. Finally, patients who count calories gradually lose interest in doing so as they gain confidence in their ability to follow a food plan and accurately assess and respond to their hunger and fullness signals.

Diet Foods

As foods modified to reduce calorie, sugar, or fat content are widely used by normal eaters, it is difficult for us to rationalize banning these foods from the food plans of ED patients. Continuing to use diet foods, however, may reinforce an obsessive, fearful approach to eating. Clearly it is counterproductive for patients who are having difficulty gaining weight to use artificially sweetened foods and reduced-fat foods. We approach these issues in a collaborative fashion, allowing patients to make choices among reasonable alternatives. Parents are often surprised that we don't "ban" diet drinks. We query about family use of diet drinks and, unless the family has previously disallowed them, we encourage a lenient approach as long as the food plan is followed and the non-caloric items are not consumed excessively. "You must get your fat somehow," we tell patients who choose non-fat foods to the exclusion of foods that contain fat. We appreciate the irony but support the choice of a non-fat yogurt and a slice of bread and butter for a snack. For example, if a patient needs to increase calories, we may suggest considering substituting juice, milk, or non-diet soda for a diet drink. We are happy to compromise and collaborate with patients as long as they are making progress. Through these negotiations, we keep in mind that, in most outpatient settings, we can at best give advice.

Supplemental Drinks and Bars

Meal-replacement drinks, high-calorie energy drinks, instant breakfast drinks, and protein, sports, and other snack bars can fit into the RO3s. These supplements, typically sold in convenient, portable, single-serving packages, can be used to increase calories (usually 200–300 calories) and replace a serving of protein (if they contain 20 g of protein). Tucker did not like eating off the school lunch menu and was not a fan of sandwiches. He incorporated a 300-calorie energy bar (nearly equal to a serving of protein and carbohydrate) into his lunch plan. We have a flexible approach which tolerates the use of supplemental foods in the RO3s; however, our aim is to ultimately rely less on supplements and more on consumption of basic whole foods.

Nutrient Supplementation

At the time of writing, we find no consensus in the evidence-based research about the use of nutritional supplements by ED patients (Lock & Fitzpatrick, 2009). Regardless of lack of evidence, it is standard practice to recommend AN patients take multivitamin and mineral supplements (Reiter & Graves, 2010, p. 131). Our consistent theme, however, is that nutrient needs are met by the categories of foods and the portions in the RO3s. At best, multivitamin and mineral supplements are an extra insurance policy. As stated above, our long-term goal is for patients to rely less on supplements and more on consumption of basic whole foods. Nevertheless, we do not discourage patients from using standard formulations of multivitamin and mineral supplements when taken in safe non-toxic doses that do not interact with other nutrients or medications. Multivitamin and mineral supplements may possibly benefit patients who have an aversion or intolerance to a food group, or who are consuming less than 1,500 calories/day. For our patients who take single-nutrient supplements, we carefully assess intake from diet sources to guard against overdose. Recently, we have found patients oversupplementing with calcium in the form of chocolate or flavored calcium candy chews or gummies. Too much calcium can cause constipation and inhibit absorption of other important nutrients.

Forbidden or Fear Foods

Including forbidden or fear foods is not a priority during early weight restoration, but it is essential for long-term recovery (Schebendach et al., 2011). When it is clear that nutrient and caloric needs are consistently being satisfied, we encourage patients to increasingly vary their food choices and to consume foods they have previously avoided, otherwise known as "forbidden foods" or "fear foods." These foods are characteristically high in fat or carbohydrates, which the patient avoids for fear of bingeing or weight gain. Common forbidden foods include French fries and other fried foods, pizza, pasta, sweets, and desserts. Without prior improvements in the nutritional quality of the patient's food plan, however, the introduction of forbidden foods can lead to bingeing. While it is important not to tolerate restrictive eating habits that can lead to feelings of deprivation and to food cravings, it is equally important not to overwhelm apprehensive patients by insisting that they eat anxiety-provoking foods. The depth of the typical patient's phobia, however, should guide how cautiously to proceed in this area. Focusing first on directing the patient to improve her or his intake of other food groups is usually prudent. Too much pressure to broaden food choices early in treatment can lead to resistance to food planning altogether.

Success in making dietary improvements increases the patient's trust and confidence in her or his nutrition counselor so that later suggestions to add high-fat forbidden foods are likely to be well received. We wait for a timely opportunity to propose the introduction of forbidden foods. When patients complain of fullness, yet need to eat more calories to gain weight, the suggestion to add a higher fat food may be well received. Likewise, when patients complain of distress by urges to binge after eating low-fat meals, the recommendation to increase the fat content of meals is opportune. Patients are often intrigued by the prediction that "someday fat will be your friend."

We let patients know early on that part of the work of recovery is to address and incorporate forbidden food. Patients, nevertheless, are usually eager to disclose these foods to us. We tell patients, "Over time, we're going to have to work on incorporating forbidden foods, so give me your forbidden food list." We record in the patient's chart when they have successfully consumed a forbidden food then keep track of continued consumption. To demonstrate he or she has overcome the fear of eating a particular forbidden food, the patient needs to be comfortably eating the forbidden food on more than one occasion. Overcoming the fear of eating forbidden foods is an important sign of recovery.

We may suggest eating a forbidden food as homework; the patient will need to eat the forbidden food at least once before their next session. "Which forbidden food do you want to work on this week?" To help the patient complete the homework, we may do cognitive restructuring. (For more information see Chapter 4: Counseling Interventions, pp. 79–104.) We reiterate the concept that all foods fit in a healthy diet and that labeling a food "bad" makes us crave it more. We present the notion that regular consumption of moderate servings of forbidden foods "inoculates" against bingeing on these foods. In other words, food plans that completely exclude anxiety-provoking foods are not likely to protect against bingeing. Patients may choose to eat a small quantity of the forbidden food initially or they may practice a mindful diaphragmatic breath before each bite so as to be calm, centered, and non-judgmental. When forbidden foods are matter-of-factly written into a customized food plan, patients make the most progress. We simply ask, "What do you want to have for your fat (or fun food serving) at dinner?"

Summary Points

- The food plan is a key tool in the treatment of EDs, providing practical guidance on how to normalize food intake.
- The RO3s template presumes three meals and three snacks, with no longer than 3 hours between eating times. This is a biologically sound guide countering the common tendency of ED patients to either undereat or to overeat.
- It is of utmost importance to "sell" patients on the benefits of the RO3s food plan and to recommend no more than a few food-related behavioral changes at each session in order to help patients experience success.
- The RO3s food plan is designed to maintain a BAW and to move patients into attunement with hunger and fullness.
- Focusing on reading hunger and fullness cues waits until patients are confident and competent with the RO3s; when they reach a stable weight; and when they are physically aware of these cues.
- The patient's trust and confidence in her or his nutrition counselor is key to making anxiety-provoking changes to food intake.

6

SELF-MONITORING

Introduction

Self-monitoring by recording eating behaviors and associated thoughts and feelings in daily journals is basic to cognitive–behavior therapy (CBT). In nutrition counseling, self-monitoring proves beneficial for both nutrition counselor and patient. For nutrition counselors, food journals provide detailed descriptions of eating patterns and the circumstances of eating problems, and is a concrete way to assess progress. For patients, self-monitoring increases awareness of eating problems and precipitating events. Pike, Garner, & Vitousek (1997) find journaling is a way for patients to communicate about their experiences between sessions and to help identify and differentiate between eating situations that are difficult or manageable. Some patients may have exaggerated the extent of their eating-disordered behaviors, and self-monitoring provides a more realistic picture that is reassuring.

In this chapter, we provide instructions for when and how to use self-monitoring, and give some caveats. Of note, we use the term "food journal," while others use "food record," "food diary," or "monitoring record."

What is Self-Monitoring?

Self-monitoring is a key component in the CBT-Enhanced approach developed by Fairburn, which he describes as in the moment or "real time" recording of relevant eating behaviors, thoughts, feelings, and events (Fairburn, 2008, p. 57). Self-monitoring is most precise and has the most potent effect on behavior if it is done immediately after eating and eating-disorder (ED) behaviors. Nevertheless, patients who choose to record food behaviors at the end of day seem to still benefit from self-monitoring.

Food journals solve mysteries and suggest solutions. For example, when a patient's weight is not responding as expected, food journals can help determine the cause. Food journals provide information about the patient's food patterns and about which foods are acceptable to the patient. They also provide undeniable evidence that restrictive eating increases the likelihood of binge eating.

Self-monitoring also helps make clear to the nutrition counselor the particular difficulties a patient faces in following a food plan. We try to find ways to make self-monitoring clearly beneficial to patients. For example, when patients feel immobilized by fear of eating too much or of gaining weight too fast, an in-session review of food journals often provides relief or even a therapeutic breakthrough.

Box 6.1 gives an idea of the written or verbal instructions we give to patients who have agreed to self-monitor food-related behaviors.

BOX 6.1 VERBAL INSTRUCTIONS GIVEN TO PATIENTS WHO HAVE AGREED TO SELF-MONITOR FOOD-RELATED BEHAVIORS

Using one page per day, list all the foods you ate or drank and the amounts consumed.

Record the time of day or night.

Indicate specifically where you ate the food. For example, if you were at home, specify the room in which you ate.

Leave blank spaces between eating events (meals and snacks) to indicate foods that are eaten together.

Before and after eating, rate your perception of hunger and fullness, using the numerical scale.

The Feelings/Mood column is the place to comment on thoughts, feelings, and mood that influenced eating or exercise behaviors.

Record intentional exercise bouts (exercise beyond the movement necessary in everyday life), in chronological order. Identify the exercise activity and the number of minutes devoted to it.

Mark any binges, subjective or objective, by a "B". Objective binges are eating events in which you eat more food than a normal eater would in a similar situation. Objective binges are associated with feelings of being out of control and guilt. Subjective binges are eating events in which you also feel out of control and guilty, but eat a normal amount of food.

If food was purged, indicate with a "P" and also record how (e.g. vomiting, laxatives).

HUNGER SCALE

S M T W Th F S

Date _____

		0	starved
		1	very hungry
		2	hungry
		3	slightly hungry
		4	balanced
		5	
		6	slightly full
		7	
		8	full
		9	very full
		10	stuffed

Food or Drink (Description, Amount)	Time	Hunger Level	Where	With Whom Doing What	Feelings/Mood	Fullness After Eating	Physical Activity	B/P

FIGURE 6.1 Food journal.

Self-monitoring saves time in sessions otherwise spent obtaining 24-hour food recalls. See Box 6.2 for sample questions to ask during a recall. Verbal food recalls during sessions can only describe a few days' worth of eating behaviors, and patients may not remember to mention a significant eating event. On the other hand, 24-hour recalls give patients a chance to talk in detail about their daily eating behaviors. When patients have trouble remembering what they ate yesterday, we may suggest "working backwards," starting with the most recent meal or snack. If patients still draw a blank, we say, "Just walk me through a typical day." It is usually necessary to prompt for amounts, beverages, snacks, condiments, and whether foods were fat- or sugar-free. Having food models and measuring cups available can help patients visualize portion sizes. Patients should be asked directly about bingeing and purging behaviors. As is standard in conducting food recalls, counselors should be neutral in their responses to food choices and amounts.

BOX 6.2 SAMPLE QUESTIONS TO ASK DURING A 24-HOUR FOOD RECALL

- Tell me everything you ate and drank yesterday (or in the last 24-hours).
- Walk me through a typical day.
- Start with the first thing you ate or drank yesterday morning. What was the next thing you ate?
- Did you add milk to your cereal? How much? What percent fat was the milk? Did you have anything to drink with that meal?"
- Did you add cheese, mayonnaise, or butter to your sandwich (or bread, toast, or bagel)?
- Did you have anything to drink or eat between meals or after dinner?
- Did you have dessert or a fun food?
- Did you have a snack before bed?
- Did you eat anything in secret (particularly effective for assessing binge-eating behaviors)?

Introducing Self-Monitoring

We tell our patients that self-monitoring is always helpful to the nutrition counselor because written journals provide a detailed picture of the patient's situation. Careful review of food journals allows the nutrition counselor to individualize treatment strategies and propose interventions, the efficacy of which can be evaluated at subsequent sessions. "Let's see what happens if you eat dessert with dinner." Food journal data is very useful in design of effective eating plans that strategically reduce urges to restrict, binge, and purge. "Saturday really worked well for you, let's use this day as basis for your new food plan." As treatment progresses, food journals permit both patients and nutrition counselors to concretely assess progress. "Wow! Look at this—only one binge/purge this week."

We also discuss the difficulties associated with self-monitoring: time, effort, shame, embarrassment, and the initial increase in preoccupation with food. We use an importance and confidence rating (see Chapter 4: Counseling Interventions, p. 79–104). "How confident are you on a scale of 1 to 10 that you can keep a week-long food journal?" "How important is it to you on a scale of 1 to 10 to keep food journals?"

We query about any negative past experiences with self-monitoring. We have encountered patients who enter treatment adamantly opposed to self-monitoring, either because they have "failed" a CBT-based treatment or have attempted unsuccessfully to keep records on their own or for other practitioners. We often respond, "Let's see how treatment goes for you, if it goes well, then food journals clearly are not necessary."

We have seen how the collaborative nature of a therapeutic counseling relationship can be hampered when patients are unable to complete self-monitoring assignments. We assure patients they do not have to self-monitor to be engaged in treatment with us. If patients are not engaged in self-monitoring, however, it is important to ascertain dietary patterns by conducting 24-hour dietary recalls (see above, p. 143) at each session.

How to Self-Monitor

Although research shows that real-time monitoring is most effective (Fairburn, 2008), patients who have full-time employment, who are full-time students, or who are reticent to record in public, may not be able to commit to this level of rigor. In our clinical experience, even journaling just once a day is therapeutic. For some patients a simplified approach to self-monitoring is more realistic. We often suggest recording just foods and amounts consumed over the course of a day in a discrete pocket-size notebooks. Other patients prefer to create their own journaling formats; still others elect to use a computer or phone app to chart food behaviors and e-mail to share their records. Be aware that most online food recording programs and apps are designed for calorie counting and weight loss and usually are not appropriate. An even less-demanding technique, but surprisingly effective, is the use of stickers. Patients affix a sticker to a calendar to signify days on which they followed their food plan or did not binge or purge.

We find that patients are most likely to embark on self-monitoring if we offer a variety of record-keeping tools (e.g., a spiral notebook, a packet or folder consisting of 7 days of food journals, a selection of stickers) for the taking. It is best to advise patients not to try to change food behaviors during the initial week of self-monitoring. Rather, we instruct patients to approach self-monitoring as an anthropologist would, aiming to make non-judgmental, open-minded, and accurate observations.

When to Self-Monitor

Self-monitoring is effective if patients are committed to recovery (i.e. in an action stage of change, see Chapter 4: Counseling Interventions, pp. 79–104) and are interested in using the technique. Such patients benefit from self-monitoring from initial sessions throughout treatment. Others find an increase in awareness of food intake, hunger, and fullness and a significant decrease in eating-disordered behaviors after a few weeks of self-monitoring. We do not oppose these patients' wishes to discontinue self-monitoring as long as there are no obvious impediments to progress. We suggest a return to self-monitoring when patients report unexplained or unresolved difficulty, such as continued bingeing behaviors.

Standard CBT practice is to assign self-monitoring to all patients at the first session. We, on the other hand, tend to not assign food journals this early in treatment. We usually wait until patients volunteer to (or ask "May I?") self-monitor or until patients have exhibited problems that remain unresolved. When we are asked, "Should I do food journals?" We reply, "There are pros and cons, but they are always helpful to a nutrition counselor. The important question is: are they helpful to you?" We find that our soft-sell approach over time reduces resistance to journaling.

Most patients naturally discontinue food journals as eating-disordered behaviors subside and are replaced by normal eating habits. Patients, however, should be advised to err on the side of caution when considering discontinuing self-monitoring. It is better to look back, they can be told, and say, "I could have stopped a month ago" than to stop prematurely and risk a relapse. As long as patients report eating-disordered behaviors and thoughts, they should persevere with self-monitoring. Before terminating treatment, Fairburn (2008, p. 187) recommends that patients stop monitoring several weeks before treatment ends in order to get used to not monitoring while still receiving professional support.

Anorexia Nervosa

Self-monitoring is less effective in the treatment of anorexia nervosa (AN) than it is in bulimia nervosa (BN) or binge-eating disorder (BED). Most AN patients do not possess enough motivation to sustain self-monitoring. In addition, self-monitoring can seem superfluous to patients who are dogmatically following a food plan, are gaining weight, and are not engaging in bingeing and purging behaviors. Furthermore, AN patients rightfully complain that self-monitoring of food consumption can aggravate ED-related obsessions and anxieties. For this reason, relatively uncomplicated food journals are preferred in the treatment of AN (e.g., a small notebook to record only what and how much they consume and, if germane, to also note time devoted to exercise). In the face of consequences associated with unmet weight-gain goals (e.g., limitations on physical activity or school), AN patients can be quite amenable to self-monitoring. Food journals can also provide a sense of security: "At least my nutrition counselor will tell me if I am eating too much."

Bulimia Nervosa and Binge-Eating Disorder

Self-monitoring is a standard intervention in nutrition treatment of BN and BED, and is a requisite in CBT treatment for these EDs (Fairburn, 2008; Ozier & Henry, 2011). The well-documented efficacy of CBT as a treatment for BN and BED infers that requiring patients to self-monitor is productive. In clinical practice, BN food behaviors often improve with no other intervention save the record-keeping associated with self-monitoring. For some patients, self-monitoring will almost immediately and substantially reduce bingeing and purging, particularly when the patient also complies with a food plan. Self-monitoring helps "end" an eating episode before it progresses to binge proportions. Journaling about feelings and the details of binge episodes diminishes the urge to purge. Furthermore, recording the details of binge-eating episodes helps patients face up to the reality of their binge-eating behaviors. Some bulimic patients report that, prior to self-monitoring, they were unaware of what and how much they ate while bingeing. Furthermore, self-monitoring proves to patients that vigilantly following a food plan reduces vulnerability for binge eating.

Reviewing Self-Monitoring Food Journals

Reviewing self-monitoring records in sessions allows for collaborative problem-solving, for the development of new strategies, for assessing progress, and for opportunities to provide encouragement. For instance, counselors can extract examples from a patient's records to illustrate that skipping meals and snacks or inadequate eating predestines the patient to binge. Food journals also document specific situations that can be used to practice problem-solving skills.

If self-monitoring is prescribed, food journals need to be reviewed or at least scanned in every session and kept on file to emphasize their value. At the very least, counselors should ask to peruse patients' food records at the beginning of each session. We make a routine of saying, "Let me take a quick look at your food journals before we start talking." Positive feedback for completion of detailed food journals should be routinely dispensed. We verbalize our appreciation for the effort required to self-monitor consistently and thoroughly, commenting on how much courage and hard work self-monitoring requires. Until the patient is monitoring proficiently, we show more interest in the adequacy of the monitoring than in the patient's actual food behaviors.

We ask patients to give us a synopsis of their week before we begin in-depth review of food journals; otherwise we risk missing the big picture. In an inquisitive mode, we begin the discussion by asking where they did well or had difficulties:

- "What stands out for you?"
- "What did you learn from journaling this week?"
- "What worries you?"
- "Where do you see that you need some assistance?"
- "Walk me through your week using your food journal."

When reviewing food journals, we commend patients for consuming meals and snacks that fulfill their food plan (see Chapter 5: Food Planning: Rule of Threes, pp. 107–139) and comment on any positive trends in food behaviors. "I see that you only binged four times last week compared to seven times the week before." We also encourage patients to learn from their shortcomings. We inquire "What is missing?" when we observe eating that deviates from the food plan. We encourage patients to look for patterns and "causes and effects" in their journals. We are careful to respond to maladaptive food behaviors with curiosity, not exasperation. For example, "What are your hunches as to why you binged Friday afternoon?" We point out any obvious patterns in thoughts and emotions that result in eating-disordered behaviors. For patients who are having difficulty following a food plan, food journals can be used to "build" a plan on the "foundation" of current food intake.

Some patients enter treatment having kept self-initiated food journals. We encourage patients to bring such records to sessions for collaborative review. Our standard practice is to keep completed food journals in each patient's chart. Occasionally previous journals are useful when comparing progress over time.

A few caveats:

- Guard against spending a disproportionate amount of time reviewing journals at the expense of using other treatment approaches and addressing other issues.
- Guard against expressing disproportionate positive feedback about "healthy food" choices.

Fairburn, Marcus, and Wilson (1993, p. 371) remind practitioners that the quality of a patient's monitoring is directly related to the degree of attention that the practitioner pays to food journals. A sure way to discourage regular completion of journals is failure on the part of the nutrition counselor to ask about them at subsequent sessions.

Compliance

Patients may resist self-monitoring because they imagine that record keeping will increase the shame they feel about their behaviors. They may be apprehensive that the counselor will be appalled at the details of their eating behaviors. Because they themselves are often overly self-critical, patients worry about being harshly criticized. Nutrition counselors should reiterate that they have "seen it all" and have a genuine interest in the patient's particular eating behaviors. We say we are most interested in the "less than perfect days" as those are the ones that are most helpful to examine. "The more forthcoming you are in accurately describing your eating behaviors, as difficult as that can be, the greater the likelihood that I will suggest effective solutions."

Once reassured as described above, most patients are painfully honest about the details of their difficulties. Patients who are unable to comply with self-monitoring despite these assurances, however, may be particularly affected by the humiliation associated with binge eating. This impasse can be overcome by the suggestion that they do not record the details of their binge, but rather just write "binge food" when they binge. At a later time, gently explore in a general way the patient's experiences with binge-eating behaviors: which foods are typically binged on, how much is usually eaten, and so forth.

Another approach is not to "require" self-monitoring, but to introduce it to solve a specific problem or to address lack of progress if that occurs. If at a Monday appointment a patient declares, "I don't know why I binged last Thursday." To be truly helpful, the nutrition counselor will need to know what was eaten at prior meals; what was the interval between meals and the binge; and what the patient was thinking and feeling during the binge. The patient's likely inability to recall pertinent details makes the case for the institution of a stint of self-monitoring. Other patients will continue to make behavioral progress without self-monitoring, indicating that self-monitoring is not a requisite for their recovery.

It is clearly not productive to "fight" with patients over non-compliance with self-monitoring. The "monitoring" requirement of CBT is one reason patients drop out of CBT treatment and report difficult relationships with CBT practitioners. Paradoxically, self-monitoring may also be the reason CBT "works" for patients who stay in treatment. Consider adopting the CBT instruction to practitioners: "Sympathetically" insist that patients conscientiously self-monitor or risk undermining the effectiveness of the treatment program. Another approach is to remind patients that half-hearted attempts at self-monitoring are unlikely to change eating-disordered behaviors.

Summary Points

- Self monitoring is a key component in the CBT approach developed by Fairburn (2008), which he describes as "in the moment" or "real time" recording of relevant eating behaviors, thoughts, feelings, and events. It is the key intervention associated with remittance of bingeing and purging.
- Self-monitoring "speeds-up" treatment; frees sessions from fact-gathering so more time can be spent on problem-solving; and facilitates behavior change between sessions.

- Self-monitoring is not useful for all patients, especially anorexic patients who may lack motivation or who may obsess about food journaling.
- Nutrition counselors should always review self-monitoring assignments and show appreciation for completed food journals.
- 24-hour recalls during sessions can be used in place of self-monitoring.

7

LEVELS OF CARE

Introduction

This book is devoted to describing appropriate nutrition outpatient care for those with eating disorders (EDs). In this chapter, however, we focus on the continuum of care beyond outpatient care. Higher levels of care are important treatment options and should be recommended when outpatient treatment has not led to observable progress. We describe how we prepare patients who leave our care for higher levels of care and how we treat patients who are returning to outpatient care after a stay in an inpatient facility or from an intensive outpatient program. We add a few words about relapse and recovery because these are related concepts. Finally, we provide guidelines for helping patients secure third-party reimbursement so more patients can afford the full level of care they need.

Beyond Level 1

The American Psychiatric Association (American Psychiatric Association, 2006) has established level of care guidelines for patients with EDs. We, in consultation with other treatment team members, consider these guidelines, but also use our collective professional judgment when making recommendations for higher levels of care for a particular patient (additional considerations for higher levels of care are given in Chapter 9: Restoring Weight, pp. 191–228). American Psychiatric Association levels of care guidelines for patients with EDs, range from one to five:

    Level 1: Outpatient
    Level 2: Intensive outpatient program
    Level 3: Partial hospitalization or full-day outpatient care

Level 4: Residential treatment center
Level 5: Inpatient hospitalization

Simply put, Level 1 care is outpatient care for patients who are above 85% of a healthy body weight (for more information on healthy body weights see Chapter 8: Assessing Weight, pp. 169–190). Level 2 care is for patients who are above 80% of healthy body weight. Level 2 typically consists of treatment at a specialized center with outpatient services or treatment from a group of professionals who can provide frequent appointments and team treatment. Patients attend two to three times a week for sessions lasting up to 3 or 4 hours each time. Intensive outpatient programs are often associated with residential treatment centers and double as "step-down" programs. Level 3 treatment is full-day outpatient care, specifically defined as 8 hours a day, 5 days a week. Level 3 is appropriate for patients above 75% of healthy body weight. Level 4 care consists of live-in residential treatment. It is appropriate for patients who are suicidal but have no plan, and weigh less than 85% of a healthy body weight. Level 5 is inpatient hospitalization. Level 5 care is for patients who are less than 75% of a healthy weight, medically unstable (e.g., heart rate less than 40 bpm, blood pressure less than 90/60 mmHg, glucose less than 60 mg/dl, potassium less than 3 meq/L), or are suicidal. Various terms such as "hospitalization," "residential" and "inpatient" are widely used to refer to levels of care above Level 1. All these terms loosely, but inaccurately, refer to placement at a higher level of care beyond outpatient care. Inpatient hospitalization is technically Level 5 care in which a patient is admitted to a hospital due to medical or psychiatric instability.

Nutrition counselors should be familiar with local, regional, and national inpatient treatment programs, as well as residential and intensive outpatient programs. With this knowledge, we can help other members of the treatment team make appropriate clinical decisions. We also can convey to patients and their families the benefits of higher levels of care and how to begin the process of finding an appropriate program (Case Example 7.1).

CASE EXAMPLE 7.1: LILY

Lily is a top cross-country runner and a junior in high school (restricting, thin but with a body mass index (BMI) above 17.5, amenorrheic, runs to relieve stress in addition to training with the team, and vegetarian). She entered outpatient treatment for an eating disorder not otherwise specified (EDNOS) in January, seeing a nutrition counselor every other week and a pediatrician monthly (Level 1). Both practitioners are specialists in eating disorders. Neither Lily nor her parents felt that mental health counseling was necessary, though the nutrition counselor and the pediatrician recommended it. Lily

---

CASE EXAMPLE 7.1 (continued)

achieved her minimum weight goal just before spring track and was allowed to return to sports. Over the summer, Lily was too busy to continue nutrition counseling, but she continued to see her doctor, who did occasional weight checks (Level 1). Lily's weight dropped 5 lb over the summer, but Lily was allowed to do cross-country, her favorite sport. She was given a talking to by her parents and doctor about the need to get her weight up and she gained a pound or two. In October, Lily passed out after a practice run. The next day she saw her doctor, who found her heart rate to be dangerously low. Lily was evaluated several days later by a cardiologist, who recommended immediate hospitalization at a regional children's hospital (Level 5). Lily was kept on bed rest for 9 days until refeeding normalized her heart rate. She remained hospitalized until her weight was again at her minimum, and was then sent home. Lily's community lacks a treatment center, but she was to enter *ad hoc* intensive outpatient treatment (weekly appointments with a therapist, a nutrition counselor, and a doctor, and monthly team meetings which included parents; Level 2) and was not allowed to return to sports until she was able to maintain at or above her minimum weight for 6 weeks. Heart monitoring was required before and after practice runs. Lily is hoping to return to Level 1 care because "intensive treatment takes up so much time." Lily's treatment team is considering a Level 4 residential program if Lily does not make progress, because intensive day treatment (Level 3) would require a 3-hour drive. Lily's family is worried about the expense and being able to be involved in her treatment, as the nearest program is also 3 hours away.

Level 2

Lily's situation in Case Example 7.1 is common. The best her family could do was to approximate Level 2 care by putting together an ad hoc intensive outpatient program team (medical provider, mental health provider (individual or family or both), and nutrition counselor). Lily lives at home and goes to school and attends hourly sessions in her providers' private offices, with at least one appointment most days of the week. Ideally, intensive outpatient care would also include group psychotherapy, but availability of such services is rare outside of major population centers. Lily and her family are fortunate as their community has excellent outpatient providers, thanks in large part to being near a college campus.

Level 3

The full-day treatment programs recommended by the American Psychiatric Association (2006) for Level 3 care are rarely available outside of larger cities, and therefore not practical for many patients as they do not provide overnight accommodation. Level 3 programs with the best outcomes involve patients in treatment at least 5 days a week for 8 hours a day (American Psychiatric Association, 2006). Admission to or continuation of Level 4 treatment (i.e., residential treatment) may be necessary when access to a Level 3 care (i.e., partial hospitalization) is lacking because of geography or a lack of resources (third-party payers are more likely to approve and pay for Level 4 care than for Level 3 care). (See pp. 158–166 for more discussion of third-party reimbursement strategies.)

Level 4

Level 4 residential treatment typically ranges from several weeks to months. Patients need to know that residential treatment is a likely alternative if outpatient treatment fails to bring control to bingeing and purging behaviors, to excessive exercise, or to continuing weight loss. When ED behaviors have proven to be unrelenting in nature, it makes clinical sense to intensify treatment with a residential placement rather than continue long-term unproductive outpatient treatment. Moreover, chronic eating-disordered behaviors in a child can devastate family relationships. Parents are either completely unnerved by watching their child literally and figuratively waste away despite treatment, or are angry about their child's resistance to or failure in outpatient treatment. Families of disruptive bulimic children may have difficulty coping with their child's unrelenting ED-related behaviors. A residential stay can provide needed respite, protecting family relationships so that in the future the patient and the family can live together more effectively. Longer duration residential treatment (Level 4) should also be considered if patients refuse food, or have difficulty following a food plan or complying with other aspects of outpatient treatment.

Patients must come to understand that higher levels of care will be considered if they become medically unstable or are unable to make progress. One indicator of medical stability is body weight, although the weight criterion should be individualized to take into account the patient's overall health status and age. Residential programs should also be considered for any patient whose weight loss cannot be arrested. Similar considerations should be given to very low-weight patients who are unable to gain weight despite intensive outpatient treatment. We have seen how the "threat" of Level 4 care can be an effective motivator for progress, particularly in weight restoration.

Level 5

Level 5 inpatient hospitalization should be considered early on for children and adolescents, as they are at higher risk than adults for acute medical emergencies. They are also at risk for irreversible effects on physical growth and development, even when weight loss is not severe (American Psychiatric Association, 2006). The American Psychiatric Association (2006) practice guidelines recommend hospital-based programs for nutritional rehabilitation when weight has deviated below growth curves in children and adolescents. American Psychiatric Association practice guidelines also recommend Level 5 treatment in cases of rapid weight loss or food refusal, even if the patient is above 75% of a healthy body weight. Hospitalization should also be considered if restoration of body weight stymies and in cases of serious medical risks such as dilatation of the stomach or, in the case of Lily, low heart rate or other acute problems such as low body temperature (less than 97.0°F), electrolyte imbalance, dehydration, or signs of hepatic, renal, or cardiovascular compromise. (For more information on medical complications to consider when considering higher levels of care see Chapter 1: Clinical Features of Eating Disorders, pp. 3–31.) A brief period of hospitalization may help patients to fully grasp that they have a serious condition and that engagement in outpatient treatment (Level 1 or 2) is necessary for recovery.

Level 5 hospitalizations may range from a few hours in order to normalize potassium levels or for rehydration, to a week or longer to restore nutritional homeostasis. After patients are medically stabilized, it may be reasonable for them to return to intensive outpatient treatment. However, longer hospitalizations, possibly followed by admittance to a residential program, can be very effective. In essence, extending Level 5 care can "jump start" outpatient treatment. Another positive effect of Level 5 care is that patients often conclude that outpatient treatment is more palatable in comparison. But, following a hospital stay, patients are more likely to experience the outpatient treatment team as "serious" about safety, treatment, and recovery.

Transition from Inpatient to Outpatient

It is expected that patients admitted to higher levels of care programs eventually return to outpatient nutrition treatment. Rarely do relatively short inpatient stays, or even the longer stays in a residential programs, help patients make substantial behavioral progress. Patients may remain wedded to their eating-disordered behaviors looking forward, in fact, to resuming these behaviors once released from hospital or residential programs. Other patients, though ready to build on the "abstinence" obtained in the protective and structured environment of the residential treatment setting, often face a discouraging relapse on release. Most patients have not had any or sufficient opportunity to practice recovery behaviors in a free-living, independent setting, due in part to a lack of stepped-down care or an intensive outpatient program. It is, therefore, important to appreciate that most patients are far from fully recovered on release from higher levels of care.

The majority of such programs prepare discharge summaries and plans. Ideally, these reports include psychological and weight histories, the current food plan, and discharge goals. We, and other outpatient team members, evaluate the appropriateness of inpatient discharge goals and keep in mind that such plans are intended to be no more than recommendations. Many patients are released from higher levels of care at weights that are lower than those that support full recovery. We are aware that it is not unusual for third-party payers to terminate coverage for inpatient treatment once weight is above "85% of expected."

Patients usually return to outpatient treatment with a food plan designed by the inpatient treatment staff. Unless the patient has lost all faith in this plan, we help him or her develop strategies to adhere to it. It is not uncommon for inpatient programs to utilize food plans based on the Exchange List system or, at the time of this writing, the MyPlate/MyPyramid. Initially we make every effort to use the "language" and schema of the inpatient plan and to consult with the inpatient nutrition counselor if necessary and if consent is granted. When patients have difficulty following their "inpatient" plan, we say, "What would your inpatient nutrition counselor say about that?" Eventually though, most patients will need to be guided into the use of a food plan that is more suitable to life outside of a treatment center (see Chapter 5: Food Planning: Rule of Threes, pp. 107–139).

See Box 7.1 for the protocol we have developed to guide our work with patients recently released from higher levels of care.

BOX 7.1 PROTOCOL TO GUIDE WORK WITH PATIENTS RECENTLY RELEASED FROM HIGHER LEVELS OF CARE FOR RELAPSE

Phase 1: First month after release from inpatient program

- Provide patients with "seamless treatment" during the first month of transition to outpatient treatment.
  - Request discharge plan from inpatient program if not already received.
  - Use inpatient food plan until patient having trouble following it or it interferes with recovery.
- Focus on restoring patients to a minimal safe weight (BMI of 20 for females, BMI of 22 for males) as quickly as possible.
  - Rapid weight gain is a normal response to the starvation of anorexia nervosa (AN).
  - Remind patients that rapid weight gain is associated with complete recovery.
- Transition to a more family-style food plan. (See Chapter 5: Food Planning: Rule of Threes).

Phase 2: Begins as the patient reaches a minimal healthy weight

- Treatment is focused on:
  - Hunger and fullness .
  - Eating with family and friends .
  - Eliminating food fears.

BOX 7.1 (continued)

Phase 3: Begins when the patient is maintaining a minimal healthy weight

- Treatment is focused on:
  - Maintenance food plan: three meals/day, two protein servings/day, two fun foods .
  - Weight maintenance.
  - Adding sports, exercise, other activities, and away-from-home eating experiences.

Relapse

One of our most effective practices is to recommend a "quick" return to a higher level of care if patients regress within the first month in outpatient care. On the other hand, we understand (and share this understanding with our patients) that the road to recovery includes lapses and relapses. Fairburn (2008) recommends emphasizing that there is a difference between a lapse and a relapse. We conceptualize a lapse as a setback that can be corrected by the patient, but relapses require professional help. In either case, special attention should be paid through the first 6 months after intensive treatment, as this is when serious relapses are most likely to occur. In Box 7.2 we list the relapse triggers and risk factors that we watch for and help our patients handle or avoid. Box 7.3 contains the strategies we use to help patients reduce vulnerability for relapse.

BOX 7.2 RELAPSE TRIGGERS AND RISK FACTORS

- Incessant thoughts about body weight, shape, and size.
- Critical of body and food and exercise behaviors.
- "Feeling fat."
- Heightened interest in dieting or exercise .
- A rekindling of the desire to overeat or purge.
- Comments from others about weight or appearance.
- Stress of any kind.
- Holidays.
- New or difficult personal relationships.
- Major life transitions.

BOX 7.3 STRATEGIES TO HELP PATIENTS REDUCE VULNER-ABILITY FOR RELAPSE

- Encourage realistic expectations, including the possibility that patients may have an occasional setback. It is important that patients understand that recovery usually includes a series of ups and downs but that "slips don't lead to slides." Expecting to be instantaneously free of ED thoughts or behaviors is not realistic and increases vulnerability for relapse. Lapses and relapses provide the opportunity for the development of more effective food and coping strategies.
- Educate on how to recognize the signs and symptoms of impending relapse, namely, binge eating, purging, restrictive eating or dieting, loss of body weight, or missing a menstrual cycle. Encourage patients to interpret resurgence of ED thoughts as a possible signal of emotional distress or an indicator that food-related behaviors need attention.
- Emphasize the importance of adequate social support (e.g., friends, family, and community members). Having a confidante or accountability partner can sustain patients in times of relapse.
- Review cognitive–behavioral therapy (CBT), dialectical behavior therapy (DBT; see Chapter 4: Counseling Interventions, pp. 79–104) and problem-solving skills learned in prior sessions for identifying and managing "triggering" behaviors, thoughts, or situations (and their antecedents).
- Reiterate that dieting and obsessive self-weight checks are risky behaviors that can trigger an ED relapse.
- Sell adherence to the Rule of Threes (RO3s) or another food plan to the patient (for life?) as the key to continued recovery. Although some chafe at the structure imposed by a food plan and are eager to eat in a more carefree way as they recover, lapsing patients should immediately return to a more structured plan. Lapsing patients should be instructed to pre-plan meals in detail so that they know exactly what and when they will be eating. If helpful earlier in treatment, encourage resumption of self-monitoring.

We teach that returning to more frequent nutrition counseling sessions or other supportive treatment because of lapse or relapse is not a sign of failure, but one of wisdom. For example, we tell anorexia nervosa (AN) patients to return to treatment if they lose more than 5 lb or drop below their minimum safe weight goal (for more information see Chapter 8: Assessing Weight, pp. 169–190). A follow-up visit, if not a return to treatment, should be considered if the patient or others notice an increased in self-criticism and or obsession with food or weight. Patients, parents, and professionals should have a low threshold for determining when it would be prudent to return to treatment. Allison, a weight–recovered anorexic, is a case in point. Her parents recommended a return to treatment the summer prior to entering her freshman year in high school. They suspected that the well-known social pressures that favored thinness in Allison's high school would put her at risk for a relapse.

Recovery

Patients often ask, "Do people completely recover from an ED?" and "How long does recovery take?" Most patients feel reassured when we review the recovery literature with them, starting with what recovery looks like. In research studies recovery is defined by some as being symptom-free for at least 4 months and by others as up to 3 years without symptoms. "Symptom-free" is defined as when low weight, dieting, binge eating, purging, and other compensatory behaviors are no longer present (Von Holle et al., 2008). Because the risk for relapse is greatest within 1-year post treatment, one symptom-free year is another measure of recovery (Bardone-Cone et al., 2010). Although most recovery studies do not assess psychological recovery, it is thought to take twice as long to achieve as does physical and behavioral recovery (Couturier & Lock, 2006). Psychological recovery has not been definitively defined, but continuing to fear weight gain and poor body image predicts relapse despite abstinence from ED behaviors (Bardone-Cone et al., 2010).

To answer the question about whether people can recover, we summarize the latest research statistics as follows: After 5 years of treatment, nearly all patients with BN, BED, and other eating disorder not otherwise specified (EDNOS) and 50% of patients with AN are fully recovered (Agras, Crow, Mitchell, Halmi, & Bryson, 2009; Keel & Brown, 2010). Other reviews found that 75–90% of AN cases eventually recover, but up to 30% may only achieve partial recovery (Johnson, Lund, & Yates, 2003; Miller, 2011). The only significant predictor of recovery from AN is intervention within 2 years of onset (Clausen, 2008). In conclusion, we define recovery as being free of behavior and physical symptoms and related psychological issues for at least 2 years. We tell our patients that recovery means being free of physical and psychological symptoms, including low body weight, dieting, bingeing, purging and other compensatory behaviors, and being at peace with one's body weight and appearance as well as with food and eating for over 2 years.

Third-Party Reimbursement Issues

Here we describe the process we use for obtaining third-party reimbursement for nutrition counseling services. Of note, the only professionals allowed to directly bill for nutrition counseling are registered dietitians (RDs). RDs must have a tax identification number (TIN), also known as an Employer Identification Number

(EIN), and a National Provider Identifier (NPI) to participate with insurance companies. (For more information on applying for TIN, EIN, and NPI contact http:// www.irs.gov/Individuals/International-Taxpayers/Taxpayer-Identification-Numbers-%28TIN%29.)

The first step is to investigate the possibility of becoming an in-network provider (also known as a credentialed, contracted, or participating provider) with the health insurance companies serving your area. Many insurance policies only cover visits with in-network providers. Some will cover out-of-network providers, but usually require subscribers to pay a higher deductible or co-pay for each visit. As a contracted provider, one agrees to the insurance company's reimbursement fees (we ask for written disclosure of fees before proceeding), to submit claims for patients, and to wait for the company's reimbursement (usually about 30 days). On the plus side, as a participating provider one does not have to discuss paying for services with patients. To become an in-network or contracted provider, complete the credentialing process, which requires the dietitian to submit a simple but tedious application and typically wait several months for notification of approval. The details of the credentialing process are usually outlined on each insurance company's website. Of note, dietitians are considered medical providers by insurers for credentialing and billing purposes. To determine the economic feasibility of contracting with a particular company, ask for reimbursement rates per unit (15 minutes) of nutrition counseling using procedure codes 97802 (first visit), 97803 (second visit), and 97804 (group counseling). We also participate with the Council for Affordable Quality Healthcare (CAQH), a well-respected web service that allows dietitians and other healthcare providers to complete one application for credentialing by many insurance companies (http://cagh.org).

There is no question that becoming a participating provider is of benefit to patients. Helping patients and their families secure third-party payments for nutrition counseling helps reduce stress in an already overwhelming situation and positions the nutrition counselor as a supportive member of the team. All this may sound quite time-consuming, and it is. Ways to reduce the time necessary to obtain reimbursement for services include: hire or contract staff to manage obtaining insurance coverage information and for billing; participate in electronic billing options; or contract with an online billing service. When problems arise around insurance reimbursement, we inform patients or parents and suggest that they call their insurance company and advocate for themselves.

Unless nutrition counseling is provided on fee-for-service with payments due each visit, during initial contacts with the prospective patients (via phone or e-mail or during the first visit), obtain the patient's first and last name, date of birth, source of referral, primary care provider, reason for visit, name of insurance company, insurance identification number, insurance provider information number, email address, and credit card information. Before contacting the patient's insurance company to confirm benefits, have in hand the patient's first and last name, date of birth, and insurance identification number and the provider's tax ID and NPI. We either call or check the company's website (another benefit of being a participating provider) to determine the patient's eligibility (whether his or her policy is active) and benefits (whether nutrition counseling is a covered benefit) and deductible and co-pay requirements, and any limitations on diagnoses or requirements. We occasionally ask patients to obtain this information, but it is best if the provider contacts the insurance company directly as the lingo can be difficult to understand. Important information to obtain from the insurance company representative or their website includes:

- Is a primary care provider's referral required?
- How many nutrition counseling sessions are allowed per year? Ask what the perimeters are of the patient's contracted year?
- Is a deductible or patient co-payment required and, if so, what are the details?
- Which ED diagnoses are covered?

We phone or email the patient after we have obtained the above information to schedule an appointment. If the patient requires a primary care provider referral, we request the patient contact his or her medical provider to request that the referral be faxed to us. The date of the referral must be on or before the first scheduled session. If the patient's insurance company does not offer nutrition counseling benefits or offers a limited number of visits, we discuss with the patient the process of appealing to the insurance company (see The Appeal Process below). We inform the patient about our fees and discuss other payment options such as flexible spending accounts, monthly billing, and using a credit card. We either collect payment (i.e., co-pays or visit fees if the patient has not met deductibles or doesn't have nutrition coverage) at the beginning of each session. Or, we wait for insurance payments while keeping a copy of the patient credit card (or credit card number and expiration date) on file in case there is a problem with the reimbursement. Having credit card information on file is also helpful when patients come unprepared to pay fee-for-services or co-pays. Credit card information also expedites payments for missed appointments as per our policy (i.e. 48-hours notice is required to cancel an appointment, otherwise the patient is charged for the cost of the visit because insurance companies cannot be billed for visits that patients miss.) Depending on circumstances, we occasionally offer a sliding scale.

When insurance companies deny our claims it often is because they have mistakenly billed our services under mental health. In these cases, we contact the insurance company (using the number on the back of the patient's insurance card) to explain that we are required to use mental health diagnoses codes (307.1 for AN, 307.51 for BN, and 307.50 for BED and EDNOS) despite being required to bill for a medical service.

The Appeal Process

If the patient's insurance company does not offer nutrition counseling benefits or offers a limited number of visits, we offer the family (as only rarely do patients have the energy for an appeal) our help and support in appealing for coverage (Case Example 7.2). Of note, we have had most success with appeals when the patient is underweight. We warn families that appealing to an insurance company for coverage is a lengthy process and may feel like a part-time job. While the steps we describe below may seem easier said than done, we have had families gain coverage using each one of described strategies. Ideally, treatment should begin while the appeal is in process. Some families are able to afford to pay for nutrition visits out-of-pocket. At the very least, we encourage patients in this situation to begin treatment with a medical provider and a mental health provider. Insurance coverage for these providers is usually more generous.

CASE EXAMPLE 7.2: DIANNA

Dianna, I suggest you call your insurance company and ask to speak to a supervisor. Explain that your daughter has AN, a serious mental disorder (that is where the 307.1 mental health diagnosis comes in) with potentially life-threatening medical complications that I as a registered dietitian am trained to treat. You can also say standard treatment for AN is team treatment with a medical doctor (the doctor cannot treat the medical complications only assess them), a psychotherapist (for the mental problems associated with AN), and a dietitian (treats the underweight and the food fears). This team treatment is the approach that is most likely to keep your daughter out of the hospital and ensure complete recovery. You can also suggest that the supervisor talk to me--either give them my contact information or find out how I can reach them.

The first step is for the family to call their insurance company and ask to speak to a case manager about a "benefit exception." In this call, the family member should emotionally and forcefully state their case. If they are met with an emphatic "no," they should ask to talk to a supervisor. Supervisors have more leeway than do "representatives" who field such calls. Talking to a supervisor provides an opportunity to restate their case and to request an explanation of the options for pursuing coverage. We often follow up with our own call to the company's provider services to explain our view of the case and to ask what documentation the company requires from the nutrition counselor to consider a benefit exception. In the best-case scenario, the insurance company assigns a case manager who gathers facts about the patient's medical history and negotiates with the company for approval of nutrition visits. Usually visits are approved in batches of six visits or more. Once a benefit exception has been approved for a batch of visits, approval for more visits usually becomes routine and is accomplished by the nutrition counselor in a call to the case manager. Providers and families should document the date and content of each conversation with the insurance company, along with the insurance company employee's name and any case reference numbers provided. If still unsuccessful, families should ask the company about how to initiate an appeal. This is an even more arduous process that will involve the patient, family, referring physician, nutrition counselor, and possibly the mental health provider. The National Eating Disorders Association (NEDA) Parent Toolkit (http://www.nationaleatingdisorders.org/information-resources/parent-toolkit.php) has detailed advice on how to manage an appeals process and sample letters to use with insurance companies. Box 7.4 lists the points we make when we write in support of an appeal.

BOX 7.4 POINTS TO MAKE WHEN WRITING IN SUPPORT OF AN APPEAL

- Providing comprehensive nutrition services is a cost-effective means to treat an ED and to prevent complications.
- The semi-starvation that results from AN, and the medical complications associated with BN, are physiological complications that, if untreated, will likely result in an expensive hospitalization or residential treatment.
- EDs are medical illnesses. This is important to stress because nutrition counseling is considered a medical service not a psychological treatment. The most likely medical complications resulting from an ED are cardiovascular events [even in patients with normal electrocardiograms (ECGs)], growth failure in pre-pubertal patients, irreversible osteopenia, high fracture rates, and even sudden death (American Psychiatric Association, 2006).
- Any abnormal medical findings should be mentioned. For example, restricting patients often have ECGs that show marked bradycardia. This data is objective information that is difficult for the insurance company to deny. If the patient hasn't had an ECG, talk to the medical provider about the benefits of ordering this test. Because ECGs improve with refeeding, follow-up ECGs can be used to prove that nutrition counseling is beneficial.
- All ED diagnoses, including EDNOS, have elevated mortality rates similar to that of AN (Crow et al., 2009) . Similarly, all ED diagnoses have increased rates of suicide (Crow et al., 2009).

If the appeal fails, families should be advised to inform the subscriber's employer as it is the employer who actually determines which benefits are included or excluded in the company's insurance policy. Employers sometimes are willing and able to request an exception. We also advise the patient's primary care provider to write a letter of appeal or call the insurance company, stating emphatically that, without nutrition counseling, the patient will likely end up in hospital or a residential treatment center. With the patient's permission, we then offer to write up a case summary for the insurer, and sometimes for the primary care provider who may not be sure how to proceed. See Box 7.5 for a sample letter and the diagnosis-specific treatment guidelines we include when requesting nutrition coverage.

BOX 7.5 SAMPLE PROFESSIONAL LETTER FOR REQUESTING INSURANCE COVERAGE FOR NUTRITION COUNSELING

Provider's Letterhead

Date of Request
Patient's Name
Date of Birth
Insurance ID #
Subscriber's Name
Diagnosis Code (*307.1 or 307.51 or 307.50*)
Procedure Code (*97802 or 97803*)
Re: Benefit Exception

Clinical History

(*Patient's name*) is a (*age of patient*)-year-old (*gender*) with a (*number of months or years*) history of an eating disorder (ED). *He or she* presents with (list clinical findings, other diagnoses, treatment providers, and medications). *If significant, include graphs showing the patient's growth curve, weight, or BMI history from childhood and or from a pre-morbid period.*

Recommendations

(*Patient's name*) needs continued nutrition counseling support to make progress with her weight, eating habits, and food beliefs and to avoid residential treatment or inpatient hospitalization. I recommend that a Benefit Exception for Nutrition Counseling Visits be (*approved/extended*) to cover (*number of visits*) nutrition counseling visits from (*month, day, year*) through (*month, day, year*) with nutrition services provided by (*your name and ADA/ AND registration number*).

Treatment Guidelines

The American Psychiatric Association's (APA) Practice Guideline for the Treatment of Patients with EDs, 3rd edition (2006) recommends nutrition counseling as a crucial aspect of treatment for EDs. The APA guideline cites research evidence that nutrition counseling improves clinical outcomes by reducing behaviors related to an ED. According to the APA, "A primary focus for nutritional rehabilitation is to help the patient develop a structured meal plan as a means of reducing the episodes of dietary restriction and the urges to binge and purge. Adequate nutritional intake can prevent craving and promote satiety. It is important to assess nutritional intake for all patients, even those with a normal body weight (or normal BMI), as normal weight does not ensure appropriate nutritional intake or normal body composition. Among patients of normal weight, nutritional counseling is a useful part of treatment and helps reduce food restriction, increase the variety of foods eaten, and promote healthy but not compulsive exercise patterns.

Role of the Nutrition Counselor

The nutrition counselor is a vital member of the interdisciplinary treatment team for a patient with an ED. No other member of the team has the nutritional expertise and medical nutritional skills to assess the patient's caloric and macronutrient intake for adequacy, for variety of food choices and to correct nutrient deficiencies. The nutrition counselor is the team member who designs a food plan to maintain the patient's biologically determined weight range and to support his or her physiological and emotional stability. The nutrition counselor monitors and treats binge-eating and purging behaviors, episodes of food restriction, and excessive exercise patterns. The nutrition counselor provides psycho-education, evidence-based nutrition advice, and counseling for body-image concerns, weight-related fears, and nutrition misinformation. He or she provides ongoing patient and ED treatment team support.

(Depending on the patient's diagnosis we add from the following)

Anorexia Nervosa

Anorexia nervosa is a serious illness that increases severity of a variety of physical and psychological problems. The American Psychiatric Association's Practice Guideline for the Treatment of Patients with Eating Disorders (2006) provides the following information: Anorexia nervosa has serious consequences for adolescents, with mortality rates of 5.6% per decade. Estimated death rates of females with anorexia nervosa are up to 12 times those of age-matched females and up to twice those of females with other psychiatric disorders In a 2011 meta-analysis, mortality was 5.86-fold higher in anorexia nervosa than expected from the general population (Arcelus, Mitchell, Wales, & Nielsen, 2011). Intensive treatment of adolescents greatly reduces mortality to nearly nil. The American Psychiatric Association's Practice Guideline for the Treatment of Patients with Eating Disorders (2006) recommends nutritional treatment for anorexia nervosa. Nutritional treatment restores weight, normalizes eating patterns, achieves normal perceptions of hunger and satiety, and corrects biological and psychological sequelae of malnutrition.

Bulimia Nervosa

The American Psychiatric Association's Practice Guideline for the Treatment of Patients with Eating Disorders (2006) recommends nutritional treatment for bulimia nervosa. In cases of bulimia nervosa, nutritional treatment is used to reduce behaviors related to the eating disorder, minimizing food restriction, correcting nutritional deficiencies, increasing the variety of foods eaten, and encouraging healthy but not excessive exercise patterns. Treatments for bulimia nervosa that include nutrition counseling have been proven to be more effective than programs that do not include nutrition counseling. Mortality is 1.93-fold higher in bulimia nervosa than expected from the general population and 1.92-fold higher in patients with the diagnosis of Eating Disorder Not Otherwise Specified (Arcelus, Mitchell, Wales, & Nielsen, 2011).

Eating Disorder Not Otherwise Specified (EDNOS)

EDNOS includes early-stage anorexia nervosa and bulimia nervosa. Without treatment, 80% of EDNOS patients are likely to develop full-spectrum eating disorders, particularly anorexia nervosa (Agras et al., 2009; Eddy et al., 2008). Mortality rates for diagnosis of EDNOS is similar to those for anorexia nervosa and bulimia nervosa (Arcelus et al., 2011).

If an appeal is still not granted, we advise the family to inform the insurance company that they will be notifying their state insurance commissioner of the steps the family has taken to get coverage and of the difficulties they have encountered. To find out how to contact the state commissioner, we recommend checking: www.insuranceclaimsconsult.com/Ins.Commissioner.htm. After the insurance commissioner has been contacted, a follow-up letter to the insurance commissioner and copies to the insurance company should be sent. This letter should restate the patient's situation and needs and include documentation of the family's previous efforts. Copies of all correspondence and other pertinent documents should be kept on file. If the insurance commissioner is not helpful, the next step is for the family to send a similar letter to local and state senators and Congress representatives. If this proves unsuccessful, we advise contacting the state governor.

Reduced-Fee Treatment Options

When all else fails, the nutrition counselor may be able to offer sliding-scale fees based on the patient's ability to pay. Another option is to suggest to the patient or family no-fee research treatment programs, which are offered periodically throughout the United States. A research study may be underway at a college or university near the patient. Although there may be no fee for part of the treatment, there may be fees for certain non-research portions of the study. There are inclusion and exclusion criteria for acceptance into these programs. At the time of writing, the following research program is accepting applicants: The Eating Disorders Clinic at New York State Psychiatric Institute at Columbia Presbyterian Medical Center in New York City.

Summary Points

- The American Psychiatric Association has established levels of care guidelines for patients with EDs, ranging from one to five, the lowest being outpatient care and the highest level being hospitalization.
- Patients must understand that higher levels of care will be considered if they become medically unstable or are unable to make progress.
- Recovery means being free of physical and psychological symptoms, including low body weight, dieting, bingeing, purging, and other compensatory behaviors. It means being at peace with one's body weight and appearance, as well as with food and eating for over 1 year.
- A lapse is a setback that can be corrected by the patient, but relapses require professional help.
- Nutrition counselors can provide help and support patients and their families in securing third-party reimbursement for ED treatment.

PART III

Treatment

8

ASSESSING WEIGHT

Introduction

In this chapter we outline how to estimate a patient's biologically appropriate weight (BAW), how to talk about weight issues, how to use body mass index (BMI) categories, and how to appropriately monitor weights throughout treatment. This information provides a framework for the following chapters on restoring weight, managing weight and managing bingeing, purging, and exercise behaviors. Although all team members address weight issues, usually it is the nutrition counselor's responsibility to assess and monitor weights and to educate patients about the biological facts that influence body weight. Weight monitoring is a helpful gauge of the adequacy of a particular food plan and it can reassure patients who worry that improving eating patterns will cause undesired changes in weight.

Whichever team member conducts weight monitoring, he or she must keep other team members up to date about the patient's weight status. If weight is monitored by another professional, it is imperative that arrangements be made for the nutrition counselor to have access to current weight data at the time of each visit. It is also important that the patient's psychotherapist is kept up to date on weight changes. There are a few instances that patients' self-report of weights on a home scale might be useful (for phone sessions and in family-based treatment (FBT) by parents). In general, though, it is best to not rely on weights that cannot be verified.

Biologically-Appropriate Weight (BAW)

We have chosen to use our own term "biologically appropriate weight" (BAW) instead of more familiar terms such as, "healthy weight," "expected body weight," or "ideal body weight". Below we lay out the evidence for our view that that the major determinant of body weight is genetic and that BAW is maintained with ease without dieting or other inappropriate food and exercise behaviors, and supports normal growth and function. Box 8.1 lists the characteristics of BAW.

BOX 8.1 CHARACTERISTICS OF A BIOLOGICALLY APPROPRIATE WEIGHT

- Absence of:
  - restricting or dieting
  - bingeing
  - excessive exercise

- Supportive of:
  - normal physical and psychological function
  - normal growth in young patients

- Consistent with:
  - pre-morbid weight
  - gender
  - ethnicity
  - family history

Genetics

The genetic basis for BAW is supported by twin and adoptee studies, which show that adopted children's weight is more closely correlated with their biologic parents' weight than to their adopting parents' weight, and that twins show a much stronger correlation in body weight to an identical twin than to a fraternal twin or other siblings (Hainer, Stunkard, Kunešová, Parízková, Štich, & Allison, 2001; Stunkard, Foch, & Hrubec, 1986; Stunkard et al., 1986). These studies and others indicate that the heritability (proportion of a trait that is determined by genetics) of BMI could explain up to 40–75% of an individual's body weight (O'Rahilly & Farooqi, 2008; Schousboe et al., 2004).

Set Point

Set point theory asserts that a genetically-based control mechanism regulates metabolism so that weight is maintained at a genetically-predetermined level, despite variability in energy balance. Set point is thought to protect against life-threatening weight loss in a famine. It also provides an explanation for why weight can remain stable with very low caloric intakes and for why underweight patients in recovery return to pre-morbid weight and younger patients return to their pre-morbid BMI-for-age percentile.

Metabolic Efficiency

Related to set point is metabolic efficiency. Survival in primitive conditions favors metabolically efficient individuals who have high set points and, therefore, are able to maintain body weight on relatively low caloric intake. This trait is genetically determined and runs in families. It was an evolutionary asset, as metabolically efficient individuals are more likely to survive in times of unreliable food supplies (Dokken & Tsao, 2007). Such individuals are prone to gain weight during positive energy balance and not likely to lose weight during negative energy balance (Müller, Bosy-Westphal, & Heymsfield, 2010). Metabolic efficiency also explains why individuals with similar energy intakes and outputs may maintain significantly different body weights. Understanding the survival advantages of metabolic efficiency can help patients accept the hard truth that weight loss is, for them, problematical. Koenig (2008) tells her patients who are frustrated that they cannot reach or maintain a desired weight that "willpower cannot override biology."

On the other hand, we are careful not to estimate the level of metabolic efficiency for an individual. First, there are too many factors to make an accurate prediction about the efficiency of an individual's metabolism. Secondly, patients can easily become discouraged if they are not prepared to hear that they have a low metabolic rate. Of note, we prefer to use the more affirmative phrase "metabolic efficiency" over "low metabolic rate."

Muscularity, Gender, and Ethnicity

Muscularity, gender, and ethnicity illustrate other reasons why BAW varies between individuals, and especially between the genders. In 1943, the Metropolitan Life Insurance Company introduced gender-specific height–weight tables for adults. In general, men are more muscular and taller than women, and they have denser bones and bigger and heavier frames. Athletes of both genders are more muscular than average.

It is no surprise that recent studies show that many Asian individuals have smaller frame size and less muscle mass than do Caucasians (WHO Expert Consultation, 2004). In the United States, African Americans and Hispanic/Latino Americans, especially females, have larger body frames than do Caucasian Americans. Asian American females are significantly smaller. Although these same differences among ethnicities are seen in males, they are less pronounced (Boykin, Diez-Roux, Carnethon, Shrager, Ni, & Whitt-Glover, 2011).

For children and adolescents, the National Institutes of Health (NIH) provides gender-specific BMI percentile calculators (Centers for Disease Control and Prevention, 2011). Another tool is an online service (https://mygrowthcharts. com) for tracking BMI data for individual patients.

Normal Eating and Exercise Behaviors

Normalized eating and exercise patterns practiced over time lead to maintenance of BAW. Once achieved, unless the patient is still growing BAW is stable and resistant to change, despite variations in daily intake and caloric expenditure. Another sign of reaching BAW is a considerable improvement in obsessions and preoccupations with food, shape, and weight (Golden, Jacobson, Sterling, & Hertz, 2008).

Normal Physiological Function

Normalized blood chemistries, such as testosterone, estradiol, IGF-1, and cortisol levels, along with weight stability, normal body temperature (hands are not cold most of the time), and no dizziness upon standing (Tyson, 2010) are associated with weights near BAW. In both male and female adolescents and young adults with anorexia nervosa (AN), achieving BAW is associated with arresting bone loss, and possibly some bone density recovery (Mehler, Sabel, Watson, & Andersen, 2008). In adult females and older girls, BAW is a stable weight at which normal menstruation and ovulation are maintained. Secondary amenorrhea (the absence of three consecutive menstrual cycles), however, may occur at higher weights when weight loss is sudden, as in the case example of Sally (Case Example 8.1; Genazzani, Riccieri, Lanzoni, Strucchi, & Jasonni, 2006) or when a caloric deficit from excessive exercise, dietary restrictions, or both, leaves too little energy for the body to maintain a regular menstrual cycle (see Chapter: 12 Managing Exercise, pp. 260–276). The most common instances of this phenomenon are heavy individuals who lose weight through extreme dieting, or athletes who eat modestly and exercise intensely. In males, return of normal testosterone is important indicator of reaching BAW, as in the case example of Jake (Case Example 8.2; Wabitsch et al., 2001).

CASE EXAMPLE 8.1: SALLY

Sally (a 36-year-old, white female) came from a family where both parents and two brothers were morbidly obese. At 5'4" tall, Sally weighed 260 lb until she joined an Overeaters Anonymous (OA) group that encouraged weighing and measuring. A sponsor gave her a food plan, which Sally followed religiously over the next 6 years, losing 80 lb. At 180 lb, menses stopped, and a bone scan showed osteoporosis. Menses resumed after Sally gained back 20 lb in 3 months when work-related travel made it impossible to weigh and measure her food. Returning to OA, Sally quickly lost the 20 lb she had gained and her menstrual cycle. When Sally sought help from Larkin, she presented with many of signs and symptoms of AN, including amenorrhea.

CASE EXAMPLE 8.2: JAKE

Jake, a 37-year-old white male from big-boned farm family (5'10"), had lost 40 lb (from 220 lb to 180 lb, BMI = 26.5 kg/m^2) in 6 months before seeking professional nutrition counseling. Jake achieved weight loss by restrictively eating a low-fat vegan diet, with occasional consumption of fish in sushi. He complained of low energy, lack of food variety, inability to focus, and erectile dysfunction. An endocrinologist prescribed medication for hypothyroidism, low testosterone levels, and vitamin D deficiency. Jake scored 25 out of 26 on the EAT-26 test (see Chapter 2: Course of Treatment) and met the criteria for eating disorder not otherwise specified (EDNOS). With dietary improvements and an increase in calories, Jake's thyroid and testosterone levels were restored, his physical symptoms were alleviated, and his weight increased to 190 lb (BMI = 27.3 kg/m^2).

Settling Point

Settling point, like set point, "defends" the body against weight loss. Settling point theory helps clarify why binge eaters who stop bingeing may not lose weight. When food is abundant, body weight tends to drift upward and "settle" at a weight that is consistent with current energy intake. Settling point is stable as long as there are no changes in energy balance. Unlike set point, which is thought to be a genetically predetermined body weight, settling point theory predicts the likelihood of several different stable weights an individual could maintain depending on energy balance. Settling point "drifts downward" if changes in energy balance are modest and long-term enough to not trigger a decrease in metabolism (Dokken & Tsao, 2007). The body defends a settling point weight when faced with a drastic reduction in calories by thwarting weight loss and becoming more metabolically efficient. We see the effects of settling point in high-weight binge-eating disorder (BED) patients who stop binge eating but do not lose weight. Weight loss can be achieved in these patients with small changes in caloric intake over the long term. Similarly, settling point may explain some of the weight gain that often occurs in the menopause, when metabolic rate drops, and energy intake is not adjusted (Tam, Fukumura, & Jain, 2009).

Normal Growth and Development

In children and adolescents, BAW supports normal growth and development, as evidenced by consistent and predictable growth patterns that are consistent with the patient's pre-morbid and age-adjusted growth curve (for copies of growth charts, see http://www.cdc.gov/growthcharts/clinical_charts.htm). Boxes 8.2

and 8.3 list expected height and weight milestones associated with normal pubertal development in girls and boys. The most obvious sign of normal development in girls is age-appropriate menstrual physiology, and in boys it is physical signs of sexual development and expected growth in height. In girls, however, height growth is delayed during the pubertal weight-gain period. We have seen patients and parents often wrongly interpreting this normal change in weight in girls as excess weight gain.

BOX 8.2 INDICATORS OF NORMAL ADOLESCENT FEMALE GROWTH

- 7–13 years old: pubertal changes begin in girls
  - noticeable perspiration, body odor, and acne
- 10–16 years old: growth spurt
  - 40 lb gained
  - 6–9 months of increases in body fat before growth in height
  - 13 years old: average age of onset of menses
  - 11–15 years: average range of first menses
- 16–20 years old:
  - 10–20 lb gained
  - weight gain continues until height growth stops

BOX 8.3 INDICATORS OF NORMAL ADOLESCENT MALE GROWTH

- 9–14 years old: pubertal changes begin in boys
  - noticeable perspiration, body odor, and acne
  - 12 years is the average age for onset of puberty
- 12–16 years old: growth spurt
  - 45 lb gained
  - simultaneous increase in muscle development and height
- 16 years to early 20s:
  - weight gain continues until height growth stops
  - 20 lb gained

Delayed Puberty

In cases of delayed puberty, 20% are the result of excessive exercise, low energy intake, low body weight, AN, bulimia nervosa (BN), or another systemic illness such as hypothyroidism, inflammatory bowel disease, or celiac disease (Palmert & Dunkel, 2012, p. 445). Delayed puberty is defined as the absence of testicular enlargement in boys or breast development in girls at an age that is 2–2.5 standard deviations (SD) later than the age of 14 years in boys and 13 years in girls. At 16 years old, girls who have not started menses (primary amenorrhea) are at high risk for loss of bone mass. Boys older than 15 years with few signs of pubertal development and delayed growth in height are equally at risk for poor bone mass.

Menopause

Menopause is yet another factor to be considered in determining BAW. In older women, menopause is associated with increases in body weight, fat mass, and waist circumference; and decreases in skeletal muscle mass and metabolism (Soni, Conroy, Mackey, & Kuller, 2011; Sowers et al., 2007). Longitudinal studies show that weight gain averages 5–10 lb around the time of the menopausal transition (Macdonald, New, Campbell, & Reid, 2003). Menopausal weight gain is hypothesized to be biologically adaptive (Freeman, Sammel, Lin, & Gracia, 2010). When ovaries no longer manufacture estrogen, estrogen is produced by adipose tissue, providing heavier women with protection from heart disease, hypertension, osteoporosis, and loss of cognitive abilities. Researchers have found an association between weight gain during the menopause and mortality, showing that "lean women" who gain at least 20 lb experience a three-fold drop in mortality (Singh, Haddad, Knutsen, & Fraser, 2001). This same protection, however, is not afforded to older men. Men who gained significant weight with age experienced higher rates of mortality than lower weight peers (Singh, Haddad, Knutsen, & Fraser, 2001). Given this data, we expect that premenstrual patients at BAW may gain up to 20 lb over the course of menopause.

Predicting Biologically Appropriate Weight

As nutrition counselors, we are often asked by patients to predict a goal, ideal, or healthy weight. We answer the question by first introducing the concept of BAW as "your genetically predetermined natural weight" or "your weight when you have normal eating and exercise behaviors and your body is healthy" or "your best weight." We then add, "Only your body knows for sure, but by working together we will discover your BAW." We talk about clues that indicate when one has reached BAW: absence of disordered eating behaviors; regular menses or normal testosterone levels; absence of feeling cold and tired; adequate food intake in response to hunger and fullness signals; and weights that are consistent and stable as per a growth curve or an adult weight map. Patients often worry whether past restriction or dieting "damages metabolism beyond repair" (Koenig, 2008, p. 86). Research on this question suggests that low metabolism persists perhaps indefinitely in people who maintain a reduced body weight through dieting but, once caloric restriction stops, metabolism returns to its previous rate (Rosenbaum, Hirsch, Gallagher, & Leibel, 2008; Weinsier, 2001).

The following points help patients understand the concept of BAW:

- Weight is genetically regulated.
- A remarkably wide range of weights are natural, biological, and healthy.
- "All you need to do is just take good care of your body by listening to and attending to its needs."

Although BAW is best "discovered," we do discuss the following indicators of BAW (barring any food or exercise behavior problems). We also explain that the wide ranges in BAW indicators account for differences in gender, frame size, and genetic predisposition.

- BAWs are at least 10–20 lb heavier than high-school graduation weights.
- Weight at college graduation is usually nearer a BAW.
- BAWs are usually higher than minimum menstrual weights.
- For adult females, BAW usually falls between BMI of 20 kg/m² and 30 kg/m², roughly a 60-lb range.
- For adult males, BAW usually falls between BMI of 25 kg/m² and 35 kg/m², roughly a 65-lb range.
- For children and adolescents, BAWs are usually between the 25th percentile and the 85th percentile, and should be consistent with each individual's growth curve.

Weight History

Nutrition counselors must obtain a weight history to be able to predict a BAW. The components of a weight history are listed in Box 8.4.

BOX 8.4 COMPONENTS OF A WEIGHT HISTORY

- Growth curves
- Menstrual weights

  – Weight and age at which menses began
  – Weights associated with amenorrhea

- High-school graduation
- College graduation

- Weight at age 25 years (and so on, by decade)
- Highest weight
- Lowest weight
- Family weight history (e.g., big-boned, slight)

In younger patients, having access to growth curves is essential. Counselors or parents can request growth history from primary care providers. If growth curves are unavailable, historical height and weight data can be entered at https://mygrowthcharts.com to create a curve for individual patients. Ideally, nutrition counselors also have access to the weight and menstrual histories of adult patients. For adult patients, we often create, from self-reports, a "weight map" on graph paper, consisting of the patient's weight at year of menarche, high-school graduation, college graduation, age 25 years, and so on by decade. At the very least, the nutrition counselor should ask adult patients to recall their recent highest and lowest body weights.

We usually do a "family weight history" by asking questions such as: "Are you from a big-boned family?" "Is there a lot of differences or variations in body weight among family members?" "Whose body shape and size did you inherit?" When exploring weight histories with patients, it is important to remain neutral, non-judgmental, and empathetic.

For patients with BN, BED, and eating disorder not otherwise specified (EDNOS) whose weights are in normal ranges, weight is not a medical health concern. AN patients and, to a lesser extent, obese eating-disordered patients, however, do have medical health risks associated with weight. The nutrition counselor should determine the level of concern about the patient's weight from the medical provider and from the patient. "What are your concerns about your weight?" "What are your medical provider's concerns about your weight?" Adolescent patients often comment, "I've never been this heavy before." We respond, "But you've never been this old before."

BMI Weight Categories

The BMI is the weight in kilograms divided by the square of height in meters (kg/m^2). It is well-established numeric measure of body size. (See Box 8.5 for BMI online calculators.)

The NIH BMI categories are widely accepted in the medical, health, and research fields as an accurate, simple, and low-cost system for assessing the degree of health risk associated with either low or high body weight and for assessing nutritional status in adults. The Centers for Disease Control (CDC) developed a similar approach to assess the nutritional status, general health and well-being of children and adolescents up to age 20 years. The CDC BMI-for-age percentile

---

BOX 8.5 ONLINE CALCULATORS FOR BMI

- Subscription growth curve plotting application: https://mygrowthcharts.com
- BMI percentile calculator for children and adolescents: http://apps.nccd.cdc.gov/dnpabmi
- BMI calculator for adults: http://www.nhlbisupport.com/bmi

---

curves are used to detect deviations from previously established growth curves and to compare growth to the expected parameters of children of the same age and gender. (See Table 8.1 for the CDC BMI-for-age weight categories.)

BMI weight categories, nevertheless, have their limitations and are not to be "interpreted in isolation but in combination with other risk factors of morbidity and mortality" (WHO Expert Committee on Physical Status, 1995). Such categories are fundamentally arbitrary and do not account for an individual's ethnicity, pre-morbid weight history, frame size, and muscle mass, or, in the case of adults, gender. Still, BMI calculations provide a practical correlation between weight and height, and BMI-based categories provide clinical parameters that often are of value to clinicians (Flegal & Ogden, 2011).

We, and others, believe that the current NIH BMI weight categories for adults (Table 8.2) are problematic in many areas, particularly if applied indiscriminately to ED patients. These BMI categories underestimate the presumed health consequences of lower weights and overestimate the presumed health consequences of higher weights (Bacon & Aphramor, 2011; Copeland, Sacks, & Herzog, 1995, p. 121; Golden et al., 2008). Consequently, we have modified the NIH BMI categories so they are more clinically appropriate for assessing ED patients for

TABLE 8.1 CDC BMI-for-Age Weight Categories

Weight status category	Percentile range
Underweight	Less than the 5th percentile
Healthy weight	5th percentile to less than the 85th percentile
Overweight	85th percentile to less than the 95th percentile
Obese	Equal to or greater than the 95th percentile

TABLE 8.2 NIH BMI Weight Categories

Weight status category	BMI range
Underweight	Below 18.5 kg/m²
Healthy weight	18.5–24.9 kg/m²
Overweight	25–29.9 kg/m²
Obese	30 kg/m² or greater

TABLE 8.3   DSM-IV and DSM-5 Weight Categories for Diagnosis of Anorexia Nervosa

DSM-IV AN for adults	DSM-5 AN for adults
Less than 17.5 kg/m² Less than 85% of normal of Metropolitan Life Insurance tables	Less than 18.5 kg/m²
DSM-IV AN for children	*DSM-5 AN for children*
Less than 85% of expected of pediatric growth charts	Less than the 10th percentile in pediatric growth charts

weight-related problems. Our revisions (Table 8.3) are based on a thorough review of the literature and account for gender and musculature (American Psychiatric Association, 2010; Fairburn, 2008; Flegal, Graubard, Williamson, & Gail, 2007; Golden, et al., 2008; Swenne, 2008). We have used these revised BMI categories with success for over 15 years in our clinical practices.

As many patients are fully aware of how their weight corresponds to national BMI standards, we find it is therapeutic to explain the development and limitations of the NIH BMI categories. Until 1998, standard BMI categories considered men underweight with a BMI < 20.7 kg/m² and women underweight with a BMI < 19.1 kg/m². Men with a BMI ≥ 27.8 kg/m² and women with a BMI ≥ 27.3 kg/m² were considered overweight. In 1998, NIH lowered its BMI categories to match the international categories developed by the World Health Organization (WHO), despite the fact that WHO encouraged individual countries to make alterations in BMI categories to reflect different associations between BMI and health risks for their particular populations (WHO Expert Consultation, 2004).

We tell our patients we do not use the adult NIH BMI weight categories because these categories are used on a worldwide basis to primarily to assess the health of people living in developing countries. Since North Americans make up only 5% of the world's population and Asia and Africa account for over 75%, we feel that international BMI categories are not appropriate for evaluating the health of individuals living in the United States. However, we often consult the NIH BMI categories for patients of Asian descent.

We cite the number of recent studies of mortality rates in the United States which find that people in the overweight and obese NIH BMI categories have lower mortality rates than have been previously estimated (Flegal et al., 2007). Flegal et al. (2007) found the lowest all-cause mortality in the NIH BMI "overweight" category (BMI 25–29.9 kg/m²) even when compared to people in the "normal weight" category (18.5–24.9 kg/m²). We conclude that the differences in ethnicity, access to adequate food supplies, and health risks make the WHO and the indistinguishable NIH BMI weight categories not useful in the treatment of ED patients.

CDC BMI for Age–Weight Categories

Of note, the CDC percentile categories for children aged 2 to 20 years old are derived from studies of American children. Ironically, WHO has adopted and uses the U.S.-derived percentiles as worldwide growth standards for children and adolescents.

NIH BMI Weight Categories for Adults

Under the latest NIH guidelines (see Table 8.2) released in 2000, gender distinctions were removed and BMI categories lowered by about two BMI units (one unit is 7 lb). Now a BMI of 25 kg/m² or more is considered "overweight," and 30 kg/m² or more is considered "obese" for both men and women. When this change was enacted, 35 million more normal-weight Americans immediately were labeled as overweight. One of Herrin's patients said, "I went to sleep one night at a healthy weight and woke up the next morning overweight!"

DSM BMI Weight Categories

Although both DSM-IV and DSM-5 include BMI-based guidelines for diagnosis of AN (see Table 8.3), the proposed DSM-5 will leave the judgment of whether weight is inappropriately low to the clinician to evaluate in light of all relevant information, including frame size and weight history.

Ideal Body Weight

A recent review of current clinical and research practices identified 10 different methods in use to calculate ideal body weight (IBW) in the diagnosis of AN, each of which produced a different weight (Thomas, Roberto, & Brownell, 2009). These discrepancies varied as much as 15 lb for female patients and 25 lb for male patients. Furthermore, weight categories that are termed "healthy" or "ideal" (including IBW) are not strongly associated with health benefits; nor are there any data that prove any particular weight ranges are ideal (Flegal et al., 2007; Golden et al., 2008).

Nevertheless, since IBW is still widely used, it is useful to know how IBW might be calculated. A simple formula for calculating IBW that has been used since the mid-1970s, and has been virtually unchanged since, is given in Box 8.6. The formula's purpose at the time was to provide a calculation for estimating weight-based dosages for medication (Pai & Paloucek, 2000).

BOX 8.6 APPLYING THE IDEAL BODY WEIGHT FORMULA TO EATING DISORDERS

The well-respected clinician and researcher Philip S. Mehler, MD (Mehler, Winkelman, Andersen, & Gaudiani, 2010) argues that, although the IBW formula is dated and does not reflect ethnicity and age, it is a reasonable estimate. Mehler classifies ED patients as mild, moderate, severe, or critical based on whether they are 10%, 20%, 30%, or more below IBW, respectively.

For women: allow 100 lb for the first 5 feet and 5 lb for each additional inch

For men: allow 110 lb for the first 5 feet and 5 lb for each additional inch.

Revised BMI Weight Categories

Our revised BMI weight categories are given in Table 8.4. Readers will notice that many of the revised categories overlap, accounting for the wide variation in individuals and reminding us that even the revised BMI weight categories are arbitrary. Next we elucidate the research and clinical experiences we used in the development of these weight categories: risky low weight, low weight, minimum

TABLE 8.4 Revised BMI Weight Categories

Weight status category	Percentile range
Children and adolescents	
Risky low weight	Less than the 10th percentile
Low weight	10th percentile to the 25th percentile
Minimum safe weight	25th percentile to the 50th percentile
Safe weight	25th percentile to the 85th percentile
Risky high weight	Equal to or greater than the 95th percentile
Adult females	
Risky low weight	Below $18.5 \, \text{kg/m}^2$
Low weight	18.5–$19.9 \, \text{kg/m}^2$
Minimum safe weight	20–$24.9 \, \text{kg/m}^2$
Safe weight	20–$29.9 \, \text{kg/m}^2$
Risky high weight	$30 \, \text{kg/m}^2$ or greater
Adult Males	
Risky low weight	Below $20 \, \text{kg/m}^2$
Low weight	20–$24.9 \, \text{kg/m}^2$
Minimum safe weight	22–$30 \, \text{kg/m}^2$
Safe weight	25–$34.9 \, \text{kg/m}^2$
Risky high weight	$35 \, \text{kg/m}^2$ or greater

safe weights, safe weights, and risky high weights. We also say a few words about using BMI weight categories in individuals who do not fit neatly in to the usual categories, i.e. menopausal women, muscular women, adult men, and members of many ethnic groups.

Risky Low Weight Category

Risky low weights are defined as below the 10th percentile for children and adolescents, and below $18.5\,kg/m^2$ for women and below $20\,kg/m^2$ for men. These parameters match the DSM-5 proposed BMI guidelines for AN for children and adolescents and women (see p. 184 for BMIs of adult men). Risky low weights are associated with the likelihood of medical instability and of long-term health consequences. For outpatients who enter treatment at or fall below a risky low weight limit, a higher level of care should be seriously considered (see Chapter 7: Levels of Care, pp. 150–166).

Low Weight Category

Low weights are defined as between the 10th percentile to the 25th percentile for children and adolescents, $18.5–19.9\,kg/m^2$ for women, and $20–24.9\,kg/m^2$ for men. Low weights are usually associated with stable medical status. Most adolescent and adult females will not have initiation or resumption of menses at lower weights. This is a weight at which a higher level of care is usually not considered unless there are extenuating circumstances, such as: instability in vital signs and laboratory findings, unremitting ED behaviors, or restoration of body weight stymies. It cannot be over emphasized that low-weight patients who are treated as outpatients need regular medical monitoring to ensure that continued outpatient treatment is prudent. Low-weight limits are often used as interim treatment goals (see Chapter 9: Restoring Weight, pp. 191–228).

Minimum Safe Weight Category

Minimum safe weights are defined as between the 25th percentile to the 50th percentile for children and adolescents, $20–24.9\,kg/m^2$ for women, and $22–30\,kg/m^2$ for men. We define the minimum safe weight as the lowest weight at which a patient can maintain healthy function and growth, meet nutritional needs, and experience a substantial decline in ED behaviors and thinking. In children and adolescents, a minimum safe weight would be consistent with each patient's pre-morbid growth curve.

Safe Weight Category

Safe weights are defined as between the 25th percentile to the 85th percentile for children and adolescents, $20–29.9\,kg/m^2$ for women, and $25–34.9\,kg/m^2$ for men. In our clinical experience, BAW usually falls into the safe-weight category. The wide range of weights in this category accounts for genetic and ethnic differences.

Risky High Weight

Risky high weights are defined as equal to or greater than the 95th percentile for children and adolescents, 30kg/m^2 or greater for women, and 35kg/m^2 or greater for men. We struggled most with setting limits for the risky high weight category, as there is little evidence that BMI in higher weight patients is a scientifically-based proxy for health. For example, Wildman et al. (2008) analyzed a nationally representative sample of Americans for cardiovascular abnormalities and found that 50% of overweight people and 30% of obese people were healthy, while 25% of normal-weight Americans had cardiovascular abnormalities. We have known patients who fall into our "safe weight" category but have high blood pressure, blood cholesterol, and blood sugars, and we have patients in the "risky high weight" category who are healthy on these measures. Clinically, we try to assess each patient individually, taking into account pre-morbid weight or growth curve, food behaviors, and mental and medical status. We have treated BED patients who fall into our risky high weight category and have well-established weight-related problems (i.e., type 2 diabetes, hypertension, cardiovascular disease, joint problems, breathing problems). Our patients who lose 5–10% of their body weight, but remain in the risky high weight category, report significantly improved blood pressure, blood cholesterol, and blood sugar levels. With weight loss in the range 10–15%, patients report improvements in sleep apnea and joint pain. These results match published reports of moderate weight loss leading to reductions in risk factors for a wide range of weight-related illnesses (Lindström et al., 2003; Wing et al., 2011).

Menopause

In postmenopausal women, we adjust BMI weight categories up by one to two BMI units (about 7 lb) to account for expected weight gain at this time (Sowers et al., 2007). Sue, in Case Example 8.3, is a good example.

CASE EXAMPLE 8.3: SUE

Sue, who had suffered from AN since age 25 years, managed to keep her BMI between 19 and 20 kg/m^2 until she went through the menopause in her mid-fifties. Eating virtually the same, she steadily gained weight over 2 years. Sue's BMI was 23 kg/m^2 when she saw me out of frustration: Her weight was higher than it had ever been, but Sue did not want to reduce her caloric intake. We worked on variety and balance but left her 1,500 calorie intake the same. Sue's weight stabilized but she did not lose weight. Hearing about the biological drive in the menopause to protect the female body from heart and bone disease helped her eventually to accept a higher postmenopausal weight.

Muscular Females

We are likely to consult the adult male BMI weight categories when assessing BMI or formulating weight goals for muscular female patients. Athletic or muscular females often do not resume menses until reaching a BMI of at least $22\,kg/m^2$, two BMI units higher than usually predicted for females (Christo et al., 2008). Our clinical experiences and the research on this issue leads us to conclude that a BMI between 22 and $30\,kg/m^2$ is an appropriate minimum safe weight for muscular women (Ode, Pivarnik, Reeves, & Knous, 2007). As is our standard practice, if menses do not return within 3 months of maintaining a minimum BMI, estimation of BAW should be reassessed and, most likely, raised by 5 lb.

Adult Males

Because the NIH does not provide gender-specific BMI categories for adults, epidemiologists have recommended that clinicians use a BMI that is two to three units higher in adult males than is indicated by the NIH for adults (Gallagher, Visser, Sepúlveda, Pierson, Harris, & Heymsfield, 1996). This increase in BMI units accounts for the greater muscle mass and heavier bones that most males have compared to females. Our clinical experiences, coupled with the research on this issue, led us to conclude that a BMI between $22\,kg/m^2$ and $30\,kg/m^2$ is a more appropriate range for defining minimum safe weights for men. As is our standard practice, if normalized testosterone levels do not return within 3 months of maintaining a minimum BMI, BAW should be reassessed and, most likely, raised by 5 pounds.

Again our patient Jake (see Case Example 8.2) is a good example of low testosterone levels, indicating that his weight is below the BAW. Jake's BMI is $27.3\,kg/m^2$ and falls into the standard BMI category for overweight in adults ($25–29.9\,kg/m^2$). At a BMI of $26\,kg/m^2$, which falls into our BMI category of "safe weight" for men, Jake had all the signs of malnutrition. We estimate that Jake's BAW is at least a BMI of $27\,kg/m^2$.

Ethnicity

WHO and others have documented evidence that suggests that Asian populations have different associations between BMI and health risks than do Caucasians (WHO Expert Consultation, 2004). Specifically, Asians are healthier at lower BMIs but tend to develop weight-related illnesses at lower than expected BMIs. We agree with the WHO recommendation to use NIH BMI "normal" category for Asian adult females, namely a BMI of $18.5–24.9\,kg/m^2$. We estimated that BAW for Aspera, in Case Example 8.4, was below the lower limit of the NIH BMI "healthy weight" category.

CASE EXAMPLE 8.4: ASPERA AND SHAUNIQUA

Aspera, a Thai college student, came for an evaluation because her counselor was worried that she was too thin at 16.5 kg/m². Aspera believes her weight has been stable since she was 17. She is now 20 years old and reports that her age of menarche was 12, she is menstruating regularly, is not on oral contraceptives, eats three large meals a day and a bedtime snack, exercises rarely, and comes from a family of thin people. Recent lab results (blood chemistry, CBC, celiac screen, and thyroid) are all normal. We explained to her counselor that our hunch is that Aspera is genetically and culturally programmed to be healthy at her current weight. Shauniqua, also a college student, is African American. She was hospitalized with cardiac abnormalities after losing 30 lb at 21 kg/m². Cardiac function didn't return to normal until Shauniqua's BMI reached 26 kg/m².

Hispanic and African American women have lower percent body fat at higher BMI than do Caucasian women, implying that women of these ethnic groups are healthier at higher weights (Rahman & Berenson, 2010). Unfortunately, no published research can be found on recommendations for revising BMI categories for African American or Hispanic populations. The heart problems that Shauniqua (see Case Example 8.4), experienced show the need for appreciating the necessity of considering higher BMI, especially in African American or Hispanic patients.

Fluctuations and Ranges

Body weights fluctuate for a variety of reasons. Weight can vary by as much as 5 lb within 24 hours with no change in energy balance (Lask & Frampton, 2009). Weights taken first thing in the morning are generally 5 lb lighter than weights measured before bed. Other variables are "time of the month," type of clothes, in season/out of season for athletes, hydration, timing of meals and exercise, bowel habits, variances between scales, and measurement error. One of Herrin's patients dropped 5 lb because she had cut off her heavy dreadlocks. Weight maintenance has been defined in a variety of ways (a range of 2–11 lb; a range equal to 5–10% of body weight; and a range of one BMI unit), yet the field lacks an agreed upon variation in weight that indicates weight maintenance (Stevens, Truesdale, McClain, & Cai, 2006). We do not presume to know or to be able to calculate a weight range for our patients. Instead, we feel more confident that we can predict a minimum weight above which patients will range according to their individual tendencies. We have been in the untenable clinical situation of working with patients who have previously been given a weight range and have become anxious about nearing the "top of my range."

At the risk of being redundant, we remind our readers that our limits and goals should not be used arbitrarily or simplistically, but be taken into consideration along with each patient's particular situation. We often remind ourselves, "Until we get to know the patient, we cannot predict about weight goals." (For more on weight goals for underweight patients see Chapter 9: Restoring Weight, pp. 191–228.)

Weight Checks

Weight monitoring provides concrete evidence about the impact of the patient's food and exercise behaviors on body weight. When weight gain is a goal of treatment, weight changes are essential indicators of medical status and treatment progress. We practice what Fairburn (2008, p. 63) calls "collaborative weighing." In other words, the nutrition counselor and patient check weight together in a "calm and matter-of-fact manner." Patients are discouraged but not "forbidden" from checking weight themselves between sessions, but if weight is checked at home it should be reported. Patients usually discover that leaving weight monitoring to treatment sessions makes it easier to practice normal eating and exercise.

Data from weight monitoring sets the stage for therapeutic discussions. We invite patients to explore thoughts, feelings, and fears about their weight. And in return we provide objective feedback, advice, and information. Weight data also helps dispel common misconceptions about diet and weight interactions, such as eating dessert, fat, or increasing calories necessarily causes weight gain. Patients also learn that, when weight is up 1 lb it does not indicate weight gain. We remind patients that trends in body weight take at least 4 weeks to be clear (Fairburn, 2008, p. 63). Restricting weight checks to office visits also teaches patients to tolerate some degree of uncertainty about their weights.

Weight monitoring reassures underweight patients that weight gain is not too fast or too much and is under the control of a skilled and trustworthy professional. In normal-weight patients, weight monitoring can also provide reassurance. Such patients are often anxious that weight will increase as a result of normalizing eating and exercise behaviors. They benefit from having factual data.

Patients typically become fraught with ambivalence, anxiety, and resistance when weight monitoring is addressed. If weight issues are ignored, however, patients may feel their concerns are not being taken seriously. Involving patients as active participants in the management of their weight is an effective antidote to these feelings, as long as involvement does not include renegotiating clinically-determined weight goals (see Chapter 9: Restoring Weight, pp. 213–214). Cloak and Powers (2010) advise that, when dealing with weight issues, counselors "attend to both sides of the conflict." This can be done by expressing concern about the patient's well-being and about whether the patient may feel coerced, controlled, or misunderstood. Cloak and Powers (2010) further recommend that counselors state their rationale for treatment decisions, such as goal weights, but do not insist that patients have to agree. Asking the patient, "How can we deal with this?" may help develop and preserve the therapeutic alliance. The nutrition counselor should keep in mind that the patient's self-esteem is based heavily, and often exclusively, on the ability to control weight and shape and that he or she has internalized media messages that portray attractive, successful people as unrealistically thin.

Introducing Weight Checks

Weight monitoring should be sensitively introduced and conducted. We approach weight monitoring as a standard part of practice for underweight patients, but we make it optional for normal-weight patients. In reality, most patients expect to be weighed as part of treatment. Like Fairburn (2008), we recognize that, if we accede to a fearful patient's plea to forego the in-office weight checks, rarely will the patient agree later in treatment to weight monitoring (p. 55). We explain to patients that weight monitoring is essential because "the weight check is how your body speaks to me about how it is reacting to our treatment plan."

Discussions about the benefits of weight monitoring and the various ways weight can be monitored can help patients feel included in the treatment process. Patients may argue against weight monitoring, claiming it will increase their anxiety. We assure patients that increases in obsessive thinking stirred up by weight checks usually dissipate in short-order. We explain that office weight checks provide accurate measurements of body weight (home scales are rarely accurate or reliable) and help patients resist the compulsion to self-check multiple times during the week or even multiple times over the course of a day. When a carefully spelled-out rationale as to the necessity of office weight checks is provided, most patients agree, albeit reluctantly for some, to forego self-weight checks.

In our many years of treatment, we have had only one patient refuse to have her weight checked. As this girl was at a dangerously low weight, we could not in good conscience agree to provide nutrition treatment without reliable weight data measured in our office or by another treatment provider.

Procedure for Weight Checks

At an initial visit, first spend time taking the patient's history, establishing a relationship, and summarizing the scope of treatment, including purpose of weight checks. Well before the end of this visit, outline the "whys and hows" of weight monitoring, allotting time to weigh the patient near the end of the visit. At subsequent visits, greeting the patient and moving directly to a weight check provides the information the nutrition counselor needs to have a productive session and makes it less likely the patient will be distracted by anxiety about the upcoming weigh-in. Some patients, however, may prefer first to have the opportunity to interact before the weight check.

It is standard outpatient protocol to check weight at each nutrition visit. Stable patients may benefit from less frequent checks (e.g., monthly). In AN, patients are weighed at least weekly. Very low-weight patients may need weight checks every several days. It is a common practice to weigh ED patients standing on the scale backwards (also called "blind" weight checks). This approach keeps the patient from seeing his or her weight in the hope of making body weight and weight checking more neutral and to keep the patient less focused on the number on the scale. Another approach is an open weight check in which the patient stands forward on the scale seeing the number.

We make a decision based on discussions with each patient, and the particulars of her or his situation, whether to weigh a patient "backwards" or "frontwards." Our usual approach is to discuss the pros and cons of both methods and to let the patient decide. We usually say, "It is up to you, we can try it one way, and if you don't like it we can do it the other way. If you choose backwards weight checks, I would never keep the number from you if you wanted to know. The one thing I won't do is tell you your weight at the end of a session. We need the option of having plenty of time to discuss it." As treatment progresses, desensitize patients to weight issues by routinely conducting frontwards weight checks. Of note, there is not much benefit in backwards weighing a patient who insists on checking her or his own weight.

Weight checks are best done in a private room or in screened off area and early in each session to allow plenty of opportunity for the patient to discuss feelings and thoughts about the weigh-in. Use either balance-beam scales, which can be easily calibrated, or research-quality electronic scales. To avoid embarrassing higher weight patients, we recommend high-quality professional scales, which can weigh patients to 600 lb or more, rather than the more typical scale limit of 250 lb.

Ideally, patients are weighed on the same regularly calibrated scale after they have voided and at about the same time of day. In actual outpatient practice, it may not be possible to have parents void or to schedule weight checks at the same time of day. Keep in mind that a full bladder and a bowel movement can contribute 1–2 lb of weight, and that body weight increases over the course of a day by as much as 5 lb from morning to night. Fluid retention associated with a woman's menstrual cycle can account for 2–5 lb. We note at each weight check: the time of day; whether the patient used the bathroom prior to the weight check; and whether the patient wore a gown or dress, shorts, or pants. Because even individual good quality scales vary in accuracy and appointments may occur at varying times of day, team members should be hesitant to compare weights taken on different scales at different times of day.

Patients who need to gain weight should be weighed in a gown (also known as a patient gown or johnny) with only underwear on underneath so that even modest changes in weight can be gauged. In normal-weight patients, street clothes can be worn, though some patients may prefer to wear a gown. Street clothes (with shoes, jackets and other similar outer garments removed and pockets emptied of keys, wallets, cell phones, etc.) typically weigh 2 lb for women and 3–4 lb for men. A gown weighs 0.3-0.5 lb.

Use of BMI requires that height be accurately measured. In as much as self-reported heights are not likely to be accurate, re-check each patient's height. Because height changes rapidly in young patients, height should be reassessed every 3–6 months (Golden, Jacobson, Schebendach, Solanto, Hertz, & Shenker,, 1997). In severe AN, which can cause growth and height retardation, projected height rather than measured height, should be used when assessing weight (Golden et al., 2008).

We advise against using a scale's height-measuring rod because it is easily bent. If it is used, patients should stand backwards on the scale. The recommended method for measuring height is to attach either a height-measuring device or non-stretchable measuring tape or stick to a wall. Instruct patients to remove their shoes, face away from the wall, stand "tall" with their heels together, and look straight ahead. The patient's heels, buttocks, shoulders, and head should touch the wall. Place a book, block, or ruler on top of the patient's head and at a right angles to the wall. In the event the patient is tall, stand on a stool to ensure an accurate measurement.

Discussing Weight Checks

Inferences about trends in body weight should be based on no less than four weekly weigh-ins. Graphing or charting weight helps identify trends. As most ED patients tend to overreact to changes on the scale, it is crucial that communication about trends in body weight be approached in a collaborative and matter-of-fact manner. Fairburn (2008) emphasizes to patients that "one cannot interpret a single reading" on the scale (p. 63). In our underweight patients, however, we "micromanage" weight changes. We "overreact" to weight drops and "underreact" to weight gains. It is important for backwards-weighed patients to receive at least general feedback about their weight, but we try to be non-specific about how much weight has varied. These matter-of-fact, but somewhat vague, responses help patients focus on their food plans and not their weight. Feedback, such as "Your weight is within your range," is appropriate for patients who are in weight maintenance. We often say "looks like we need to tweak your food plan" to patients whose weight check indicates an unintended trend.

Summary Points

- It is usually the nutrition counselor's responsibility to assess and monitor weights, as well as to use weight as a gauge of the adequacy of a particular food plan.
- Obtaining an accurate weight history is an important assessment tool. Knowing that self-reported weights are the least valuable, the nutrition counselor

should obtain child and adolescent growth curves and adult weights, as well as, for women, a menstrual history from the patient's medical provider.

- BMI is somewhat arbitrary and does not account for an individual's ethnicity, pre-morbid weight history, frame size, muscle mass, and gender in adults. Despite these limitations, BMI-based definitions provide practical guidelines that are of clinical value.
- BAW is a weight that is easily maintained without the practice of dieting or other inappropriate food and exercise behaviors. BAW reflects pre-morbid weight, normal physical and psychological function, genetic predisposition (ethnicity), gender, and family history.
- Weight checks provide concrete evidence about the impact of the patient's food and exercise behaviors on body weight. When weight gain is a goal of treatment, weight changes are essential indicators of the patient's medical status and treatment progress.

9

RESTORING WEIGHT

Introduction

We begin this chapter by defining weight restoration and by describing the well-documented metabolic and physical challenges to weight restoration. Next, we discuss the four phases of the weight restoration protocol we have developed over the course of years of clinical practice. We also include a detailed section on the art and science of setting weight goals. The chapter concludes with a discussion of weight restoring food planning based on the rule of threes food plan [(RO3s) detailed in Chapter 5: Food Planning] and other approaches that support weight restoration.

Definitions and Descriptions

Weight restoration is signified by the carefree maintenance of a healthy stable body weight and is fundamental to recovery from AN. Weight restoration also restores physical, emotional, and cognitive function and resolves most medical complications. Although weight restoration alone is not sufficient to assure full psychological recovery, a biologically appropriate weight [(BAW) see Chapter 8: Assessing Weight, pp. 169–190] is essential for recovery from the cognitive and emotional symptoms characteristic of an ED. An expeditious approach to weight restoration prevents disordered eating behaviors (restriction, bingeing, and purging) and compulsive exercise behaviors from becoming entrenched. When weight is restored, patients are able to eat a wider variety of foods and they exhibit less obsessive food-related thoughts and behaviors.

Of note, outpatient providers are treating more low-weight AN patients in part because insurance companies are now, more than ever, limiting admissions to and lengths of stay at inpatient eating disorders programs. Previously, low-weight patients were routinely treated as inpatients.

Challenges to Weight Restoration

The Caloric Conundrum

The "caloric conundrum" in AN is that caloric needs are low in the weight-loss phase but high in the weight-gain phase. Basal metabolic rate prior to weight restoration treatment is lower than would be predicted for subjects of similar height, weight, and age (Golden & Meyer, 2004). Changes in thyroid hormones, adrenal hormones, leptin, and the loss of lean body mass are major contributors to the drop in metabolism (El Ghoch, Alberti, Capelli, Calugi, & Dalle Grave, 2012). Patients have reported to us that intakes as low as 300 calories/day maintains their weight. The restrictiveness required to maintain weight loss does not prepare patients for the prospect that they will need to increase substantially caloric intake to gain weight. The calories needed to sustain weight gain have been documented up to 4,500 calories/day (Mehler, Winkelman, Andersen, & Gaudiani, 2010). Once caloric intake improves, metabolic rate increases almost immediately.

Bottom line: Most patients need to consume substantial amounts of calories to gain weight. As occasionally a patient will be able to gain weight on normal (rather than elevated) caloric intake, it is important to discuss this possibility as well. Mehler, Winkelman, Andersen, & Gaudiani (2010) found some patients gaining on 1,800 calories/day. Patients for whom this is the case can be reassured with statements like, "You are lucky your metabolism appears to be unaffected by your ED."

Famine Metabolism

Directing patients to imagine a "famine in the land" and the associated compulsory hunt for food can help them grasp the effect food restriction has on the body and behavior. We explain that essential to surviving famine is the capacity to make metabolic adaptations and behave appropriately. In a famine, food becomes of utmost interest and is consumed when available. The body aims to keep metabolism low and to increase body fat stores in order to survive the next famine. "You are on high alert; all of your focus is on food. If you see food, you are interested in it because there are no guarantees about when you will eat again. The smart thing to do is to eat as much as you possibly can. Your body is smart, too. Famine lowers your body's metabolism so that when you feast, which you do whenever you can, your body is able to store many of the calories you eat as fat. The body does this so that you are ready and able to survive the next famine which will surely come." Box 9.1 describes the Keys' starvation studies which further illustrates this point.

BOX 9.1 STARVATION STUDY

Familiarity with Keys' classic study of starved young male conscientious objectors during World War II provides ample data on the effect of starvation on physical and mental functioning and food behavior (Keys et al., 1950). Keys' study is often used to illustrate that most symptoms associated with anorexia nervosa and bulimia are the result of starvation.

Keys' subjects entered the study in good physical and psychological health. After 6 months of consuming one-half of their normal food intake, the subjects exhibited labile mood, cognitive dysfunction, poor concentration, social withdrawal, obsessive and ritualized eating behaviors, insatiable appetites, binge eating, food cravings, apathy, anxiety, depression, irritability, and frequent outbursts of anger. These young men became negative, argumentative, and withdrawn, and developed low self-esteem and relationship problems. Physical changes included: hair loss, gastrointestinal discomfort, edema, dizziness, headaches, increased fatigue, cold intolerance, lowered body temperature, decreased heart and metabolic rates, and decreased need for sleep. Cognitive changes included: impaired concentration, comprehension, and alertness. Food became the principal topic of conversation, reading, and daydreams. Food behaviors changed; of note were an increased interest in cooking, an inordinate amount of time spent meal planning, food hoarding, increased gum chewing, increased consumption of liquids, and eventual bingeing. A very readable summary of Keys' study can be found in *Garner and Garfinkel's Handbook of Treatment for Eating Disorders* (2nd ed.; Garner & Garfinkel, 1997, pp. 153–161).

Refeeding Syndrome

Another challenge during the first two weeks of improved food intake and weight restoration is the risk of refeeding syndrome. Patients at risk typically present with abdominal pain, nausea, vomiting, abdominal distention, and abnormal blood chemistries. Ironically, this potentially fatal syndrome is triggered by improvements in metabolism, tissue repair and cellular turnover which, in turn, increases nutrient needs and depletes already low stores to dangerous levels (Setnick, 2010). Particularly at risk are patients who have not eaten for 5 to 10 days; who weigh less than 70% of ideal body weight; or who are aggressively refed by feeding tube or total parental nutrition (TPN). A history of abuse of alcohol, drugs, insulin, antacids, or diuretics increases risk (Mehler & Andersen, 2010). Refeeding syndrome is associated with sudden and unexplained death, presumably secondary to cardiac arrhythmia. Sudden onset of abdominal pain, nausea, vomiting, and abdominal distention can indicate dilation of the stomach which can also be fatal.

Abdominal pain, nausea, and vomiting can indicate pancreatitis, another complication seen in early refeeding.

Also catastrophic, but less common, are rapid increases in serum sodium in undernourished patients in early refeeding. A spike in sodium levels may cause central pontine myelinolysis (CPM), destruction of the myelin sheath covering nerve cells in the brainstem. Early symptoms are difficulty speaking and swallowing. At its most severe, coma and death are possible (Mehler et al., 2010).

Patients with concerning levels of liver enzymes are usually monitored in a hospital and prescribed a reduced carbohydrate and dextrose diet (Stanga et al., 2008). Unusually high levels of liver enzymes (i.e., aspartate aminotransferase (AST), alanine aminotransferase (ALT), alkaline phosphatase and bilirubin) are not likely to be dangerous unless they reach three times normal values. In such circumstances, the risk is of hepatic steatosis (fat accumulation in liver cells).

Low-weight patients can experience post-prandial hypoglycemia due to malnutrition. In this situation, the liver having been depleted of glycogen cannot manage the elevated insulin response to increased food intake. Symptoms are faintness, sweating, and pallor several hours after eating meals. Usually the symptoms are relatively mild and can be used as evidence of improved food intake but incomplete recovery. Consuming a sweet drink (i.e. juice, sweetened tea, "real" soda) or a small sweet dessert usually alleviates these symptoms.

Edema is common, but usually only a minor problem, as insulin production increases with improved food intake (Mehler & Andersen, 2010). Insulin, however, increases sodium retention which, in very low-weight patients, can cause heart failure. One indicator of concerning fluid problems is weight gain greater than two to three pounds a week in patients who are not constipated. Another sign is stretched, puffy skin or skin that retains a dimple after being pressed for several seconds in ankles or shins (indicating edema). Blood chemistry levels of potassium, phosphorous, magnesium, sodium, glucose, and liver enzymes should be checked as often as daily in early treatment of very underweight patients (Mehler et al., 2010). With consistent weight gain and normal values, testing is gradually reduced. We find discussions about edema and blood chemistry as measures of medical risk or recovery help motivate our patients. For example, we tell our patients that dropping levels of potassium, phosphorous, or magnesium usually mean that muscle is being synthesized. Next, we emphasize, muscle restoration will not commence without adequate consumption of these nutrients and enough calories.

There are two reasons inpatients are more likely to be at risk for refeeding syndrome than outpatients. Inpatients tend to be more malnourished than outpatients. Inpatients programs are able to improve food intake quickly compared to outpatient nutrition counselors, who have to take a more cooperative approach. Although with the development of more aggressive outpatient feeding methods, namely, family-based therapy (FBT; see Chapter 13: Working with Families, pp. 277–298), and the rise of low-weight patients in outpatient settings, outpatient counselors may well be faced with patients at risk for refeeding syndrome. It is imperative to proceed with caution when refeeding very low-weight patients by increasing calories gradually every 24 to 48 hours in 100 to 300 calorie increments and insisting on frequent medical monitoring (Boateng, Sriram, Meguid, & Crook, 2010; Golden & Meyer, 2004; Mehler & Andersen, 2010). Weight, vital signs, and fluid and electrolyte levels should be measured frequently in the first several weeks. Nutrition counselors should be alert to patient reports of symptoms that may indicate this dangerous syndrome.

Although a number of protocols designed to prevent refeeding syndrome can be found, at the time of writing no evidenced-based research supports specific caloric guidelines that protect against refeeding syndrome. Protocols for refeeding range from an initial rate of 10 to 60 calories/kg (Kohn, Madden, & Clarke, 2011; Waterhous & Jacob, 2011). The use of specific vitamin or mineral supplements as preventative measures for refeeding syndrome is not yet established as efficacious due to limited evidence and lack of clinical consensus (Lock & Fitzpatrick, 2009). The judicious approach of suggesting a multiple vitamin and mineral supplement (which helps ensure adequate phosphate, thiamin, and magnesium intake) is recommended by the Academy of Nutrition and Dietetics in a 2011 practice paper, Nutrition Intervention in the Treatment of Eating Disorders (Waterhous & Jacob, 2011). It is clear that requirements for phosphate, thiamin, and magnesium increase during refeeding because of their essential roles in carbohydrate metabolism. Another approach is to keep carbohydrate intake to 50 to 60% of calories to help minimize phosphate depletion (Khan et al., 2011). Higher carbohydrate intakes early in refeeding can shift phosphate into intracellular space and into newly synthesized tissue leading to hypophosphatemia. Hypophosphatemia increases the heart's vulnerability to arrhythmias and heart failure. Binge eating in patients with AN also creates risk of hypophosphatemia.

Gastrointestinal Discomfort

Since various gastrointestinal (GI) symptoms are corollaries of EDs, most patients have been plagued with GI discomfort since the onset of the disorder. Moreover, even normal sensations of satiety and other normal gastrointestinal sensations may be experienced as unpleasant by AN patients. Additionally, most AN patients experience significant gastric discomfort with improved food intake. These symptoms may make patients "feel fat" leading to limitation of food intake or purging (see Chapter 11: Managing Purging, pp. 246–259). In patients consuming a vegetarian diet high in fiber, bloating can be severe. Forewarning patients helps them tolerate the symptoms associated with refeeding (i.e., early satiety, delayed gastric emptying (DGE), bloating, indigestion, abdominal pain, constipation, and excessive gas). Heartburn, nausea, and vomiting are less common, but do occur. We stress that most acute GI symptoms resolve within four to six weeks as eating patterns normalize and weight restored.

Some helpful strategies for early satiety and DGE are to eat smaller meals more frequently; to use high calorie liquids instead of solid foods especially early in a meal; and to decrease fruit, vegetable and fiber intake (Mehler & Andersen, 2010). Very compromised patients may experience symptoms of low blood pressure or "early" dumping syndrome (i.e., epigastric fullness, flushing, and faintness) after meals. In such cases, we recommend rest after meals and visualization of the body readjusting to improved food intake. "Your tummy is doing the best it can."

Constipation is common among anorexics and can become a preoccupation for some. Chronic constipation is caused by restricted food intake, restriction of fluids, or overuse of laxatives. Certain medications used to treat co-morbid diseases may also cause constipation, namely, tricylic antidepressants. Hypokalemia and hypomagnesemia as a result of malnutrition or purging may slow colonic transit time and interfere with nerve function in the bowel wall also contributing to constipation. Some AN patients with constipation are diagnosed with disordered rectal evacuation; a condition that improves with refeeding (Hadley, 2003; Waldholtz & Andersen, 1990). Like other GI symptoms, bowel functions normalize within three to four weeks of following a food plan and with steady weight gain. We inform our patients that normal bowel patterns range from two to three times per day to two to three times per week and that it is "normal" for reduced food intake to result in less frequent bowel movements and constipation (Mehler & Andersen, 2010). We ensure that our constipated patients have six to eight cups of fluid per day but only rarely do we suggest an increase fiber due to risk of bloating. Before laxatives of any kind are prescribed, AN patients should be evaluated for potentially serious GI complications such as gastric dilation, bowel impaction, and gallstones. We, therefore, usually leave questions about using over the counter (OTC) bulking or fiber-containing laxatives to medical providers. We also keep in mind that patients with EDs can have other medical explanations for GI complaints unrelated to the ED. We are quick to refer for medical evaluation any patient who has unremitting diarrhea, constipation, or abdominal pain.

We use complaints about constipation as an opportunity to educate about the dangers of laxatives and their ineffectiveness in reducing caloric absorption (Steffen, Mitchell, Roerig, & Lancaster, 2007; see Chapter 11: Managing Purging, pp. 246–259). In the final analysis, our job is to help patients come to understand that whatever gastric sensations they are experiencing, these must be tolerated, as food intake must be increased.

Changes in Body Shape and Size

Weight restoration magnifies patients' underlying dissatisfaction and distortion of their body size and shape. Patients' fears of weight gain are intensified by the inherent overestimate body size and weight in AN. On the other hand, patients are happy to know that when they feel less sensitive to cold it is a sign that muscle mass is being restored and that muscle restores before fat mass. We mention the research of Forbes et al. (Forbes, Kreipe, Lipinski, & Hodgman, 1984) which showed that about two-thirds of weight restored during the acute phase of re-feeding of adolescents with restrictive AN was lean body mass.

We frequently hear complaints about how huge a patient feels subsequent to gaining minimal amounts of weight. Most disconcerting is abdominal weight gain. A number of studies show that weight restoration in AN leads eventually to fat deposits to the abdomen, a hypersensitive area for most patients (Mayer et al., 2009). Adolescents are less likely than adults to experience the increase in central adiposity, but we have seen this phenomenon in our teenaged patients (Misra et al., 2003). The good news is that abdominal weight redistributes to normal after BAW (Biologically Appropriate Weight) weight is maintained for at least a year (Lund et al., 2009; Mayer et al., 2009). We empathize with our patients about the initial abdominal changes and reassure them that this body change is common and normalizes with recovery. We often commiserate by saying, "I can't think of anything that would make recovery harder than to have weight restoration show up first on your tummy. I know this is hard now but also I know from the research and from working with other patients that it always goes away with recovery."

Changes in Hunger and Fullness

Patients complain that eating according to a weight restoration food plan leaves them in a constant state of uncomfortable fullness and never hungry. We respond that it takes significant time before normal appetite returns. Hunger and fullness signals are not likely to return until weight is nearly restored. Making gradual increases in food plans or moving to smaller portions eaten more frequently helps at least a little to alleviate uncomfortable fullness. Reducing dietary fiber and adding lower volume but calorie-dense foods helps as well. In the meantime, we advise "eating by the clock." We reiterate with sympathy about how difficult it is to increase calories when one feels full.

Sensations of hunger do eventually return. Patients tell us that this phenomenon feels like a voracious hunger lurking just below the surface destining them to binge-eat unless they carefully restrict food intake. The hunger, more than likely, is the body's way of ensuring that there are enough nutrients and calories to begin the backlog of biological repair work (and growth in younger patients) that was put on hold during periods of undereating. Together with the patient, we revisit the food plan and consider whether urges to overeat indicate lack of compliance or that the food plan is no longer adequate (see The Rule of Threes Food Plan, pp. 108–109). If we conclude the food plan is inadequate, adjustments must be made immediately by augmenting intake by 200 to 300 calories. If overeating occurs because of undereating, we urge a quick return to the food plan and to immediately report any future episodes.

Urges to binge may be especially acute when food intake is first augmented, particularly if only minimal improvements are made. AN patients will remain at high risk for binge eating until their caloric intake begins to approach biological needs. When AN patients binge, the amounts eaten are generally considerably less than is characteristic of an authentic binge (an amount of food definitely larger than most people would eat; Peat, Mitchell, Hoek, & Wonderlich, 2009). Patients, nevertheless, are quite distressed about these episodes, which may be as insignificant as eating one unplanned cookie. They will report feeling out-of-control and guilty for consuming more than they usually do or for eating foods they used to make a point of avoiding. Whether AN patients act on their urge to binge or not, the fear of succumbing reinforces restrictive eating patterns. We explain that binge eating is *a natural response* to undereating and low-body weight. We have found it most effective to respond with concern about binge eating behaviors, no matter how insignificant the caloric contribution of the binge eating. Not surprisingly, AN patients abhor binge eating and are often very embarrassed about it. One strategy is to present the RO3s plan as a protection against bingeing. We also remind our patients that weight gain prevents binge eating.

AN patients may come into treatment with purging behaviors, or purging may develop as a compensatory response to the onset of bingeing. Patients with a longer duration of AN are more likely to exhibit purging behaviors than those with a shorter duration ED (Miller et al, 2005). Many AN patients will stop compensatory purging spontaneously, without having to addressed it in treatment, when bingeing stops (Fairburn, 2008). We remind patients of the physical consequences and the ineffectiveness of purging on caloric consumption and weight. (See Chapter 11: Managing Purging.)

Resistance

The nutrition counselor should be ready to provide guidance and solutions when patients reach a roadblock or when they show resistance. For example, some patients have difficulty being honest about their ED behaviors. (See Chapter 1: Process of Counseling, pp. 3–31). We find that patients are more forthcoming when we "roll with resistance," acknowledging rather than challenging it. When patients do admit to difficulties, we explore what happened and why. Past difficulties are viewed as "grist for the mill" or "water under the bridge." We maintain our focus on developing solutions to patients' present problems. This is not to say that patients should be spared the consequences of weight loss (i.e., activity restrictions or consideration of higher levels of care).

Unique to treating AN patients is coping with intentional fluid and sodium loading. We warn our patients about the dangers of augmenting weight checks by overconsumption of fluids or salt or both. Overconsumption of liquids is also used to allay hunger or as a misguided attempt to rid the body of calories through increased urination. Extreme fluid loading, also known as "water intoxication," has been linked to ataxia (loss of muscular coordination), seizure, and coma. Consumption of 6 to 10 liters of water over the course of 24 hours can result in sudden death, or in the case of Herrin's patient, Sadie, extreme embarrassment.

Sadie drank a gallon of fluid before she weighed in, but lost control of her bladder during the session. Her mother insisted on paying for cleaning the couch and rug. Of note, weight augmentation is associated with treatment resistance and poorer outcomes (Santonastaso & Sala, 1998).

AN patients have a well-deserved reputation for attempting to boost weight in deceptive manners. It is not unusual for patients to conceal heavy objects, such as nuts and bolts, in their underwear, or to tape weights to their bodies. We try to be in the habit of visually scanning for hidden weights. It is predictable that some patients will drink extra fluids to temporarily increase or maintain weight. One clue to this behavior is the patient who needs to be excused to go to the restroom after weight checks.

Most patients respond well to candid discussions about attempting to "cheat the scale" and the resulting moral dilemmas for intrinsically truthful patients. Early in treatment, we inform our patients that they will probably face the temptation to augment weight in one of the ways described above and how it can backfire. We tell our patients about the girl who urinated all over the scale. We narrate the story of the mother who became irate upon discovering that strap-on weights were missing from her home gym, suspecting her daughter was trying to deceive her nutrition counselor. Another patient managed to gain 10 pounds by sewing buckshot filled packets into her bra. The increase in her weight was so drastic that her doctor became suspicious and the patient confessed. Yet another patient managed to consume enough of what she called "heavy foods" (melons, yogurts, cottage cheese and liquids) right before weight checks to augment her weight by almost 6 pounds and to also painfully distend her stomach.

We inform patients that water loading can cause seizures and death. We routinely have patients go to the restroom just prior to weigh-ins. If we suspect water loading, we can arrange to have patients weighed in a facility where specific gravity of urine can be tested. A urine specific gravity of less than 1.010 indicates the patient may be over-consuming fluids (Kreipe & Uphoff, 1992, p.53). We remind patients that once they begin augmenting weight they will feel obligated to continue. We also point out that there is a limit to how much weight can be successfully hidden; eventually the patient will have to actually gain weight. Finally, we keep in mind that chronic augmentation of body weight legitimately raises the question of whether a patient can be effectively and safely treated as an outpatient.

It is also common for AN patients, many of whom are excessive exercisers, to have difficulty adhering to limitations on activity. If weight is not increasing as expected, we quiz our patients about exercise behaviors. If patients are not able to adhere to activity limitations, a more structured treatment environment may need to be considered. (See Chapter 12: Managing Exercise.)

We are prepared to talk with our patients about seeking higher levels of care (see Chapter 7: Levels of Care) if weight loss continues or does not improve. Patients should understand that if a reasonable amount of weight is not restored in 2 to 3 months of outpatient treatment, and sooner if weight is lost, more intensive treatment must be contemplated. A brief hospitalization may be necessary for patients to fully grasp that they have a serious condition and that their outpatient treatment team is determined to find an approach that will result in recovery. Residential treatment must also be considered if patients refuse food or have difficulty following a food plan or complying with other aspects of outpatient treatment. The APA (2006) summarizes these concerns in its recommendation for higher levels of care when there is a failure to respond to outpatient treatment. We have seen how the "threat" of hospitalization can be an effective motivator for weight restoration.

Solutions

In this section we detail our weight restoration protocol. The protocol's first phase, "setting the stage for weight restoration," establishes the relationship between nutrition counselor and patient and educates the patient about the challenges associated with weight restoration. The next phase "weight stability" highlights the first weeks of weight restoration, and the third phase "weight restoration" follows the patient as he or she is actively restoring weight. The "weight maintenance phase" details the process of normalizing eating and preventing relapse.

Weight Restoration Protocol

Our basic protocol (see Box 9.2) helps manage the unpredictable nature of weight regain by basing caloric additions on the patient's current intake. Initially some patients are able to gain weight with relatively small "adds." To sustain weight gain, sooner or later, every patient will need to consume an increased number of calories as "metabolism recovers." Because our protocol is based on the patient's current food intake, we avoid underfeeding patients who sometimes enter treatment consuming relatively high amount of calories (e.g., 1,500 to 2,000 calories/day) and we avoid overfeeding patients at risk for refeeding syndrome. Others use a similar approach. The APA Practice guideline (2006) advises beginning with 200 to 300 calories above the patient's usual caloric intake. British nutritionists, Cockfield and Philpot (2009), also report adding increments of 200 to 300 calorie to achieve adequate weight gain. Fair-

---

BOX 9.2 PROTOCOL FOR ADDING CALORIES FOR WEIGHT RESTORATION

- No additional calories if sufficient weight is gained
- Add 200–300 calories if weight gain has stymied
- Add 500 calories if weight is lost
- No more than three adds per week

burn (2008) recommends adding 500 calories/week to intake for weight gains of about a pound a week.

Appointment Frequency

Most patients will need frequent appointments to create a food plan that is both acceptable to them and effective in delivering the necessary rate of weight gain. Although weekly appointments are the "gold standard" in nutrition counseling, most underweight patients need more frequent visits to increase motivation for change, to manage the anxiety weight gain engenders, and to adjust caloric intake to match the often volatile metabolic changes. Very low-weight patients should be seen every other day until weight is consistently improving. We agree with Fairburn (2008) who recommends twice weekly sessions until weight is consistently improving. We offer additional support for dangerously low-weight or anxious patients via phone, e-mail, or a supplementary appointment. Once patients are maintaining an acceptable weight, appointments can be scheduled on a less frequent basis. There is little advantage, however, to reducing the frequency of visits as long as patients remain anxious or have not made considerable progress. For patients who find nutrition counseling somewhat aversive and therefore are eager to decrease the frequency of visits, we suggest experiments to test whether patients can make acceptable weight-gain progress with greater intervals between appointments.

Setting the Stage for Weight Restoration

We inform new patients that our responsibility as nutrition counselors is to manage weight restoration by providing education, structure, organization, and monitoring. We assure them that we are expert in these matters and are capable of directing the rate of weight gain so that it is not too fast or too much. We flat out tell our patients that we have absolutely no interest in making them fat, overweight, or obese. "I am not interested in making you fat. I don't think you would be happy fat; I am interested in getting you healthy at the thinnest weight possible." We point out that we would not be in the nutrition counseling business very long if even one of our patients became obese. We are equally committed to helping patients avoid overweight as we are to helping them restore weight. Furthermore that if, in the unlikely event, too much weight gain does occur, we have the skills to restore weight to the thinnest possible healthy weight.

Establishing a Collaborative Relationship

We are mindful that underweight patients are likely to be fearful, anxious, and distrustful about receiving our help and that they usually are significantly ambivalent about weight gain as a goal of treatment. Our first order of business, therefore, is to develop a therapeutic alliance (see Chapter 3: Process of Counseling, pp. 59–78) where we sometimes play coach or teacher and at other times, cheerleader. We agree with Nicholls, Hudson, and Mahomed (2011) that it is particularly important as we begin the process of weight restoration to treat patients with respect, to provide information, and offer as much choice and involvement in decision-making as possible. We acknowledge our patients' fear of weight restoration and affirm the courage it takes to increase food intake. We are generous in providing praise, understanding, support, and encouragement.

Although anorexic patients are often adamant about their lack of interest in gaining weight, nutrition counselors should make it crystal clear that their "job" is to help underweight patients improve health by helping them regain weight. Patients must come to understand that correction of underweight is a "nonnegotiable part of treatment" and the primary assignment for the nutrition counselor. Treasure (2009) softens this message by giving patients choices for where, when and what to eat. In making this same point, we have said, "You can eat at home or in a residential center, but you have to eat. You can eat with a school nurse or with your friends, but you have to eat. You can eat with your family; or with just one parent, but you have to eat." We are especially careful about how we refer to "weight gain." Instead of telling patients they must "gain weight," Fairburn (2008) advises telling patients they must "regain weight" (p. 148). We generally use the terms "regain weight" or "weight restoration."

From the start, we are careful about how we approach patients who need to improve weight, emphasizing the benefits of weight restoration rather than merely telling patients that they must gain weight. Making the connection between weight restoration and resolution of distressing symptoms is often helpful. We identify which symptoms the patient finds most worrisome then discuss how weight restoration will resolve those symptoms. Patients are often particularly concerned about brittle hair and nails; loss of scalp and pubic hair, and even eyelashes; dry and discolored skin; dizziness; cold extremities; cold sensitivity; impaired concentration; preoccupation with food, eating, and weight; sleep disturbances; episodes of binge eating; and gastrointestinal problems. We explain how weight restoration has resolved similar problems for other patients.

Many patients, however, are unaware that many of their symptoms are directly caused by low-body weight or disordered eating behaviors. They are also unaware that these conditions can pose risks to vital organs such as bones and brain. We explain how bone density improves when patients reach a weight at which menses resumes (and for men when testosterone levels increase; Mehler & MacKenzie, 2009; Schulze, Schuler, Schlamp, Schneider, & Mehler-Wex, 2010, pp. 196–201). We tell adolescent patients that building bone is like a savings account. The patients must make all the money they will make in a lifetime by the ages of 22 to 25 years. After this age, they can only live on what they have made.

Bone density is the same. They can only build bone up to this age; after this age they can only maintain bone. Herrin tells the story of how a DEXA bone scan for a young medical student coming back with results similar to those of an elderly woman serving as a decisive wake-up call.

We inform patients how concentration and other brain functions are noticeably enhanced with weight restoration. Our student patients, in particular, are intrigued when we describe the effects of weight loss and regain on brain tissue. Significant losses of grey and white matter volumes have been found in low-weight patients which likely explain the many cognitive symptoms of AN. Recent studies indicate that to fully restore brain volume requires weight regain to at least BMI of 20 (Roberto et al., 2011). Also of interest to patients is the fact that weight restoration improves metabolic rate and decreases binge eating (Golden & Meyer, 2004). Nonetheless, many patients do not fully grasp the long-term risks associated with an ED. These patients believe that serious consequences of EDs only befall those who have EDs much worse than their own. In other cases, patients report finding solace in physical symptoms that confirm they are undereating. Feeling weak, observing the emergence of prominent bones, and even fainting can be reassuring to patients who have a morbid fear of weight gain, a relentless drive for thinness, and a distorted body image. It is important that discussions about the hazards of low body weight and the benefits of weight restoration do not become debates or arguments. These discussions must remain cordial and respectful of each patient's predicaments and choices. The nutrition counselor's task is to merely report what is known about the consequences of maintaining a below-normal weight compared to the advantages of maintaining a healthy body weight.

Progress can be derailed if patients are not prepared for the likelihood that they will experience uncomfortable symptoms that are secondary to weight restoration. We aim to communicate these clinical realities without unduly alarming patients. We have observed that when patients understand what to expect, they feel less anxious, and they are more likely to be compliant. We also reassure patients that most physical symptoms subside with weight gain and that it is our responsibility to help them manage any adverse reactions associated with weight restoration. Herrin often says, "We are in this together and I will do my best to help keep you safe and comfortable."

Weight Monitoring

It is not unusual for younger patients with a short course of illness to have a genuine interest in gaining weight. Such patients may benefit from forward-facing weight checks or quite specific information about their weight progress. In most cases, however, backwards weigh-ins are more effective. See Box 9.3 for the type of feedback we give patients who are weighed backwards.

BOX 9.3 FEEDBACK FOR BACKWARDS-WEIGHED PATIENTS

- To patients who are progressing on a weight-gain regime, we might comment, "Your weight is fine."
- To patients who have gained the requisite amount since last weight check, we note, "You have gained just the right amount of weight."
- To the patient who has gained over a pound, we remark, "Your weight is right where it should be; keep up the good work."
- If a patient has lost weight, we say, "It looks like we need to add some things to your food plan or revisit your exercise pattern."
- When weight is lost by an underweight patient we tend to more specific. For example, we might observe, "You have lost 2 pounds so it looks like you need to be eating more."
- Feedback, such as "Your weight is within your range," is appropriate for patients who are in weight maintenance.

Low-weight patients are discouraged and strongly advised against self-weight checks. AN patients, like David in Case Example 9.1, often have difficulty complying with this guideline if a scale is assessable. One mother in Herrin's practice drove over her scale with the family pickup truck after her daughter dug it out of the garbage. Most patients are willing to abide by limits on self-weighing and are often relieved to turn over monitoring of their weight to the nutrition counselor or medical provider. (See Chapter 8: Assessing Weight, for more information on weight monitoring, pp. 169–190.)

CASE EXAMPLE 9.1: DAVID

Fourteen-year-old David's story provides a good example of how we manage these kinds of issues with our patients: Struggling with AN, David needed to gain weight before his physician would allow him to participate in the upcoming lacrosse season. At his first nutrition visit, David confessed that, even though he had been advised against self-checking weight by his doctor, he had been getting on the scale whenever his family visited his grandparents. "Does it help to check your own weight?" asked his nutrition counselor. "Not really," David reflected. "I don't know if that old scale is accurate, but I always skip a meal after I stand on the scale just to be extra sure." "It sounds like we should ask your parents to get rid of that scale," the nutrition counselor suggested. "Most home scales, even brand new ones, aren't very reliable."

Julie (see Case Example 9.2) shows how this approach can help patients make progress. Julie's situation also makes the point that it crucial that treatment team members agree on general weight-related goals (i.e., to lose, to gain, or to maintain) and not make changes in any related parameters without team consensus.

CASE EXAMPLE 9.2: JULIE

Julie, a 15-year-old field hockey player, is resistant to adding anything to her food plan. Julie sent the following e-mail to Herrin after her weight dropped 2 lb below the "field hockey weight goal" set by her doctor:

Julie: I was wondering if you could talk to my doctor so I could play field hockey. My team just barely has enough members to play with me on it, and I hate the feeling of letting them down.

Herrin's reply: Julie, the only way you can play field hockey is to be at the weight your doctor says is safe. If you make the food adds that we talked about for the rest of the week, I bet your weight would be OK. If your weight is OK you can play. Basically you are being asked to sacrifice for your team. Your sacrifice is eating more than you want to and to being fuller than is comfortable, but you care so much about your team that I think it is worth it to you.

Self-Monitoring

At most sessions devoted to weight restoration, we obtain a 24-hour recall and ask about day-to-day eating (see Chapter 6: Self-Monitoring, pp. 140–149). We tend, however, not to assign self-monitored food journals. Most AN patients either have no interest in completing food journals or they already obsessively self-monitor or they have difficulty being honest in self-monitoring. We do not insist on self-monitoring if the patient is making consistent progress with weight restoration. When self-monitoring appears necessary, we follow the advice of Pike et al. (2010) by presenting food journals as a way for patients to communicate about their experiences between sessions and to help identify and differentiate between eating situations that are difficult or manageable. We try to find ways to make self-monitoring obviously beneficial to patients. For example, when patients feel immobilized by fear of eating too much or of gaining too fast, we demonstrate how in-session review of journals often provides relief or even a therapeutic breakthrough (see Chapter 6: Self-Monitoring).

Weight Stability Phase

Medical stabilization rather than weight gain is our primary goal during the first week of treating the low-weight outpatient. A slow start helps patient's adjust to following a food plan and to working with a nutrition counselor. A slow approach to increasing caloric intake further protects against refeeding syndrome (see pp. 193–195 for more on refeeding syndrome). It is particularly important for very low-weight patients to devote the first 7 to 10 days of treatment to arresting weight loss, achieving weight stability, and slowly increasing calories. For example, at the first session we generally assign a specific food addition to the patient's current diet to prevent further weight loss. Any foods that contribute the necessary calories are good choices. As much as is reasonable, patients should be allowed to decide what to add to their diet. We invite the patient to describe current eating patterns, fears, and difficulties, and his or her ideas on how to increase caloric intake. If the patient's ideas are reasonable, we include them as we develop an individualized food plan based on current eating patterns taking care to not directly challenge food fears.

For example, it was agreed that Jena's suggestion for adding either a caloric drink or a granola bar to her school lunch (approximately 150 calories) was a reasonable addition. Our practice in this phase is to aim for an increase of 100 to 300 calories above current intake at the initial visit. The size of the first addition is dependent on the patient's weight (additions closer to 100 calories are recommended for patients at risk for refeeding syndrome), level of motivation, support, and supervision. Any weight loss during this phase must be taken seriously and corrected immediately with an increase in food consumption. Once risk of refeeding syndrome has past, weight restoration proceeds as described below.

As mentioned above (see Caloric Conundrum, p. 192) very low-weight patients have a unique metabolic profile. Metabolic rates tend to be exceptionally low ranging from 50 to 70% of normal until caloric intake is improved. As patients increase food intake, metabolic rates become remarkably elevated, well above those documented in any other disease state (Golden & Meyer, 2004; Polito et al., 2000; Rigaud et al., 2007). The high-calorie costs of growing lean body tissue and restoring depleted fat stores explain this phenomenon. Increases in protein synthesis, muscle mass, bone formation, heart rate, and heat dissipation (all associated with improved nutrition) also contribute to increased caloric needs (Sum, Mayer, & Warren, 2011; Van Wymelbeke, Brondel, Marcel Brun, & Rigaud, 2004; Yamashita et al., 2010). In 4 to 6 weeks of improved caloric intake, metabolism usually improves to near normal (Forman-Hoffman, Ruffin, & Schultz, 2006). Consequently, we are not surprised if a patient loses some weight with initial improvements in food intake. Importantly, we do not automatically attribute weight loss to not complying with the food plan. It is of utmost importance, however, to immediately add to the food plan to cover this spike in metabolic rate. We tell our patients that weight restoration is difficult and that it will take concentrated effort on their part to gain weight: "You will have to work at weight restoration; it won't happen in spite of you." Patients tell us such statements are reassuring.

We have adopted Mehler's principal for adding calories "start low and advance slow." Like Mehler and colleagues, we rely on changes in body weight to indicate caloric adequacy (Mehler, Winkelman, Andersen, & Gaudiani, 2010). For instance, if the patient has lost weight, we add calories, or more precisely assign "food" additions. If the patient has gained weight, we keep caloric intake the same until the next visit.

Weight Restoration Phase

In the weight restoration phase patients are actively gaining weight. The rate at which weight is gained varies. Some patients may gain 2–3 lb one week and none the following week. Weekly weight gain averaging 1–2 lb is regarded as optimal. There is evidence; however, that slower pace in the range of half a pound to one pound per week may lead to better outcomes (Cockfield & Philpot, 2009; Herzog, Zeeck, Hartmann, & Nickel, 2004). Weight restoration approaches usually result in gains of 1–3 lb/week. Outpatients can generally tolerate, but rarely achieve, gains of up to 4 lb/week. When patients gain at higher rates, we rule out binge-eating behavior, water or salt loading, or water retention. Sustained weight gain at rates greater than 3 lb/week may indicate edema or bowel impaction (Mehler & Andersen, 2010). In either case, patients should be referred for a medical evaluation.

Some patients make steady progress, but gain at much lower rates. Nevertheless, if rate of gain is less than half a pound a week, we increase caloric intake. Exercise and activity levels, which usually are already limited for medical reasons, should be reassessed in patients who are not gaining at least a half a pound a week.

Food Choices

In the weight restoration phase, it is important not to become distracted by patients' fears of specific foods or nutrients. These issues must remain subordinate to the primary goal of achieving weight restoration. If we can come up with alternatives which provide the necessary calories, we do not push patients to eat foods they fear eating. It is not uncommon for patients to have made progress consuming a limited selection of "safe" foods. Once they are consistently gaining weight, we begin to encourage food choices that lend nutritional balance and normalcy to patients' diets. In general, we advise patients to choose well-balanced meals focused on generous servings of normal foods and to use snacks to provide additional calories. Typical food plans usually include large portions and side dishes at meals, several servings of high-fat foods and two to three servings from the fun food group. At this stage, it is less likely that we need to add to the patient's food plan as steady weight gain is the norm.

It is not uncommon for patients to anticipate that recovery will require them to consume certain foods. Asking about foods they are afraid to eat or have never liked indicates sensitivity to and respect for patients' concerns. We explain that there is no one food that patients must consume to meet their nutrient needs, though meet their nutrient needs they must. For example, we say, "It is really no problem that you do not like milk since yogurt and cheese are equally good sources of calcium." Over time, however, the patient's food plan should evolve to include foods (see "feared food," p. 210) that were excluded on account of the patient's the ED. When weight gain is clearly progressing, we address this issue by asking patients to talk about the foods they fear, hate, or "feel gross eating." In fact, we note the particular foods mentioned and use them in future "fear food challenges."

Standard practice in the past was to disallow AN patients from the use of any diet or low-calorie food. Today, however, these foods are ubiquitous in the food supply and are freely used by many people. For a significant number of patients, lower calorie foods were consumed prior to the onset of their eating disorder. Patients who choose to continue to consume such foods should be guided as to their appropriate use. First and foremost, consumption of diet foods should not be allowed to hinder the achievement or maintenance of a healthy weight. Secondly, diet foods should not take the place of foods that provide necessary nutrients. For example, a diet soda consumed with a small bag of chips may be a reasonable snack. However, a diet soda which takes the place of a glass of milk at a meal is not as good a choice. On the other hand, a glass of skim milk is as reasonable a choice as a glass of whole milk if patients have other sources of fat at the meal. It should be kept in mind that in the throes of an eating disorder, patients often use "diet" foods to assuage hunger. Be particularly alert to a resurgence of these behavior patterns in recovering patients.

Patients who are under the supervision of parents may ask permission to leave some food on their plates because they like the feeling of control that comes with leaving "one bite." We are not inclined to make any concessions that endorse eating less than the patient's food plan. Xenia liked to tear up food as she ate it and to leave crumbs on her plate. Her parents, who supervised Xenia's meals and snacks, found themselves in the untenable situation of trying to define a "crumb." Xenia balked at our principle of designating a clean plate (as defined by her parents) "non-negotiable." We countered that when she is steadily making progress and is out of danger, we will slowly hand the decision-making and responsibility for food intake back to her. When that occurs, she will notice that her parents no longer pay much attention to how much she leaves on her plate. We advised Xenia's parents to ignore odd food behaviors such as "tearing food into bits" or eating one thing at a time, assuring them that such behaviors usually resolve as weight is restored. (See Chapter 13: Working with Families, pp. 277–298.)

Reinforcing Weight Gain

We find that rewarding weight gain improves motivation, decreases surreptitious food behaviors, and helps create positive attitudes toward treatment and recovery. Moreover, meaningful rewards distract patients from the often-incapacitating preoccupation with weight and body changes. Potent motivators are permission to more freely partake in sports, school, and other activities such as overnights with friends. To avoid reinforcing erratic weight changes, we usually require patients maintain weight gains for at least two weeks before major privileges or rewards are granted. The same can be said for negative consequences meted out for weight loss. For instance, in medically stable patients, we may allow a grace period of 1 to 2 weeks to rectify minor weight losses before limiting or denying certain activities.

Providing rewards for weight gain is far more effective than rewarding increases in caloric intake or improved food behaviors. When food behaviors are directly rewarded, patients may feel compelled to covertly dispose of food by vomiting or by other means or to become disingenuous about reporting food intake. Rewarding weight gain also helps avoid fruitless discussions and arguments with patients about the subjective nature of what constitutes improved food behaviors. Nevertheless, families of younger patients often are successful in finding imaginative ways to reward the patient for improvement of specific food behaviors such as allowing access to cell phone or television after a good meal. We advise families to require evidence (the best evidence being observational) of sustained behavior change before rewarding new behaviors. We also advise parents to be cautious about rewarding minor behavior changes when their child is not gaining weight and that major rewards should be reserved for substantial changes in weight. All the same, improved eating behaviors deserve praise from nutrition counselors and significant others. We keep in mind, though, that some patients feel demeaned or even bullied by such reactions especially from parents. Fifteen-year old Jeremy told us, "It is weird for my parents to say 'good job' every time I take another bite. They don't talk that way even to my younger sister." (See Chapter 13: Working with Families for more information, pp. 277–298.)

Weight Maintenance Phase

With maintenance of BAW, physiological functions and tissues are restored to normal or near-normal states. Bone restoration, basal metabolic rate, and abdominal fat distribution take longer to normalize, usually requiring a year or more after BAW has been achieved (Mayer et al., 2009; Nicholls, Hudson, & Mahomed, 2011). In this phase, patients learn to tolerate body weight fluctuates throughout the day, week, and year. Preoccupation with food and distortion of body image, however, often are last to improve.

We also review what current eating-disordered behaviors and attitudes patients would like to change. We have had patients "confess" that they still count calories.

We are sympathetic about how tedious calorie counting is and remind them as their ED resolves, they will gradually lose interest in keeping track of calories. To buoy up such a patient, we may tell the story of Sami who came into her nutrition session in a very excited state: "I bought crackers without comparing calories or even looking at the food labels!"

When patients seem to falter and lose motivation, we often borrow Fairburn's (2008) technique of reviewing the reasons patients want to recover. We have patients write down how their life is impaired by AN, what has improved during treatment and what are their hopes for the future. Fairburn suggests patients write out at their reasons for recovery on sticky notes post them in their bedrooms. We keep a selection of colored note cards and sticky notes in office for just this purpose. One of our patients wrote down that she was enjoying her new body and personality and was proud of the fact that she had broken many of her AN food rules. Research, however, indicates that patients with AN, especially restricting type, are relatively insensitive to rewards of any kind compared to healthy controls and patients with bulimia nervosa and AN-binge/purge type (Harrison, O'Brien, Lopez, & Treasure, 2010).

Feared Foods

The issue of feared foods is tackled using a CBT approach (see Chapter 4: Counseling Interventions, pp. 79–104). We direct patients to articulate evidence and facts to support their apprehensions about the food in question and then to consider evidence that casts doubts on the original concerns. Next, we guide them toward a "reasoned conclusion" about the food. Finally, a feared food is incorporated into the food plan and patients are encouraged to tolerate the feelings they cannot reason away. We often introduce this assignment by saying "Which food fear do you want to work on this week?" When patients consistently approach food in this manner, formerly feared foods lose their power. Note that it may require numerous discussions before patients feel ready to experiment with a feared food. Even then, we often suggest patients begin by consuming feared foods in small quantities. Nutrition counselors should keep in mind that patients are not recovered from an eating disorder until they no longer have fear foods. We note that patients who regularly eat higher calorie foods and have significant variety in food choices have better outcomes than patients who avoid many foods, particularly energy dense foods (Schebendach et al., 2008).

Normalizing Eating

When patients are comfortably maintaining a healthy weight, food plans should become less specific. Usually, directing patients to the type of guidance provided by the general RO3s food plan (i.e., specifying which food groups to be consumed at meals) and to attune to physical cues of hunger and fullness is sufficient.

At this stage, patients should be enjoying foods and experiencing satisfaction with eating. Yet, some may wonder if they should ban fun food from their plans since "I have gained my weight." We respond, "No, you will be eating two fun foods per day for the rest of your life. The RO3s is your recovery plan. You'll be following it the rest of your life, too." We are ready, nevertheless, to refer patients back to a more explicit food plan if they express difficulty in making food choices or become anxious about weight gain or report binge-eating episodes. We notice that weight-recovered patients lose weight quickly if caloric intake dips even slightly or just occasionally.

At first, patients will be apprehensive about a maintenance food plan. They may long for the days when following their weight restoration plan meant "they couldn't eat too much." Provisions for another year of nutrition counseling will help avert bouts of restrictive eating and ensure continued compliance with a maintenance plan and, eventually, development of carefree eating behaviors. Patients who maintain BAW, are symptom-free, and continue intermittent nutrition sessions or at least weight checks over several years are most likely to completely recover. Some patients worry they will be abandoned by treatment professionals after weight has been restored. These patients should be reassured, that as long as they need support to maintain a healthy weight, it will be available. Most patients recover and stay well after five years of treatment (Keel & Brown, 2010). When it becomes evident that patients are maintaining weight comfortably through normal food behaviors, nutrition sessions are slowly reduced and finally terminated. Rachel, a college student, is a good example of a patient who benefitted from continued nutrition treatment. Rachel still needed a specific plan for each day of the week (see Box 9.4) and had a number of feared foods she had not yet worked into her plan. Yet, Rachel was able to eat on campus with an occasional meal at a restaurant in town and was maintaining what her treatment team assumes is her BAW.

BOX 9.4 RACHEL'S WEEKLY FOOD PLAN

Monday
Breakfast: plain yogurt, blueberries, coffee
Snack: fiber one bar
Lunch: turkey and cheese sandwich with mustard and pickles, cheez-its, diet soda
Snack: fat-free chobani yogurt with fruit, carrots with hummus
Dinner: Indian stir-fried tilapia, cauliflower, rice
Snack: rice pudding, decaf chai

BOX 9.4 (continued)

Tuesday
Breakfast: multi-bran chex with 2% milk, coffee
Snack: fat-free chobani yogurt with fruit
Lunch: turkey and cheese sandwich on wheat with pretzels, diet soda
Snack: fiber one bar, carrots and hummus
Dinner: Homemade chicken soup (made with rice and vegetables)
Snack: rice pudding, decaf chai

Wednesday
Breakfast: eggs with spinach, clementine, plain yogurt, coffee
Snack: nothing if not hungry
Lunch: pizza (3 slices), carrots, diet soda
Snack: apple with cottage cheese
Dinner: baked chicken, roasted vegetables, baked sweet potato
Snack: rice pudding, diet soda, decaf chai

Thursday
Breakfast: bran flakes with milk
Snack: nuts and raisins to equal ½ cup
Lunch: favorite chicken with roasted vegetables
Snack: all-bran crackers + cheddar cheese + apple
Dinner: meatloaf with sautéed vegetables + roll
Snack: rice pudding, diet soda

Friday
Breakfast: 2 sugar-free oatmeal packets (made with milk), coffee
Snack: nothing unless hungry
Lunch: 3-egg omelet with spinach/onions/peppers, bowl of plain yogurt with equal, 2 clementines
Snack: ½ cup of Ben & Jerry's ice cream, diet soda
Dinner: (Thai restaurant) Beef bulgoki, sushi roll, seaweed salad, pickled vegetables
Snack: rice pudding, diet soda

Saturday and Sunday
Brunch: (restaurant) 3-egg omelet with asparagus, tomatoes, cheddar, English muffin with butter, fruit, coffee
Snack: plain yogurt with equal, 2 clementines
Dinner: meatloaf, vegetables, mashed potatoes (1 cup), cupcake or an equivalent meal
Snack: fat-free chobani yogurt with fruit

Preventing Relapse

Because relapse rates are as high as 50% in AN (Laurel et al., 2007), we focus on recognizing behaviors that predict elapse (weight loss; bingeing; delaying or skipping meals, snacks, or fun food; and increasing exercise and body checking (Laurel et al., 2007). We also establish a BAW which if weight should fall below signals a risk for relapse. To prevent relapse, we encourage our patients to continue with weight checks and nutrition support, but less frequently, for at least a year after reaching BAW. It is essential that anorexic patients develop confidence in their ability to maintain their weight gain on their own. Fears of overshooting weight goals and impending obesity are likely to surface at this juncture. If patients do gain beyond predetermined weight goals while following a maintenance food plan, it is likely that their BAW is above the estimated weight goal. Unless BAW goals are recalculated to reflect patients' physical reality, relapse is likely. We tell our patients in this situation that they will not indefinitely gain weight, but will reach a stable healthy weight that is correlated with physical and mental health and with normal eating and exercise behaviors. We reiterate our willingness to help patients maintain BAW by saying to the effect, "I will work as hard at helping you maintain a healthy weight as I did in helping you gain weight."

Ideally, termination is, not before patients have maintained BAW for a year. We make it clear to our patients and their families, however, that if weight drops below a certain minimum or if troubling eating behaviors reappear, we would always be available for a consultation or another bout of nutrition counseling.

Weight Goals

Success in restoring weight in underweight ED patients depends on the establishment and regular revision of weight limits and goals. We use the standards described below. Our revised BMI categories, indicated in parentheses and discussed in Chapter 8: Assessing Weight (p. 181) provide numerical guidance.

- Risky Low Weight Limit (BMI category: risky low weight) is the weight below which the patient would be referred for higher level of care.
- Interim Goal Weight (BMI category: low weight) helps pace treatment.
- Minimum Safe Weight Goal (BMI category: minimum safe weight) is the lowest weight at which a patient can maintain healthy function and growth.
- Menstrual Weight or Testosterone Restoration Goal (BMI category: safe weight) is the minimum weight at which females start or resume regular menses and men have normal testosterone levels.
- Activity-Based Goal (BMI category: minimum safe weight) is the weight at which safety of activity is presumed.
- BAW Goal (BMI category: safe weight) is the weight that is maintained with ease and supports normal growth, function, and mental health.

Establishing weight goals and regular monitoring of weights helps pace treatment and reassures patients that treatment will not lead to obesity. This process considers the importance of the patient's medical and psychological status as well as his or her food and weight behaviors. It is an on-going, collaborative process, involving all members of the ED team. It is the nutrition counselor, however, who typically takes the lead on establishing, reviewing and communicating weight limits and goals. Although medical providers on our treatment teams often say, "Let me wear the black hat when it comes to weight goals." All team members need to understand the rationale for various weight goals as it is expected that patients will challenge each team member (Olmstead et al., 2010). Team members can express concern about the patient's physical health while referencing the medical provider's weight goals. The mental health provider focuses on what patients feel, think and want to do about weight goals. The nutrition counselor works on food and exercise behaviors that will help the patient reach these goals.

Risky Low Weight Limits

We define "risky low weight limits" as weights below which serious medical problems are likely (i.e., if the patient falls below a risky low weight limit, a higher level of care may be necessary). Weights below this limit (typically set at the 10th percentile for children and adolescents and below 18.5 kg/m^2 for women and below 20 kg/m^2 for men) are associated with rapid weight loss, rapid and persistent decline in food intake, physical complications of severe malnutrition, cardiac disturbances, psychosis, high suicidal risk and usually indicate the need for more supervision than outpatient services can provide (American Psychiatric Association, 2006). Unless the patient is making sustained progress on the parameters mentioned above, higher levels of care should be seriously considered. It is important to note that because of greater risk of compromised medical status and growth, weight limits for children and adolescents should be recalculated every three to six months (Golden, Jacobson, Sterling, & Hertz, 2008). It cannot be over emphasized that very low weight outpatients need regular medical monitoring to ensure that continued outpatient treatment is prudent.

Interim Weight Goals

Early in treatment, many patients are not ready to discuss predicted long-term weight goals. Concentrating on interim goals instead can avoid overwhelming such patients. On the other hand, nutrition counselors must be careful that interim weight goals are not mistakenly taken for long-term goals. In fact, interim goals must include the expectation of continued weight gain. Once an interim weight goal has been met, the patient may be allowed more activity such as a return to school or sports with the expectation that weight would continue to improve. In children and adolescents, an interim weight goal could be a return to the highest weight the patient has experienced to date. Another example of an interim goal for a young patient might be reaching a weight at or above the 10th percentile. A BMI of 19 kg/m² for older patients or return of menses are often used as interim goals.

Interim goals help pace treatment. Clinical consensus is that a realistic target for outpatient treatment is one half to one pound per week (American Psychiatric Association, 2006). One strategy is to show patients a graph mapping out how long it will take to reach an interim goal while gaining on average about one half to one pound per week (Fairburn, 2008, pp. 63–66). Some patients gain at slower rates because of metabolic reactions to improved food intake. In other cases, the patient's resistance to behavior change and weight gain makes for slower progress. As long as the patient is gaining measurable weight, making behavioral changes, and is medically stable, low rates of gain can be tolerated. Meeting interim weight goals, however, are often required before allowing less supervised situations such as attending boarding school, summer camps, or taking overnight trips.

Minimum Safe Weight Goals

We define minimum safe weight goal as the lowest weight at which a patient can fluctuate above, but not below, and maintain healthy growth and function, meet nutritional needs, and experience a substantial decline in ED behaviors and thinking. Minimum safe weight goals for children and adolescents are likely to be around the 25th percentile of BMI for age or consistent with each patient's growth curve. Of note, in children and adolescents, a minimum safe weight must take into account expected growth. Otherwise, children and adolescents who reach a static minimum goal weight will have, in essence, lost weight compared to the expected weight gain for age over the course of treatment (Lask & Frampton, 2009). Younger patients who have not matured can also lose linear height percentiles. We extrapolate from pre-morbid BMI percentiles to estimate the percentile had growth not been interrupted by AN.

Minimum safe weight goals for older adolescent females and older adult females are usually at or above a BMI of 20 kg/m². At weights above a BMI of 20 kg/m², many females are free of the physical and emotional consequences of being underweight, start or resume menses, and can eat normally (Fairburn, 2008). We do not have as strong a reference for males though normalized testosterone levels are indicative of reaching a minimum safe weight.

We advise against using inpatient discharge weights as proxies for a minimum safe weight. It should be noted that inpatient discharge weights are often well below a minimum safe weight because of insurance-mandated limits on treatment based on achieving a percentage of ideal body weight [(IBW) usually 86% to 90% of IBW]. As we discussed in Chapter 8: Assessing Weight (pp. 169–190), IBW, itself, is a dubious concept.

In summary, we agree with Fairburn (2008), Kaplan (Kaplan & Noble, 2007), Hart, Williams, Wakefield, and Russell, (2012), and others that a BMI of 20 kg/m² is a reasonable minimum safe weight goal for many female patients (with the exception of athletes) who at this weight can eat normally, have regular menses and be free from the adverse secondary effects of being underweight. Projected goal weights that require patients to restrict food intake or over-exercise to maintain should be revised.

We acknowledge that a few people are naturally very thin, and are clearly recovered physically, behaviorally, emotionally, and cognitively at a BMI lower than 20 kg/m². We also acknowledge that is less rare for patients to not be recovered with BMI well above 20 kg/m².

Menstrual Weight or Testosterone Restoration Goals

A menstrual weight goal is the minimum weight at which females start or resume regular menses. Resumption of menses (ROM) usually indicates significant improvement in nutrition and health status. This, however, is not always the case. In a significant proportion of females, menses are hormonally induced by use of oral contraceptives. Other females have the biological capability to continue menses or to resume menses at weights that are below expected despite severe weight loss and restricted food intake. Consequently, minimum weight goals for such patients, and in male patients, pre-menarche females, post-menopausal women and women with histories of reproductive surgeries should be based on BMI categories, pre-morbid weight histories, or in men, testosterone levels.

For patients with primary amenorrhea (failure to menstruate by age 15 in the presence of normal sexual development), our clinical experience and research supports the prediction that minimum menstrual weights for many adults and older adolescents begin at a BMI of 20 kg/m² (Copeland, Sacks, & Herzog, 1995, p. 121). In younger adolescents, Golden et al. (2008) found ROM occurring roughly equivalent to the 27th BMI percentile. Prediction of menstrual weights is complicated by how each patient responds or adapts to the stress of weight loss and under nutrition (Genazzani, Riccieri, Lanzoni, Strucchi, & Jasonni, 2006). Adult females with secondary amenorrhea (the absence or cessation of normal menses for three months or more) can expect resumption of menses (ROM) when they reach their premorbid menstrual weight.

To complicate matters further, once an estimated minimum menstrual weight is reached, menses do not usually return immediately. If ROM has not occurred in three to six months, we raise menstrual weight goals by five pounds. If amenorrhea continues a medical workup should be recommended. Similarly in men, if testosterone levels have not normalized, we raise weight goals by 5 pounds.

Activity-Based Weight Goals

Activity-based weight goals are usually imposed by medical providers (who attest to the safety of increases in activity) in consultation with other treatment providers and are managed by nutrition counselors. Exercise, participation in sports, and even casual activities, such as shopping or attending school, may be completely banned or severely limited until a minimum amount of weight is gained or until patients can demonstrate sustained weight gains. Sherman and Thompson (2010) the foremost experts on treating EDs in athletes recommend weight goals of at least a BMI of 18.5–19.0 for a return to sports while acknowledging BMI guidelines are arbitrary and that patients must be healthy enough to exercise regardless of achieving a specific BMI.

There is little advantage in setting the weight criteria for permission to participate in activities or athletics so high that patients feel discouraged or antagonistic toward the treatment team. Allowing patients to increase activity when they reach interim goals is motivating and helps keep them from surreptitious exercise. Limits on activity once established must be honored or else the treatment team risks loss of credibility with patients and parents.

As with other types of weight goals, activity-based goals are best if individualized. For example, an often used and reasonable, yet conservative, criterion for sports involvement is ROM. Powers & Thompson (2007), however, do not recommend using a ROM-based criterion. They point out that: One, normal menses may be delayed by up to 6 months after reaching BAW. Two, athletics may be the patient's primary source of self-esteem, social attachment, and support. And finally, organized sports provide limits, supervision, and monitoring that would be lacking if the patient resorts to exercising on his or her own. We also keep in mind the reality that it is nearly impossible to keep patients who desire to exercise from exercising in outpatient treatment.

For patients eager to return to relatively rigorous athletic endeavors additional criteria should be discussed. Patients must be agreeable to increasing caloric intake to cover exercise-related expenditures. They must also understand that if weight drops then sports participation will be prohibited until weight is restored--no matter the athletic consequences (missing an important game or meet, etc.). Lastly, activity-based goals are motivational. Permission to engage in an activity when progress in treatment is made can be withdrawn when progress is not being made.

Biologically Appropriate Weight Goals

We are convinced that "weight will take care of itself once eating is normalized" and also that BAW are typically somewhat heavier than a "minimum safe weight." To predict a child's BAW, it is necessary to obtain historical height and weight data. Generally, a normal child's growth in height and weight will follow about the same percentile curve throughout childhood. Growth curves obtained from the patient's primary care provider, therefore, can be used to predict a child's natural height and weight if not inhibited by an ED. If growth curves are unavailable, historical height and weight data can be entered at https://mygrowthcharts.com to create a curve for individual patients.

We warn our patients that aiming to maintain a weight that requires dietary restriction and or over-exercise hinders recovery from an ED as does attempting to maintain body weights that are below pre-morbid weights. If a patient was at a high weight prior to the ED, it must be ascertained whether the pre-morbid weight was the result of a genetic tendency to maintain a high body weight or the result of poor eating habits. Genetically determined body traits can be explored by inquiring, "Are your family members large and big-boned or a small and fine-boned?" In these discussions, we state that we have no interest in forcing patients or "allowing them," to become overweight or obese. Intentionally being somewhat provocative, we often say, "Do you think I would have a full caseload if my patients gained a lot of extra weight."

Discussing Weight Goals

When discussing longer-term goals, like BAW, we emphasize that it takes time for the treatment team to gather the data necessary to predict such goals. Consequently, our initial focus is on "getting weight gain moving" and on interim goals. We remind ourselves that delaying discussion of longer-term goals is often in the patient's best interest. It is best to talk gently, and somewhat vaguely, about the concept of BAW. We usually wait on discussion of goal weights with patients until they broach the subject. Instead, we focus on the fact that the patient's current weight is a serious health risk and must be remedied as quickly as possible. Again, we guard against intimidating patients with too much discussion about the eventual necessity of maintaining a significantly higher weight (i.e., a goal weight). We have noticed that after initiation of nutrition rehabilitation and some weight restoration, patients are better able to engage in such discussions.

When discussing weight goals with patients, we first review the benefits that weight gain provides. Often patients are able to acknowledge that weight gain will help lessen the concern of parents and treatment providers and gain them permission to be active and to play sports, or in some cases, return to college. Furthermore, most can appreciate that achieving weight goals usually keeps inpatient treatment from being considered. We often restate weight-gain goals to incorporate benefits articulated by patients: "Let's see, you need to weigh 'x' to play soccer... to keep your doctor happy... or to return to school."

We review individual weight gain data with patients who continue to express significant anxiety about consuming too many calories. "See, you've only gained a half a pound a week this past month. Your doctor is pushing me to get things moving faster so I know you are not eating too much." The nutrition counselor may choose to show the patient his or her BMI and growth chart percentiles to illustrate normal versus underweight or overweight status. This can reassure a patient who believes he or she is overweight when in fact is not; it can be a reality check for the patient who believes his or her weight is normal when in fact it is not. A discussion about what body weight consists of, namely, bone, water, organs, lean muscle mass, and not just body fat, is often helpful. At regular intervals during treatment, we may explore the pros and cons of regaining weight. Some benefit from writing out current and future pros and cons. We have collected in Box 9.5 some of our favorite ways to discuss weight with patients.

BOX 9.5 DISCUSSING BODY WEIGHT

- "You are back on your curve!"
- "I don't know enough about your body to really talk about weight goals at this point but we will figure that out as we go along."
- "I cannot 'promise' to keep your weight low."
- "I will work as hard on helping you maintain a BAW as I will at helping you gain weight."
- "Weight will take care of itself once eating is normalized."

Weight Restoring Food Planning

Some patients are capable of managing weight regain with little more than encouragement. Many will need, at least initially, all food decisions made for them. Introducing the RO3s plan at this point can give patients the guidance they need, but for others any all-purpose food plan is likely to be overwhelming. In low-weight AN, we usually hold off presenting a copy of the RO3s till later in treatment. When we do introduce the RO3s food plan, we often say some or all of the following: "Here is a roadmap of where we are headed. You might find this pattern of eating helpful in figuring out what to add. This plan provides all of your nutrient needs and will eventually maintain a safe weight. I use this plan for all my patients, including those I am helping lose weight." We may add in a somewhat co-conspirator tone, "I eat this way too" (because we do). We find that boundaries of the RO3s give patients the confidence to experiment with variety and to take initiative in improving intake.

Instead of individualizing the RO3s food plan, we write out an individualized plan based on the patient's 24-hour recall plus the agreed upon "adds." And of course, we talk about reasonable substitutes for items in the sample day that we may well write in. We give a copy of the plan to the patient and keep one in the patient's chart for future reference. This sample day becomes the patient's weight restoring food plan. Annabel's food plan in Box 9.6 is a good example. Annabel, a young adult, is at very low weight and has struggled with AN since a young adolescent. She admitted counting calories and requested a plan that includes calorie counts and very specific foods. For illustration, we highlighted "adds" with an italicized font. In Annabel's case the "adds" equaled about 135 calories.

BOX 9.6 ANNABEL'S WEIGHT-RESTORING FOOD PLAN

Breakfast
6 oz. non-fat yogurt (80 calories)
1 cup Kashi "7 Whole Grain Honey Puffs" cereal (120 calories) **or** 1 English muffin
1 cup sliced strawberries (50 calories)
Total 250 calories

Lunch
2 slices Vermont Bread Company organic spelt bread (70 calories per slice/ 140 calories total)
3 tbsp Tribe All Natural Hummus (25 calories per tbsp/75 calories total) [Annabel had been eating 1 tbsp]
2 slices tomato (8 calories)
1 medium-sized apple (80 calories) **or** small banana
Total 303 calories

Dinner
1 Thomas' Sahara multi-grain pita pocket (140 calories)
2 slices Kraft 2% milk sharp cheddar cheese (50 calories per slice/100 calories total)
2 tsp Annie's Naturals mustard (0 calories)
2 slices tomato (8 calories)
1 pack Bolthouse Farms baby-cut carrots (25 calories)
Total 273 calories

SNACK
6 oz. non-fat yogurt (80 calories)
1/2 cup sliced strawberries (25 calories)
Total 105 calories
Day Total 931 calories

Making "Adds"

The most effective question to ask of patients is "What would you like to add?" We try to avoid saying "Could you add 'x' or 'y'?" To the former question, patients are likely to respond with several food suggestions. To the latter, patients are apt to respond negatively, regardless of the suitability of the suggested foods. Nevertheless, there are times that our patients need concrete suggestions on what to add. An easy approach is to suggest increasing the servings of foods already incorporated into the food plan. We sometimes use Fairburn's approach (2008, p. 172) of giving patients a list of foods or combinations that equal 300 or 500 calories and letting the patient pick something at each session to add. Or, we ask patients to list foods they could imagine eating or would like to be eating. For patients who have difficulty with this task, we explore feelings, thoughts, and fears about specific foods. Later, we use these lists as suggestions for meals and snacks, beginning with the foods about which the patient has the least fears or hesitations. To the patient who says, "I want to add one slice of bread." We might say, "I can tell you this is not enough. What else do you want to add? It's easier to make a sandwich with 2 slices of bread."

When we suggest that patients add foods high in the nutrients they feel are most important, these ideas are often well received. A case in point is protein. Some patients are able to add peanut butter in service of protein nutrition. Others are only interested in adding low-fat protein powders, sports bars, or egg substitutes than more typical high-protein foods. Inasmuch as lower-fat additions contribute calories, we do not dissuade our patients from these choices. Some patients claim, and probably do, to eat a well-balanced diet which includes desserts and similar foods. Without a doubt, many exaggerate the magnitude of their intake or over-exercise, but we usually do not investigate the veracity of such claims. Instead, we reiterate time and again that if one is underweight or not gaining weight, no matter how well or how much he or she is eating or that he or she out-eats friends, current intake is just not enough to protect health. In such cases, we may take on the task of revamping a food plan by saying, "Since it sounds like your meals are good, let's add snack or increase your current snacks."

We have noticed that some patients often find it more palatable to add additional servings of desserts rather than to add yet another entree or supplementary side dishes. As long as their nutrient needs are met by inclusion of adequate servings of all food groups, they should not be discouraged from eating more than the recommended number of servings per day of any one group, except for fruits and vegetables. We watch for overconsumption of vegetables, in particular, as they offer so little in the way of calories and can contribute to uncomfortable fullness. We often say, "If you are too full, don't worry about your veggies, they are not important right now." We find that these approaches are more effective than expressing anger or scolding patients for not complying with their food plan or for losing weight. A stance that is empathetic and respectfully curious about the patient's difficulties and oriented towards problem solving is generally most productive.

When patients have no ideas of their own and resist every offered idea and strategy about what to add, we recommend increasing the serving sizes of currently eaten foods. If patients cannot agree to sufficient dietary additions, a follow-up appointment should be scheduled within several days for a weight check and for continued discussion about how the food plan can be augmented.

Occasionally patients will argue against adding despite losing weight "but I haven't followed the food plan" or "I went running every day even though I wasn't supposed to." We use clinical judgment to determine whether we make "an add" at this visit or, instead, focus on adherence to food and exercise directives, waiting until the next visit to add calories if weight loss has not been rectified. Herrin often says, "Your food plan looks as good as you are able to make it, but I am concerned that it is not enough. So let's experiment staying with your current plan, but you will have to come back for a weight check in several days to make sure you are gaining."

Weight loss between sessions indicates patients either need to commit to larger caloric increases at each appointment or to commit to more frequent food planning sessions. We say to the patient who has lost weight, "You and I know you need to add 500 calories this week, let's figure out foods you could add to equal 500 calories." To patients who do not "think in calories," we might say, "You need to add a couple of substantial food items to your daily intake." Of note, we prefer not talk about "calories in food" except when patients need to make a concrete add to their food plan or if the patient "thinks in calories."

At the close of each session we outline the agreed upon food plan verbally, and in writing (i.e., the sample day), giving patients one last opportunity to edit the plan. After handing the written plan to the patient, we say, "Take a look at this. Let's make sure we both are in agreement." Nutrition counseling sessions should be devoted almost entirely to revisions of the food plan until patients are gaining 1–3 lb/week.

The reality is that it does not usually matter in what sequence the patient makes dietary changes as long as food intake improves. Initially, nutritional balance is not a major concern. If the patient is eating inconsistently, the first order of business may be to recommend a more regular pattern. Fairburn (2008) focuses first on helping the patient establish a regular pattern of eating, three meals and three snacks without specifying what and how much the patient eats. We use this approach in very resistant patients making it clear that our goal is organized eating not necessarily adding more calories. Instituting breakfast and a morning snack helps patients break the habit of delaying food intake until later in the day. Spreading food intake out over the course of a day decreases sensations of fullness and decreases preoccupation with food. Janine, for example, had a morning snack on Monday, Wednesdays and Fridays during her economics class. A nutrition counseling session was devoted to helping her figure out how to have a morning snack on the other days of the week.

Below are specific strategies we have used to add calories:

- *Eating larger portions of same food.* Kara decided to do two scoops of rice at dinner instead of her usual "one."
- *Adding snacks.* School-aged patients who have a snack right after school may be able to also add a "before dinner snack." College students who eat dinner relatively early and stay up late may decide to add a "bedtime snack" in addition to an after-dinner snack.

- *Increasing the caloric value of food and drink.* Keith who usually drank water at meals, but was willing to drink milk instead. Jillie chose to drink a boost drink instead of milk at meals. Instead of diet bread, Will switched to regular bread.
- *Adding a supplemental drink or bar.* Ginger thought she could handle a granola bar at lunch.
- *Adding a side to meals.* We tell patients that it is old-fashioned, but many people used to have bread and butter with meals as a "side dish" in addition to a serving of potatoes or another carbohydrate. Emily decided she could add a side of baked beans or coleslaw to dinner if she didn't feel like bread and butter.
- *Adding an additional serving of fun food.* Chris, a college sophomore, ate another dessert before he went to bed.
- *Eating smaller meals and calorically dense snacks.* Ariel was more comfortable consuming normal-sized meals and high-calorie snacks.

Calories and Weight Restoration

By now the reader may surmise we add calories not based on estimations of a patient's total caloric intake but based on the patient's weight status. We are matter-of-fact about the need to increase calorie intake if the patient is not gaining weight as expected. That patients must improve their caloric intake is not, however, negotiable.

Our approach has served us well clinically for a number of reasons: One the field lacks predictive equations for determining energy needs during weight restoration in AN (Boullata, Williams, Cottrell, Hudson, & Compher, 2007; Forman-Hoffman, Ruffin, & Schultz, 2006; Mehler, Winkelman, Andersen, & Gaudiani, 2010). Of note, the commonly used Mifflin-St. Jeor and Harris-Benedict equations tend to over-predict energy needs in very low-weight patients and under-predict energy needs when patients began to gain (American Dietetic Association, 2011; Forman-Hoffman, Ruffin, & Schultz, 2006). Two, the clinical literature suggests that there is significant variation among individuals as well as differences due to gender and ED subtype. Published caloric recommendations for initial food plans range from 500 calories/day to over 2,000 calories/day (American Dietetic Association, 2011; American Psychiatric Association, 2006; Cockfield & Philpot, 2009; Royal College of Psychiatrists, 2005). Recommendations for calorie levels to support ongoing weight gain range from 2,200–4,000 calories/day for adolescent girls (Lock & Fitzpatrick, 2009; Mehler, Winkelman, Andersen, & Gaudiani, 2010; Royal College of Psychiatrists, 2005). Mehler et al. (2010) finds that male patients generally need as much as 4,000 calories/day and females as much as 3,500 calories/day with a range of 1,800–4,500 calories/day. Restricting AN patients require higher caloric levels to gain weight than do AN-binge/purge patients (Sunday & Halmi, 2003).

Another often-used method is to base caloric levels on an estimate of calorie needs per pound of body weight. Published accounts of initial caloric needs vary from 2–27 calories/pound for severely malnourished patients to 15–50 calories/lb/day for better nourished patients (American Psychiatric Association, 2006; Boateng, Sriram, Meguid, & Crook, 2010; Khan, Ahmen, Khan, & Macfie, 2011; Kohn, Madden, & Clarke, 2011; Lock & Fitzpatrick, 2009; Mehler, Winkelman, Andersen, & Gaudiani, 2010). According to the current Practice Guideline for the Treatment of Patients with Eating Disorders (2006) some female patients will eventually require intakes as high as 30–45 calorie/pound/day.

The bottom line, we remind ourselves, is that if our patients are losing weight, they are not eating enough no matter what we might predict for calorie levels. We do not assess the caloric intake of our patients and discourage patients from keeping running totals though many of our patients, like Annabel (see Box 9.6), do. If patients, nevertheless, persist in totaling their caloric intake, we ask that they report the totals to us. There are many reasons we do not calculate caloric intakes. First and foremost, we "don't have a clue as to the calorie requirements" of any particular individual. Second, patients are often poor estimators of food intake. They may already be consuming more calories than reported or expected yet not meeting energy needs or they may over estimate intake. Another reason is that myths abound about calories though we are quick to debunk the most confusing ones (see Box 9.7). Yet another reason is that in general we do not support calorie counting as it supports ED approaches to food behaviors.

BOX 9.7 THE 3,500 CALORIES = 1 POUND MYTH

This myth arises from the misuse of logic applied to biology. There are 3,500 calories in a pound of fat. Regaining a pound of muscle, heart, lungs, brain, and bone tissues takes far more calories than it does to regain a pound of fat (an essential body component but relatively simple to maintain). It is universally agreed that it is not possible to calculate calorie needs of individuals outside of a metabolic lab. These needs vary considerably between individuals and day to day. Major factors include: age, gender, height, weight, health status, fitness level, physical activity, lean body mass, stress level, and basal metabolic rate. Even the most widely used equations do not account for that dynamic physiological adaptations that occur when a patient is underweight and needs to regain. On the other hand, it is well established that if a patient loses weight between weight checks, add 500 calories to usual intake. If weight is maintained rather than gained, add 300 calories. This is the reason we talk "calories" only when we are talking about additions to a food plan.

Supplemental Drinks and Bars

Supplemental drinks and bars are often well tolerated by patients who can more easily think of them as "medicine" or who find supplements more comfortable to consume than regular foods. Besides calories (on average 200–300 calories/ serving), many of these products contain protein (usually in amounts similar to a cup of milk or yogurt), vitamins, and minerals. For our patients who consume more than two to three servings a day of such drinks and bars, we assess for excessive intakes of vitamins and minerals. The fact that these foods are advertised as health-promoting, able to improve sports performance, or effective for weight loss lends a sense of security. Supplemental drinks and bars are particularly useful in helping AN patients who are apprehensive that they will become too comfortable consuming a high-calorie diet. Patients who recently discharged from higher levels of care may be accustomed to using supplements or used to the common residential setting rule that if a meal or snack is not finished, a supplemental drink must be consumed. Some patients, but not all, find that supplemental drinks result in less gastric discomfort than do calorically equivalent solid foods. For patients who would rather drink a supplement than eat a larger meal, we advise drinking the supplement after the meal because they can be filling for some patients. We assure our patients that supplemental foods can easily be discontinued when weight gain goals are achieved and over time we will help them return to consumption of normal, everyday foods. We always keep in mind, nonetheless, that it is quite possible to achieve weight gain even in the most emaciated patient, relying solely on normal, everyday foods.

Vitamin and Mineral Supplements

The RO3s food plan provides adequate vitamin and mineral levels, including adequate calcium and vitamin D (unless patients avoid dairy products, egg yolks, and fatty fish like salmon and tuna). Initially, we usually do not complicate our focus on weight restoration and the message "food is your main medicine and it is sufficient to heal your body" with advice to add various supplements. To date, there is no evidence of benefit for AN patients in taking multiple vitamin and minerals, calcium, vitamin D, or any other supplements. A literature review by Rock (2010) found that adequate food intake and weight gain corrected possible nutrient deficiencies in AN patients. Calcium and vitamin D supplementation has not proven to increase BMD in acute AN (Mehler & MacKenzie, 2009).

Later in treatment after weight gain and improved nutrition increase the possibility that bone-related hormones are normalizing, we recommend assessing whether patients are consuming 1,000 mg (RDA for 19 to 50 years old) to 1,300 mg of calcium/day (RDA for 9 to 18 years old) from either foods or supplements and 600 IU/day (the current recommended daily allowance for children up to age 70) for vitamin D. These intakes match the Dietary Reference Intakes (DRIs) developed by the Food and Nutrition Board (FNB) at the Institute of Medicine of The National Academies (formerly National Academy of Sciences) for healthy children, adolescents, and adults to maintain bone health and normal calcium and vitamin D metabolism.

High-calcium foods (milk, yogurt, and cheese) contain about 300 mg of calcium/cup serving. Patients who are consuming a reasonably varied diet usually receive another 300 mg from the traces of calcium found in other foods. The difference between the patient's intake and the age-appropriate recommendation should be made up by a calcium supplement. Diets inadequate in calcium are usually low in vitamin D as well. Milk and yogurt are the best food sources of vitamin D; 5 one-cup servings provide approximately 600 IU of vitamin D. Vitamin D needs are easily met by taking a multiple vitamin supplement containing vitamin D. If calcium supplementation is necessary, we recommend using one with added vitamin D unless the patient is taking a multiple vitamin supplement that contains vitamin D.

We advise caution in the use of all supplements including vitamin D and calcium as interactions with other nutrients or toxicities can be serious. High doses (above the tolerable upper intake level 4,000 IU/day) of vitamin D, for example, can raise blood levels of calcium and increase the risk of kidney and heart problems. Calcium doses greater than 1,500 mg (from either food or supplements) may inhibit absorption of other important nutrients such as iron, magnesium, phosphorus, and zinc. Additional problems associated with large doses of calcium include urinary tract stones and kidney damage. Even moderate doses of calcium can cause constipation, intestinal bloating, and excessive gas. Nutrition counselors should be aware that ED patients have been known to consume large quantities of calcium chews or flavored calcium tablets (also marketed as anti-acids) because of their negligible calorie content, mouth-feel, and flavor.

This is not at all to say we discourage patients from using vitamin and mineral supplements as there is no evidence of harm not contain as long as doses do not exceed 100% of daily values for the various nutrients. We are particularly cautious with AN patients who may be more sensitive to toxicities or other adverse effects (Rock, 2010). Of note, it has become routine to recommend a daily multiple-type supplement and 1,500 mg of calcium/day and 400 to 600 IU of vitamin D/day to AN patients.

A few clinical trials point to possible benefits in the use of supplemental essential fatty acids, antioxidants, probiotics, magnesium, iron, zinc, riboflavin, thiamin and other nutrients in the treatment of eating disorders, particularly in AN (Greenblatt, 2010; Setnick, 2010). More research is needed to clarify benefits and hazards before these supplements should be used clinically.

Referrals

Before patients have significantly improved nutritional intake and before weight gain has begun, they are usually unable to fully engage in psychotherapy (APA,

2006, p. 17). Nevertheless, we find that concurrent psychotherapy can be helpful and that making a psychotherapy referral is much harder to sell to patients and families if the patient is experiencing improved mood and cognitive functioning as they often do after first improving nutritional intake.

Psychotherapy helps patients understand and accept nutrition interventions. Psychotherapists can add an additional source of support, and empathy, encouragement in the intensive phases of weight restoration and later help address cognitive distortions and body image issues. As patients recover, they benefit from exploring the antecedents of their disorder and in finding other ways to cope with emotions and life issues. A course of psychotherapy is usually necessary to minimize risk of relapse and for recovery (APA, 2006, p. 17).

Psychotropic Medication

Selective serotonin reuptake inhibitors (SSRIs) antidepressants are often prescribed for patients receiving outpatient treatment for AN. These SSRIs include: fluoxetine (Prozac), sertraline (Zoloft), paroxetine (Paxil), fluvoxamine (Luvox), and citalopram (Celexa), escitalopram (Lexapro), and venlafaxine (Effexor). Of note, some research shows that SSRIs are "do not appear to confer advantage regarding weight gain in patients who are concurrently receiving inpatient treatment in an organized eating disorder program" (APA, 2006, p. 18). As a result, it has become a common adage that SSRIs are not helpful in AN. Our clinical experience and that of others is that an SSRI confers significant advantages to AN patients early in outpatient treatment. It is hypothesized that one reason these medications are effective in AN is because they are also effective in treating common co-morbid problems, such as: depression, anxiety, phobias, panic attacks, and obsessive-compulsive disorder (OCD). The effective dose for SSRIs in AN is usually over twice as high as doses typically prescribed for depression and anxiety (e.g. fluoxetine 60 mg/day; APA, 2006, p. 20). As nutrition counselors, we often find ourselves in the position of recommending the consideration of a trial of SSRI therapy to patients, parents, and other team members. Of note, antipsychotics may also be prescribed for patients who continue to resist weight restoration or to help very distressed patients manage mealtimes.

Summary Points

- The nutrition counselor should affirm patients' fear of weight restoration along with their courage to increase food intake, providing ample praise, understanding, support, and encouragement.
- It is helpful to prepare patients for the obstacles they may face during weight restoration such as cognitive, behavioral and emotional issues, gastrointestinal discomfort, changes in body composition and metabolism, and potential medical concerns.

- Medical stabilization rather than weight gain is the primary goal during the first few weeks of treating a low-weight patient. A slow start helps patients adjust to following a food plan and to working with a nutrition counselor.
- Patients who have not eaten for 5–10 days or who weigh less than 70% of ideal body weight (IBW) are a risk for refeeding syndrome. With the development of more aggressive outpatient feeding methods, namely, family based therapy (FBT), and the flux of low-weight patients in outpatient settings, nutrition counselors should be alert to the symptoms of refeeding syndrome.
- The caloric protocol for weight restoration is based on patient's current intake and caloric additions are made one to three times a week: start with 200 to 300 calories above the patient's usual caloric intake; add 300 calories if weight gain has stymied; 500 calories if weight is lost.
- Weight restoration approaches usually result in gains of 1–3 pounds/week. Outpatients can generally tolerate, but rarely achieve, gains of up to 4 pounds/week.
- Success in correcting underweight in ED patients depends on the establishment and frequent revision of weight goals. Establishing weight goals and frequent monitoring of weights helps pace treatment and reassures patients that treatment will not lead to obesity.
- Once patients achieve BAW, caloric intake can be stabilized unless present intake does not allow for provision of adequate nutrients. When patients are comfortably maintaining a healthy weight, food plans should become less specific. Usually, directing patients to the type of guidance provided by a general food plan (specifying food groups to be consumed at meals) and to the physical cues of hunger and fullness is sufficient.
- Concurrent psychotherapy and SSRI medication should be considered.

10

TREATING BINGE EATING

Introduction

Binge eating is defined as eating unusually large amounts of food while experiencing a lack of control over eating. Loss of control is assessed by asking, "Did you have a sense of loss of control at the time?" "Could you have stopped eating once you had started?" "Could you have prevented the episode from occurring?" (Wolfe, Baker, Smith, and Kelly-Weeder, 2009). Patients who binge eat may have a diagnosis of anorexia nervosa (AN), bulimia nervosa (BN), or binge-eating disorder (BED). Some are overweight or obese and some not. Entrenched AN, especially if the body mass index (BMI) is less than 17.5, almost always includes bouts of binge eating (Lowe et al., 2011). It is important to note that binge eating is found in over 60% of AN patients and is known to delay or inhibit full recovery in AN (Tenconi, Lunardi, Zanetti, Santonastaso, & Favaro, 2006).

Definitions and Descriptions

Binges have been differentiated into subjective and objective binges. Subjective binges have been tentatively defined as less than 500 calories/episode (Wolfe et al., 2009). Some of our patients find this distinction helpful in decreasing purging: "This isn't really a binge so I don't have to purge." Both types of binges are associated with the compunction to purge. Patients are often oblivious to the potentially immense caloric contribution of an objective binge. In one study, binges averaged between 1,000–2,500 calories/episode, with the largest recorded at 10,500 calories (Alpers & Tuschen-Caffier, 2004).

A number of studies show that that most direct cause of binge eating in BN and BED is dietary restraint (Lowe, Thomas, Safer, & Butryn, 2007). Nearly all binge-eating patients enter treatment with a strong desire to lose weight and are profoundly discouraged about their prospects for recovery. Many are perfectionistic and have attempted multiple times to abstain from bingeing only to experience relapses that further erode their confidence. They are ashamed of their eating behaviors and suffer extreme body dissatisfaction. In this chapter we offer some reflection on the challenges of working with binge-eating patients and present solutions that we have found helpful in our practices.

As with other eating disorders (EDs), there is a strong suspicion that the tendency to engage in binge eating is inherited. An interesting variant on this theory is that an inherited tendency for higher body weight increases risk for bingeing (Cooper, 2009, p. 44).

Challenges

The Restriction–Binge Cycle

It is well known that food restriction increases the likelihood of binge eating. It is not uncommon for binge-eating patients to virtually starve during the day in order to save up calories for an expected evening binge. Patients also restrict food intake to compensate for calories previously ingested while bingeing. When this cycle becomes a habit, patients tolerate restrictive eating during the day in order to enjoy the freedom of eating whatever they want later. For some, the initial phase of the binge is pleasurable. Free from dietary restraint at last, they are relaxed, happy, and their selective focus on food tunes out other troubling thoughts. Patients also report that bingeing helps relieve stress, boredom, depression, anxiety, and anger. Other patients describe how they use bingeing to reduce vague feelings of uneasiness associated with transitional periods such as coming home from work or school, getting ready for bed, or beginning a study session. It is not unusual to dissociate while bingeing. For example, Sadie said, "I was surprised to see so many food wrappers when I cleaned up after my binge."

Restrictive eating and the tremendous willpower required when the body is in need of food depletes reserves of self-control. It leaves patients deprived of nutrients and calories and from the sensory pleasure food naturally provides. Furthermore, along with chronic denial and the disregard of hunger comes the proclivity to override and become insensitive to fullness signals. We explain this using our feast and famine analogy. Restrictive eating (famine) creates physical and psychological deprivation, which naturally and eventually leads to binge eating (feasting). The modern twists are that patients use the guilt they experience when bingeing to reinforce restrictive eating; they "feel thinner" during periods of food restriction; they don't want to "give-up" feeling thinner or the dietary righteousness and the sense of control that restrictive eating delivers; yet they feel defeated by the binge eating that inevitably follows restrictive eating. Continuous restrictive eating, however, further erodes actual control the patient might have over food intake. It is not surprising that patients believe any attempt to eat normally only leads to binge eating. In this mindset, one has no choice but to continue restrictive eating in order to maintain a tenuous hold on self-control and controlling body weight. Stice, Davis, Miller, and Marti (2008) found that fasting, defined as going without food for 24 hours or more for weight-loss purposes, increases the risk of binge eating even more than general dieting. Neumark-Sztainer, Wall, Guo, Story, Haines, and Eisenberg (2006) established that adolescent girls with elevated dietary-restraint scores are at increased risk for future binge eating. Empirical evidence and clinical experience leads us to expect that restrictive food behaviors that are maintained for about 9 months or longer will lead to binge eating.

Difficulty Losing Weight

Our careful review of the literature reveals these stark facts: cessation of binge eating does not lead to significant weight loss (at best, 5% of initial weight at 2 year follow-up); and behavioral weight-loss treatments do not lead to sustained weight loss or cessation of binge eating (Wilson, Wilfley, Agras, & Bryson, 2010). Our clinical experience is similar, although we often do see weight loss in young and adolescent patients with abstinence from binge eating. The good news, we tell our adult patients, is that we see slow, but significant weight loss in adult patients who have stopped binge eating and are engaged in cognitive–behavioral therapy (CBT)-flavored behavioral weight-loss treatments (see Weight Management below, pp. 238–240).

Food Rules

Food rules contribute to the tendency to binge eat. Typical "rules" include no eating after a certain time of day, avoiding foods with more than "x" amount of fat or calories, refusal to consume foods that lack nutrition labeling, and so forth. Food rules beg to be broken. When this occurs, patients naturally try to recommit to restrictive eating, but end up thinking, "I've already blown it. Why not binge?" We call this type of response black-and-white or all-or-nothing thinking, "The 'what the hell' response." As we noted earlier, Craighead prefers "what the heck" (see Chapter 5: Food Planning, pp. 107–139)

Reduced Calorie Needs

In spite of concerted efforts to eat minimally when not bingeing, most patients who binge on a regular basis gain weight or find that they must severely restrict intake to prevent weight gain. Although little research has been published recently, older studies show that high-calorie binges override the adaptive mechanisms that normally control body weight. If bingeing is followed by periods of restriction or purging, caloric needs seem to be reduced even further (Devlin, Walsh, Kral,

Heymsfield, Pi-Sunyer, & Dantzic, 1990). This effect has been documented in bulimic patients and even in anorexic patients who binge and purge (Weltzin, Fernstrom, Hansen, McConaha, & Kaye, 1991). In other words, ED patients who binge appear to need fewer calories than normal controls to maintain a stable weight. In our and others' experience, once a patient abstains from bingeing and purging and consistently follows a food plan, metabolism adjusts and weight is relatively easily maintained (Vanderlinden, Norré, & Vandereycken, 1992).

Body Dissatisfaction

Body dissatisfaction and fear of weight gain is associated with poor compliance with normalized eating and with increased frequency of binge-eating episodes. Many patients enter treatment reporting significant body dissatisfaction, and bingeing in ways that are almost self-abusive, reporting food choices and amounts that are incongruous with weight maintenance. Patients tell us: "I hate my body so it doesn't matter how I eat." Many of our binge-eating patients are large-sized individuals who report having gained a substantial amount of weight due to bingeing. Bulimic patients are usually within normal weight parameters, but likely to be heavier than their highest pre-morbid weight.

Health Consequences

Contrary to what most patients assume, binge eating is not associated with many health problems. Patients may be bothered by abdominal pain, bloating, flatulence, and constipation but these usually are not of any serious health consequence. A full stomach can press up on the diaphragm, interfering with respiration and making breathing feel heavier or labored. Patients who present with acute onset of abdominal pain accompanied by nausea, vomiting, and abdominal distention may be at risk for stomach dilatation and should be referred for immediate medical attention (Mitchell, Pomeroy, & Adson, 1997, p. 389). Actual rupture of the stomach due to binge eating has been documented, but only rarely. One of Herrin's patients, however, was at risk for rupture after bingeing on a large bowl of cookie dough, which expanded in her stomach. In extreme pain, she was rushed to the emergency room. A binge-eating patient of Larkin's developed severe gastroparesis (delayed gastric emptying) and was in severe pain when food stopped moving through her digestive tract. Certainly, if binge eating results in obesity, patients may incur the associated health risks for diabetes, heart disease, hypertension, and osteoarthritis.

Lack of Hunger and Fullness Signals

To further confound the situation, normal sensations of hunger and fullness are disrupted by cycles of restriction and binge eating. Some binge eaters constantly feel hungry and have voracious appetites; others report having no hunger or feeling full all the time. Still others say they only feel completely satisfied after bingeing. Not surprisingly, those who regularly restrict eating are likely to feel chronically hungry. Chronic hunger naturally leads to urges to overeat or to binge, or, alternatively, to an even more restrictive approach to food in an attempt to manage the hunger that feels increasingly out of control. Several recent studies indicate that binge eating in BN may be associated with a deficit in the development of satiation (Zimmerli, Devlin, Kissileff, & Walsh, 2010). The restrictive eating that leads to binge eating appears to alter appetite by increasing interest in food and strengthening the natural drive to eat. Deprived eaters, then, are likely to become obsessed with food and have enhanced sensory reactivity to the attractiveness of food. As restrictive eating continues, resisting the drive to eat becomes increasingly problematical.

Patients who report little appetite may be experiencing a mild form of ketosis. Nutrition counselors should explain that ketosis is an adaptation to food restriction which, among other consequences, mutes hunger. Furthermore, ketosis indicates the body has had to rely on protein from its own lean tissues to supply necessary calories. Increasing caloric intake corrects ketosis and allows appetite to return.

Shame-Based Thinking

To be effective in treating binge-eating patients, nutrition counselors must be sensitive to the shame associated with this behavior. Bingeing leaves most patients feeling appalled that they have eaten so much, and many intend to immediately purge or to restrict intake the next day or both. As shameful as patients might feel about their binge-eating behaviors, many also have some ambivalence about giving up their ED routines. They may use bingeing to distract themselves from other sources of shame or use restriction to offset their shame.

The Ups and Downs of Recovery

The majority of binge-eating patients are not prepared for the incremental or "up and down" type of progress that is typical of recovery from binge eating. The perfectionism typical of ED patients makes it likely they will become discouraged when they fail to be totally abstinent from binge eating. Nutrition counselors should inform patients that treatment will likely result in step-by-step reductions in bingeing rather than abrupt cessation. Of note, bulimic patients who stop purging behaviors "cold turkey" find that, almost immediately, bingeing behaviors are much diminished. We tell bulimic patients "When you give yourself permission to purge, you give yourself permission to binge." Those who continue to purge should be prepared for slower improvements in binge eating. On the other hand, once patients stop bingeing, they are likely to stop purging as well.

The Solutions

A lifetime nutritional plan of normal eating (e.g., the rule of threes (RO3s) food plan described in Chapter 5: Food Planning: Rule of Threes, pp. 107–139) is at the core of recovery from binge eating. In addition, counselor-guided self-help (using a self-help manual), CBT, and interpersonal therapy are found to aid recovery by developing assertiveness, and interpersonal relationship and stress management skills (Ansell, Grilo, & White, 2012; Wilson et al., 2010). Antidepressant [selective serotonin reuptake inhibitor (SSRI)] medication reduces bingeing and purging, but alone does not sustain recovery (Mehler & Andersen, 2010).

The Formulation

Central to Fairburn's (2008) CBT-Enhanced treatment for ED is the development of a relatively simple "formulation" or explanation of why a patient binges. The process of creating a "formulation" is intended to be collaborative and engaging. It involves dialoguing or reviewing food journals to uncover what appears to be triggering the patient's binge eating or what purpose the binge eating serves (Cooper & Fairburn, 2010, p. 249). For example, when discussing what led up to a binge, Herrin learned that Jake did not eat lunch because, "I am fat so it's OK that I missed lunch." This formulation makes the point that there was deprivation (physical hunger) at the root of the binge rather than some defect in the patient's character such that he cannot control eating. To make matters worse, Jake's negative self-talk ("I am fat") reinforces low self-esteem and perceived lack of self-control that is characteristic of the binge cycle. Binge eating, then, turns into a self-fulfilling prophecy. With this new understanding, Jake was able to eat lunch so he could better resist bingeing.

Putting together a formulation assures patients that we understand their problem, that we respect their struggle, and that there is hope. The formulation also helps patients see that binge eating is a reasonable response to dieting, stress, and negative emotions. It helps patients to maintain a healthy distance from their problems, improves their self-esteem, and provides us with a guide to the patterns that need to be targeted in treatment. We reiterate that, to overcome binge eating, the mechanisms (i.e., dieting, managing stress and moods, and an unhealthy focus on weight and shape) that maintain binge eating must change (Cooper & Fairburn, 2010, p. 250). We remind patients that binge eating, itself, maintains the core belief about the lack of ability to control eating, shape, and weight. Fairburn's self-help book, *Overcoming Binge Eating*, (1995, p. 134) outlines additional benefits associated with recovery from binge eating: reduced depression, tension, and irritability; increased energy, self-confidence, self-respect, and self-image; a wider range of interests; improved concentration, relationships, and health; and a return of the ability to recognize hunger and fullness.

Self-Monitoring

Self-monitoring journals provide data that can confirm or revise the CBT-Enhanced formulation discussed above. Significant research shows that self-monitoring is particularly effective in changing binge-eating behaviors (Cooper & Fairburn, 2010). For some patients, self-monitoring is treatment enough to interrupt binge-eating behaviors. Others may worry about increased preoccupation with eating as a result of self-monitoring. We concur, but point out that self-monitoring is a time-limited constructive preoccupation that will eventually help overcome binge eating. Completing self-monitoring journals (as described in Chapter 6: Self-Monitoring) helps patients observe the relationship between restrictive eating and binge eating, as well as the influences of mood, time, and place. Some patients notice they are likely to binge if they have eaten past a comfortable level of fullness at a meal, or if they consume even moderate amount of foods viewed as fattening. Others observe that particular situations promote binge eating, such as eating in the car, eating alone, or eating in a certain restaurant. For others, studying or watching television leads to binge eating. Many of our patients note that feelings of boredom and loneliness are associated with binge eating.

As mentioned in Chapter 6: Self-Monitoring (see pp. 140–149 for more information), our experience shows self-monitoring (via food journals) is only effective if the patient is interested in and able to devote time to journaling. Self-monitoring, we point out, provides valuable information about eating problems, making clear binge patterns and triggers, and allows the nutrition counselor to play detective, looking for clues to solutions to binge-eating episodes. We also mention that self-monitoring immediately after bingeing makes it less likely that one will dissociate and more likely that one will have smaller binges. Patients tell us that just knowing that their nutrition counselor is going to look over their food journal keeps them "on the straight and narrow" and fosters their commitment to follow a food plan. In addition, reviewing journals give the nutrition counselor occasion to provide much needed encouragement to demoralized patients. We make the point of commending patients for completing journals and for any and all constructive behaviors. We discuss with patients how shame about binge-eating behaviors can make self-monitoring difficult, while emphasizing that, to overcome binge eating, behaviors must be faced head on.

Food Planning

CBT-Enhanced endorses a regular plan for eating three meals and two to three snacks as the fundamental solution to binge eating (Cooper & Fairburn, 2010, p. 252). Our RO3s food plan (for more information see Chapter 5: Food Planning: Rule of Threes, pp. 107–139) is such a plan. Very detailed food plans describing exactly when, what, and how much to eat are necessary for some patients but others do well with the general guidance provided by the RO3s. Provision of adequate calories and nutrients is crucial at meals and snacks, otherwise patients will remain biologically dissatisfied and at risk for bingeing. As a rule, intakes less than 1,500–2,000 calories are insufficient to meet nutrient, energy, or sensory needs and are unlikely to prevent binge eating. Food plans to treat binge eating should provide at least 1,500–2,000 calories, with additional calories for males and for very active patients. We recommend snacks in the 200–500 calories range. For patients who frequently binge, it is wiser to err on the side of generosity when designing initial food plans. We tell our patients over and over again that regular eating in this fashion does not cause weight gain and protects against binge eating. Our other refrain is, "We can't help you work on weight loss until you stop bingeing." On the other hand, underweight and or amenorrheic patients must be informed that weight gain is required before remission of binge eating can be expected.

A food plan of normally proportioned and timed meals and snacks gives patients control over binge eating by increasing general satiety. Not surprisingly, studies of appetite control indicate that meals that are well balanced in carbohydrate, protein, and fat and provide adequate calories are most satiating. Nutrient-balanced meals modulate meal size and delay the emergence of hunger and future interest in eating. Our review of the literature on nutritional control of appetite shows that, calorie for calorie, protein has the greatest satiating effect. One recent study compared diets of 20% and 30% of calories from protein and found the 30% protein diet more satisfying (Jönsson, Granfeldt, Erlanson-Albertsson, Ahren, & Lindeberg, 2010). Protein and carbohydrates are efficient appetite suppressants in that they influence meal size and delay the emergence of hunger and future interest in eating. While dietary fat seems to have little effect on appetite at the time of consumption, fat consumption clearly delays future eating. Patients who systematically avoid either protein, carbohydrate, or fat will have continued difficulty in resisting binge eating. Based on research on carbohydrate cravings, we recommend that for snacks binge eaters eat protein along with carbohydrates (e.g., cheese and crackers, peanut butter and fruit, or cottage cheese and vegetables; Corsica & Spring, 2008).

Most patients, however, are skeptical about the notion that having a plan for regular eating protects against binge eating. The knowledge, however, that guidance is provided by an experienced, competent nutrition counselor can help give the patient confidence that a food plan will provide the promised results over time: elimination of binge eating and maintenance of a biologically appropriate weight (BAW).

First Steps

Nutrition counselors may want to suggest patients make their first dietary improvements in protein intake, as foods in this group are likely to have the greatest impact on appetite regulation. Suggestions to increase consumption of protein are often well received, since fewer patients have anxieties about this nutrient. Of note, it has been supposed that following a food plan increases patients' innate fear of weight gain so much so that they are afraid to binge (Vanderlinden et al., 1992, p. 74).

Cooper (2009) provides several strategies that our patients have found helpful:

- *Decide in advance when to eat meals and snacks.* This means eating only when a meal or snack is scheduled and not eating at other times.
- *Decide in advance to end a meal with a full stop.* This means no more eating until the next scheduled meal or snack. On the RO3s plan, the meal ends after the fun food is eaten.
- *Decide in advance to problem-solve.* When a problem arises, write out the problem, produce as many solutions as possible, consider the pros and cons of each solution, choose the best solution, and at the end of the day evaluate the effectiveness of the chosen solution. If the solution is not effective, brainstorm other solutions.

Always Return to the Food Plan

Binges must not replace meals or planned snacks. We advise our patients to have meals and snacks regardless of whether they have previously binged. If bingeing occurs, patients should be instructed to immediately return to the food plan and eat the next scheduled meal or snack. Patients who abide by this instruction find that binge eating is minimized and planned eating is reinforced.

The Usual Suspect is Deprivation

If patients complain about a resurgence in binge eating, they should be quizzed about prior dietary restriction. Typical restrictive patterns include long intervals between meals and snacks, inadequate and unsatisfying snacks, and exclusion of favorite foods. We often ask, in an effort to understand why a patient binged, "I wonder if you ate enough (e.g., calories, fat, protein) at your previous meal?" We prepare our patients to expect incremental decline in the frequency and size of binges if they continue to abide by the food plan. We use the reports of occasional binges as object lessons on what "you could have done differently." Patients need to be told that the most powerful behavioral strategy for interrupting a pattern of binge eating is an immediate return to the food plan and consumption of the next scheduled meal or snack.

For underweight patients, appetite can feel so insatiable they become terrified of binge eating. We advise such patients to match their appetite by quickly increasing caloric intake through generous interpretation of the food plan. Patients who do not do so are likely to lose weight or to binge. It should be noted that, to gain at reasonable rates (1–3 pounds/week), most patients are required to eat beyond a comfortable level of fullness at meals. Patients in these circumstances may worry that this level of fullness means they are binge eating. We maintain that, without question, eating scheduled meals and snacks despite lack of hunger and feeling 'stuffed' after an evening snack is not bingeing. We have several underweight patients whose plans specify snacks of 1,000 calories. Hunger before meals, on the other hand, may indicate the need to increase caloric intake yet again. Once normal weight is achieved, patients can expect both hunger and satiety to normalize. It is important to keep in mind that most people, whether they have an ED or not, are able to perceive hunger more accurately than satiety, as basic health and wellness is more threatened by undereating than overeating.

Hunger and Fullness

We assure our patients that a well-regulated appetite-control system will arise when an orderly pattern of eating is practiced. Furthermore, we inform them that it may take as long as 6 months of following a food plan for "recalibration" of hunger and satiety cues to occur. One way to summarize these facts is to say, "At the moment, you cannot rely on your feelings of hunger or fullness as they are corrupted by your eating disorder. If you consistently follow a biologically sound food plan (e.g., RO3s plan), your appetite will recalibrate and once again become a trustworthy guide to when and how much to eat." One aim of our RO3s plan, we tell our patients, is to adjust appetite so that it accurately reflects biological needs. To achieve this we say, "You must eat no less and no more than the prescribed food plan" (Fairburn, 2008, p. 77). We interpret continued binge eating as indicating that the food plan is not biologically or psychologically satisfying and needs to be revised. Although patients will be apprehensive about weight gain, food plans should be gradually modified to include more calories, particularly from protein and fat, until binge eating subsides.

Foods with Boundaries

Initially, patients often benefit from use of pre-portioned foods. These are foods with intrinsic "boundaries," either pre-packaged in single servings, like many snack foods, or microwavable dinners or naturally proportioned foods like potatoes or bagels. When it is clear patients have confidence in their ability to follow a food plan, we begin to encourage increasingly varied food choices, including former "binge" foods. This strategy prevents feelings of deprivation, lessens food cravings, and helps patients stop categorizing food as safe or dangerous, all of which, if unaddressed, can trigger a binge-eating event.

Weight Management

As one would expect, binge-eating behaviors interfere with behavioral weight-loss treatments. Behavioral weight-loss treatments also interfere with efforts to decrease binge eating (Wilson et al., 2010). We tell patients, "Bingeing guarantees you won't lose weight." While we respect the patient's intent to lose weight, we emphasize that normalization of eating behaviors must be established before we can work on weight loss. We tell our patients that recovery from binge eating is an absolute prerequisite for successful long-term weight management (Gorin et al., 2008).

BED is strongly associated with severe obesity (BMI 40; Hudson, Hiripi, Pope, & Kessler, 2007). Consequently, we have a good number of binge-eating patients seek treatment primarily for weight loss. We inform patients there is no more effective first step toward weight management than to learn how to abstain from bingeing. In discussing this issue with patients, we aim to be empathetic and collaborative ("We'll figure this out together"), supportive ("I know how worried you are about your weight"), confident ("I am not going to let your weight get out of control"), and guardedly optimistic ("It can be a long process, but we will figure out how you can reach and maintain your BAW"). We reiterate that focus on weight management must wait until eating behaviors are under control.

We hold closely to the position of the Academy of Nutrition and Dietetics (Ozier & Henry, 2011) that nutrition counselors should support body acceptance and health-centered behaviors rather than weight-centered dieting. Our approach to weight loss is akin in many ways to Health at Every Size (HAES), Size Acceptance, Intuitive Eating and Mindful Eating programs. These non-diet approaches focus on weight-neutral outcomes and improving eating and exercise behaviors by encouraging size acceptance, unrestricted eating, and a heightened awareness of and response to hunger and fullness. Our review of the literature indicates that non-diet programs lead to clinically significant improvements in physiological measures (e.g., blood pressure, blood lipids), health behaviors (e.g., eating and activity habits, and dietary quality), and psychosocial outcomes (e.g., self-esteem and body image; Bacon & Aphramor, 2011; Bacon, Stern, Van Loan, & Keim, 2005; Provencher et al., 2009). It is likely that non-diet methods have gained acceptance in large part due to the poor results of standard weight-loss programs in achieving sustainable weight loss and their potential for adverse consequences such as binge eating, weight cycling, reduced self-esteem, eating disorders, and weight stigmatization (Bacon & Aphramor, 2011).

Once binge eating has been extinguished, we "tinker" with the RO3s plan, gradually reducing portion sizes to help large-sized patients achieve weight loss at a rate of about 1 pound/month. Faster rates may be seen in larger patients. We find slow weight loss is least triggering for relapse of ED behaviors. In our clinical experiences, we find that weight stabilizes after losing 10–40 pounds or about 5–20% of initial body weight. These results are significantly better than standard behavioral weight-loss treatment. Literature reviews of behavioral weight-loss treatment for obesity indicate that 5–10% loss of initial weight can be expected, but most subjects were not able to maintain losses beyond a year (Franz et al., 2007; Jain, 2005). The patients who remain in nutrition counseling and follow the RO3s plan often maintain lost weight or continue to lose weight. We have also found it helpful to explore the impact of the prevailing cultural preference for thinness.

As most patients remain skeptical, nutrition counselors need to continually state that following the RO3s plan will not cause weight gain even when servings of foods previously avoided by the patient are included. Patients who have gained weight as the result of their ED find they slowly lose weight once they consistently abide by a food plan. Only rarely will patients gain weight following the RO3s plan. Usually, these patients had previously restricted food intake. We assure them that this effect is small and transitory and will quickly disappear once their metabolism is rejuvenated by normalized food intake (Vanderlinden et al., 1992, p. 70; Rosenbaum, Hirsch, Gallagher, & Leibel, 2008).

Somewhat tongue in cheek, we refer to the RO3s plan as the "Dessert Diet: The sweetest way to lose™." We find that this slowly paced, patterned, all-foods-are-allowed approach gives patients the opportunity to resolve self-esteem, food behaviors, weight, body shape, and size issues. If binge eating reappears, we increase portion sizes and refocus on ED behaviors and thoughts.

Weight Monitoring

Regular weight monitoring is recommended in CBT for binge eating as a method to reduce obsessive self-weight checking. Weight monitoring also provides assurance that instituting regular meals and snacks does not result in weight gain (Cooper & Fairburn, 2010). We tell our patients that weight checks "allow your body to give me feedback on the food plan." Marion reported obsessing constantly about her body weight. "Sometimes," she said, "I binge out of worry about my weight." After several weight checks during nutrition visits, Marion reported less concern about her weight and was able to eat more modestly.

We find that our patients, whether normal weight or larger sized, benefit from being involved in discussions about the most efficacious way to monitor their weight. Many choose in-office weigh-ins, standing on the scale backwards in street clothes, with general feedback about weight trends. Others do better checking their weight facing forward on the scale. Some patients report having made a commitment to avoid weight checks of any kind. This commitment should be respected. If, however, weight concerns begin to dominate nutrition sessions, in-office weight checks should be suggested. Others weigh themselves at home or the gym daily, weekly, or monthly and are willing to report weights to their counselor, or they also want an in-office weight checks to confirm home weight data. We do not discourage these practices unless they becomes obsessive, but we do recommend that self-weight checks occur no more than once a week, at the same time of day, and in similar attire. (See Chapter 8: Assessing Weight, pp. 169–190.)

Behavioral Strategies

A number of tactics have been developed to manage the various problems patients are likely to encounter as they work at controlling binge eating. We have created our own list (see Box 10.1) based on the strategies that have worked for our patients. A number of these strategies have been developed by patients, themselves. It

---

BOX 10.1 ALTERNATIVES TO BINGE EATING

Eat three satisfying meals and one-to-three snacks/day

Do not get overly hungry

Eat one normal serving if you eat when you aren't hungry

Do not skip meals

Increase protein

Be alert if you are "feeling fat"

Plan your days to avoid unstructured time

Talk to a friend

Eat with a friend

Exercise in a healthful manner

Keep busy

Take deep breaths

Explore the internet

Engage in a non-food-related passion (find one if you don't have one)

Dance

Sleep

Take a walk

Meditate

Do a hobby

Knit or crochet

Journal

Make a collage

Delay (e.g., wait 10 minutes or longer if you can) if you choose to binge

Do positive self-talk

Have a plan (preferably something enjoyable) for immediately after

Talk yourself out of it

Repeat helpful phrases

Leave a tempting situation

Avoid triggering situations or foods

Do e-mail

Listen to music that makes you feel good

Do a sport

Relax

Imagine yourself in a beautiful place

Rest

Treat yourself with something other than food

Paint

Do your nails

Yoga

Take a class

Read a book

Draw

Write a story

Make an iTunes playlist

If you do overeat or binge

Do not berate yourself for urges or failures

Eat your next scheduled meal or snack

Do not weigh yourself

Learn from your failures

Do not purge

Practice loving kindness

should be noted that, even though these tactics are often effective, few of them are likely to be practiced by normal eaters. These behavioral approaches, therefore, should be used prudently and targeted at specific problems, but never at the expense of efforts to normalize food behaviors.

Alternatives to Overeating or Bingeing

In cases of recurring bingeing, we have had success advising patients to pick three to four things from the alternatives to bingeing list that they must do before allowing themselves to binge. Recording the "alternative behaviors" on self-monitoring forms allows for assessment of the strength of this strategy. We instruct patients who binge because of unpleasant feelings, such as loneliness, restlessness, boredom, anxiety, and the like, to substitute other behaviors for bingeing. (For more discussion on distress tolerance and emotional regulation see Chapter 4: Counseling Interventions, pp. 79–104.) For example, if the patient is lonely, she or he should arrange to be in the company of others or phone a friend. With a touch of humor, we commiserate with patients that very few alternatives are truly incompatible with eating, though patients have reported that knitting, woodworking, and oil painting are just such activities. We help our patients formulate a personalized list of pleasurable, simple, and distracting activities or provide them with a list of alternative activities others have found helpful. We also work on pre-empting binge-eating behaviors by suggesting a commitment to engage in an alternative activity at specified times of the day. We may draw up an individualized plan of alternative activities for a number of days in advance (Case Example 10.1).

CASE EXAMPLE 10.1: ABIGAIL

After lunch, go for a walk.
After snack, call or text a friend.
After dinner, brush teeth and spend 30 minutes on a hobby.
Go to bed before 10 p.m.

Programmed Binges

For some patients, the paradoxical approach of programming binges is necessary to achieve a decrease in binge-eating behavior. This approach allows patients to experience success because controlling binge-eating behaviors is usually more feasible than eliminating them altogether. Programmed binges designate the amount and kind of food and times and places that patients are allowed to binge.

Another related approach is to suggest patients pick the amount of time they know they can abstain before bingeing. For example, wait 5–10 minutes, and then longer spans of time, before bingeing. Patients who are bingeing multiple times a day may be able to agree to limit binges to once a day. Other patients may be able to promise to binge every other day in the afternoon, but not in the evening. Designating specific times and places for bingeing has proven to be beneficial. For example, a patient commits to only allowing binge eating if seated at the kitchen table. This is particularly helpful for those who previously binged in bed or sitting in the living room watching television. A specific intervention that many of Herrin's patients have found helpful is the "tuna solution." Patients are instructed to keep cans of tuna available and to eat one can "straight up" (i.e. no bread, crackers, or mayonnaise) before they allow themselves to binge. This dose of nearly pure protein biologically reduces urges to binge and, as many patients have reported, "I realized that I didn't want to binge badly enough to do the tuna solution first."

We occasionally suggest patients prepare a "binge bag" which is stored out of sight (e.g., in the trunk of the car). Instructions are to buy and store in the binge bag $10 to $20 worth of any food or combination of foods. Older patients may intentionally limit their access to cash in order to reduce bingeing; buying something nice with the funds that would have been spent on binge foods. With adolescents, parents offer an allowance dedicated to buying binge foods, leaving the child free to use the left money as he or she pleases. Some families have success making the kitchen off-limits outside of specified times. Others lock the refrigerator or put binge-provoking foods in a locked cabinet or box. Although these approaches can help ease tensions that arise when a family member binges regularly, when such extreme measures are deemed necessary, the possibility that the patient may benefit from a higher level of treatment should be considered.

We also remind our patients that each person has limited reserves of self-control. These reserves should not be "wasted" on restrictive eating. In fact, most patients need all the self-control they can muster to withstand the temptation to binge. It can be a relief for patients to hear that binge eating is a normal, expected response to restricted eating behaviors. Binge eating does not mean patients lack will power (Winocur, 1990, p. 67). On the contrary, patients can be told they demonstrate exceptional control over food except when they binge. Exploring the possibility that a patient may feel ashamed or ambivalent about binge-eating behaviors can help her or him feel understood and less resistant to treatment (Siegfried & Mullins, 2009). Through the process of helping patients manage binge-eating behaviors, we remind ourselves to be generous in offering emphatic understanding and to acknowledge the necessary bravery and trust and the resulting pain in disclosing a behavior that normally causes shame.

It is characteristic of patients to pair bingeing with other activities such as reading, studying, using the computer, or watching television. Patients who do so usually describe a dissociated quality during binge episodes. These patients can experiment by avoiding these distractions while eating. Not surprisingly, many patients find that if they eat with others they are able to remain focused on their food plan and are unlikely to binge.

Guided Self-Help

We have found, as published research supports, that guided self-help adds power to interventions aimed at reducing binge eating (Wilson et al., 2010). Our approach is to recommend or lend one of the following books listed in Box 10.2 to patients to read and "work on" between sessions.

BOX 10.2 SUGGESTED RESOURCES

Cooper, P. J. (2009). *Overcoming bulimia nervosa and binge-eating.* New York: Basic Books.

Fairburn, C. G. (1995). *Overcoming binge eating.* New York: Guilford Press.

Koenig, K. R. (2005). *The rules of "normal" eating: A commonsense approach for dieters, overeaters, undereaters, emotional eaters, and everyone in between!* Carlsbad, CA: Gurze Books.

Matz, J., & Frankel, E. (2006). *The diet survivor's handbook.* Naperville, IL: Sourcebooks.

Tribole, E., & Resch, E. (2012). *Intuitive eating: A revolutionary program that works* (3rd ed.). New York: St. Martin's Griffin.

Referrals

Nutrition counseling often allows patients to become aware of emotional states that are associated with binge episodes. Patients who continue to exhibit psychological distress despite having resolved eating-disordered behaviors should be referred for psychotherapy. Referrals for psychotherapy should also be considered for patients who continue to binge despite having corrected nutritional intake and food patterns. Many patients benefit from conjunctive psychodynamic psychotherapy that allows an opportunity to express and understand feelings and conflicts, to gain insight into the meanings and functions of binge-eating behaviors, and to develop more appropriate coping skills (Wilson et al., 2010).

Psychotropic Medication

The same selective serotonin reuptake inhibitor (SSRI) antidepressant medications that are beneficial in the treatment of AN are used in BN and BED (see Chapter 9: Restoring Weight, pp. 191–228). SSRI treatment for BN has significant research evidence for efficacy (American Psychiatric Association, 2006, p. 20). It is hypothesized that one reason these medications are effective in BN is because they are also effective in treating common co-morbid problems such as depression, anxiety, phobias, panic attacks, obsessive–compulsive disorder (OCD), premenstrual dysphoria (PMS), post-traumatic stress disorder (PTSD), and impulse-control disorders. There is much less research, but, nonetheless, substantial evidence indicates that SSRI are modestly efficacious for binge eating in BED over the short term (McElroy, Guerdjikova, Mori, & O'Melia, 2012). Researchers in this area also hypothesize that SSRI's usefulness may stem from its impact on the depressive symptoms and other co-morbid problems that may occur in BED. As in AN, effective doses of SSRIs in BN and BED are usually over twice as high as doses typically prescribed for depression and anxiety. The American Psychiatric Association (2006, pp. 20, 83) suggests fluoxetine in doses of 60–80 mg/day for BN in adolescents and adults. Similar doses of fluoxetine were used in the BED clinical trials (McElroy et al., 2012). As nutrition counselors, we often find ourselves in the position of recommending the consideration of a trial of SSRI therapy or an increase in dose to an effective level.

Summary Points

- Recovery from binge eating is absolutely necessary for successful long-term weight management.
- Bingeing helps relieve stress, boredom, depression, anxiety, and anger. Patients use bingeing to reduce vague feelings of uneasiness associated with transitional periods such as coming home from work or school, getting ready for bed, or beginning a study session.
- Food restriction increases the likelihood of binge eating. It is common for binge-eating patients to virtually starve during the day in order to save up calories for the evening.
- Body dissatisfaction and fear of weight gain is associated with poor compliance with normalized eating and increased frequency of binge-eating episodes.
- Normal sensations of hunger and fullness are disrupted by cycles of restriction and binge eating.
- Exploring the possibility that a patient may feel ashamed or ambivalent about binge-eating behaviors can help her or him feel understood and less resistant to treatment.
- Most often, cessation of binge eating does not cause weight gain and may lead to modest weight loss of about 5% of initial weight at 2-year follow-up.
- Behavior strategies should be used prudently and targeted at specific problems, but never at the expense of efforts to normalize food behaviors.
- Concurrent psychotherapy and SSRI medication should be considered if bingeing behaviors do not quickly resolve.

11

MANAGING PURGING

Introduction

Purging, especially self-induced vomiting, is a difficult behavior to extinguish. Patients usually agree when we say that purging is the eating-disorder (ED) behavior that is most addicting. We respectfully acknowledge that purging may seem like a logical solution to a number of problems. Besides an ersatz weight-management tool, purging provides short-term relief of anxiety, resulting in relaxation, exhilaration, and even a sense of "purity." To be effective with patients who purge, we find that we must be sympathetic, tolerant, and understanding of each patient's difficulties, particularly his or her embarrassment about purging. We keep in mind that correcting purging behaviors takes much effort on the patient's part and constant encouragement and help with problem-solving on our part. In this chapter, we define and describe purging behaviors (see Chapter 1: Clinical Features of Eating Disorders, pp. 3–31) and then devote the rest of the chapter to describing approaches we use to help patients become free of the compulsion to purge.

Definitions and Descriptions

Purging behaviors (self-induced vomiting, laxative, and diuretic abuse) are compensatory measures aimed at preventing weight gain, eliminating calories consumed during regular meals and binge-eating episodes, feeling empty, and restoring a flat stomach after bingeing. Patients accept as true that purging gets rid of calories and frequently report that purging allows them to lose weight despite significant binge-eating episodes. Over time, however, the majority of patients find that their body weight increases; it is then that they usually seek treatment.

Self-induced vomiting is by far the most common purging method. Patients may binge and purge numerous times per occurrence. Some patients purge normal-sized meals; some purge if they feel even slightly full or if they have eaten something they feel is fattening; and still others purge everything they eat.

Some, who chronically self-induce vomiting, find they do not have to gag to purge: they regurgitate at will (e.g., leaning over, pushing on abdomen) or even involuntarily. Patients may normalize involuntary behavior, concluding it means that their body really does not want or need the food since the vomiting was not self-induced. They may come to believe that purging in this manner is not associated with an ED. We have had patients who sought medical evaluation for gastro-esophageal reflux disease instead.

Laxative abuse leaves a uniquely empty feeling that is reassuring. Patients often believe that over-the-counter laxatives are benign. The laxative that is most often abused is Ex-Lax (Steffen, Mitchell, Roerig, & Lancaster, 2007). Bulk-forming laxatives (such as Metamucil) are infrequently abused, but we have patients who are dependent on them. Diuretics are used in the hope of reducing bloating and body weight. Our patients who use diuretics say they feel "lighter" and thinner. Diuretic use leads to a temporary loss of 2–4 pounds of fluid that can be mistaken for weight loss (Mehler, 2011). Other purging methods include misuse of prescription medications (e.g., prescription thyroid medications), enemas, spitting (chewing and spitting out food without swallowing), rumination (regurgitating food into the mouth and re-swallowing it), fasting, extended breast-feeding, and overuse of saunas and sweat suits. Diabetic eating-disordered patients may omit doses of insulin, thereby interfering with glucose metabolism. Ipecac may be misused. Ipecac is rarely stocked by drugstores since an expert panel at the U.S. Food and Drug Administration recommended, but did not rule, that ipecac syrup be available only by prescription (Pfister, 2010). Of note, ipecac remains available on the internet. Excessive exercise when used to compensate for ingested calories or eating episodes is considered a method of purging. Exercise is deemed excessive when it interferes with important activities, occurs at inappropriate times and in inappropriate settings, or when patients exercise despite injury or other medical complications. Patients may purge by abusing diet pills and appetite suppressants (see Box 11.1 for more information). Of note, using multiple methods of purging indicates a more serious ED (Edler, Haedt, & Keel, 2007).

BOX 11.1 THE DANGERS ASSOCIATED WITH DIET PILLS AND APPETITE SUPPRESSANTS

Abuse of diet pills and other appetite suppressants in EDs is well documented, with prevalence estimates reported as high as 50% in patients who use other methods of purging (Celio et al., 2006). Nearly all ED patients who take appetite-suppressing diet pills will discontinue use as the ED progresses because they are found to be relatively ineffective compared to other ED behaviors (de Zwaan & Mitchell, 1993, p. 64). We remind our patients that most diet pills and appetite suppressants are considered "dietary supplements" by the U.S. Food and Drug Administration and do not have to have demonstrated safety or efficacy. Roerig et al. (2003) illustrates the risk by recounting a misformulated diet pill compounded in Belgium that left 70 people in complete renal failure and 50 individuals with kidney damage. The 37 individuals who had a kidney removed were found to have either cancer or precancerous lesions. Currently, popular ingredients in over-the-counter diet pills and supplements include: hoodia, caffeine, guar gum, green tea extract, chromium, acai fruit, and bitter orange. Many of these ingredients cause gastrointestinal symptoms or stimulant-like effects that could pose serious health risks, especially to those who are medically compromised by an ED. Except for the modest effects of Orlistat or Xenical (prescription gastrointestinal lipase blockers), which cause diarrhea and carry warnings about potential liver complications, there is no clinical evidence for the efficacy of diet pills. Alli is the half-strength over-the-counter version of Orlistat (Mayo Clinic, 2010; U.S. Food and Drug Administration, 2010).

Challenges

Purging "Feels Good"

For many patients, purging has its own rewards. Purging temporarily relieves the anxiety and fear of weight gain associated with bingeing. Purging also serves as an emotional release for other negative feelings such as anger, frustration, and anxiety. Patients report that purging helps them feel back in control of their eating after a binge; the purge "wipes the slate clean" or "corrects eating mistakes," so to speak. Other patients say: "It just feels good to get the food out of my system." "It's a control issue. If I can't control what goes in my mouth, I can control what comes out of it."

After a purge, patients tell us they feel calmer and more organized. Purging quite easily becomes a compulsion and a solution for a wide range of food and emotional issues, as well as a form of self-punishment and abuse (Fairburn, 2008, p. 84). We often acknowledge to patients that the only actual benefits are the temporary "flat stomach" after self-induced vomiting and the also fleeting concave abdomen associated with serious laxative abuse.

Purging Creates a Vicious Cycle

Eventually, most patients feel trapped in a vicious cycle in which they must purge (to get rid of binge calories) and they must binge to feel full enough to purge. Most patients find that it is easier to induce vomiting if they have just consumed a large amount of food. Eventually purging results in feelings of dietary deprivation, the consequences of which are strong urges to binge eat. Patients who purge are more likely to binge eat than those who abstain from purging. Moreover, patients who purge consume more food when they binge than those who do not purge. In a typical scenario, once deciding to purge a patient has permission to continue to binge, "I might as well eat more since I am going to rid of it."

Purging also sets in motion a cycle of weight fluctuations associated primarily with dehydration and rebound water retention. Patients characteristically interpret a gaunt-looking face or flat stomach after purging as signs of weight loss rather than dehydration. On the other hand, when patients see signs of the ensuing water retention, namely, a puffy face or swollen extremities, they erroneously assume they have gained weight. Moreover, the enlarged salivary glands associated with self-induced vomiting also gives the impression of weight gain.

The situation is further complicated by the need for secrecy to engage in purging behaviors. In some cases, patients feel "obligated" to purge when they are alone or have the opportunity. Patients who live with others may have interpersonal conflicts resulting from purging behaviors. It is not uncommon for vomiting to clog plumbing; housemates may complain about odors and dirty bathrooms. The considerable costs in time and money associated with maintaining the binge/purge cycle can be burdensome as well.

Solutions

If self-induced vomiting does not cease when binge eating is discontinued, it must be tackled head on through self-monitoring (see Chapter 6: Self-Monitoring, pp. 140–149), food plans (see Chapter 5: Food Planning: Rule of Threes, pp. 107–139), and the strategies we describe below.

Psycho-education

Psycho-education regarding the negative effects of purging on health and appearance and the futility of purging to manage weight can be motivating enough for some patients to stop these behaviors (Vanderlinden, Norré, & Vandereycken,

1992, p. 92). (For more about using psycho-education see Chapter 4: Counseling Interventions, pp. 79–104.) With correction of common misconceptions and the creation of sufficient motivation, patients often can just stop abusing laxatives, diuretics, appetite suppressants, and diet pills, even if they have been using these substances for a long-time. Self-induced vomiting, a more entrenched behavior pattern, usually requires additional treatment strategies to extinguish.

Effects on Health

Purging is associated with significant health problems, many of which are life threatening especially for low-weight patients (See Chapter 1: Clinical Features of Eating Disorders, pp. 3–31). A good number of patients are unaware that purging can cause serious problems. Some feel immune to the consequences of purging because they have not yet experienced any negative symptoms. Repeated warnings about the dangers of purging to these patients is usually ineffectual.

Nevertheless, all patients should be informed about the potential health risks of purging behaviors. Thanks to our years of clinical practice, we have many stories of other patients' experiences to help make our points about the dangers of purging. The dramatic story of Eliza who binged on a large batch of cookie dough is compelling (we mentioned her story in Chapter 1: Clinical Features of Eating Disorders, p. 28). After trying without success to purge, the dough expanded in the warmth of Eliza's stomach. Her father, a nurse, knew she had to be rushed to the hospital to have her stomach pumped before it ruptured. Josie, like many other patients, developed a weak gag reflex due to chronic self-induced vomiting. We explain a weak gag reflex as "a door opened too many times the wrong way." As a result, Josie, had to resort to using elongated objects (toothbrushes, spoons) in increasingly vigorous efforts to self-induce vomiting; the toothbrush she swallowed subsequently needed to be surgically removed.

Over-the-counter diuretics rarely cause medical complications. Although if misused, the substantial amounts of caffeine many diuretics contain may lead to headaches, trembling, and rapid heart rate, among other caffeine-related symptoms. Despite the fact that non-prescription diuretics have few side-effects, their use should be discouraged, for several reasons: their use may evolve into abuse of more dangerous prescription diuretics; and the use of diuretics perpetuates the binge/purge cycle and unhealthy approaches to weight control.

Effects on Appearance

Although warnings about potential health risks of purging behaviors appear to have minimal effects on behavioral change, problems related to appearance are usually of greater interest. We describe how purging can cause: puffiness; sores around the mouth; red, rough hands; red spots around the eyes; swollen face and neck; and yellow teeth and other unsightly dental problems.

Edema is the likely explanation for feelings of "puffiness" and abrupt increases in body weight. We often see patients with painful sores (cheilosis) at the angles of the mouth, hoarseness, and sore throats. Red, rough abrasions and calluses on the dorsum of the hand and knuckles (Russell's sign) is a classic indicator of the habit of forcibly inserting fingers into the throat to induce vomiting. The strain of vomiting can cause hemorrhages on the cornea and petechial (tiny red spots) hemorrhages on the face. While these can be unsightly, they are not of medical significance. Salivary gland enlargements are common in patients who binge and vomit. The hypertrophy of these glands gives those afflicted swollen faces and puffy-looking jaws. The swelling, which is painless and apparently harmless, disappears when purging stops.

Dental complications are also at the top of the list of appearance concerns (see Chapter 1: Clinical Features of Eating Disorders, pp. 3–31). We tell our patients who purge to expect an increased rate of dental caries and other dental problems. The first sign is slight yellowing of the front teeth. Over time, teeth appear worn, ragged, chipped, thinning, and discolored as stomach acids wear away tooth enamel.

We warn patients that brushing their teeth just after purging, a common practice, can cause permanent damage to tooth enamel made soft and fragile by contact with stomach acid. To protect tooth enamel, we advise waiting several hours before brushing. Instead, immediately after a purging episode, patients should rinse their mouths with a fluoridated mouthwash or baking soda dissolved in water, or even just plain water, or suck on an antacid (e.g., Tums or Rolaids). All of these techniques neutralize stomach acid to some extent and permit at least some remineralization to occur. The best protection, dentists have told us, is to wear a sports mouthguard sprinkled with baking soda while vomiting. Prior to purging, rinsing with a fluoridated mouthwash or spreading fluoridated toothpaste over teeth can make enamel more resistant and tooth roots less sensitive. As long as vomiting occurs regularly, tooth enamel will remain soft and susceptible to erosion. Individuals who purge should avoid raw fruit and fruit juice and, at the very least, wait several hours after consuming fruit or fruit juice before brushing teeth.

In order to receive the best possible preventive dental care, patients should inform their dentists about purging behaviors. Early dental damage is subtle and difficult to assess by an unsuspecting dental professional.

Effects on Weight and Calories

We make a point of providing patients with facts that counter the belief that purging protects against weight gain. Studies show that patients who binge and purge eventually gain weight, and do not lose weight until they abstain from purging (Carter, Mcintosh, Joyce, Gendall, Frampton, & Bulik, 2004). Patients lose weight when they stop binge eating (Agras & Apple, 1997, p. 42). Research shows that self-induced vomiting, laxatives and diuretics are relatively ineffective in eliminating consumed calories (Bo-Linn, Santa Ana, Morawksi, & Fordtran, 1983; Kaye, Weltzin, Hsu, McConaha, & Bolton, 1993). We also know that purging does not guarantee weight loss or empty all stomach contents. The distinct feeling of emptiness after purging is just a passing phenomenon. Some patients eat highly colored marker foods first (e.g., carrots, tomatoes, corn) purging until they see remnants of the marker food. One of Herrin's patients said that after bingeing in the afternoon, she purges until she can see some evidence of food she ate for breakfast in her vomitus. "Then I know I have got it all up." Herrin responded that because the stomach's function is to mix and liquefy food; whatever food is eaten first, does not necessarily come out last. Even when we share relevant information and research studies with patients, many do not accept this data on face value.

Excessive exercise has a limited affect on calorie balance. ED patients usually are unaware of the modest caloric expenditures associated with exercise: 5 and 10 calories/minute for walking and running, respectively (Ainsworth et al., 2011). (For more information, see Chapter 12: Managing Exercise, pp. 260–276.)

To make these points, we often e-mail or give skeptical patients copies of relevant research articles. When we discuss in detail the research on the amount of calories retained after purging, patients find the information very compelling. Kaye et al. (1993) found that 1,200 calories are retained after self-induced vomiting, regardless of whether the binge was relatively small (1,200 calories) or large (3,500 calories). It is unknown how many calories are retained from normal-sized meals and snacks that are purged, but it is logical to assume that up to 1,200 calories are preserved then. The fact that frank nutrient deficiencies are rarely, if ever, found in bulimic patients suggests that at least a minimum amount of nutrients are absorbed. Our patients are quite interested when we tell them that a 1,200-calorie diet, if very well chosen, provides the bare minimum of nutrients necessary for life, and that is exactly the calories that the body holds on to when vomiting is self-induced. To further illustrate that intakes of 1,200 calories are minimal and inadequate, we tell the story that, as dietetic students, we were assigned to design a 1,200-calorie diet that met the recommended daily allowances of nutrients, but it was so difficult we had to rely on a computer to ensure a well-balanced diet (Fontana, Klein, Holloszy, & Premachandra, 2006). We also discuss the research by Bo-Linn et al. (1983), which showed that laxatives decreased caloric absorption by only 12% even when purging produced 4–6 liters of diarrhea. Nutrient losses are likely to be minimal since their absorption occurs in the small intestine, while laxatives work on the lower bowel. Diuretic abuse has no known effect on caloric or nutrient absorption.

When presented with the above information, our patients counter, "But I lost a lot of weight when I first started purging, so I know it works." "Exactly right!" we respond. "Novice purgers" are likely to be convinced that purging, in its various forms, is a potent weight-control method because most do initially lose weight. But, eventually, most individuals who purge experience gain weight. One possible explanation is that the gastrointestinal tract adapts as purging continues and learns to compensate by "capturing" calories before they are purged. Or, more frequent and larger binges overwhelm the capacity of purging to rid the body of excess calories. Without a doubt, most patients who purge tend to engage in larger and more caloric binges as the ED progresses and, as a consequence, they gain weight. With recovery from bulimia nervosa (BN), however, 50% of patients lose weight, while the rest maintain weight (Carter et al., 2004). Of note, the restriction of food intake typical of anorexia nervosa (AN), when coupled with purging, is often associated with significant weight loss.

Of utmost interest to patients are the possible metabolic changes associated with purging. There is good evidence that purging reduces caloric needs (Devlin, Walsh, Kral, Heymsfield, Pi-Sunyer, & Dantzic, 1990; Sedlet & Ireton-Jones, 1989). This effect has been documented in bulimic patients and even in anorexic patients who binge and purge (Weltzin, Fernstrom, Hansen, McConaha, & Kaye, 1991). Some studies, however, show that metabolic rates in BN are similar to normal controls (Kotler, Devlin, Matthews, & Walsh, 2001).

Initially, patients who abruptly stop purging may experience short-term weight fluctuations associated with rebound edema. Increases of as much as 10 pounds have been noted, though much smaller changes in weight (2–6 pounds) are more the norm. Patients who are very underweight and are purging multiple times a day are the most likely to experience larger rebound weight changes. While it may be helpful, and necessary in the case of underweight patients, to discuss the possibility of temporary weight gain with cessation of purging behaviors, we are circumspect about emphasizing the possibility of temporary changes in weight since clinical experience indicates that most normal-weight patients usually do not experience any gains at all. We have concluded, therefore, that there is little clinical benefit in routinely forewarning all bulimic patients about possible weight gain if they stop purging.

Our strategy is to be ready to provide information about how hydration affects body weight when otherwise unexplained shifts in weight occur. We remind our patients that "a pint is a pound" which puts fluid fluctuations in perspective. We also mention that actual changes in body mass occur gradually (1–2 lb/week) and are due to increases or decreases in muscle and fat stores. Changes in body weight due to hydration shifts, if they do occur, happen relatively quickly, and are often similar to the patient's usual premenstrual weight changes. Weight gains of 5 to 10 pounds over a few days should be taken seriously, particularly in underweight patients, and reported to the medical provider.

The Rule of Threes Plan

Purging gives false signals regarding hunger and satiety, impelling patients to eat or binge when they are not hungry or to be hypersensitive to feelings of fullness.

It takes several months of regularly following the rule of threes (RO3s) plan (eating three meals and two to three snacks per day) without bingeing or purging to re-establish sensations of hunger and fullness (Fairburn, 2008, p. 78). In the meantime, the RO3s plan provides biologically appropriate guidance on what, when, and how much to eat (see Chapter 5: Food Planning, pp. 107–139).

Although no food, in and of itself, prompts bingeing or purging, we query patients about trigger foods (i.e., foods that, when consumed, elicit bingeing or purging urges). This exploration gives us the opportunity to correct misconceptions about specific foods and to expound again on the underlying theme: restriction and deprivation lead to overeating (or the perception of overeating) setting in motion the binge/purge cycle. Usually patients express concerns about the caloric or fat content of "trigger" foods, and they have come to believe these food cause weight gain. Our mantra is that a normal serving of any food, including trigger foods, does not cause weight gain. Nevertheless, we often recommend temporarily excluding these foods in first renditions of the RO3s to reduce anxiety. Designating "safety" meals or snacks is helpful for some. These are meals or snacks that patients agree will not be purged. Usually safety foods are items that patients feel no need to purge, have never purged, or are hard to purge. We instruct our patients to rely on these meals and snacks when they feel at risk for purging. In time, we encourage patients to include trigger and other forbidden foods in their food plans. Some patients are inclined to "replace" the meals and snacks they purge. As this practice is likely to start a series of binge/purge episodes or lead to weight gain, we advise our patients to wait until the next planned meal or snack to eat.

Since alcohol and recreational drug use may be associated with bingeing or purging, we explore this subject with patients (Bruce et al., 2011). Binge drinking is highly prevalent in individuals who binge eat. Rates of problematic drinking as high as 13% in AN, 49% in BN, and about 39% in eating disorder not otherwise specified (EDNOS) have been published (Khaylis, Trockel, & Taylor, 2009). It is not unusual for patients to include binge drinking in self-monitoring records or to disclose this behavior in nutrition sessions. We find that patients are often unaware of the caloric contribution of alcoholic drinks. When presented matter of factly, caloric information can inspire a pledge to reduce consumption. We also point out, with examples from the patient's own experiences, that binge drinking reduces inhibition and also therefore increases the risk for bingeing on food and purging. We often use this opportunity to provide information on the dangers of alcohol abuse and to provide referrals for substance abuse treatment.

Behavioral Strategies

In Chapter 4: Counseling Interventions (pp. 79–104) we outlined approaches to managing ED behaviors: problem-solving, chain analysis, emotion regulation, reducing cognitive vulnerability, cognitive restructuring, mindfulness, and distress tolerance. Any of these approaches can be applied to purging behaviors. Below we describe specific behavioral strategies we use to address purging behaviors.

Swallow It Back

Patients may describe spontaneously vomiting and not recognize this behavior as purging. We have patients so entrapped that they rationalize purging in several ways: "It is not under my control." Or, "It means my body does not really want or need the food I ate." First, we inform patients that when the sphincter between the esophagus and stomach relaxes with overuse, it readily lets food back up into the esophagus. Second, we advise swallowing back any vomitus that spontaneously enters the mouth. Patients who do this dutifully find that spontaneous regurgitation diminishes quite rapidly. Third, we caution about leaning over after eating, and may advise eating a little less at meals and snacks.

Throw Away Purgatives

We ask if patients can throw away their purging supplies or turn over these medications to us or to someone else. Many patients find that a symbolic act of "throwing away" purgatives enhances motivation to abstain. We take advantage of any opportunity to ask patients to bring their laxative supplies into a session for ceremonial disposal.

Go Cold Turkey

We tell patients how brave, radical, and immediately effective it is to stop purging while still being troubled with bingeing. Bulimic patients who are able to commit to stopping purging behaviors, however, find that almost immediately bingeing behaviors are much diminished. Conversely, once patients stop bingeing, they are likely to stop purging as well (Fairburn, Marcus, & Wilson, 1993, p. 379). Others have noted that patients who stop vomiting usually experience a marked decline in bingeing, even though the urge to overeat may remain (Garner, Rockert, Olmsted, Johnson, & Coscina, 1985, p. 546).

Many patients are willing to immediately stop using laxatives once they understand how ineffective they are at eliminating calories and how dangerous they are. Phasing out laxatives extends the period of discomfort and is not recommended unless patients use them on a regular basis or are hesitant to stop all together. Fairburn (2008, p. 83) recommends a schedule of reducing each week by half the number of pills taken per episode or per day.

We agree with Agras and Apple (1997, p. 67) who advise an immediate halt to diuretic use and who direct patients to dispose of their supplies rather than tapering their use. Non-prescription diuretics are so mild that stopping rarely causes any problems and continued use supports binge eating and other eating-disordered behaviors.

Stop Bingeing

If patients stop bingeing, they usually stop purging. Initial treatment efforts directed toward eliminating binge-eating behaviors such as compliance with a food plan may well be an effective approach and, if successful, not much attention in treatment needs to be paid to purging. Typically, when patients categorize an eating event as a binge, they eat more and purge. Here, we might point out the difference between a subjective and objective binge (see Chapter 10: Treating Binge Eating, pp. 229–245).

Delay Purging

Some patients find the strategy of "delaying" a purge an effective technique. After 30 minutes, self-induced vomiting is much more difficult, if not impossible to accomplish. Other patients, however, claim they can purge a meal, at will, no matter how long it has been since they have eaten. In either case, advising patients to wait at least 30 minutes, and longer if they can, before purging can be an effective strategy (Vanderlinden, Norré, & Vandereycken, 1992, p. 72). During the "waiting period" patients often find that they regain control and can choose not to purge. At the very least, delaying the purge allows patients to practice abstaining from purging. Additionally, the 30-minute wait allows for some digestion to occur. Having digested some food, patients feel more satisfied and are less likely to eat more or binge after they purge. They may also conclude, "What's the point? The food is already digested."

Program Purging

Another approach that helps patients begin to take control of the binge/purge cycle is to suggest "programmed" purging. This is a purge that is preplanned: "I purge only on Mondays and Fridays." "I purge only between 6 and 7 p.m." "I only purge into a specific bowl or bucket instead of the toilet or shower." Programming purging makes purging less automatic. Of note, patients report back that, when they purge in these manner, purging behaviors become indisputable and repugnant.

Self-Monitoring

Self-monitoring food and purging behaviors helps patients understand their binge eating and purging cycles as well as the situations and factors that trigger purging episodes. In-the-moment self-monitoring allows for examining and addressing bingeing and purging behaviors as they occur (Cooper & Fairburn, 2010, pp. 250–251). When we review self-monitoring journals, we particularly look for triggering foods and situations. We use these examples to illustrate how the patient might make use of the technique of engaging in alternative activities, "What could you have done instead of purging?" (For a list of alternative activities see Chapter 6: Self-Monitoring, pp. 140–149, and Chapter 10: Treating Binge Eating, pp. 229–245.)

Find Alternatives

We often collaborate with patients on creating a written list of activities that can serve as "alternatives to purging" for when they feel most at risk. Effective activities must be engaging enough to distract patients from their urge to purge. (For a list of alternative activities see Chapter 10: Treating Binge Eating, pp. 229–245, and Chapter 4: Counseling Interventions, pp. 79–104.) We have discovered that many patients are less likely to purge if they brush their teeth first. Furthermore, brushing teeth can replace purging as a ritualistic end of a binge. Another effective ritual is using a calendar to mark off any days free from purging. Some patients relish picking out attractive stickers to use for this purpose.

Expect Discomfort

Laxative abusers should be told to expect some constipation, bowel discomfort, and cramping which dissipates within a week or so when laxatives are discontinued. Some patients may have attempted to stop using laxatives in the past, but found that they were bothered by constipation, so resumed use. We may suggest increasing intake of insoluble fibers (e.g., fruits, legumes, vegetables, and whole grains) and fluids to restore health to their digestive tract and to provide solace that there is a remedy. We are, however, cautious about advising supplementary fibers like wheat bran or Metamucil, though these products may minimize discomfort; some of our patients misuse these products as well or do not adequately increase fluid intake. Patients who do not have a normal bowel movement within 2 weeks should be referred for medical assessment to rule out an obstruction, and sooner if they do not have evidence of bowel activity (flatus). We are prepared to help explain to our patients who are heavy users of laxatives that over the first several weeks they may experience transient weight gain due to rehydration. When laxatives are withdrawn, the resulting rebound peripheral edema usually resolves in 10 days or less (Mitchell, Specker, & Edmonson, 1997, p. 419).

We advise patients to expect some "reflex" water retention with discontinuation of prescription diuretics. Indicators of water retention are increased thirst, reduced urinary output, and swelling and puffiness of the fingers, ankles, and face. Patients, who may be inclined to restrict fluid intake in light of these symptoms should be informed that reducing fluids aggravates the problem. Restricting sodium intake and drinking plenty of fluids may help. Of note, diuretics are more likely to be abused by older patients with access to prescription diuretics than by younger patients who are less likely to be aware of the relationship between water retention and weight.

Weight Management

We find that a well-crafted weight-management plan and the reassurance it provides, coupled with information about the ineffectiveness of purging on body weight, helps make it feasible for patients to stop purging. With weight managed by a competent nutrition counselor, patients begin to decrease purging behaviors and discover that they do not gain weight. In this regard, we find weight monitoring useful. It provides realistic feedback about the effect of changes in eating patterns and purging behaviors on body weight. Bulimic patients purge or diet because they fear weight gain or hold the irrational belief that certain foods cause weight gain. We take an experimental stance, "Let's see if ceasing to purge causes a change in your weight." Or, "Let's see if eating a modest breakfast causes weight gain." Patients often imagine that weight is increasing when it is stable. We constantly find ourselves reassuring patients that only by consuming substantially more calories than the body needs on a long-term basis will body weight increase beyond what is normal. Most of our patients require regular weight monitoring before they can accept this fact.

Referrals

We take seriously any reported physical complaints and explain the likely relationship to purging. Although we feel it is imperative that patients be informed about medical symptoms, we also stress that most problems quickly resolve once purging stops. If necessary, we are prepared to make referrals for medical evaluations. Prescription diuretics are so dangerous, on the other hand, we routinely insist on medical evaluations for possible kidney damage. We also insist on medical assessments for patients with troubling reports such as reports of blood in vomitus or severe abdominal pain. Blood can indicate serious esophageal or gastric tearing, though it is more likely that the blood is from minute lacerations in the esophageal or gastric walls and not of any medical consequence. Abdominal tenderness may be the result of the strain of vomiting or, more seriously, from pancreatitis. When patients describe increased thirst, decreased urination, dizziness, lightheadedness, and weakness, we suspect potentially dangerous dehydration due to purging.

Purging behaviors that are not greatly reduced in outpatient treatment may confirm the need for higher levels of care (American Psychiatric Association, 2006; see Chapter 7: Levels of Care, pp. 150–166.) This matter-of-fact statement can serve as a wake-up call to those who are complacent about reducing purging behaviors. Although the decision to continue outpatient treatment is based on the patient's overall level of physical health and on whether the patient is making progress, very low-weight patients who purge are at elevated medical risk and are very likely to be referred to a higher level of care.

Psychotherapy may benefit patients for whom purging has become a coping mechanism for stress, boredom, transitions, depression, anxiety, or anger (Garner et al., 1985, p. 538). Psychotherapy referrals should be particularly considered for laxative abusers, as laxative abuse appears to indicate more severe psychopathology than is typical of ED patients (Herzog, Keller, Lavori, & Sacks, 1991; Weltzin, Bulik, McConaha, & Kaye, 1995).

Psychotropic Medication

As mentioned in Chapter 10: Treating Binge Eating (pp. 229–245) selective serotonin reuptake inhibitor (SSRI) antidepressant medications have been shown to be beneficial in the treatment of BN (American Psychiatric Association, 2006, p. 20). Patients who are prescribed antidepressants should be told that such medications require at least 2 hours for digestion. If purging occurs within this timeframe, the medication may not be absorbed. The best strategy is to take medications before bed or at a time when the risk of purging is less likely.

Summary Points

- Purging behaviors (self-induced vomiting, laxative, and diuretic abuse) are compensatory measures that are erroneously thought to prevent weight gain by eliminating calories consumed during regular meals and binge-eating episodes.
- Eventually, most patients feel trapped in a vicious cycle in which they must purge (to get rid of binge calories) and must binge to feel full enough to purge.
- Psycho-education regarding the harmful effects of purging and the futility of relying on purging to manage weight can be motivating enough for some patients to stop purging behaviors.
- Self-induced vomiting, laxative and diuretic abuse, and diet pills have been proven to be relatively ineffective in eliminating consumed calories and reducing body weight.
- Many patients, in fact, lose some weight when they stop purging because, once purging ceases, so too does bingeing.
- Alternative activities, self-monitoring, and the RO3s food plan are helpful tools to reduce and eliminate purging.
- Weight monitoring provides reassurance to patients who resist making changes in food behaviors for fear of weight gain.
- Concurrent psychotherapy and SSRI medication should be considered if purging behaviors do not quickly resolve.

12

MANAGING EXERCISE

Introduction

In this chapter we provide strategies and protocols for managing exercise, definitions of "healthy activity" (of benefit for all patients), and its antithesis, "compulsive/excessive exercise." Permitting exercise during weight restoration may reinforce weight gain, but it can also increase health risks and portray exercise or sports participation as more important than recovery. In eating disorders (EDs), exercise is used to regulate mood, weight, and shape, but only rarely are patients aware that excessive exercise can jeopardize health. In this regard, we discuss the clinical features of the "female athlete triad" and review the health consequences associated with excessive exercise.

Definitions

As we assess the ED-related exercise behaviors of our patients, we are regularly asked to define "healthy exercise." We explain that we prefer the term "healthy activity" as it does not imply that health requires one to be regularly engaged in vigorous exercise. Though patients usually do not ask, we also define compulsive/excessive exercise (the term we prefer) as exercise that is detrimental to both physical and mental health. Below we expand on our definitions of both healthy and compulsive/excessive exercise in the context of the treatment for ED.

Healthy Activity

Calogero and Pedrotty (2004) show that healthy activity (defined in Box 12.1) can improve compliance and decrease relapse among patients with anorexia nervosa

(AN). They emphasize that exercise must be redefined and reconceptualized for purposes other than weight loss, or engaging in exercise will lead to relapse. A low heart rate can trigger limits on even low-intensity activity like horseback riding (see Chapter 9: Restoring Weight, pp. 216–217).

BOX 12.1 COMPONENTS OF HEALTHY ACTIVITY

Healthy activity is:

- for purposes other than weight loss
- functional, mindful, healthy, and safe
- in the context of reconnecting to the body
- engaged in a safe therapeutic environment
- accompanied by food behaviors that provide the fuel and nutrition nec-essary to sustain activity

---

Healthy Exercise

Healthy exercise, on the other hand, is often defined as 20–60 minutes of exercise 3–5 days/week. The current recommendations for fitness-promoting exercise is: 30 minutes/day, 5 days/week (Garber et al., 2011). However, in AN, aiming to practice even "healthy exercise" can be contraindicated. We, repeatedly, and in no uncertain terms, remind our patients that it is unhealthy to exercise if one is underweight and undernourished.

Compulsive/Excessive Exercise

In Box 12.2 we list the characteristics of exercise that is compulsive/excessive.

BOX 12.2 CRITERIA INDICATING COMPULSIVE/ EXCESSIVE EXERCISE

When deprived of exercise, the patient:

- experiences feelings of anxiety, depression, and guilt (Goodwin, Haycraft, Willis, & Meyer, 2011)

Outside of participation on a coached athletic team, the patient:

- exercises more than an hour per day
- has less than 2 rest days/week
- exercises more than 4 days/week without a break for more than 3 months (Dalle Grave, Calugi, & Marchesini, 2008)
- more than is typical for someone of similar age and circumstances (e.g., a 10-year-old who runs for 45 minutes before school)

BOX 12.2 (continued)

Engaging in exercise that:

- is significantly more than required or recommended by an athletic coach
- increases the risk of injury
- increases risk for short- and long-term medical complications (American Psychiatric Association, 2000)
- interferes with medically necessary weight gain
- significantly interferes with important activities (American Psychiatric Association, 2000)
- occurs at inappropriate times or in inappropriate settings (American Psychiatric Association, 2000)
- requires significant modification of other activities
- is accompanied by intense guilt and extreme feelings of failure if the exercise is postponed or there is deviation from routine (Mond, Hay, Rodgers, & Owen, 2006)
- is obsessive (driven to do "extra" exercise)
- aggravates attitudes (Seigel & Hetta, 2001), motivation (Beumont, Arthur, Russell, & Touyz, 1994), and emotions (Steffen & Brehm, 1999) associated with ED psychopathology
- cannot be controlled (Davis et al., 1997, pp. 322–323)
- requires a rigid exercise schedule (Adkins & Keel, 2005)
- requires detailed record keeping (Adkins & Keel, 2005)

The patient engages in exercise to:

- solely purge calories
- solely influence weight or shape (Mond et al., 2006)
- reduce or manage general anxiety
- manage an obsessive preoccupation with weight gain (Shroff et al., 2006)
- alleviate negative emotions
- minimize fear and anxiety about eating

The patient engages in exercise:

- without proper nutrition
- despite injury, illness or medical complications (American Psychiatric Association, 2000; Pinheiro et al., 2007)
- in unsafe situations (e.g., running alone at night)
- in a self-punishing way
- with little or no attempt to suppress inappropriate amounts, times and places of the behavior (Pinheiro et al., 2007)
- despite interference with social relationships or educational and work activities

Literature Review

According to a recent review by Taranis and Meyer (2011), ED-related exercise behaviors are a common features of AN and bulimia nervosa (BN), with an estimated lifetime occurrence of up to 84% of patients. Urges to excessively/compulsively exercise may be the last ED symptoms to abate (American Psychiatric Association, 2006). The American Psychiatric Association's *Diagnostic and Statistical Manual of Mental Disorders* (DSM-IV; American Psychiatric Association, 2000) does not define "excessive" quantitatively in terms of exercise frequency, duration, or intensity. Instead in DSM-IV, exercise is defined qualitatively as excessive if it "significantly interferes with important activities, when it occurs at inappropriate times or inappropriate settings, or when the individual continues to exercise despite injury or other medical complications" (American Psychiatric Association, 2000, pp. 590–591; 2010). In addition, consensus is lacking on which term or terms to use to describe exercise behaviors in EDs. We found the following terms proposed as replacements for DSM-IV's "excessive exercise": unhealthy exercise, unbalanced exercise, exercise abuse, disordered exercise, compulsive exercise, ritualistic exercise, overexercise, extreme exercise, rigid exercise, driven exercise, exercise addiction, exercise dependence, exercise craving, exercise anorexia, activity anorexia, activity-based anorexia, anorexia athletica, excessive activity, and exercise-dependent symptomatic.

Adkins and Keel (2005) recommend the term "compulsive exercise" because it underscores the compulsory quality of exercise in ED patients. Dalle Grave et al. (2008) point out that both the amount and intensity of exercise, along with the degree of guilt experienced whenever exercise must be postponed, are important criteria. We believe that "compulsive/excessive exercise" best captures the pathological activity found in ED.

Clinical Examples

In our practices, we observe that some patients may be compulsive about exercise that is not excessive. An example is a thirty-something female patient who gets up at 5:00 a.m. to run 3 miles with no consideration of the weather, darkness, safety, or how she feels. Or the young mother who leaves her toddler napping while she jogs. Zunker, Mitchell, and Wonderlich (2011) and others propose that "excessive exercise" is exercise that exceeds 6 hours/week. In our practices, we have patients who have required sports practices that total over 6 hours/week. We also work with other patients who are worn out by their commitment to spend one hour in the gym every day.

Our patients are likely to engage in solitary aerobic pursuits such as distance running, or they may spend hours "working out" on aerobic exercise equipment. Some maximize the caloric expenditure of everyday activities, such as taking multiple trips upstairs when one trip would do. Rebekkah told Herrin why she refuses to sit; she knows that standing burns more calories than sitting. Very low-weight patients (body mass index (BMI) of 15 kg/m² or below) often exhibit restless, aimless physical movements, such as rocking, toe tapping, pacing, or standing instead of sitting; these behaviors are thought to be uncontrollable biological adaptations to starvation. With continued weight loss, all exercise, including hyperactive activity, usually decreases. A good example is Sasha. She was required to take a medical leave from a prestigious university when her dramatic and severe weight loss and obvious compulsive and excessive exercise caused a campus stir. A month later, Sasha was taking the elevator to Herrin's third floor office. Six months later, after weight restoration and nutrition rehabilitation, Sasha bounded up the three flights, but said she had no interest in returning to her strenuous running schedule. As patients normalize weight to a safe range, interest in excessive physical activity usually diminishes. Of note, a return to excessive exercise is a significant predictor of relapse (Zunker et al., 2011). Unremitting compulsive/excessive exercise is associated with poor treatment outcomes, often requiring high levels of care (Taranis and Meyer, 2011).

Assessment

We explore each patient's exercise history, current activity patterns, and beliefs about and interest in exercise. Throughout the course of treatment, we regularly inquire about exercise behaviors, particularly if the patient is not gaining weight as expected. We keep in mind that, although not every AN patient overexercises or has a history of exercising, some may develop hyperactive behaviors during treatment that interfere with weight gain. Exercise assessments should be individualized, as the functional aspects of exercise behaviors vary among patients. Quantifying "how much exercise is too much" needs to be considered, along with whether the patient is an athlete versus a non-athlete, injured versus uninjured, which type of sport he or she participates in, as well as the intensity of the exercise effort. We also discuss with patients the reasons why they exercise (De Young & Anderson, 2010). One difference between ED females and non-ED females is that in an ED, exercise manages negative affects such as anxiety and sadness. Non-ED females find that exercise improves positive moods (Bratland-Sanda, Sundgot-Borgen, Rø, Rosenvinge, Hoffart, & Martinsen, 2010).

Athletes

Competitive athletes are at greater risk for ED than age-matched populations (American Psychiatric Association, 2006). Particularly at risk are female athletes in sports that emphasize a thin body or appearance, such as gymnastics, figure skating, dance, and distance running. The same is true for male athletes in sports such as bodybuilding and wrestling and other sports that have weight limits. Pressure for increased training, dieting, and weight loss may come from teammates, parents, or coaches who hope to help improve an athlete's competitiveness. Nevertheless, we have worked with athletes in sports without obvious demands for thinness (e.g., football, field hockey, basketball). Then again, sports may offer protection to some from ED risk when involvement is approached in a sensible way and when healthy pride and self-esteem result (American Psychiatric Association, 2006).

Assessments in athletes must consider the context of the sport and the athlete's level of involvement (e.g., middle-school athletes may practice 1–2 hours several days a week; collegiate athletes may be expected to train much more). Many athletes are required to devote hours every day to their sport. The athlete who is not compulsive about exercise will be able to respond to advice to limit activity outside mandatory practices, to improved nutrition, and to increase rest. Compulsive exercisers struggle to moderate any exercise-related behaviors.

We use the questions in Box 12.3 to assess exercise compulsion (Dalle Grave et al., 2008; Davis, Brewer, & Ratusny, 1993; Mond, et al., 2006).

BOX 12.3 COMPULSIVE EXERCISE ASSESSMENT

- How is your exercise schedule impacting your social life? Are there times when you turn down an invitation to an interesting social event because it interferes with your exercise schedule?
- How do you feel if, for one reason or another, you are unable to exercise? Do you feel guilty that you have "let yourself down" when you miss an exercise session?
- What do you do if you miss one or more exercise sessions? Do you try to make up any missed sessions by exercising more later?
- Tell me about your exercise routine. Do you have a set routine for your exercise sessions (e.g., the same time of day, the same location, the same number of laps, particular exercises)?
- Do you keep detailed records of your exercise sessions?
- What happens if you are too tired or sick to exercise? Do you continue to exercise at times when you feel tired or unwell?
- What do you do if you develop an exercise-related injury? Do you continue to exercise even when you have sustained an exercise-related injury?
- What are "rest days" like for you? Do you become anxious at the suggestion you take a planned "rest day"?

Challenges

Patients live in a cultural environment that values exercise as a major influence on weight, shape, and appearance. A major misconception is the overestimation of the intensity and duration of exercise necessary to support fitness and health. Most patients share the same misconceptions about the relationship between health, fitness, caloric intake, body weight, and exercise with the much of the population. Often parents, teachers, coaches, peers, and teammates place a high premium on fitness and exercise, increasing the pressure to continue high levels of exercise.

Occasionally compulsive/excessive exercise is not a component of the patient's clinical picture. These patients may never have engaged in regular exercise or sports and may continue to have little interest in formal exercise in spite of their ED. As counselors are often idealized by patients, we must be careful not to impose our own value judgments about the benefits of regular exercise in maintaining health. It is likely that, as patients recover and increase their social involvements, just having "fun" (bike riding with friends, swimming, skiing, and the like) will provide enough activity to maintain health. Addressing lack of regular physical activity is best done at the patient's request and some time after the ED has been resolved.

Exercise can be Bad for Your Health

Although it is an ingrained truism that exercise is good for the human body and that weight-bearing exercise improves bone mineral density (BMD), there is no evidence that exercise improves BMD in anorexic patients. In fact, it is more likely that exercise interferes with improvements in BMD in ED (Mehler & MacKenzie, 2009). Waugh, Woodside, Beaton, Coté, and Hawker (2011) found that high amounts of moderate exercise (such as walking) were negatively associated with BMD in ED patients (defined as amenorrheic and with a BMI less than 18.5kg/m^2 for at least 1 year). Because weight gain and full recovery is the only known treatment for anorexia-induced osteopenia (significantly reduced bone mass) and osteoporosis (osteopenia associated with non-traumatic pathological fractures), exercise recommendations must support weight-gain goals. Extended bed rest, however, is not recommended, as inactivity at that level is associated with further skeletal calcium loss. One study found rapid disruption in bone turnover within 5 days of bed rest in AN, especially in younger adolescents (DiVasta, Feldman, Quach, Balestrino, & Gordon, 2009). Patients who complain of bone pain while exercising should be advised to stop exercising and to seek medical assessment, as they may have sustained a stress fracture.

The majority of AN patients are already at high risk for a variety of serious medical complications (e.g., bone fractures, electrolyte imbalances, sudden death). (For more information on medical complications see Chapter 1: Clinical Features of Eating Disorders, pp. 3–31.) Even moderate physical activity may be hazardous for patients with impaired cardiac function, electrolyte abnormalities, osteopenia, or osteoporosis (American Psychiatric Association, 2000, p. 33). Because a course of AN of as little as 6 months can cause significant bone loss, exercise restrictions should be considered early in treatment (Becker, Grinspoon, Klibanski, &

Herzog, 1999, p. 1094). Those at greatest risk for osteopenia, and who may benefit most from exercise restrictions, are patients with primary amenorrhea (never
having had menses), amenorrhea that began in adolescence, and a long duration
of amenorrhea (Biller, Saxe, Herzog, Rosenthal, Holzman, & Klibanski, 1989,
p. 553). Moreover, it is not uncommon for eating-disordered patients to exercise
despite chronic fatigue or even injury. Patients who cannot comply with exercise
limitations require close medical monitoring and may warrant consideration of a
higher level of care.

Metabolic Issues

A number of metabolic factors create additional challenges. First, anorexic
patients require higher than expected calories to achieve weight gain (Krahn,
Rock, Dechert, Nairn, & Hasse, 1993; Salisbury, Levine, Crow, & Mitchell,
1995, p. 341). Second, exercise itself is known to increase overall caloric requirements by raising metabolic rate. Exercise-induced metabolic changes are insignificant for most people. But in underweight patients, any exercise increases overall caloric requirements, particularly weight-training-type activities that increase
muscle mass. This is due to the simple fact that muscle cells are more metabolically
active than fat cells. Endurance-type activities (e.g., running and swimming) have
an additional impact on metabolic rate by elevating caloric needs for some time
after the exercise session.

The increase in caloric expenditure may last from minutes to hours, depending
on the intensity and duration of the exercise. Even low-intensity exercise, like
walking, expends calories. Since caloric costs associated with specific activities
are also affected by exercise intensity and the fitness level of the individual, it
cannot be overemphasized that these are just estimates. A clinically useful guide
is to assume that the caloric expenditure for jogging or other common aerobic-
type exercise is about 10 calories/minute. For activities like walking, calculate
the caloric cost as about 100 calories/mile. Nevertheless, the magnitude of the
increase in caloric needs for an AN patient engaged in exercise is impossible to
predict precisely outside of a research facility. Yet another challenge is that ED
patients tend to underreport the amount of exercise they do (Bratland-Sanda et
al., 2010).

Female Athlete Triad

The term "female athlete triad" has been coined to describe a unique set of
health challenges among female athletes. The triad consists of three components, each on a continuum: low energy availability (LEA), menstrual dysfunction, and low BMD. The extreme end of the triad continuum is manifested
in eating disorders, amenorrhea, and osteoporosis. Among collegiate athletes,
nearly one-third of females not using oral contraceptives met the criteria for

the triad (American Psychiatric Association, 2006). It is not unusual for athletes to have different degrees of intermediate or "subclinical" symptoms of one or more of the triad components. Most at risk are athletes in "thinness-demand" sports such as gymnastics, ballet, and long-distance running (Nattiv et al., 2007). LEA seems to be the primary mechanism that predisposes female athletes to menstrual dysfunction and the resulting detrimental effects on bone (Feingold & Hame, 2006). Extreme training, especially when combined with LEA is a risk factor for AN. Even if an ED is ruled out, athletes should be advised to increase caloric intake and decrease exercise. "Overtraining syndrome," sometimes related to the triad, is described as a state of exhaustion, depression, and irritability during which athletes continue to train while performance diminishes.

Energy Availability

Energy availability is defined as the amount of energy that is available for an individual to fuel basal metabolic functions and non-exercise activities of daily living. Energy availability is affected by low caloric intake or high energy expenditure, or both. As it is not clinically practical to calculate energy availability (i.e., dietary energy intake minus exercise energy expenditure divided by fat-free mass), we rely on the athlete's presenting clinical features to assess energy availability. LEA is indicated by weight loss, a decline in athletic performance, a change in mood, frequent injuries or illnesses, fractures, low BMD, or menstrual dysfunction.

Menstrual Function

Menstrual function may vary from normal menstrual cycles and oligomenorrhea (i.e., intervals longer than 35 days) to amenorrhea (i.e., no menstrual cycle in 3 months or more). Amenorrhea may be normalized by some coaches and athletes as a sign that training is appropriately intense and successful. Regular menses may make some athletes feel fat or complicate training (Thompson & Sherman, 2010). Inadequate calorie intake seems to be the primary mechanism that predisposes female athletes to menstrual dysfunction and the resulting detrimental effects on bone (Feingold & Hame, 2006).

Bone Mineral Density

In the female athlete triad BMD can range from healthy bones to low BMD or osteoporosis. Because athletes participating in weight-bearing sports typically have a greater BMD than do non-athletes, it is recommended that athletes be further evaluated if z scores are less than −1.0 (the usual standard for further evaluation is a z score less than −2.0; Lanser, Zach, & Hoch, 2011). The triad increases risk for stress fractures, especially in cross-country and track athletes (Feingold & Hame, 2006).

Solutions

Psycho-education

Excessive Exercise is Dangerous

An important theme is that exercising over the activity limits established by a treatment team is dangerous, particularly for patients with compromised cardiac status or low bone density. We echo Treasure, Smith, and Crane's (2007) point that, with an ED, the body has few reserves and is so "out of balance" that elective physical activity can cause harm. We highlight the physical complications each patient is experiencing as evidence that exercising may be using resources the body desperately needs. We discuss the medical risks of premature return to exercise: short- and long-term risks to muscles, bone fractures, and the litany of other medical concerns (i.e., weakness, thinning bones, disrupted blood sugar levels, dehydration, and electrolyte imbalances). At the same time, we are sympathetic that compulsive or excessive exercise may have been a way to cope or distract from hurt, pain, and injustice. We also discuss studies that food deprivation increases activity (i.e., running in rats; Exner et al., 2000), to make the point that biology is part of what drives the compulsion to exercise. Our drumbeat is that, for underweight and undernourished patients, exercise is not conducive, and is even counterproductive, to regaining health.

Compulsive Exercise is Dangerous

To make the point about the dangers of compulsive exercise we may tell the story of Trisha Meili who published her first-person account in *I am the Central Park Jogger: A Story of Hope and Possibility* (Meili, 2004). Meili's story is powerful, but we use it judiciously because of its disturbing content (Box 12.4).

Modest Exercise is Sufficient

We make our patients aware that only a modest amount of exercise is necessary to sustain health and that exercise is not a significant factor in managing body weight. We remind patients that 20–60 minutes of exercise 3–5 days/week is sufficient. Herrin often gives patients a copy of the well-researched 2009 *Time* magazine cover story, "Why exercise won't make you thin," in which Cloud (2009) says, "exercise for fun, flexibility, for strength, health, to enjoy nature, so your dog can do his business, so you can hike the Grand Canyon, but not for weight control because it does not work." Once patients understand the relevant

---

BOX 12.4 FIRST-PERSON ACCOUNT OF THE DANGERS OF COMPULSIVE EXERCISE: THE CENTRAL PARK JOGGER

Both AN and BN patients may risk personal safety to satisfy their compulsion to exercise. Andrea's boyfriend was so worried about her running alone at night on campus that he called campus police. When safety is an issue, we may give patients a brief synopsis of the terrible story of the Central Park Jogger. In 1989, a young woman nearly died after a brutal assault and rape while jogging in New York's Central Park at night. Fourteen years later, in a first-person account, Trisha Meili published *I am the Central Park Jogger: A Story of Hope and Possibility* (Meili, 2004). Meili says in the first chapter, "There was no chance I'd forgo the run. I was obsessed with exercise … maybe there were deeper issues that drove me to take the risk … back then, I was compulsive about it. I had an ED." Later in the book, Meili says that her rehabilitation after the attack included treatment for her ED.

---

scientific facts, some are able to manage their own exercise responsibly. Finally, we assure our patients they will have the choice to include moderate or more intensive exercise with recovery.

Exercise Limitations

For patients who experience unremitting weight loss and for those whose weights are at or below the level that is diagnostic of AN (e.g. a BMI of $18.5\,\text{kg/m}^2$ for adult females), it is medically necessary to consider limits on exercise. We make every effort to collaborate with patients, if possible, in devising exercise limits and prescriptions. In crafting exercise restrictions, we keep in mind the following precepts:

- Exercise cannot interfere with weight gain.
- Prescriptions for exercise must be individualized.
- Weight should be maintained for at least a month before allowing or increasing exercise (Pike et al., 2010).
- Medical providers can limit exercise by denying permission to participate in school-sponsored sports and other activities.
- Parents can withhold privileges and reward compliance. (See Chapter 13: Working with Families, pp. 277–298.)
- It is counterproductive to prohibit exercise when compliance cannot be guaranteed (Beumont, Beumont, Touyz, & Williams, 1997).

At this point in time, however, establishing weight limitations is more of an art than a science, as there are no established treatment guidelines (Zunker et al.,

2011). Limitations on exercise range from banning all but limited daily tasks, to allowing mild to moderate exercise, as long as weight restoration is on schedule.

Determining an "exercise weight" (the weight at which exercise is allowed) should be done as pragmatically as possible. Exercise weights are usually based on medical status, progress, and pre-morbid exercise practices. Significant weight-bearing exercise may be restricted until menses returns, as resumption of menses indicates a theoretical minimal weight associated with restoration and protection of bone health (Mehler & MacKenzie, 2009). Note, however, that this rule should not be applied to patients who have regular menses at low BMIs. Maintenance of a minimally safe weight (e.g., a BMI of 20kg/m^2 for adult females) is another parameter used as an exercise-weight threshold. (See Chapter 8: Assessing Weight for more discussion on menses and weight, p. 216, and BMI weight categories, p. 181.)

If at all possible, exercise limits are discussed among and agreed to by all treatment-team members. Typical exercise limits are given in Box 12.5. A united front is particularly essential on this issue. To emphasize the medical gravity, the patient's medical professional ideally conveys the limitations or bans on exercise or participation in sports to patients and their families. The truth is that medical professionals often consult with nutrition counselors in establishing exercise limits. In any case, we often find ourselves in the role of discussing or explaining limits with patients. Once weight goals and exercise parameters are set, there is no advantage to "caving in," though there is wisdom in regularly re-evaluating goals and limits. There is also little advantage in setting the weight criteria for permission to exercise or participate in sports so high that patients feel discouraged or antagonistic toward the treatment team. It is rarely productive to attempt to limit activity unless it is likely the patient will be compliant or the treatment team can control access to the activity.

BOX 12.5 GUIDELINES FOR ESTABLISHING EXERCISE LIMITS

No exercise if:

- not complying with the food plan
- losing weight
- at risky low weight
- below "exercise weight" (see pp. 270–273)
- excessive when exercises

Exercise allowed if:

- a weight goal has been maintained for at least a month (Pike et al., 2010, p. 99)

BOX 12.5 (continued)

- the patient can comply with exercise prescriptions (see pp. 274–275)

  – no more exercise than a coach requires

Definition of terms

No exercise:

- limited daily tasks
- rearranging the home so that extraneous walking or stair climbing are minimized
- school and work may be limited
- gym and exercise classes banned

Risky low weight:

- adult female patients at a BMI less than 18.5 kg/m2
- adult male patients at a BMI less than 20 kg/m2
- children below the 10th percentile BMI for age
- any weight-associated medical concerns

  – low heart rate
  – low blood pressure
  – other medical concerns

Excessive exercise:

- more than an hour per day
- has less than two rest days a week
- without a break over the past 3 months if exercising more than 4 days/week (Dalle Grave et al., 2008)
- more than is typical for someone of similar age and circumstances (e.g., a 10-year-old who runs for 45 minutes before school)

Athletes

To be effective in treatment and in working with exercise limits for ED athletes, counselors must value sports participation and the traits that make for good athletes, and be ready to consult, if necessary, with coaches and other sports personnel. Thompson and Sherman (2010, pp. 148–150) find benefit in allowing athletes to train and compete while in treatment as long as involvement is in the best interest of the patient. They argue that continued sports participation allows for additional support, oversight, and monitoring (i.e., by coaches, trainers, team-mates); and provides a natural incentive for recovery. Without athletic involvement, patients may become depressed and feel lost without the identity and focus of being an active athlete. A number of our adolescent patients have benefitted from being allowed to attend practices and games as long as they only sat on the sidelines. Thompson and Sherman (2010, pp. 153–154) reiterate that treatment should never be subordinate to sport and that patients should not miss treatment sessions in order to train or compete.

Bulimia Nervosa and Binge-Eating Disorder

In BN exercise is often part of a pattern of behaviors used to compensate for binges. BN patients who use exercise as a purgative will need special assistance to avoid restricting food intake as they reduce exercise. BN and binge-eating disorder (BED) patients often have many misconceptions about exercise. Some patients assume that healthy patterns of exercise require higher intensity and greater frequency than guidelines actually recommend. Others are so demoralized about their eating behavior and their body weight that they have given up incorporating even moderate activity into their lifestyle. Because admonitions to exercise or increase exercise are commonplace in society, few patients respond positively to similar guidance. On a clinical level, it is more effective to be empathetic and supportive of the patient's current approach to exercise, whatever it is. Some binge-eating patients are overly focused on their inability to engage in regular exercise. These patients erroneously conclude that the lack of exercise, not the binge eating, is the reason why weight has increased. We help such patients direct their attention to correcting their food behaviors by saying, "Food behavior has a more potent effect on your weight than exercise does. Regular activity will improve your health so we will want to incorporate that in the future, but for the time being we need to focus on your food behaviors." At this juncture, we often offer a copy of the *Time* article, "Why exercise won't make you thin" (Cloud, 2009; see pp. 269–270).

Presenting Exercise Limits

On reflection, many patients are distressed regarding their unmanageable exercise habits and are relieved when they are required to "take a break" from exercising. Patients often tell us that they are grateful that they are not allowed to exercise; otherwise, they feel obliged to exercise compulsively. Limitations can give patients a graceful way out of a sport they are participating in to please others or an acceptable excuse not to overexercise (Thompson & Sherman, 2010, p. 150).

Pike et al. (2010, p. 99) present exercise limits as an "experiment in what is like to not exercise." At the same time, they tell patients that abstaining from exercise is a necessary, but temporary, treatment much like "wearing a cast on a broken limb." Most patients are able to understand and accept, albeit grudgingly, that weight must be increased before they are medically stable enough to return to pre-morbid activity levels. Particularly young patients and those in the early stages of an ED can be quite amenable to exercise limitations. Behavioral strategies to help patients refrain from exercise include the distraction and delay techniques and reframing cognitions described in Chapter 4. (See Chapter 4: Counseling Interventions, pp. 79–104). Patients may be well advised to cancel gym memberships, hide running shoes, disable exercise equipment, and self-monitor thoughts on what it is like to not exercise. We assure patients that we will help them manage weight gain and deal with body-image challenges that are sure to arise.

Monitoring Exercise Limits

Another reality is that the "policing" required to limit exercise often strains therapeutic relationships. It is not unreasonable then, if patients are not medically compromised and if their level of exercise does not obviously compromise quality of life, to exclude exercise from direct clinical management. Lila is a good example. Her nightly regimen is 15 minutes of sit-ups and push-ups in her bedroom. Patients like Lila benefit from discussions about the compulsion to exercise, but they make more progress if the initiative to limit or manage exercise is left to the patient.

Monitoring of exercise behaviors, however, is difficult if not impossible in outpatient settings, even for patients who are supervised by parents, school personnel, or coaches. Of note, non-compliance with exercise guidelines or returning to excessive exercise is associated with relapse (Olmsted, Carter, & Pike, 2012; Zunker et al., 2011). If patients, especially very underweight patients, are not able to adhere to activity limitations, a more structured treatment environment may need to be considered, such as a higher level of care.

Exercise Prescriptions

Exercise prescriptions for eating-disordered patients must be individualized, reasonable, and clinically defensible based on health status or lack of progress with weight restoration. What might be excessive for one patient may not be for another. For example, the patient who is a competitive athlete may have physical capacity for more extensive exercise than would a non-athlete. Presumably, athletes are able to engage in heavier levels of exercise without becoming obsessional or compulsive because their exercise routines are purposeful and overseen by a coach. A reasonable exercise guideline for athletes is: no more exercise than the coach recommends. Yet, for a "non-athletic" patient, two 10-minute walks on weekdays might suffice. Exercise prescriptions are usually graded for lower weight patients. Patients at minimally safe weights and above are usually allowed full permission to exercise and to engage in activities.

Graded Exercise Prescriptions

Our clinical experience supports that rewarding improvements in body weight with permission to increase exercise usually helps patients make progress. Klein Schebendach, Gershkovich, Bodell, Foltin, & Walsh (2010) found that allowing even modest amounts of physical activity in response to weight gain had a positive effect. Permission to return to jogging and other more strenuous activities should be granted gradually and be contingent on weight gain, medical stability, and menstrual status. For patients who are gaining weight consistently, moderate exercise can help them accept associated body changes (Fairburn, 2008). Other studies show that use of a supervised moderate exercise program, such as non-aerobic yoga, may be beneficial during the weight-gain phase (American Psychiatric Association, 2006). The inpatient program developed by Bratland-Sanda et al. (2010) incorporated a variety of exercise approaches in 60-minute group sessions, 4 times/week. Each session included a skilled trainer leading the group in a combination of stretching, posture, yoga, Pilates, partner exercises, strength training, balance, exercise balls, aerobic activity, and recreational games. Patients in the exercise group gained 33% more weight than non-exercisers.

Examples of graded exercise prescriptions that we have used include:

- no additional exercise besides that associated with school or work
- taking the dog for a 10-minute walk in the evening
- 30 minutes of window shopping at the mall 2 days/week
- 15 minutes of swimming or exercise biking every other day.

Unrestricted Exercise Prescriptions

Full permission to exercise is contingent on the individual's physical condition and successful achievement of weight goals. Permission should be rescinded if these conditions are not met. Caryn is a good example. As an up and coming college tennis player, Caryn's physician set a minimum weight goal she had to meet before she would be allowed to play in competitive matches. As the first match approached, Caryn's efforts to follow her food plan took on a new intensity, but she was 3 pounds short of the minimum on the day of the match. True to her word, the physician let the tennis coach know that Caryn would have to sit out the match. Caryn made steady progress from that day forward and did not miss another match the rest of the season.

Unrestricted exercise prescriptions for patients who have reached a safe weight should be focused on maintaining health, restoring a positive relationship with the physical body, and receiving pleasure from physical activities (American Psychiatric Association, 2006). Ideally, these activities would not be solitary, but social and enjoyable (e.g., ice skating with friends or gentle yoga classes).

Summary Points

- At this time, the field lacks unambiguous criteria and established treatment guidelines for defining or managing excessive exercise.
- Compulsive/excessive exercise is associated with poor treatment outcomes, requiring high levels of care and demonstrating an increased risk of relapse.
- The term "female athlete triad" has been coined to describe the physical complications of excessive exercise among athletes. The triad consists of three component parts on a continuum: LEA, menstrual dysfunction, and low BMD.
- Patients who are malnourished and underweight should know that exercise is not conducive and counterproductive to restoration of health. Once they understand the relevant scientific facts, some patients are able to manage their own exercise responsibly.
- Permission to return to jogging and other physically strenuous activities is usually granted gradually, and is contingent on weight gain, medical stability, and menstrual status.
- "Exercise weights" are determined pragmatically based on each patient's medical status, progress, and pre-morbid body weights. For patients whose weights are at or below the level that is diagnostic of AN, it is reasonable to consider limits on strenuous exercise.
- Healthy exercise is 20–60 minutes of exercise 3–5 days/week.

13

WORKING WITH FAMILIES

Introduction

This chapter describes our Parent-Assisted Meals and Snacks (PAMS) approach, a nutrition-counseling approach derived from the family-based treatment (FBT) research first conducted at the Maudsley Hospital in London in the 1980s and 1990s. Beginning in the mid-1990s, Stanford University launched a research initiative on FBT also known as the Maudsley approach or the Maudsley method. Published studies demonstrate the effectiveness of FBT for anorexia nervosa (AN) in children and adolescents, with full remission at both 12 months and 5 years (Lock, Le Grange, Agras, Moye, Bryson, & Jo, 2010). Recent studies show that the most powerful aspects of FBT lie in the parents taking control, being united, not criticizing the patient, and externalizing the ED (Ellison et al., 2012). The publication of several FBT treatment manuals for AN and bulimia nervosa (BN; Lock, Le Grange, Agras, & Dare, 2001; Le Grange & Lock, 2007) led to the establishment of FBT programs in university centers in the United States, Canada and Australia. FBT is a based on the five tenets listed in Box 13.1 (Lock, 2011, p. 232).

The Original FBT Model

According to the "original" FBT model, a family counselor, with support from a medical provider, a psychiatrist, and a dietitian, conducts a relatively short intensive treatment consisting of three phases for adolescent AN and BN. In an early session, parents bring a meal into the counselor's office for the patient and attending family members to eat. The aims of this "coached" meal are to allow the counselor to observe family food dynamics and to coach parents on how to help their child eat one more bite than he or she intends.

BOX 13.1 THE FIVE TENETS OF FBT

1. An agnostic view of what causes EDs; focusing on what can be done to treat the ED instead of what caused the ED; no assumption that parents caused the ED.
2. First focus on disrupting ED behaviors as is done in inpatient programs (e.g., by normalizing food behaviors, increasing calories, and limiting exercise).
3. The counselor is, first and foremost, a consultant to the family (rather than an authority), providing information, possible strategies, and help in evaluating results.
4. Parents can effectively change their child's behaviors if they are empowered to make changes in their own thinking, behaviors, and environment.
5. The counselor maintains a relationship with the patient. The ED behaviors and thought processes and not part of the patient's identity; an ED is not a choice.

The first phase of FBT entails teaching parents how to normalize their child's eating behaviors. Normalizing eating involves "refeeding" the patient (i.e., ensuring that the patient consumes an adequate variety of food to meet his or her nutritional needs to support complete weight restoration and eliminating binge and purge behaviors). Key to success of phase one is heightened anxiety in family members about the seriousness of the current situation and about the gravity of the long-term impacts of the eating disorder (ED). Also conveyed is that all family members are needed to overcome the ED. Lock calls this "a paradoxical stance" in which parental anxiety is promoted but also contained by the confidence the family has in the calm, experienced counselor. The second phase focuses on restoring the child to physical health and returning control of eating to the child. Once the child is eating independently, has reached a stable healthy weight and has stopped bingeing and purging, phase three of FBT concentrates on family dynamics and individuation.

While the original FBT model (conducted by a family counselor with a team of consultants) is limited to a few university medical centers, the use of FBT techniques is spreading as inpatient programs and outpatient psychotherapists, nutrition counselors, and others attend trainings (Training Institute for Child and Adolescent Eating Disorders: http://www.train2treat4ed.com) and apply the treatment manuals mentioned above.

We adhere to the core principles of FBT shown in Box 13.2 (Lock, 2011).

BOX 13.2 CORE PRINCIPLES OF FBT

- The entire family is an essential resource.
- The family is not held responsible for causing the ED.
- Parents are capable of helping their child re-establish normal eating behaviors.
- Parenting is age appropriate except in regards to food and weight-related behaviors.
- EDs are serious and potentially fatal medical conditions.
- The child's development is arrested by the ED.
- The patient has little control over their eating-disordered behaviors; parents must take charge of their child's eating and exercise behaviors.

Parent-Assisted Meals and Snacks (PAMS)

Herrin first became acquainted with FBT at the First International Eating Disorder conference in London in 1999. Having involved parents in the treatment of children and adolescents since the early years of her practice, Herrin knew first hand that when she collaborated with parents outcomes improved. Because no FBT clinics or trained FBT therapists existed in her community, she sought out additional research, trainings, and workshops. Her knowledge and enthusiasm continued as she studied the first FBT treatment manual (Lock et al., 2001) and completed two FBT trainings. Determined to apply her newfound knowledge and skills, Herrin successfully modified FBT for use in her nutrition counseling practice. This modified version is called Parent Assisted Meals and Snacks (PAMS) and is detailed in Herrin's book *The Parents' Guide to Eating Disorders* (Herrin & Matsumoto, 2007). At the core of PAMS and all of our eating disorder work are the five tenets of FBT (see Box 13.1) and the FBT core principles (see Box 13.2). Another way of conceptualizing PAMS is that it is a parent training programming teaching the inpatient refeeding techniques that are used in ED facilities, namely, supervision of food intake.

PAMS and Team Treatment

PAMS relies on a nutrition counselor and a psychotherapist working in tandem. We have observed, as did Strober and Johnson (2012), how low-weight patients benefit from concurrent psychotherapy that supports weight change, acquiescence to parents on food-related matters, and "submission" to the food plan (as one of Herrin's psychologists puts it). In PAMS, the nutrition counselor utilizes FBT phase one and phase two techniques focused on helping the patient reach and maintain a biologically appropriate weight (BAW) and to eat in an age-appropriate way. The psychotherapist works concurrently with the patient during the first two phases, providing counseling that supports and encourages compliance to the food plan and weight gain, and then becomes the lead provider for phase three, which is focused on adolescent development.

It is important that the psychotherapist and the physician on the treatment team understand and support PAMS. When all members of this interdisciplinary team support the family's efforts to do PAMS, parents become increasingly empowered to refeed their child. It is equally important that the nutrition counselor work closely with parents, spending significant time with them at each session, helping them problem-solve how to help their child, supporting their relationship with their child, and modeling for parents how to set clear and reasonable expectations, and how to be firm but caring as they insist on compliance (Lock, 2011, p. 237).

PAMS Rationale for Using a Food Plan

PAMS also provides a food plan. In the original FBT model, food planning is left up to the parents to manage: parents figure out what and how much to feed their child to achieve weight restoration. Parents in our program use the Rule of Threes Food Plan (RO3s) as detailed in Chapter 5: Food Planning: Rule of Threes. Our experience and others (K. Boutelle, University of California–San Diego Adolescent Day Treatment Program for Eating Disorders, personal communication, February 24, 2012) confirms that parents are relieved to have some professional guidance on designing a food plan for their child because it makes refeeding easier and safer. With a food plan and professional guidance, parents do not have to figure out how to increase caloric intake on their own and can instead concentrate on implementing the food plan. They do not have to worry that they are over- or underfeeding their child. Using PAMS, parents not only receive from the nutrition counselor instructions about the refeeding process and educational information about EDs, but also obtain support for their care-giving efforts and reassurance they are on the right track.

Assessing Whether to Use PAMS

The decision to use PAMS depends first and foremost on whether patients are able to follow a food plan. PAMS is an unnecessary intervention (as it is intense) for patients who are able to follow an food plan, to gain weight on schedule, and to engage in resolving ED behaviors.

Of equal importance, PAMS requires that parents have the time and energy to devote to their significant role. In some cases parents may not able or ready to commit to the effort required to attend appointments, to oversee meals, and to settle food battles. Parents may have already adopted a hands-off approach to dealing with their child's eating behaviors. They may have been told by other practitioners to leave treatment up to the professionals or that parental involvement will result in additional problems for their child.

Adolescents with AN

Research indicates that FBT techniques are most effective (90% recovery rates) for AN patients 18 years old and younger with a short duration of illness, but we and others have used it successfully with patients in their mid-twenties who live at home (Le Grange & Eisler, 2009). Best outcomes are in newly diagnosed (i.e., diagnosed for less than 1 year) AN patients whose family members are willing and able to have meals together. Although research is scant on the efficacy of FBT for BN and is even less for binge-eating disorder (BED), we and others have used it effectively with these patients (Le Grange, Crosby, Rathouz, & Leventhal, 2007). Similarly, PAMS is most appropriate and effective for patients who are undereating and are underweight and have supportive and available parents. It is less effective for overeating or overweight children. PAMS is more difficult, but not impossible, for families with fewer resources, such as single-parent families or families with other significant constraints.

Adult Patients

Adult patients can benefit from PAMS if they are open to accepting a "support team," consisting of people willing to provide long-term food-plan support. New research supports using FBT with college-aged patients and with couples (Bulik, Baucom, Kirby, & Pisetsky, 2011; Le Grange & Eisler, 2009). We have had young adult patients move back home to live with their parents so they could engage in PAMS. Parents who are financially assisting an adult child (e.g., paying for college or living expenses) are in an especially advantageous situation to implement PAMS, but any parent who provides emotional support or guidance to an adult child may successfully employ PAMS techniques. Parents and counselors, however, need to pay particular attention to the independence needs of adult patients.

Contraindications

Patients and parents who are not likely to be good candidates for PAMS are those with a history of extreme aggression or hostility, bipolar disorder, substance-use disorder, or other serious psychiatric problems. We confidently use PAMS, knowing that our general treatment philosophy is to experiment; if PAMS techniques are not working, we stop, evaluate, and revise, and may well try another approach.

PAMS Philosophy

We use the PAMS philosophy in all of our work with children, adolescents, and their families. For patients who do have difficulty following a food plan, we find that implementing PAMS techniques early in treatment helps parents become competent and confident in overseeing their child's eating, which ultimately increases the pace of recovery. But we also use PAMS techniques with good results for patients who have had months of treatment but are not making progress.

Whether PAMS is unnecessary or parents are unable to fully put into practice PAMS techniques or PAMS is contraindicated, we continue to apply the key principle of FBT: involving parents in some way with nearly all ED patients who are 18 years old or younger and living at home with parents. It is our general practice to meet with the parents at the end of most sessions to review the food plan and possibly to revise the food plan based on the parents' feedback.

PAMS: Phase One

Phase one is focused on initiating weight gain and putting parents in charge of their child's eating. Parents are involved in each session and are taught to supervise their child's food intake. Phase one may include a coached family meal or a snack (see Coached Meal pp. 285–292). Once we have determined that PAMS is appropriate, we introduce the model to the patient and the parents. In this introductory session, we explain that PAMS is based on FBT, a promising new approach that teaches parents how to help their child recover at home. Herrin often says to parents, "My job is to guide and support as you intervene at home to help your child recover." We inform parents that at least one of them will be required to come to each session for at least the first several months and that parents will prepare and supervise (or arrange for preparation and supervision of) all meals and snacks. To patients we say, "PAMS gives you the best shot possible of recovering without having to do an inpatient program. I am going to train your parents to be my at-home staff."

If parents are separated or divorced, we occasionally recommend that the child live temporarily with the parent who can be most available for PAMS. We have also worked with patients who go back and forth between two sets of parents. Of note, in these situations, we often develop two different plans and advise against one set of parents policing how the plan is managed by the other household. For occasional meals or snacks, some families rely on a grandparent, neighbor, or (but only if there are not other options) an older sibling. School nurses or counselors often can be recruited to supervise meals and snacks at school. It is important in this first session and throughout PAMS to emphasize the seriousness of the child's ED and the likelihood of grave medical problems if the ED is not quickly resolved.

A PAMS session begins with the nutrition counselor and patient in a private segment. We use this time to develop rapport, to show interest in the patient's situation, to check weight, and to revise the food plan if necessary. Discussion may digress briefly to school, friends, and how things are going at home. We elicit from patients any concerns they want discussed with parents. Herrin's patient, Alexis, gave a typical report. Her stepfather is too busy reading the newspaper to notice that Alexis is having trouble finishing her breakfast and often pours the milk from her cereal down the sink. "Well, that explains your weight drop," Herrin replies. If the patient has lost weight as Alexis did, we explore possible explanations and confer with the patient about possible additions or changes to her food plan or parental supervision. In Alexis' case, the problem at breakfast was a likely culprit. The last few minutes of this segment are spent hammering out a revised food plan that will support weight gain and, in time, include trigger or fear foods.

Parents are then invited into the session to provide their impressions about how refeeding is progressing. The nutrition counselor inquires about any difficulties parents are having in this process and reiterates that parents must work together for refeeding at home to be successful. If we feel the child has been less than forthcoming in previous private segments, we invite parents in at the beginning of the next session to share their concerns and then move into the private segment with the patient. The patient is then invited to present the revised food plan to parents for their approval. Alexis disclosed to her mom and stepdad that she needed more help at breakfast, but needed Herrin to provide the details. The nutrition counselor mediates if necessary, keeping the focal point of the discussion on developing a course of action that ensures recovery rather than deteriorate into a "blame game." Along with solving eating and behavioral problems, the nutrition counselor models compassion and remains non-judgmental. Some children prefer not to attend the parent section of a session because it feels too intense or too embarrassing. In these cases, we oblige the child, meet alone with the parents, and then invite the child to rejoin the session for a few minutes for a summary.

Each session ends with the nutrition counselor, the family, and the patient agreeing upon a plan for the next week that will lead to the necessary rate of weight gain or a reduction in bingeing or purging. Alexis' session ended with her stepfather complimenting her on her honesty and thanking her for helping him do a better job.

Psycho-education for Parents

One important task of nutrition counselors is to educate parents about the medical gravity of a serious ED. Parents should be encouraged to think of their role as one of helping their child convalesce from a serious illness. Point out that a child with an ED often behaves in ways that are typical of children with life-threatening diseases. Understanding that an ED often "regresses" a child developmentally so that emotional responses are more typical of a much younger child can help parents move beyond the unproductive "blaming" of themselves or their child for the child's current difficulties.

Motivational Advice for Parents

Examples of the motivational advice we give to parents are given in Box 13.3.

BOX 13.3 PAMS ADVICE FOR PARENTS

Your child's recovery from this life-threatening illness depends on refeeding at home.

Your child's medicine is PAMS and you are your child's inpatient nursing staff.

You will find that your child recovers quicker and more completely when you initially make all food decisions.

You taught your child how to eat well when he or she was younger, now you have to teach him or her again.

You should not worry about treading on your child's autonomy around the issue of eating enough to recover.

Your child cannot have the option of undereating.

You should guard against caving in to your child. If in doubt, aim on the side of more eating rather than less.

You do not need to focus on how many calories your child is eating or needs. Your nutrition counselor will give you a food plan that is just what your child needs nutritionally.

You, as parents, are biologically programmed to know how much your child needs to eat. Mothers especially seem to know how much to feed their child.

You should expect your child to regress—most do—but the regression is temporary and the need to do PAMS is temporary.

You should expect more emotional outbursts during the weight-gain phase. Children may have tantrums or throw food. If this happens we will help you develop a plan to deal with it. As weight approaches normal, your child's mood will improve and there will be less hostility.

You may hear about techniques in sessions that you have already suggested to your child. You should try to refrain from saying, "I told you so" or "I was right," instead be verbally hopeful and optimistic that PAMS will be effective.

You should guard against responding angrily or irritably toward your child during PAMS.

The Coached Meal

The coached meal is such a powerful intervention it usually is necessary to do it only once for each patient. Parents bring a meal to a session to eat with the patient and his or her siblings. The nutrition counselor uses this session to coach and guide parents as they experiment with various interventions aimed at getting their child to follow the food plan or just to take one more bite than the child intends.

We consider using a coached meal intervention if a patient is not making progress or the family is struggling to take control of food behaviors at home. The first step is to discuss the benefits of scheduling a coached meal with the patient and his or her parents. We tell patients that a coached meal allows the nutrition counselor to help parents understand and follow the food plan. Of note, most patients respond well to the idea that the nutrition counselor will be guiding their parents. We tell parents that a coached meal helps the family better understand how to implement the food plan and to handle food-related issues at meals and snacks.

The earlier in treatment the coached meal is scheduled, the less likely it is that families will develop non-productive refeeding tactics. Direct observation during a coached meal reveals the strengths and weaknesses of each family's approach to refeeding and enhances assessments based on self-reports from patients and families. Ideally the coached meal illustrates the point that the child's ED is so strong and pernicious that he or she is captive to it. Parents, therefore, must learn to temporarily take over managing eating and food issues for their child. In the original FBT model, a coached meal is routinely scheduled for the second session. As bringing a family together for a coached meal (90 minutes is an ideal amount of time for this session) can be difficult to schedule for all concerned, we may schedule a "coached snack," which takes 60 minutes, or we wait on scheduling until it is clear a coached meal necessary.

Although in our practices, we find that families often make progress with PAMS regardless of partaking in a coached meal, we also have seen how this one intervention mobilizes parents who otherwise felt like they needed to "walk on eggshells" around their child when it came to eating. In this one session, parents go from feeling powerless and frustrated to having the confidence that they can manage their child's eating. Parents also come to grips with the significant time and effort they must devote to overseeing meals and snacks. Siblings learn to help by playing the role of playmate or non-critical confidant, but they are not to be involved in direct management of the ED.

A coached meal has a paradoxical effect on the patient. Being "forced to eat" allows the patient to "save face," preserving his or her dignity, and de-escalates resistance to parental oversight. Let us explain: the coached meal, or PAMS itself, is designed not to challenge the child's ED identity or need for ED behaviors. When the child is not fighting to hold onto his or her ED or needing to prove he or she has a serious ED, intense parental supervision of food intake is easier to tolerate. Patients have told us, "I don't want to eat, it makes my ED mad that I eat, but I have to eat because my parents are making me." At this point, the child usually does not want to or is not able to renounce his or her ED identity. We have seen how relinquishing accountability for food intake to the parents provides a sense of relief for the patient. Although coached meals often evoke strong emotions, parents are usually optimistic by the end of the session. In fact, it is our job to make sure parents leave the coached meal feeling confident that they can insist their child comply with the food plan, and the child is more resigned to following the food plan.

At least an hour-long segment is necessary for a coached meal. We recommend that counselors who are new to PAMS schedule a full 90 minutes. All family members (siblings, grandparents, etc.) who regularly share meals with the patient should attend the session if possible. If two sets of parents are involved, we schedule two different coached meal sessions. Instruct parents to bring to the counselor's office a meal or a snack that is typical of what is served at home, as well as necessary plates and utensils. The meal should include enough food for attending family members, and the type and amount of food the parents believe the child needs to eat. In some cases, we ask parents to bring a food that would be clearly challenging for their child to eat. We also tell parents that there is no need to bring food for the coach as we will be too occupied with coaching to eat.

We begin the session by greeting the family and expressing enthusiasm about the coaching intervention. For example, "I am so glad we are doing the coached meal today. It is the most effective technique I know of in turning around an ED." We then direct the family to set up the meal while the counselor meets privately with the patient, checking weight and explaining the patient's role in the coached meal. We tell our patients in our private segment, "Don't be polite because you are in my office. I want to see what meals are like for you and your parents. I need to see how hard eating is for you. My job is to help your parents figure out how best to help you eat enough. If you are just polite, no one will learn anything." We advise patients to behave as if they were at home, but if they can't that is OK, too. The unfortunate reality, we tell patients and sometimes their families, is that the coached meal may feel age-inappropriate and demeaning, "The coached meal may feel humiliating to you, but it is important because it will help me show your parents how to fight your ED."

We begin the coached meal by saying, "Everyone is probably going to feel a little awkward and unnatural, but I want you all to sit down, begin eating, chatting, and behaving as much like you do at home as possible." As the nutrition counselor is most effective standing behind the parents to prompt them rather than sitting with the family, we usually explain, "I won't be joining you for the meal because I will be too busy observing and coaching." As the family begins to eat, we engage them in general conversation, looking for opportunities to speak to each family member. For example, "What do you usually talk about at meals?" "Is this meal typical of what you usually eat at home?" To siblings we say, "Your brother or sister is sick. My job is to show your parents how to help him or her get well at home." Then we add, "It may be hard to watch but is very important that you do not interfere with your parents as they do their job, rather you can support, comfort, and even distract your sibling." Throughout the coached meal, we check in with each member of the family about the process and remind siblings and other family members not to interfere with the parents' efforts to feed the patient.

The counselor's primary task is to encourage parents to take an increasingly insistent series of actions until the patient is eating a reasonable amount or at least one more bite than he or she intended to eat. As is often the case, everyone quickly serves themselves and begins to eat, but the patient just sits staring at an empty plate. If he or she does not begin to dish up a reasonable plate of food within a few minutes or the parents do not step in to help, we direct, in a stage whisper, the nearest parent to say, "Would it help if I served your plate?" If the patient does not respond, parents are to serve the amount that fits the food plan as they understand it. If the patient does not begin eating at a normal pace, we ask the parents in the same whisper, "Do you think she should eat more now?" "Can you ask her to take another bite?" Or we suggest parents say, "We want you to finish that." "You are going to have to take another bite." If the patient still doesn't begin eating in a reasonable way, we suggest the following tactic. If the child has not picked up a utensil, we suggest to the parents that one parent move his or her chair closer to the child. If the child does not start eating, then the other parent is also directed to move closer. One parent directs the child to pick up the spoon or fork. Once the child starts eating, parents can move back to their original positions, unless the child prefers parents to stay close.

Some patients, even after going through the steps outlined above, still refuse to eat or, instead of eating, just push food around on their plate. Patients sometimes feel they are "letting down" or disappointing their ED when they are too willing agree to eat. When faced with this kind of resistance at the coached meal, the nutrition counselor, with kind, patient, calm, repetitive, and insistent suggestions, compels parents to take action and models the approach parents should take with their child. We have found it helpful to ask parents, "If your child was younger, what would you say or do to get him or her to take a life-saving medicine?" In the same vein, we encourage parents to commit to "sticking it out" in their attempts to get the child to finish his or her meal. In this context, we suggest that parents try sequentially the steps in Box 13.4. Once the child starts eating parents should stop intervening, unless the child stops eating. Usually the child says something like, "I'll keep eating if you just move away from me." We advise the parents not to take offense, but to move back to their original seat and pick up the conversation as if nothing had happened.

BOX 13.4 STEPS TO TAKE TO GET YOUR CHILD TO EAT

- Sit close to the child.
- Repeat calmly and insistently "You have to take a bite/eat/finish."
- If another parent is present, this parent moves his or her chair close to the child and joins in the refrain "You have to take a bite."
- Be prepared for a long meal, your child can't leave the table until she eats.
- Put a loving hand on the child's arm, leg, or shoulder.
- Guide the child's hands while he or she takes a bite.
- Gently hold the child's hands while the other parent feeds him or her.
- Position the child on one parent's lap while the other parent carefully spoon-feeds him or her.

PAMs does not involve physically forcing the child to eat, but parents are to be persistent and not deterred by crying or pleading. We have had patients say that when parents spoon-feed them it is calming and it feels like permission to eat. Still others say, "I can eat if my mother forces me." In rare cases, we have had a child suddenly leave the table. We instruct parents to calmly escort the child back to the table. Sometimes, a child is so resistant and the session becomes so emotionally charged that the best course of action is to end the session on a positive note. Jessie, for example, kicked, screamed, and swore as her parents attempted to bring her back to the table. "Let's just stop here. What we have learned tonight is that Jessie cannot cooperate because of the seriousness of her ED. Let's meet again soon for another try at a coached meal. In the meantime, please let me know how Jessie does with her eating over the next several days."

Occasionally, parents do not manage to get their child to eat even one bite during the coached session. In these cases, we praise parents for their participation in the coached meal and encourage them to continue to work at getting their child to eat at home. A relatively passive, but effective at-home technique, is for a parent to say (if they actually can), "I am going to sit here all day with you if that is what it takes." Another passive approach is to say, "If you can't finish your meal, you need to lie down on your bed or on the couch until your next meal or snack. Oh, and by the way, no TV or texting or cell phone until your eating is OK."

During a coached meal, Mollie clamped her jaw shut, refusing to eat despite her parents' best efforts to use all of the advised strategies. If this happens at home, we suggest that parents matter of factly experiment with one of the following tactics:

- Insist the child drink a "Boost" or "Ensure Plus" (or a similar high-calorie drink) if he or she doesn't finish his or her meal.
- Put the child to bed, and try again tomorrow.

- Keep the child on bed rest (no school or activities) until he or she is complying with the food plan.
- Make appointments with members of the child's treatment team as soon as possible.
- Begin exploring inpatient treatment options and tell the child that if he or she can't eat then he or she is too sick for home-based treatment.

Andrea, a high-school senior, was accompanied by her single mom and younger brother to a coached meal. After slowly eating the meal her mother had fixed for her without needing much coaxing, Andrea proceeded to vomit up most of her meal just after she took her last bite. Although such a reaction is not the norm, nutrition counselors need to be able to remain composed, supportive of parents and the patient, and optimistic about eventual recovery regardless. In this case, Herrin encouraged Andrea to try to swallow the vomitus back down. When she couldn't, Herrin held back her hair and made soothing comments such as, "I understand how hard this is for you." When Andrea finished, she was instructed to clean up the mess. To mom and brother, Herrin said, "This sort of thing does happen. If it does happen again, it means Andrea may need to eat smaller meals and more snacks. Taking her on a walk half-way through a meal may help the food settle." This type of event provides the opportunity for the nutrition counselor to make the point, "It is the ED that makes Andrea behave this way. She really needs your help to control the vomiting." Another difficult situation is when the patient becomes hostile and aggressive. Jessie, whom we mentioned above, was one such patient. After abruptly leaving the table, Jessie yelled, kicked, and swore at her parents when they tried to bring her back. All the while, Herrin encouraged the parents not to lose their tempers and to separate their anger at the ED from their feelings toward Jessie. "Remember that Jessie cannot control what she says or does with regard to food."

We watch for one parent to side with the child and against the other parent. If this happens we gently point out that siding is a classic response but it is counterproductive. Parents must remain united in their efforts to get their child to eat and to keep private any conflicts they have about managing their child's eating. We let parents know that we are available for parents-only sessions to advise and mediate any conflicts. All should be cautioned not to lose their tempers and to work at separating their anger at the illness from their feelings for the child. If the coached meal elicits strong emotions, conflict, and antisocial behavior among family members, it is likely that the PAMS approach is too taxing for this family. The same is true if the family reacts physically or angrily towards a child who is having difficulty eating at home. Charlotte reported that her parents would grab her by her hair when she refused to finish her meal. Evan reported that his parents ignored his older brother's yelling and swearing at him. The nutrition counselor needs be prepared to respond with statements conveying that, though understandable, these reactive behaviors are unacceptable and dangerous. The nutrition counselors should consider whether the parents and other family members may benefit from traditional family therapy and the patient may do better in a higher level of care. We also recommend that the nutrition counselor pass on any reports of physical or emotional abuse to the team psychotherapist and medical provider.

Difficulties also arise if a child is too cooperative during the coached meal. In these cases, parents do not have the chance to be guided through and to practice refeeding techniques and patients miss out on the therapeutic experience of having parents taking charge of refeeding. We respond to such situations by saying, "I know that really strong EDs can go underground occasionally. But I also know that having us all gathered here in an attempt to 'outwit, outplay, and outlast' an ED can overwhelm a powerful ED at least for a little while. Let's assume that is what happened here."

It is important to keep an eye on the time so that the session ends with the patient eating at least one more bite than he or she intended to. We remind parents that, while this meal's time is limited by the length of the counseling session, they need to be prepared to set aside as much time as it takes to get their child to eat appropriate meals at home. The ultimate goal, however, is for the child to eat a normal amount of food in a normal amount of time. If parents are unsure they have the ability to manage their child's eating, encourage them to do the best they can with the food plan over the next few days at home and return for another coached meal. To close the coached family meal session, we summarize, as the following statements illustrate, the family's achievements as positively as possible, regardless of actual success.

- "Everyone did a great job in a difficult situation. You helped your child eat a little more than he or she wanted to eat. Your child struggled, but did eat. The siblings did a good job staying out of the fray or cheerleading."
- "I have great confidence that you as a family can beat this ED."
- "I am glad you all got to see how strong this ED is. I was also glad to see that you (parents) could overpower the ED enough to get your child to eat a little more than he or she wanted. Remember that it is the ED you are fighting, not your child's stubbornness."

We cannot overemphasize the importance of ending the coached meal session on a positive note. To self-doubting parents, we say, "I know you can do this at home; you really can help him or her follow the food plan." At the very least, we remind parents that, prior to their child's ED, they were successful at feeding their child. We recommend that parents continue to use the above coached meal techniques at all meals and snacks. We reinforce the message that their child's ED is potentially life-threatening and will require a concerted family effort to overcome. The family is encouraged to remain in touch with the counselor about their progress. If the family reports that their child is not complying with the food plan at home, the counselor should schedule a nutrition session and possibly another coached meal as soon as possible. We reassure parents that we will recommend admission to an inpatient ED program if their child continues to have difficulty eating enough to be physically safe.

We send families home with instructions for parents to remain firmly in charge of when and how much the patient eats. Most patients need at least one "savvy" adult present at every meal and snack. Families may need help with the logistics of providing this level of supervision. It is not unreasonable to recommend that the patient take a leave from school and parents rearrange work schedules so that one of them is available to supervise meals and snacks. If the patient remains in school, staff at the school (e.g., lunch monitors, guidance counselors, or school nurses) can be asked to supervise meals either in the lunchroom or in their individual offices and report back to the parents each day. We have had parents arrive at school lunchtime so that they can eat lunch with their child in the car or join him or her in the school cafeteria.

At coached meals and subsequent sessions, we reiterate that parents are in charge of buying food, preparing food, and deciding when, what, and how much food the child should eat to adhere to the food plan. We provide nutrition advice as needed, but, if at all possible, we concur with parents on food questions and advise parents to agree together in advance on the amount of food the child needs to eat. If the meal or snack provided at the coached event is insufficient to support weight gain or does not contain some high-calorie or high-fat foods, we gently point this out to parents and talk about alternatives. We encourage parents not to lecture their child about nutrition or the dangers of EDs (most usually "tune-out"), instead we advise parents in a simple and redundant way (much like the PAMS approach) to focused on refeeding using strategies, such as:

- "You can't leave table till we say you are finished."
- "I will sit here with you as long as it takes for you to finish eating."
- "You can't use have the privilege of using your xx (e.g., cell phone, TV, computer, socializing, sports, after school activities, wearing favorite clothes, shoes, boots) if you don't finish."
- "We have to follow the food plan your counselor gave you."
- "You don't have to worry. Your counselor is managing your weight."
- "Following the food plan will stop the bloating, improve your digestion, hair loss, insomnia, etc."
- "Following the food plan will give you your life back."
- "Following the food plan will get you back to school, exercising, sports, travel, etc."

We do not recommend sneaking high-calorie ingredients into foods served to the patient or lying about how food is prepared. It is best not to discuss food preparation or caloric composition of foods with the patient. Parents should calmly inform their child that "this meal is according to the food plan." We have had parents openly share their worries about gaining weight if they eat what their ED child is eating. We encourage parents to eat the variety of foods indicated in the food plan, including fun foods, desserts, and snacks, according to their individual appetites. It is unproductive to engage in conversation comparing how much each family member is eating. Parents should validate their child's concerns about being portioned more than others and acknowledge that it may not seem fair. They should explain that the amount served to the child is necessary for recovery.

Privileges

Traditional behavior-modification strategies that reward desirable behaviors and provide consequences for undesirable behaviors usually are not helpful. But making privileges such as use of a cell phone or computer, or going out with friends contingent on positive eating behaviors is often effective. For example, Elena refused to eat an afternoon snack. Mom told her it was her phone or a snack. Elena threw her phone at mom. To make matters worse, mom was driving Elena to her horseback-riding lesson. Mom slowly turned the car around saying "We'll need to go straight home so you can have your snack, and Thursday we'll have the snack at home and if it goes well I'll take you to your lesson. I can't let you have your phone until you can eat without creating a dangerous situation."

Managing Mealtimes

It is important for parents to know that it is not unusual during the early stages of refeeding for their child to act aggressively and resist eating by yelling, swearing, hitting, screaming, and throwing things. Parents may feel that they are damaging their relationship with their child by strictly adhering to the food plan. Taylor refused to come to the table for dinner, promising he would eat just fine if he could only be alone. His parents were tempted to agree, as meals have been difficult, but remembered the coaching about not allowing eating alone. They needed to nag Taylor for about 15 minutes, but he did come to the table.

Parents are advised to do everything in their power to get their child to eat without resorting to force or undue coercion (Lock, 2011, p. 231). We reassure parents that their child's resistance should improve with refeeding and continued treatment, and that deep down most children know that their parents are doing the right thing. Patients often tell us that when they are allowed to cheat on the food plan they feel like their parents don't care or aren't worried about them, or that their ED is not very serious.

Some illustrative examples of the use of PAMS are given in Case Examples 13.1 to 13.3.

CASE EXAMPLE 13.1: KIRSTEN

Kirsten's parents made a frantic call to Herrin. Kirsten was pouting in her room and refusing to finish her lunch. Herrin advised, "Take her meal up to the bedroom and sit with her till she finishes." Kirsten ate the next few meals in her room, but before long she was joining the family at the table.

CASE EXAMPLE 13.2: OLIVIA

Olivia's 24-hour food recall indicated that she did not consume the planned morning snack (Luna bar) and her milk at dinner. Further conversation indicated that the family had run out of Luna bars and no substitute was provided. At dinnertime, Olivia poured herself a glass of water in place of milk, without the family noticing. Additional discussion revealed inconsistent compliance with the food plan on most days. Herrin addressed this problem with the parents. "I am really concerned that Olivia was not able to follow the food plan. What was the problem?" Olivia's father complained about his busy week. "We had no time to shop for food this week. Dinnertime is so crazy with the three younger children at the table so we forgot about Olivia's milk." Herrin helped the parents problem-solve, reminding them of the need to be more diligent about keeping food available and monitoring their child's food intake. "It is really important for Olivia's recovery to follow the food plan to the 'T'."

CASE EXAMPLE 13.3: CARRIE

Carrie's outbursts, tantrums, and cursing whenever her parents talked about eating or the food plan worried her parents. Herrin advised Carrie's parents to handle Carrie's outbursts as they would any other behavior unrelated to eating. In this case, her parents sent Carrie to her room until she could be pleasant and resume eating again. Herrin suggested that they intervene in a matter-of-fact way to avoid escalating the conflict. The parents decided that if this happened again they would warn Carrie that if her outbursts did not stop she would have to see one of her providers as soon as possible.

A Sample PAMS Plan

A typical PAMS plan is based on the RO3s plan (Box 13.5). The plan might stipulate which family member will be supervising which meal. It may include a shopping list. If the patient has exercise restrictions, the plan would reiterate the restrictions. The plan would spell out the agreed upon consequences for non-compliance with the food or exercise plan, and possibly rewards for complying with the food plan. It may include instructions to parents to help prevent bingeing or purging.

BOX 13.5 A SAMPLE PAMS PLAN FOR OLIVIA

Breakfast (Mom supervises)
- 3 Pancakes with butter and syrup, or 1 big bowl of cereal with 2% milk
- 1 cup 2% Milk or juice
- 2 slices of bacon or an English muffin with butter and honey

Snack (school nurse supervises)
- Luna bar, or 1 cup of trail mix, or a bagel

Lunch (social studies teacher supervises)
- Thick sandwich
- Carton of school milk
- Fruit (e.g., whole banana or apple)
- 4 Oreo cookies

Snack (Mom supervises)
- Greek yogurt or pudding
- 3 Fig Newtons or granola bar

Dinner (Mom and Dad supervise)
- Dad-sized serving of protein
- Dad-sized serving of carbohydrates
- Veggies (optional)
- 1 cup 2% Milk (double check that it is not skim milk)
- Mom-sized dessert

Snack (Dad supervises)
- 3 Graham cracker squares spread with nut butter
- 1 cup 2% Chocolate milk or juice

Exercise: Can, but doesn't have to take 15-minute walk with a parent.

Other: Lock up cookies and crackers and anything else that Olivia wants secured. No bathroom visits (unless supervised) for 1 hour after meals or snacks.

Shopping list: Luna bars, cookies, trail mix, 2% milk

Consequences: If Olivia follows her food and exercise plan every day for a week, she can download two songs from iTunes. If Olivia doesn't finish a meal or snack, she loses her cell phone, computer, and TV "rights" for 24 hours.

PAMS: Phase Two

Phase two begins when (for at least a period of 1 or 2 months), the patient is adhering to the food plan, abstaining from bingeing and purging, maintaining near a BAW, and when the mood of the family has improved. Parents are less involved in day-to-day food issues, as there are fewer struggles at meals and snacks. The child takes more initiative with eating and requires less parental cajoling to eat. In phase two the focus is teaching the patient to eat independently and helping parents transition to a more age-appropriate feeding relationship with their child.

As in phase one, the counselor weighs the patient and continues to meet with the patient privately, and with parents jointly at the end of the session. But, in phase two, the counselor spends the majority of each session with just the patient. During this segment, the nutrition counselor encourages the patient to follow the food plan independently and helps the patient adapt the food plan to a variety of situations outside the home. Contrary to phase one where the counselor is seriously emphasizing the dangers of EDs, in phase two the counselor is hopeful and optimistic about eventual recovery. Throughout phase two, the counselor is watchful for signs of relapse as parents decrease supervision. Once food behaviors are normalized, the parents instructed to adopt a less directive and more supportive role. As the patient progresses, the counselor schedules less frequent appointments and decreases time spent with parents at the end of each session. It is important to decrease dependency on professional relationships while supporting the family's improved capacity to resolve eating problems. Phase two concludes when the patient is maintaining a BAW and is (without supervision) eating and abstaining from bingeing and purging. The family is no longer focused exclusively on the ED and the child has resumed normal unsupervised eating activities.

Andrea, who is maintaining a BMI of 20kg/m^2 for the first time in her recovery, illustrates the type of progress typically seen in phase two. At her session, Andrea took the initiative to write up her revised food plan and present it to her mother. Andrea no longer needed the supervision of the school nurse to complete her lunch and was able to easily resume eating with her friends in the cafeteria.

Bulimia Nervosa and Binge-Eating Disorder

Using FBT in BN is a new development. Only a few studies to date have been published on FBT in BN, but they are promising (Le Grange, 2011, p. 292). Even less is known about the efficacy of any treatments for BED in children and adolescents (Campbell & Schmidt, 2011, p. 305–306). Given the lack of available evidence for BED, we assume that FBT is applicable to BED too. The aim of PAMS in BN is to stop binge eating and purging behaviors and to promote the eating of regular meals and snacks (Le Grange & Lock, 2007, pp. 78–79). Using PAMS in BN requires that the parents and child are willing and able to cooperate. The adolescent with BN, in particular, will need to feel understood and respected by both their parents and the nutrition counselor to be able to accept the PAMS approach. Because BN and BED are ego-dystonic behaviours (unacceptable and cause anxiety), patients can be more productively involved in treatment approaches than in AN (Hoste, Stiles-Shields, Labushagnee, & Le Grange, 2012). In contrast to FBT for AN, where parents are in charge of food, in FBT for BN the adolescent is encouraged to actively collaborate with parents in exploring and implementing solutions. Coached family meals should include a food or foods the patient sees as forbidden or that usually trigger a binge or a purge or both (Le Grange & Lock, 2007, pp. 88–89). We usually suggest the family bring a fun food (e.g., chips, dessert) that the patient needs encouragement to eat in "public." The five tenets of FBT for BN are given in Box 13.6 (Le Grange, 2011, p. 294).

BOX 13.6 THE FIVE TENETS OF FBT FOR AN

1. An agnostic view of what causes EDs (neither the adolescent nor the parents are to blame).
2. Initial focus on symptoms (pragmatic approach to treatment).
3. The parents and the adolescent are responsible for normalizing eating (collaboration).
4. Non-authoritarian therapeutic stance by the therapist (joining).
5. Separation of the adolescent and the disorder (respect for the adolescent).

Often parents present with significant anger towards their child for engaging in bulimic behaviors. It is important for the nutrition counselor to reiterate that bulimic patients are not acting out or intentionally being difficult when they binge, purge, or leave a mess in the kitchen or bathroom. We explain that patients engage in these behaviors due to their pathological fear of weight gain. Hearing such explanations helps parents become more empathetic and helps patients experience the nutrition counselor as someone who really understands. As in AN, we encourage parents of BN and BED patients to take control of what eating-disordered behaviors they can, to be a united front, to not criticize the patient, and to look at the ED as an illness that is no different than any other disease that may strike in adolescence, such as cancer or diabetes. We also expect parents of adolescents to ensure that their sick child is following treatment recommendations.

It is difficult for some parents to see the wisdom of taking control of adolescent eating behaviors. Increasingly, most adolescents are allowed considerable age-appropriate personal freedoms (time, clothes, music, and food) commensurate with their developing a sense of autonomy. We point out that an adolescent with BN often finds parental control of food intake reassuring, but parents are only to control eating-disordered behaviors, not anything else. It can be a benefit to have parents limit the supply of foods available at home. Some parents are comfortable barring access to the bathroom for a certain amount of time after a meal or in providing bathroom supervision or keeping the door open. Other effective strategies are for parents to provide distractions, such as going for a walk or watching a movie, for about an hour after meals.

The Lockbox Technique

Because bingeing is often triggered by certain foods, the lockbox technique can be helpful. The patient lists foods he or she wants locked up at home in a box, cabinet, toolbox, or trunk. When the patient feels ready, the parents can portion normal serving sizes of the locked-up food as part of planned meals or snacks. Specific foods may go in the box or come out of the box as the patient's relationship with the food changes. We encourage families to experiment with moving foods out of the box and back into kitchen cabinets or regular storage places. If the patient binges on the food, back into the box it goes.

Summary Points

- Parent-Assisted Meals and Snacks (PAMS; developed by Herrin) is a nutrition-counseling approach derived from family-based treatment (FBT) research which puts parents in charge of feeding their child.
- Research indicates that FBT techniques are very effective (90% recovery rates) for AN patients 18 years old and younger with a short duration of illness.
- In PAMS, the nutrition counselor utilizes FBT phase one and phase two techniques; a psychotherapist working concurrently with the patient takes

the lead in FBT phase three, which is focused on adolescent mental health issues.

• The coached meal helps the family better understand how to implement the food plan and to handle food-related issues at meals and snacks and helps the counselor to assess feeding problems from direct observation.

• Using PAMS in BN or BED requires that the parents and child are willing and able to cooperate and that the nutrition counselor is able to develop a strong rapport with the patient and parents.

Appendix A
INTRODUCTION PACKET

Authorization for release of confidential information form

Patient's name: _____ Date of Birth: _____
Street Address: _____
City/State: _____ Zip Code:_____
Patient's SS # _____ E-mail address _____
Phone Number: (home) _____ (cell)_____ (work)_____

Permission is hereby given for (*provider name*) to <u>release or request</u> information about this patient's medical, nutritional or psychotherapeutic record from:

Practitioner's name _____

Address _____

Fax _____ Phone _____

☐ Physician/nursing notes	☐ Sexual assault
☐ Laboratory tests	☐ Mental health
☐ Complete health record	☐ Drug/alcohol
☐ History and physical exam	☐ Growth charts/weight history

I hereby release (*provider name*) from any liability or legal responsibility in connection the release of this information. I understand the risks of faxing and e-mailing medical information. I understand that I may revoke this consent in writing at any time, except to the extent that action has already been taken in response to this authorization. I understand that the potential for information disclosed pursuant to this authorization is subject to re-disclosure by the recipient other than (*provider name*), which would be beyond the control of (*provider name*) and may no longer be protected by federal law.

I request that the following information not be released:

Patient, parent or guardian signature _____

Date _____ Signature of Witness _____

HIPPA guidelines form

Description of Privacy Practices

I am dedicated to protecting your privacy. Below is a description of how I will maintain the confidentiality of your health information and the resulting records. My practices meet and exceed the requirements of federal and state privacy laws. I will not allow anyone to have access to your records or give anyone information without your written consent. If, however, you have agreed that I am to bill your insurance company for nutrition services, your signature below indicates your permission for me to discuss diagnosis, progress, and dates of services with representatives of your insurance company. If your account becomes past due, your signature below indicates your permission for me to discuss dates of service and contact information with a collection agency representative. I may, on occasion, ask for your written permission to share certain information with other healthcare providers involved in your treatment. I may consult with other clinicians in the role or consultants about your care. In this situation, I will disguise your identity. Unless instructed otherwise, there may be times that I will need to contact you or respond to you via electronic mail, voice mail, fax machine, cellular phone, or answering machine. It is important for you to realize there is the potential that these messages could be inadvertently received or overheard by an unintended third party.

I can be reached at (*provider phone number*) during office hours, at (*provider phone number*) during evenings and weekends, or at (*provider e-mail address*). I check voicemail and e-mail daily, but if you should experience a life-threatening emergency, you should call 911 or go to your nearest emergency room.

In addition, I will abide by the state and federal laws that allow disclosures of health information to improve treatment (e.g., sharing information with other professionals involved in your care), to receive payment for services (e.g., when billing insurance companies), and for healthcare operations (e.g., accounting staff who are required to protect patients' privacy). These laws also require that: Patients receive a written notice of the healthcare provider's privacy practices (that is, this document). Patients may ask for further restrictions on the ways in which I use and disclose their health information. I am not required by law to agree to further restrictions. I will agree unless I am unable to do so. Patients may ask (must be in writing) that I communicate with them at a different address, or use a different means of communication. I will make every effort to accommodate such requests. Patients may see and get a copy (such a request must be in writing) of their nutrition records or any other health information that I keep in a paper or electronic file. I may charge you a reasonable fee for copies. Patients may ask (must be in writing) for an amendment to their health records. I must decide whether the amendment is warranted, but the request and explanation of the amendment will be kept in their file. Patients may (must request in writing) receive a written account of the disclosures I have made of their health records. Patients may designate a "Personal Representative" to help them exercise their privacy rights. Patients have the right to agree or object to family and friends being involved in their care. State laws require that suspected child abuse or neglect, or suspected abuse, neglect or exploitation of a vulnerable adult must be reported.

If you believe your privacy rights have been violated, you may complain to me and to the Secretary, U.S. Department of Health and Human Services, Washington, D.C. 20201. If you have any questions about my privacy practices or confidentiality, please bring them to my attention.

Your signature below reflects that you have read and understood this statement of Privacy Practices. If you have any questions, you will discuss them with (*provider name*).

Date _____ Signature _____

Patient information form

Today's Date _____ Patient's Name _____

Date of Birth   Telephone #   Cell #

Insurance Company   Telephone # to confirm benefits   Identification #

Address to Submit Claims   Insurance Plan Name

Insured's Name   Date of Birth   Telephone #   Cell #   SS #

Insured's Address   Street   Town   State   Zip

Insured's Policy Group #   Employer's Name

Patient's Home Address   Town   State   Zip

Patient's Telephone #   Cell #   Work #   E-mail

Name of Primary Care Provider   Address   Telephone #   E-mail

Name of Psychotherapist   Telephone #   E-mail

Name of Psychiatrist   Telephone #   E-mail

Provide the following information for patients supported by parents or guardians

Name of Mother/Guardian   Address   E-mail

Mother/Guardian's Telephone#   Work #   Cell #

Name of Father/Guardian   Address   E-mail

Name of Father/Guardian's Telephone #   Work #   Cell #

Financial agreement form

Patient Name _____

Financial Agreement

Visit fees are $ . . . . . ./session. Payment is expected at the time of each visit. Cash, check, and credit cards are accepted. Make checks payable to (*provider or business name*). Co-payments required by insurance companies are expected at the time of the visit.

If arrangements have been made for (*provider or business name*) to bill your insurance company, you agree that insurance company payments can be made directly to (*provider name*). In the case that your insurance company makes payments directly to you, you will be responsible for the cost of each visit. Any fees not covered by insurance companies within a reasonable time frame are the responsibility of the patient.

To avoid the visit fee ($ . . . . . ./session) for a missed visit, cancellations must be communicated **48-hours in advance** by phone (*provider phone number*) or e-mail (*provider e-mail address*). To cancel an early morning appointment, call (*provider phone number*).

Missed visit fees are not charged for weather-related cancellations *if* you call to report your travel difficulties in a timely manner.

Any missed visit fees and overdue payments will be charged to your credit card or billed if you have made other arrangements. (*Provider or business name*) will make every effort to inform you before your credit card is charged. Overdue accounts may also be forwarded to a collection agency. A fee (30% of the account balance) is charged to accounts turned over to collections.

Your signature below indicates that you understand the above stated financial agreement.

My signature below authorizes (*provider or business name*) permission to keep my credit card number on file and to bill any outstanding balances directly to my card.

NAME (as it appears on your credit card): _____ (please print)

_____   _____
YOUR SIGNATURE (Cardholder)   Date of Signature

Appendix B

CHECKLIST FOR NUTRITION ASSESSMENT OF EATING DISORDERS

Date of first visit . . . .
Name . . . .
DOB/Age . . . .
Sex . . . .

REFERRAL SOURCE

☐ Parent
☐ Physician/therapist
☐ Friend
☐ Self
☐ Other

SOCIAL HISTORY

Current lifestyle
☐ Living arrangement
☐ Food shopping and preparation
☐ Occupation/Student
☐ Daily routine
☐ Social network

Significant family history
☐ Any family members diagnosed with eating disorders, substance abuse, depression, psychological illnesses?
☐ Medical history of immediate family members (diabetes, heart disease, cancer)
☐ Biological weight of family members

NUTRITION HISTORY

- ☐ Food allergies/intolerances
- ☐ Food likes/dislikes
- ☐ Food fears
- ☐ Religious or cultural food restrictions
- ☐ Self-imposed diets (vegetarian, avoids red meat, gluten-free)
- ☐ Medically prescribed diets (diabetic, low sodium)
- ☐ Previous diets/weight loss dieting history
- ☐ Recent changes in eating habits
- ☐ Counting: calories, grams of carbohydrate, fat, etc.
- ☐ 24-hour recall:

• Usual meal pattern skips meals grazes 3 meal/day pattern				
• Time between meals/snacks				
• Percent time spent eating				
• Calories	inadequate	marginal	adequate	excessive
• Protein	inadequate	marginal	adequate	excessive
• Carbohydrate	inadequate	marginal	adequate	excessive
• Fat	inadequate	marginal	adequate	excessive
• Calcium	inadequate	marginal	adequate	excessive
• Fluid/beverage	inadequate	marginal	adequate	excessive
• Fruits/vegetables	inadequate	marginal	adequate	excessive
• Caffeine intake	none	moderate		excessive
• Alcohol intake	none	moderate		excessive
• Diet beverages/diet food intake	none	moderate		excessive

- ☐ Eating location/environment/with whom
- ☐ Food availability/financial constraints

Nutrition counseling history
- ☐ Previous nutrition counselor's name
- ☐ Presenting problem
- ☐ What worked/did not work
- ☐ Reason for discontinuing nutrition counseling

Nutrition knowledge/beliefs/attitudes
- ☐ Internet searches/classes/magazines/books
- ☐ Beliefs and attitudes

EATING DISORDER HISTORY

Eating disorder treatment

☐ Onset of eating disorder behaviors

☐ Previous treatment, if any (inpatient and outpatient)

☐ Current members of eating disorder treatment team, if any

☐ Current reason(s) for seeking treatment

Eating disorder behaviors

☐ Restrictive eating (type, amount, frequency, and duration)

- o Food rituals and behaviors (e.g., eating in secret)
- o Refusal to chew or eat solid foods
- o Consumes only liquids
- o Rigid sensory preferences (neophobic) vs willingness to try new foods
- o Limited number of acceptable foods (safe foods vs fear foods)

☐ Binge eating frequency (type, amount, frequency, and duration)
- o Daily and/or weekly frequency
- o Typical foods consumed during a binge
- o Triggers for bingeing

☐ Purging frequency (type, amount, frequency and duration)
- o Laxatives
- o Diet pills
- o Diuretics
- o Vomiting
- o Restrictive eating
- o Exercise
- o Spitting out food or regurgitation/rumination

Physical activity

☐ Current physical activity
- o Type of exercise and duration (minutes/hours)
- o Intensity of current physical activity
- o Frequency (days/week)

☐ Patient's reasons and concerns about physical activity

☐ Past physical activity patterns

Support for eating disorder

☐ Who is aware of your eating disorder?

☐ Who is supportive or not supportive?

☐ Caregiver fatigue during feeding process (resulting in inadequate food intake)

MEDICAL HISTORY

- ☐ Date of last physical exam (electrocardiogram) and findings/treatment
- ☐ Date of last dental exam and findings/treatment
- ☐ Date of last psychotherapy session and findings/treatment
- ☐ Medical conditions

  - ○ Osteopenia/osteoporosis
  - ○ Gastrointestinal disturbances
  - ○ Bradycardia
  - ○ Orthostatic hypotension
  - ○ Hypercholesterolemia
  - ○ Other

- ☐ Psychiatric conditions
  - ○ Anxiety/depression
  - ○ OCD
  - ○ Personality disorders
  - ○ Other co-morbid conditions

- ☐ Medications currently taking (dose/frequency)
  - ○ Oral contraceptives
  - ○ Antidepressants/psychotropic medications
  - ○ Sleep aids
  - ○ Over-the-counter medications
  - ○ Illegal drugs
  - ○ Dietary supplements (vitamins/minerals/herbals)

Laboratory/test results (date)
- ☐ Bone density test
- ☐ Urinalysis: specific gravity
- ☐ Lipid panel
- ☐ Blood glucose
- ☐ Electrolytes: potassium, sodium, chloride
- ☐ Nutrients: phosphorous, zinc, iron, vitamin D
- ☐ Lymphocytes
- ☐ Hypocarotenemia

Weight history/anthropometrics
- ☐ Current height
- ☐ Current weight
- ☐ Current BMI
- ☐ Usual body weight (date)
- ☐ Lowest weight (date) at current height
- ☐ Highest weight (date) at current height

☐   Extreme weight fluctuations
☐   Growth history (thin/chubby as child)
☐   Frequency of self weight checks (by whom)
☐   Preferred weight: patient, parent, physician
☐   Expected weight for age (growth charts)

Endocrine history
☐   Date/age of first menses
☐   Date of last menstrual cycle
☐   Thyroid abnormalities/current levels
☐   Diabetes
☐   Virilization or sterility
☐   Libido in males (lack of sexual interest or a decrease in the frequency and intensity of sexual thoughts)

Current physical symptoms/complaints
☐   Heart
   o   Blood pressure: low, high
   o   Heart palpitations/arrhythmias
   o   Slowed heart rate

☐   Body fluid regulation
   o   Dehydration [ask patient the color of his/her urine (apple juice, lemonade, or pale yellow)]
   o   Dry mouth, thirst, headaches, UTIs
   o   Edema (swelling of ankles and/or feet)

☐   Body temperature
   o   Sensitive to cold
   o   Cold hands/feet
   o   Dressed in warm clothes despite mild outdoor temperature

☐   Body skin/hair/teeth
   o   Downy, fine hair on face, neck, arms, legs
   o   Brittle hair
   o   Hair loss
   o   Dry skin
   o   Yellow skin
   o   Brittle nails
   o   Finger or hand calluses
   o   Blood in stool or emesis
   o   Tooth decay
☐   Immune and hormonal function

- ◦ Frequently sick
- ◦ Depressed immune
- ◦ Amenorrhea and/or infertility
- ◦ Decreased testicular function
- ◦ Loss of libido

☐ Movement and functioning
- ◦ Dizziness/light-headed/fainting
- ◦ Muscular weakness and/or cramping
- ◦ Tiredness and fatigue

☐ Digestive function
- ◦ Bowel function: constipation or diarrhea
- ◦ Urinary: polyuria, UTIs
- ◦ Bloating
- ◦ Nausea
- ◦ Abdominal pain
- ◦ Feeling of fullness/early satiety
- ◦ Esophageal burning/heartburn
- ◦ Sore throat and/or difficulty swallowing
- ◦ Dry mouth

PSYCHOLOGICAL HISTORY

Psychotherapy history
☐ Previous therapists and presenting problem
☐ Current therapist and presenting problem
☐ Reason for discontinuing psychotherapy
☐ History of trauma or physical/sexual abuse

Behavioral symptoms
☐ Excessive dieting
☐ Fasting
☐ Avoidance of water/fluids
☐ Extreme interest in cooking/baking
☐ Refusal to eat with others
☐ Anxiety around food/eating
☐ Vegan/vegetarian
☐ Insomnia
☐ Frequent weighing
☐ Layering of clothes or excessive trying on of clothes
☐ Excessive make up
☐ Social withdrawal or extreme need for validation

☐   Self-hatred; feelings of unworthiness
☐   Substance abuse
☐   Inability to focus/impaired performance in school or at work/apathy
☐   Preoccupation with food, weight, eating
☐   Shoplifting or stealing money or credit card debt to buy food

Cognitive/emotional symptoms
☐   Intense fear of becoming fat
☐   Distorted body image
☐   Perfectionist thinking
☐   All-or-nothing thinking
☐   Depression
☐   Low self-esteem/self-worth
☐   Irritability
☐   Difficulty focusing/thinking clearly
☐   Anxiety and/or anger
☐   Constant feeling of being out of control
☐   Promiscuous or confusion about sexual identity
☐   Suicidal ideation

REFERENCES

Preface

Waterhous, T., & Jacob, M. (2011). *Practice paper of the American Dietetic Association: nutrition intervention in the treatment of eating disorders.* Chicago: American Dietetic Association. Retrieved September 14, 2012 from http://www.bhndpg.org/documents/Practice_Paper_Nutrition_Intervention.pdf.

Chapter 1: Clinical Features of Eating Disorders

Academy of Eating Disorders. (2011). *Critical points for early recognition and medical risk management in the care of individuals with eating disorders.* Deerfield, IL: Academy of Eating Disorders. Retrieved September 15, 2012 from http://www.aedweb.org/Medical_Care_Standards.htm.

Addolorato, G., Taranto, C., Capristo, E., & Gasbarrini, G. (1998). A case of marked cerebellar atrophy in a woman with anorexia nervosa and cerebral atrophy and a review of the literature. *International Journal of Eating Disorders, 24,* 433–447.

American Psychiatric Association. (2000). *Diagnostic and statistical manual of mental disorders: DSM-IV-TR.* Washington, DC: American Psychiatric Association.

American Psychiatric Association. (2010). *DSM-5 development. Proposed revisions. Feeding and eating disorders.* Retrieved September 15, 2012, from http://www.dsm5.org/proposedrevision/Pages/FeedingandEatingDisorders.aspx.

Andersen, A. E. (2006). Revising the diagnosis of anorexia nervosa will improve patient care. (cover story). *Eating Disorders Review, 17*(2), 1–3.

Anderson, D. A., Lavender, J. M., & De Young, K. P. (2010). The assessment process: Refining the clinical evaluation of patients with eating disorders. In M. Maine, B. H. McGilley & D. W. Bunnell (Eds.), *Treatment of eating disorders: Bridging the research–practice gap* (pp. 71–87). Amsterdam/Boston: Academic Press/Elsevier.

Arcelus, J., Mitchell, A. J., Wales, J., & Nielsen, S. (2011). Mortality rates in patients with anorexia nervosa and other eating disorders: A meta-analysis of 36 studies. *Archives of General Psychiatry, 68*(7), 724–731. doi:10.1001/archgenpsychiatry.2011.74.

Bahia, A., Chu, E. S., & Mehler, P. S. (2011). Polydipsia and hyponatremia in a woman with anorexia nervosa. *International Journal of Eating Disorders*, *44*(2), 186–188. doi:10.1002/eat.20792.

Benini, L., Todesco, T., Dalle Grave, R., Deiorio, F., Salandini, L., & Vantini, I. (2004). Gastric emptying in patients with restricting and binge/purging subtypes of anorexia nervosa. *American Journal of Gastroenterology*, *99*(8), 1448–1454. doi:10.1111/j.1572-0241.2004.30246.x.

Biller, B. M. K., Saxe, V., Herzog, D. B., Rosenthal, D. I., Holzman, S., & Klibanski, A. (1989). Mechanisms of osteoporosis in adult and adolescent women with anorexia nervosa. *Journal of Clinical Endocrinology & Metabolism*, *68*(3), 548–554. doi:10.1210/jcem-68-3-548.

Birmingham, C. L. (2012). Physical effects of eating disorders. In J. Alexander , & J. Treasure (Eds.), *A collaborative approach to eating disorders* (pp. 95). London: Routledge.

Bogunovic, L., Doyle, S., & Vogiatzi, M. (2009). Measurement of bone density in the pediatric population. *Current Opinion in Pediatrics*, *21*(1), 77–82.

Bo-Linn, G., Santa Ana, C. A., Morawski, S. G., & Fordtran, J. S. (1983). Purging and calorie absorption in bulimic patients and normal women. *Annals of Internal Medicine*, *99*(1), 14.

Bravender, T., Bryant-Waugh, R., Herzog, D., Katzman, D., Kreipe, R. D., Lask, B., & Zucker, N. (2007). Classification of child and adolescent eating disturbances. *International Journal of Eating Disorders*, *40*, S117–S122. doi:10.1002/eat.20458.

Chui, H. T., Christensen, B. K., Zipursky, R. B., Richards, B. A., Hanratty, M. K., Kabani, N. J., Mikulis, D. J., & Katzman, D. K. (August 2008). Cognitive function and brain structure in females with a history of adolescent-onset anorexia nervosa. *Pediatrics*, *122*(2), e426–e437. doi:10.1542/peds.2008-0170.

Crow, S. J., Peterson, C. B., Swanson, S. A., Raymond, N. C., Specker, S., Eckert, E. I. D., & Mitchell, J. E. (2009). Increased mortality in bulimia nervosa and other eating disorders. *American Journal of Psychiatry*, *166*(12), 1342–1346.

de Zwann, M. (2010). Obesity treatment for binge-eating in the obese. In C. Grilo, & J. E. Mitchell (Eds.), *The treatment of eating disorders: A clinical handbook* (pp. 428–436). New York: Guilford Press.

Dingemans, A. E., & van Furth, E. F. (2012). Binge eating disorder psychopathology in normal weight and obese individuals. *International Journal of Eating Disorders*, *45*(1), 135–138. doi:10.1002/eat.20905.

Fairburn, C. G. (2008). *Cognitive behavior therapy and eating disorders*. New York: Guilford Press.

Feldman, M. B., & Meyer, I. H. (2007). Eating disorders in diverse lesbian, gay, and bisexual populations. *International Journal of Eating Disorders*, *40*(3), 218–226. doi:10.1002/eat.20360.

Freitas, S. R., Lopes, C. S., Appolinario, J. C., & Coutinho, W. (2006). The assessment of binge eating disorder in obese women: A comparison of the binge eating scale with the structured clinical interview for the DSM-IV. *Eating Behaviors*, *7*(3), 282–289. doi:10.1016/j.eatbeh.2005.09.002.

Garner, D. M., & Garfinkel, P. E. (1997). *Handbook of treatment for eating disorders*. New York: Guilford Press.

Guillaume, S., Jaussent, I., Olié, E., Genty, C., Bringer, J., Courtet, P., & Schmidt, U. (2011). *P02-127—characteristics of suicide attempts in anorexia and bulimia nervosa: A case–control study*. *European Psychiatry*, *26*, 723. doi:10.1016/S0924-9338(11)72428-2.

Haas, V. K., Kohn, M. R., Clarke, S. D., Allen, J. R., Madden, S., Müller, M. J., & Gaskin, K. J. (2009). Body composition changes in female adolescents with anorexia nervosa. *The American Journal of Clinical Nutrition, 89*(4), 1005–1010. doi:10.3945/ajcn.2008.26958.

Horst-Sikorska, W., & Ignaszak-Szczepaniak, M. (2011). The role of anorexia nervosa in secondary osteoporosis development with the risk for low energy fractures. *Endokrynologia Polska, 62*(1), 45–47.

Hypercarotenemia. (2002). [Correspondence.] *New England Journal of Medicine, 347*(3), 222–223. doi:10.1056/NEJM200207183470317.

Joos, A., Hartmann, A., Glauche, V., Perlov, E., Unterbrink, T., Saum, B., Tüscher, O., Tebartz van Elst, L., & Zeeck, A. (2011). Grey matter deficit in long-term recovered anorexia nervosa patients. *European Eating Disorders Review, 19*(1), 59–63. doi:10.1002/erv.1060.

Kalarchian, M. A., Marcus, M. D., Levine, M. D., Courcoulas, A. P., Pilkonis, P. A., Ringham, R. M., Soulakova, J. N., Weissfeld, L. A., & Rofey, D. L. (2007). Psychiatric disorders among bariatric surgery candidates: Relationship to obesity and functional health status. *American Journal of Psychiatry, 164*(2), 328–334.

Kaye, W., Weltzin, T., Hsu, L., McConaha, C., & Bolton, B. (1993). Amount of calories retained after binge eating and vomiting. *American Journal of Psychiatry, 150*(6), 969–971.

Kaye, W. (2008). Neurobiology of anorexia and bulimia nervosa. *Physiology & Behavior, 94*(1), 121–135. doi:10.1016/j.physbeh.2007.11.037.

Keel, P. K., Brown, T. A., Holland, L. A., & Bodell, L. P. (2012). Empirical classification of eating disorders. *Annual Review of Clinical Psychology, 8*, 381–404. doi:10.1146/annurev-clinpsy-032511-143111.

Keys, A., Brozek, J., Henschel, A., Mickelsen, U., & Taylor, H. L. (1950). *The biology of human starvation* (2 vols.). Minneapolis: University of Minnesota Press.

Kim, S. T., Kang, J. S., Baek, J. W., Kim, T. K., Lee, J. W., Jeon, Y. S., & Suh, K. S. (2010). Acrodermatitis enteropathica with anorexia nervosa. *The Journal of Dermatology, 37*(8), 726–729. doi:10.1111/j.1346-8138.2010.00835.x.

Klump, K. L., Bulik, C. M., Kaye, W. H., Treasure, J., & Tyson, E. (2009). Academy for eating disorders position paper: Eating disorders are serious mental illnesses. *International Journal of Eating Disorders, 42*(2), 97–103.

Krieg, J. C., Backmund, H., & Pirke, K. M. (1987). Cranial computed tomography findings in bulimia. *Acta Psychiatrica Scandinavica, 75*, 144–149.

Marques, L., Alegria, M., Becker, A. E., Chen, C., Fang, A., Chosak, A., & Diniz, J. B. (2011). Comparative prevalence, correlates of impairment, and service utilization for eating disorders across US ethnic groups: Implications for reducing ethnic disparities in health care access for eating disorders. *International Journal of Eating Disorders, 44*(5), 412–420. doi:10.1002/eat.20787.

Matz, J., & Frankel, E.,. (2004). *Beyond a shadow of a diet: The therapist's guide to treating compulsive eating.* New York: Brunner-Routledge.

Mayer, L. E., Klein, D. A., Black, E., Attia, E., Shen, W., Mao, X., Shungu, D. C., Punyanita, M., Gallagher, D., Wang, J., Heymsfield, S. B., Hirsch, J., Ginsberg, H. N., & Walsh, B. T. (2009). Adipose tissue distribution after weight restoration and weight maintenance in women with anorexia nervosa. *The American Journal of Clinical Nutrition.* doi:10.3945/ajcn.2009.27820.

Mehler, P. S. (2011). Medical complications of bulimia nervosa and their treatments. *International Journal of Eating Disorders, 44*(2), 95–104. doi:10.1002/eat.20825.

Mehler, P. S., & Andersen, A. E. (2010). *Eating disorders: A guide to medical care and complications.* Baltimore: Johns Hopkins University Press.

Mehler, P. S., Cleary, B. S., & Gaudiani, J. L. (2011). Osteoporosis in anorexia nervosa. *Eating Disorders, 19*(2), 194–202. doi:10.1080/10640266.2011.551636.

Mehler, P. S., & MacKenzie, T. D. (2009). Treatment of osteopenia and osteoporosis in anorexia nervosa: A systematic review of the literature. *International Journal of Eating Disorders, 42*(3), 195–201.

Mehler, P. S., Sabel, A. L., Watson, T., & Andersen, A. E. (2008). High risk of osteoporosis in male patients with eating disorders. *International Journal of Eating Disorders, 41*(7), 666–672. doi:10.1002/eat.20554.

Miller, K. K. (2011). Endocrine dysregulation in anorexia nervosa update. *Journal of Clinical Endocrinology & Metabolism, 96*(10), 2939–2949. doi:10.1210/jc.2011-1222.

Misra, M., Katzman, D. K., Cord, J., Manning, S. J., Mendes, N., Herzog, D. B., Miller, K. K., & Klibanski, A. (2008). Bone metabolism in adolescent boys with anorexia nervosa. *Journal of Clinical Endocrinology Metabolism, 93*, 3029–3036.

Mont, L., Castro, J., Herreros, B., Paré, C., Azqueta, M., Magri a, J., Puig, J., Toro, J., & Brugada, J. (2003). Reversibility of cardiac abnormalities in adolescents with anorexia nervosa after weight recovery. *Journal of the American Academy of Child & Adolescent Psychiatry, 42*(7), 808.

Mühlau, M., Gaser, C., Ilg, R., Conrad, B., Leibl, C., Cebulla, M. H., Backmund, H., Gerlinghoff, M., Lommer, P., Schnebel, A., Wohlschläger, A. M., Zimmer, C., & Nunnemann, S. (2007). Gray matter decrease of the anterior cingulate cortex in anorexia nervosa. *American Journal of Psychiatry, 164*(12), 1850–1857.

Munoz, M., & Argente, J. (2002). Anorexia nervosa in female adolescents: Endocrine and bone mineral density disturbances. *European Journal of Endocrinology, 147*(3), 275–286. doi:10.1530/eje.0.1470275.

Olmos, J. M., Valero, C., del Barrio, A. G., Amado, J. A., Hernández, J. L., Menéndez-Arango, J., & González-Macías, J. (2010). Time course of bone loss in patients with anorexia nervosa. *International Journal of Eating Disorders, 43*(6), 537–542.

Ozier, A. D., & Henry, B. W. (2011). Position of the American Dietetic Association: Nutrition intervention in the treatment of eating disorders. *Journal of the American Dietetic Association, 111*(8), 1236–1241. doi:10.1016/j.jada.2011.06.016.

Preti, A., Rocchi, M. B. L., Sisti, D., Camboni, M. V., & Miotto, P. (2011). A comprehensive meta-analysis of the risk of suicide in eating disorders. *Acta Psychiatrica Scandinavica, 124*(1), 6–17. doi:10.1111/j.1600-0447.2010.01641.x.

Sachdev, P., Mondraty, N., Wen, W., & Gulliford, K. (2008). Brains of anorexia nervosa patients process self-images differently from non-self-images: An fMRI study. *Neuropsychologia, 46*(8), 2161–2168. doi:10.1016/j.neuropsychologia.2008.02.031.

Schlegel, S., & Kretzschmar, K. (1997). The role of computed tomography and magnetic resonance imaging in the diagnosis of psychiatric disorders. *Der Nervenarzt, 68*(1), 1–10.

Slevec, J. H., & Tiggemann, M. (2011). Predictors of body dissatisfaction and disordered eating in middle-aged women. *Clinical Psychology Review, 31*(4), 515–524. doi:10.1016/j.cpr.2010.12.002.

Strumia, R. (2009). Skin signs in anorexia nervosa. *Dermatoendocrinology, 1*(5), 268–270.

Sullivan, V., & Damani, S. (2000). Vegetarianism and eating disorders—partners in crime? *European Eating Disorders Review, 8*(4), 263–266. doi:10.1002/1099-0968(200008)8:4<263::AID-ERV367>3.0.CO;2-2.

Thomas, J. J., Roberto, C. A., & Brownell, K. D. (2009). Eighty-five per cent of what? Discrepancies in the weight cut-off for anorexia nervosa substantially affect the prevalence of underweight. *Psychological Medicine, 39*(5), 833–843. doi:10.1017/S0033291708004327.

Treasure, J. L., Wack, E. R., & Roberts, M. E. (2008). Models as a high-risk group: The health implications of a size zero culture. *The British Journal of Psychiatry, 192*(4), 243–244. doi:10.1192/bjp.bp.107.044164.

Tsao, S. D. (2009, May). Managing OCD in severe eating disorders. Paper presented at the annual meeting of the Multiservice Eating Disorders Association (MEDA) Conference, April 3–4, 2009.

Tung, E. E., Drage, L. A., & Ghosh, A. K. (2006). Carotenoderma and hypercarotenemia: Markers for disordered eating habits. *Journal of the European Academy of Dermatology & Venereology, 20*(9), 1147–1148. doi:10.1111/j.1468-3083.2006.01643.x.

Walsh, B. T. (2011). The importance of eating behavior in eating disorders. *Physiology & Behavior, 104*(4), 525–529. doi:10.1016/j.physbeh.2011.05.007.

Waterhous, T., & Jacob, M. (2011). *Practice paper of the American Dietetic Association: nutrition intervention in the treatment of eating disorders.* Chicago: American Dietetic Association. Retrieved September 14, 2012 from http://www.bhndpg.org/documents/Practice_Paper_Nutrition_Intervention.pdf.

Wildes, J. E., & Marcus, M. D. (2010). Diagnosis, assessment, and treatment planning for binge-eating disorder and eating disorder not otherwise specified. In C. Grilo, & J. E. Mitchell (Eds.), *The treatment of eating disorders: A clinical handbook* (pp. 44–65). New York: Guilford Press.

Chapter 2: Course of Treatment

Agras, W. S., & Apple, R. F. (1997). *Overcoming eating disorders: A cognitive–behavioral treatment for bulimia nervosa and binge-eating disorder: Therapist guide.* San Antonio, TX: Psychological Corporation/Graywind Publications.

American Dietetic Association. (2006). Position of the American Dietetic Association: Nutrition intervention in the treatment of anorexia nervosa, bulimia nervosa, and other eating disorders. *Journal of the American Dietetic Association, 106*(12), 2073–2082. doi:10.1016/j.jada.2006.09.007.

American Psychiatric Association. (2006). Practice guideline for the treatment of patients with eating disorders. In *American Psychiatric Association practice guidelines for the treatment of psychiatric disorders compendium 2006.* Retrieved September 15, 2012, from http://psychiatryonline.org/guidelines.aspx.

Beumont, P. J. V., Beumont, C. C., Touyz, S. W., & Williams, H. (1997). Nutritional counseling and supervised exercise. In D. M. Garner , & P. E. Garfinkel (Eds.), *Handbook of treatment for eating disorders* (2nd ed., pp. 178–187). New York: Guilford Press.

Garner, D.M., Olmstead, M.P., Bohr, Y., & Garfinkel, P.E. (1982). The eating attitudes test: psychometric features and clinical correlates. *Psychological Medicine, 12*(4), 871–878.

Greene, G. W., Rossi, S. R., Rossi, J. S., Velicer, W. F., Fava, J. L., & Prochaska, J. O. (1999). Dietary applications of the stages of change model. *Journal of the American Dietetic Association, 99*(6), 673–678.

Halmi, K. A. (2009). Salient components of a comprehensive service for eating disorders. *World Psychiatry, 8*(3), 150–155.

Health Insurance Portability and Accountability Act of 1996 (HIPAA). Privacy and Security Rules. Retrieved September 15, 2012, from http://www.hhs.gov/ocr/privacy.

Hill, C. E., & O'Brien, K. M. (1999). *Helping skills: Facilitating exploration, insight, and action.* Washington, DC: American Psychological Association.

Hill, L. S., Reid, F., Morgan, J. F. & Lacey, J. H. (2010). SCOFF, the development of an eating disorder screening questionnaire. *International Journal of Eating Disorders*, 43, 344–351.

Kellog, M. (2008). *Molly Kellogg's Counseling Tips for Nutrition Therapists.* Tip No. 75, Ending Treatment. Retrieved September 15, 2012, from: http://www.mollykellogg.com/archive08.html#75.

Kellog, M. (2010). *Molly Kellogg's Counseling Tips for Nutrition Therapists.* Tip No. 100, Structuring Sessions. Retrieved September 15, 2012, from: http://www.mollykellogg.com/archive10.html#100.

Kellog, M. (2010). *Molly Kellogg's Counseling Tips for Nutrition Therapists.* Tip No. 98, Making Referrals. Retrieved September 15, 2012 , from: http://www.mollykellogg.com/archive10.html#98.

Mehler, P. S., & Andersen, A. E. (2010). *Eating disorders: A guide to medical care and complications.* Baltimore: Johns Hopkins University Press.

Miller, W. R., & Rollnick, S. (2002). *Motivational interviewing: Preparing people for change.* New York: Guilford Press.

Okun, B. F. (2002). *Effective helping: Interviewing and counseling techniques.* Pacific Grove, CA: Brooks/Cole-Thomson Learning.

Peterson, C. B. (2009). *The "Top 10" biggest challenges in conducting eating disorders assessments. Perspectives*, Summer, 5–7.

Reiff, D. W., & Reiff, K. K. L. (1999). *Eating disorders: Nutrition therapy in the recovery process.* Gaithersburg, MD: Aspen.

Reiter, C. S., & Graves, L. (2010). Nutrition therapy for eating disorders. *Nutrition in Clinical Practice, 25*(2), 122–136. doi:10.1177/0884533610361606.

Schaefer, J. (2003). *Life without Ed: How one woman declared independence from her eating disorder and how you can too.* McGraw-Hill: New York.

Sloan, R. (2009). *Reba Sloan, licensed registered dietitian.* Retrieved September 15, 2012, from http://www.rebasloannutrition.com.

Williams, P. M., Goodie, J., & Motsinger, C. D. (2008). Treating eating disorders in primary care. *American Family Physician, 77*(2), 187–195.

Wilson, G. T., Vitousek, K. M., & Loeb, K. L. (2000). Stepped care treatment for eating disorders. *Journal of Consulting and Clinical Psychology, 68*(4), 564–572. doi:10.1037/0022-006X.68.4.564.

Yahne, C. E. (2004). The role of hope in motivational interviewing. *MINUET, 11*(3), 5.

Chapter 3: The Process of Counseling

AllPsych online. (2011). Retrieved September 15, 2012, from http://www.allpsych.com.

American Dietetic Association. (2006). Position of the American Dietetic Association: Nutrition intervention in the treatment of anorexia nervosa, bulimia nervosa, and other eating disorders. *Journal of the American Dietetic Association, 106*(12), 2073–2082. doi:10.1016/j.jada.2006.09.007.

American Dietetic Association. (2009). American Dietetic Association/Commission on dietetic registration code of ethics for the profession of dietetics and process for consideration of ethics issues. (2009). *Journal of the American Dietetic Association, 109*(8), 1461–1467. doi:10.1016/j.jada.2009.06.002.

American Psychiatric Association. (2000). *Diagnostic and statistical manual of mental disorders: DSM-IV-TR.* Chapter 12 Eating disorders. Retrieved September 15, 2012, from http://allpsych.com/disorders/dsm.html.

American Psychiatric Association. (2010). *DSM-5 development. Proposed revisions. Feeding and eating disorders.* Retrieved September 15, 2012, from http://www.dsm5.org/proposedrevision/Pages/FeedingandEatingDisorders.aspx.

Bays, J. C. (2009). *Mindful eating: A guide to rediscovering a healthy and joyful relationship with food.* Boston: Shambhala.

Cortese, S., Isnard, P., Frelut, M. L., Michel, G., Quantin, L., Guedeney, A., & Mouren, M. C. (2007). Association between symptoms of attention-deficit/hyperactivity disorder and bulimic behaviors in a clinical sample of severely obese adolescents. *International Journal of Obesity, 31*(2), 340–346. doi:10.1038/sj.ijo.0803400.

Davis, C., Patte, K., Levitan, R. D., Carter, J., Kaplan, A. S., Zai, C., Reid, C., Curtis, C., & Kennedy, J. L. (2009). A psycho-genetic study of associations between the symptoms of binge eating disorder and those of attention deficit (hyperactivity) disorder. *Journal of Psychiatric Research, 43*(7), 687–696. doi:10.1016/j.jpsychires.2008.10.010.

Dukarm, C. P. (2005). Bulimia nervosa and attention deficit hyperactivity disorder: A possible role for stimulant medication. *Journal of Women's Health (15409996), 14*(4), 345–350. doi:10.1089/jwh.2005.14.345.

Fairburn, C. G. (2008). *Cognitive behavior therapy and eating disorders.* New York: Guilford Press.

Garner, D. M. (2004). Body image and anorexia nervosa. In T. F. Cash and T. Pruzinsky (Eds.), *Body image: A handbook of theory, research, & clinical practice* (pp. 295–303). New York: Guilford Press.

Garner, D. M., & Bemis, K. M. (1985). Cognitive therapy for anorexia nervosa. In D. M. Garner & P. E. Garfinkel (Eds.), *Handbook of psychotherapy for anorexia nervosa & bulimia* (pp. 107–146). New York: Guilford Press.

Garner, D.M., Garfinkel, P.E., Stancer, H. C., & Moldosfky, H. (1976). Body image disturbances in anorexia nervosa and obesity. *Psychosomatic Medicine, 38*(5), 327–336.

Goodman, L. J., & Villapiano, M. (2001). *Eating disorders: The journey to recovery workbook.* Philadelphia, PA: Brunner-Routledge.

Kellogg, M. (2006). *Counseling tips for nutrition therapists, volume 1.* Philadelphia: KG.

Keys, A., Brozek, J., Henschel, A., Mickelsen, U., & Taylor, H. L. (1950). *The biology of human starvation* (2 vols.). Minneapolis: University of Minnesota Press.

Kingsbury, K. B., & Williams, M. E. (2003). *Weight wisdom: Affirmations to free you from food and body concerns.* New York: Brunner-Routledge.

Kratina, K., King, N., & Hayes, D. (2003). *Moving away from diets: Healing eating problems and exercise resistance.* Lake Dallas, TX: Helm.

Ozier, A. D., & Henry, B. W. (2011). Position of the American Dietetic Association: Nutrition intervention in the treatment of eating disorders. *Journal of the American Dietetic Association, 111*(8), 1236–1241. doi:10.1016/j.jada.2011.06.016.

Pearson, A. N., Heffner, M., & Follette, V. M. (2010). *Acceptance and commitment therapy for body image dissatisfaction: A practitioner's guide to using mindfulness, acceptance, and values-based behavior change strategies.* Oakland, CA: New Harbinger.

Sallet, P. C., de Alvarenga, P. G., Ferrão, Y., de Mathis, M. A., Torres, A. R., Marques, A., Hounie, A. G., Fossaluza, V., do Rosario, M. C., Fontenelle, L. F., Petribu, K., &

Fleitlich-Bilyk, B. (2010). Eating disorders in patients with obsessive–compulsive disorder: Prevalence and clinical correlates. *International Journal of Eating Disorders, 43*(4), 315–325. doi:10.1002/eat.20697.

Sanci, L., Coffey, C., Olsson, C., Reid, S., Carlin J. B., & Patton G. (2008). Childhood sexual abuse and eating disorders in females: Findings from the Victorian Adolescent Health Cohort Study. *Archives of Pediatric Adolescents Medicine, 162*(3), 261–267.

Stice, E. (2004). Body image and bulimia nervosa. In T. F. Cash and T. Pruzinsky (Eds.), Body image: a handbook of theory, research, & clinical practice (pp. 304–311). New York: Guilford Press.

Villapiano, M., & Goodman, L. J. (2001). *Eating disorders: Time for change*. Philadelphia: Brunner-Routledge.

Chapter 4: Counseling Interventions

Berman, M. I., Boutelle, K. N. and Crow, S. J. (2009). A case series investigating acceptance and commitment therapy as a treatment for previously treated, unremitted patients with anorexia nervosa. *European Eating Disorders, 17*(6), 426–434.

Boudette, R. (2011). Integrating mindfulness into the therapy hour. *Eating Disorders, 19*(1), 108–115. doi:10.1080/10640266.2011.533610.

Chen, E. Y., Matthews, L., Allen, C., Kuo, J. R., & Linehan, M. M. (2008). Dialectical behavior therapy for clients with binge-eating disorder or bulimia nervosa and borderline personality disorder. *International Journal of Eating Disorders, 41*(6), 505–512. doi:10.1002/eat.20522.

Courbasson, C. M., Nishikawa, Y., & Shapira, L. B. (2011). Mindfulness-action based cognitive behavioral therapy for concurrent binge eating disorder and substance use disorders. *Eating Disorders, 19*(1), 17–33. doi:10.1080/10640266.2011.533603.

Fairburn, C. G. (2008). *Cognitive behavior therapy and eating disorders*. New York: Guilford Press.

Fairburn, C. G., Marcus, M. D., & Wilson, G. T. (1993). Cognitive–behavioral therapy for binge eating and bulimia nervosa: A comprehensive treatment manual. In C. G. Fairburn, & G. T. Wilson (Eds.), *Binge eating: Nature, assessment, and treatment* (pp. 361–404). New York: Guilford Press.

Fairburn, C. G., Cooper, Z., Doll, H. A., O'Connor, M. E., Bohn, K. Hawker, D. M., Wales, J. A., & Palmer, R. L. (2009). Transdiagnostic cognitive–behavioral therapy for patients with eating disorders: A two-site trial with 60-week follow-up. *American Journal of Psychiatry, 166*, 311–319.

Garner, D. M. (1997). Psychoeducational principles in treatment. In D. M. Garner, & P. E. Garfinkel (Eds.), *Handbook of treatment for eating disorders* (2nd ed., pp. 145–177). New York: Guilford Press.

Garner, D. M., Vitousek, K. M., & Pike, K. M. (1997). Cognitive–behavioral therapy for anorexia nervosa. In D. M. Garner, & P. E. Garfinkel (Eds.), *Handbook of treatment for eating disorders* (2nd ed., pp. 94–144). New York: Guilford Press.

Heffner, M. & Eifert, G. H. (2004*). The anorexia workbook: How to accept yourself, heal your suffering, and reclaim your life*. Oakland, CA: New Harbinger.

Karbasi, A. L. (2010). Enhanced cognitive-behavioral therapy (CBT-E) for eating disorders: Case study of a client with anorexia nervosa. *Clinical Case Studies, 9*, 225–240. doi:10.1177/1534650110372541.

Kater, K. (2009). A new approach for treating eating disorders: Acceptance and commitment therapy (ACT). *Eating Disorders Recovery Today Fall, 7(4)*. Retrieved September 15, 2012, from http://www.eatingdisordersreview.com/nl/nl_edt_7_4_1.html.

Kelly, E., Wilson, K., & DuFrene, T. (2011). *Acceptance and commitment therapy for eating disorders: A process-focused guide to treating anorexia and bulimia.* Oakland, CA: New Harbinger.

Kristeller, J. L., & Wolever, R. Q. (2011). Mindfulness-based eating awareness training for treating binge eating disorder: The conceptual foundation. *Eating Disorders, 19*(1), 49–61. doi:10.1080/10640266.2011.533605.

Linehan, M. M. (1993). *Cognitive behavioral treatment of borderline personality disorder.* New York: Guilford Press.

McCabe, E. B., & Marcus, M. D. (2002). Is dialectical behavior therapy useful in the management of anorexia nervosa? *Eating Disorders, 10*(4), 335–337.

McKay, M., Wood, J. C., & Brantley, J. (2007). *The dialectical behavior therapy skills workbook: Practical DBT exercises for learning mindfulness, interpersonal effectiveness, emotion regulation & distress tolerance.* Oakland, CA: New Harbinger.

Merwin, R. M., Timko, C. A., Moskovich, A. A., Ingle, K. K., Bulik, C. M., & Zucker, N. L. (2011). Psychological inflexibility and symptom expression in anorexia nervosa. *Eating Disorders, 19*(1), 62–82. doi:10.1080/10640266.2011.533606.

Pearson, A., Heffner, M., & Follette, V. (2010). *Acceptance & commitment therapy for body image dissatisfaction: A practitioner's guide to using mindfulness, acceptance & values-based behavior change strategies.* Oakland, CA: New Harbinger.

Rollnick, S., Miller, W. R., & Butler, C. (2007). *Motivational interviewing in health care: Helping patients change behavior.* New York: Guilford Press.

Rose, G. S., Rollnick, S. R., & Lane, C. (2004). What's your style? A model for helping practitioners to learn about communication and motivational interviewing. *MINUET, 11*(3), 2–4.

Spahn, J. M., Reeves, R. S., Keim, K. S., Laquatra, I., Kellogg, M., Jortberg, B., & Clark, N. A. (2010). State of the evidence regarding behavior change theories and strategies in nutrition counseling to facilitate health and food behavior change. *Journal of the American Dietetic Association, 110*(6), 879–891. doi:10.1016/j.jada.2010.03.021.

Villapiano, M., & Goodman, L. J. (2001). *Eating disorders: Time for change.* Philadelphia: Brunner-Routledge.

Wagner, R., & MacCaughelty, C. (2011). Mentalization-based treatment and eating disorders. *Perspectives,* Winter, 6–9.

Wanden-Berghe, R., Sanz-Valero, J., & Wanden-Berghe, C. (2011). The application of mindfulness to eating disorders treatment: A systematic review. *Eating Disorders, 19*(1), 34–48. doi:10.1080/10640266.2011.533604.

Wilson, G. M., Fairburn, C. G., & Agras, W. S. (1997). Cognitive–behavioral therapy for bulimia nervosa. In D. M. Garner, & P. E. Garfinkel (Eds.), *Handbook of treatment for eating disorders* (2nd ed., pp. 67–93). New York: Guilford Press.

Wonderlich, S. (2009). An introduction to integrative cognitive affective therapy for bulimia nervosa *Perspectives,* Summer, 1–5.

Chapter 5: Food Planning: Rule of Threes

American Diabetes Association and American Dietetic Association. (2008). *Choose your foods: Exchange lists for diabetes (brochure).* Alexandria, VA, American Diabetes

Association, and Chicago, IL: American Dietetic Association. Retrieved September 15, 2012, from http://www.eatright.org/shop/product.aspx?id=4962.

Craighead, L. W. (2006). *The appetite awareness workbook: How to listen to your body & overcome bingeing, overeating, & obsession with food.* Oakland, CA: New Harbinger.

Daly A, et al. (2008). Choose your foods: Exchange lists for diabetes. Alexandria, VA: American Diabetes Association and American Dietetic Association.

Fairburn, C. G. (2008). *Cognitive–behavior therapy and eating disorders.* New York: Guilford Press.

Food and Nutrition Board. (2011). *Dietary reference intakes: Acceptable macronutrient distribution ranges.* Washington, DC: Institute of Medicine of the National Academies.

Frankenfield, D., Roth-Yousey, L., & Compher C. (2005). Comparison of predictive equations for resting metabolic rate in healthy nonobese and obese adults: a systematic review. *Journal of the American Dietetic Association, 105*(5), 775–789.

Gatward, N. (2007). Anorexia nervosa: an evolutionary puzzle. *European Eating Disorders Review, 15,* 1–12.

Gendall, K. A., Joyce, P. R., & Abbott, R. M. (1999). The effects of meal composition on subsequent craving and binge eating. *Addictive Behaviors,* 24(3), 305–315.

Guisinger, S. (2003). Adapted to flee famine: Adding an evolutionary perspective on anorexia nervosa. *Psychological Review, 110,* 745–761.

Heaney, R. P., Rafferty, K., Dowell, M. S., & Bierman, J. (2005). Calcium fortification systems differ in bioavailability. *Journal of the American Dietetic Association, 105*(5), 807–809. doi:10.1016/j.jada.2005.02.012.

Jakubowicz, D., Froy, O., Wainstein, J., & Boaz, M. (2012). Meal timing and composition influence ghrelin levels, appetite scores and weight loss maintenance in overweight and obese adults. *Steroids, 77,* 323–331.

Jönsson, T., Granfeldt, Y., Erlanson-Albertsson, C., Ahren, B., & Lindeberg, S. (2010). A paleolithic diet is more satiating per calorie than a mediterranean-like diet in individuals with ischemic heart disease. *Nutrition & Metabolism, 7.* doi:10.1186/1743-7075-7-85.

Krebs-Smith, S. M., & Kris-Etherton, P. (2007). How does MyPyramid compare to other population-based recommendations for controlling chronic disease? *Journal of the American Dietetic Association, 107*(5), 830–837. doi:10.1016/j.jada.2007.02.016.

Lock, J., & Fitzpatrick, K. (2009). Anorexia nervosa. *Clinical Evidence, 3*(1011), 1–28.

Mehler, P. S., & MacKenzie, T. D. (2009). Treatment of osteopenia and osteoporosis in anorexia nervosa: A systematic review of the literature. *International Journal of Eating Disorders, 42*(3), 195–201.

Mendez, M. A., Popkin, B. M., Buckland, G., Schroder, H., Amiano, P., Barricarte, A., Huerta, J.-M., Qúiros, J. R., Sánchez, M.-J., & González, C. A. (2011). Alternative methods of accounting for underreporting and overreporting when measuring dietary intake–obesity relations. *Journal of Epidemiology, 173*(4), 448–458.

Nestle, M., & Nesheim, M. (2012). *Why calories count: From science to politics.* Berkeley, CA: University of California Press, 2012.

Raben, A., Agerholm-Larsen, L., Flint, A., Holst, J. J., & Astrup, A. (2003). Meals with similar energy densities but rich in protein, fat, carbohydrate, or alcohol have different effects on energy expenditure and substrate metabolism but not on appetite and energy intake. *The American Journal of Clinical Nutrition, 77*(1), 91–100.

Reiter, C. S., & Graves, L. (2010). Nutrition therapy for eating disorders. *Nutrition in Clinical Practice, 25*(2), 122–136. doi:10.1177/0884533610361606.

Sacks, F. M., Bray, G. A., Carey, V. J., Smith, S. R., Ryan, D. H., Anton, S. D., McManus, K., Champagne, C. M., Bishop, L. M., Laranjo, N., Leboff, M. S., Rood, J. C., de

Jonge, L., Greenway, F. L., Loria, C. M., Obarzanek, E., & Williamson, D. A. (2009). Comparison of weight-loss diets with different compositions of fat, protein, and carbohydrates. *New England Journal of Medicine*, 360(9), 859–873.

Satter, E. (2008). *Secrets of Feeding a Healthy Family* (2nd ed.). Madison, WI: Kelcy Press.

Schebendach, J. E, Mayer, L. E., Devlin, M. J., Attia, E., Contento, I. R., Wolf, R. L., & Walsh, T. B. (2011). Food choice and diet variety in weight-restored patients with anorexia nervosa. *Journal of the American Dietetic Association*, 111(5), 732–736.

Straub, D. A. (2007). Calcium supplementation in clinical practice: A review of forms, doses, and indications. *Nutrition in Clinical Practice*, 22(3), 286–296. doi:10.1177/0115426507022003286.

Tang, A. L., Walker, K. Z., Wilcox, G., Strauss, B. J., Ashton, J. F., & Stojanovska, L. (2010). Calcium absorption in Australian osteopenic post-menopausal women: An acute comparative study of fortified soymilk to cows' milk. *Asia Pacific Journal of Clinical Nutrition*, 19(2), 243–249.

Tribole, E. (2005, Fall). Why and how to give yourself permission to eat anything. *Eating Disorders Today*, 1.

United States Department of Agriculture. (2011). *Choose my plate.* Retrieved September 15, 2012, from http://www.choosemyplate.gov.

Willett, W. C. (2002). Dietary fat plays a major role in obesity: No. *Obesity Reviews*, 3(2), 59–68.

Whitney, E. N., & Rolfes, S., R. (2011). *Understanding nutrition* (12th ed.). Belmont, CA: Wadsworth.

Chapter 6: Self-Monitoring

Fairburn, C. G. (2008). *Cognitive behavior therapy and eating disorders*. New York: Guilford Press.

Fairburn, C. G., Marcus, M. D., & Wilson, G. T. (1993). Cognitive–behavioral therapy for binge eating and bulimia nervosa: A comprehensive treatment manual. In C. G. Fairburn, & G. T. Wilson (Eds.), *Binge eating: Nature, assessment, and treatment* (pp. 361–404). New York: Guilford Press.

Ozier, A. D., & Henry, B. W. (2011). Position of the American Dietetic Association: Nutrition intervention in the treatment of eating disorders. *Journal of the American Dietetic Association*, 111(8), 1236–1241. doi:10.1016/j.jada.2011.06.016.

Pike, K. M., Garner, D. M., & Vitousek, K. M. (1997). Cognitive–behavioral therapy for anorexia nervosa. In D. M. Garner & P. E. Garfinkel (Eds.), *Handbook of treatment for eating disorders* (pp. 83–107). New York: Guilford Press.

Chapter 7: Levels of Care

Agras, W. S., Crow, S., Mitchell, J. E., Halmi, K. A., & Bryson, S. (2009). A 4-year prospective study of eating disorder NOS compared with full eating disorder syndromes. *International Journal of Eating Disorders*, 42(6), 565–570. doi:10.1002/eat.20708.

American Psychiatric Association. (2006). Practice guideline for the treatment of patients with eating disorders. In *American Psychiatric Association practice guidelines for the treatment of psychiatric disorders compendium 2006*. Retrieved September 15, 2012, from http://psychiatryonline.org/guidelines.aspx.

Arcelus, J., Mitchell, A. J., Wales, J., & Nielsen, S. (2011). Mortality rates in patients with anorexia nervosa and other eating disorders: A meta-analysis of 36 studies. *Archives of General Psychiatry*, 68(7), 724–731. doi:10.1001/archgenpsychiatry.2011.74.

Bardone-Cone, A. M., Harney, M. B., Maldonado, C. R., Lawson, M. A., Robinson, D. P., Smith, R., & Tosh, A. (2010). Defining recovery from an eating disorder: Conceptualization, validation, and examination of psychosocial functioning and psychiatric comorbidity. *Behaviour Research and Therapy, 48*(3), 194–202. doi:10.1016/j.brat.2009.11.001.

Clausen, L. (2008). Time to remission for eating disorder patients: A 2½-year follow-up study of outcome and predictors. *Nordic Journal of Psychiatry, 62*(2), 151–159. doi:10.1080/08039480801984875.

Couturier, J., & Lock, J. (2006). What is recovery in adolescent anorexia nervosa? *International Journal of Eating Disorders, 39*(7), 550–555. doi:10.1002/eat.20309.

Crow, S. J., Peterson, C. B., Swanson, S. A., Raymond, N. C., Specker, S., Eckert, E. I. D., & Mitchell, J. E. (2009). Increased mortality in bulimia nervosa and other eating disorders. *American Journal of Psychiatry, 166*(12), 1342–1346.

Eddy, K. T., Dorer, D. J., Franko, D. L., Tahilani, K., Thompson-Brenner, H., & Herzog, D. B. (2008). Diagnostic crossover in anorexia nervosa and bulimia nervosa: implications for DSM-V. *American Journal of Psychiatry,* 165(2), 245–250.

Fairburn, C. G. (2008). *Cognitive behavior therapy and eating disorders.* New York: Guilford Press.

Johnson, C. L., Lund, B. C., & Yates, W. R. (2003). Recovery rates for anorexia nervosa. *American Journal of Psychiatry, 160*(4), 798.

Keel, P. K., & Brown, T. A. (2010). Update on course and outcome in eating disorders. *International Journal of Eating Disorders, 43*(3), 195–204.

Miller, K. K. (2011). Endocrine dysregulation in anorexia nervosa update. *Journal of Clinical Endocrinology & Metabolism, 96*(10), 2939–2949. doi:10.1210/jc.2011-1222.

Von Holle, A., Pinheiro, A. P., Thornton, L. M., Klump, K. L., Berrettini, W. H., Brandt, H., et al. (2008). Temporal patterns of recovery across eating disorder subtypes [corrected] [published erratum appears in *Australian & New Zealand Journal of Psychiatry,* 2009, *43*(8), 784]. *Australian & New Zealand Journal of Psychiatry, 42*(2), 108–117.

Chapter 8: Assessing Weight

American Psychiatric Association. (2010). *DSM-5 development. Proposed revisions. Feeding and eating disorders.* Retrieved September 15, 2012, from http://www.dsm5.org/proposedrevision/Pages/FeedingandEatingDisorders.aspx.

Bacon, L., & Aphramor, L. (2011). Weight science: Evaluating the evidence for a paradigm shift. *Nutrition Journal, 10,* 9–22. doi:10.1186/1475-2891-10-9.

Boykin, S., Diez-Roux, A. V., Carnethon, M., Shrager, S., Ni, H., & Whitt-Glover, M. (2011). Racial/ethnic heterogeneity in the socioeconomic patterning of CVD risk factors in the United States: The multi-ethnic study of atherosclerosis. *Journal of Health Care for the Poor and Underserved, 22*(1), 111–127.

Centers for Disease Control and Prevention. (2011). *About BMI for children and teens.* Retrieved September 15, 2012, from http://www.cdc.gov/healthyweight/assessing/bmi/childrens_bmi/about_childrens_bmi.html#How%20is%20BMI%20calculate.

Christo, K., Prabhakaran, R., Lamparello, B., Cord, J., Miller, K. K., Goldstein, M. A., Gupta, N., Herzog, D. B., Klibanski, A., & Misra, M. (2008). Bone metabolism in adolescent athletes with amenorrhea, athletes with eumenorrhea, and control subjects. *Pediatrics, 121*(6), 1127–1136. doi:10.1542/peds.2007-2392.

Cloak, N. L., & Powers, P. S. (2010). Science or art? Integrating symptom management into psychodynamic treatment of eating disorders. In M. Maine, B. H. McGilley & D.

W. Bunnell (Eds.), *Treatment of eating disorders: Bridging the research–practice gap* (pp. 143). Amsterdam/Boston: Academic Press/Elsevier.

Copeland, P. M., Sacks, N. R., & Herzog, D. B. (1995). Longitudinal follow-up of amenorrhea in eating disorders. *Psychosomatics Medicine*, *57*, 121–126.

Dokken, B. B., & Tsao, T. (2007). The physiology of body weight regulation: Are we too efficient for our own good? *Diabetes Spectrum*, *20*(3), 166–170. doi:10.2337/diaspect.20.3.166.

Fairburn, C. G. (2008). *Cognitive behavior therapy and eating disorders*. New York: Guilford Press.

Flegal, K. M., & Ogden, C. L. (2011). Childhood obesity: Are we all speaking the same language? *Advances in Nutrition: An International Review Journal*, *2*(2), 159S–166S. doi:10.3945/an.111.000307.

Flegal, K. M., Graubard, B. I., Williamson, D. F., & Gail, M. H. (2007). Cause-specific excess deaths associated with underweight, overweight, and obesity. *JAMA: The Journal of the American Medical Association*, *298*(17), 2028–2037. doi:10.1001/jama.298.17.2028.

Freeman, E. W., Sammel, M. D., Lin, H., & Gracia, C. R. (2010). Obesity and reproductive hormone levels in the transition to menopause. *Menopause*, *17*(4), 718.

Gallagher, D., Visser, M., Sepúlveda, D., Pierson, R. N., Harris, T., & Heymsfield, S. B. (1996). How useful is body mass index for comparison of body fatness across age, sex, and ethnic groups? *American Journal of Epidemiology*, *143*(3), 228–239.

Genazzani, A. D., Riccieri, F., Lanzoni, C., Strucchi, C., & Jasonni, V. M. (2006). Diagnostic and therapeutic approach to hypothalamic amenorrhea. *Annals of the New York Academy of Sciences*, *1092*(1), 103–113. doi:10.1196/annals.1365.009.

Golden, N. H., Jacobson, M. S., Schebendach, J., Solanto, M. V., Hertz, S. M., & Shenker, I. R. (1997). Resumption of menses in anorexia nervosa. *Archives of Pediatrics Adolescent Medicine*, *151*(1), 16–21. doi:10.1001/archpedi.1997.02170380020003.

Golden, N. H., Jacobson, M. S., Sterling, W. M., & Hertz, S. (2008). Treatment goal weight in adolescents with anorexia nervosa: Use of BMI percentiles. *International Journal of Eating Disorders*, *41*(4), 301–306. doi:10.1002/eat.20503.

Hainer, V., Stunkard, A., Kunešová, M., Parízková, J., Štich, V., & Allison, D. B. (2001). A twin study of weight loss and metabolic efficiency. *International Journal of Obesity & Related Metabolic Disorders*, *25*(4), 533.

Koenig, K. R.,. (2008). *What every therapist needs to know about treating eating and weight issues*. New York: W.W. Norton.

Lask, B., & Frampton, I. (2009). Anorexia nervosa? Irony, misnomer and paradox. *European Eating Disorders Review*, *17*(3), 165–168. doi:10.1002/erv.933.

Lindström, J., Louheranta, A., Mannelin, M., Rastas, M., Salminen, V., Eriksson, J., Uusitupa, M., Tuomilehto, J., & Finnish Diabetes Prevention Study Group. (2003). The Finnish diabetes prevention study (DPS). *Diabetes Care*, *26*(12), 3230–3236. doi:10.2337/diacare.26.12.3230.

Macdonald, H. M., New, S. A., Campbell, M. K., & Reid, D. M. (2003). Longitudinal changes in weight in perimenopausal and early postmenopausal women: Effects of dietary energy intake, energy expenditure, dietary calcium intake and hormone replacement therapy. *International Journal of Obesity & Related Metabolic Disorders*, *27*(6), 669.

Mehler, P. S., Sabel, A. L., Watson, T., & Andersen, A. E. (2008). High risk of osteoporosis in male patients with eating disorders. *International Journal of Eating Disorders*, *41*(7), 666–672. doi:10.1002/eat.20554.

Mehler, P. S., Winkelman, A. B., Andersen, D. M., & Gaudiani, J. L. (2010). Nutritional rehabilitation: Practical guidelines for refeeding the anorectic patient. *Journal of Nutrition and Metabolism, 2010.* doi:10.1155/2010/625782.

Müller M. J, Bosy-Westphal A., & Heymsfield SB (2010). Is there evidence for a set point that regulates human body weight? *F1000 Medicine Reports, 9*(2), 59. doi:10.3410/M2-59).

Ode, J. J., Pivarnik, J. M., Reeves, M. J., & Knous, J. L. (2007). Body mass index as a predictor of percent fat in college athletes and nonathletes. *Medicine & Science in Sports & Exercise, 39*(3), 403–409. doi:10.1249/01.mss.0000247008.19127.3e.

O'Rahilly, S., & Farooqi, I. S. (2008). Human obesity: A heritable neurobehavioral disorder that is highly sensitive to environmental conditions. *Diabetes, 57*(11), 2905–2910. doi:10.2337/db08-0210.

Pai, M., & Paloucek, F. (2000). The origin of the "ideal" body weight equations. *The Annals of Pharmacotherapy, 34*(9), 1066–1069. doi:10.1345/aph.19381.

Palmert, M. R., & Dunkel, L. (2012). Clinical practice. Delayed puberty. *New England Journal of Medicine, 2*(5), 443–453.

Rahman, M., & Berenson, A. B. (2010). Accuracy of current body mass index obesity classification for white, black, and hispanic reproductive-age women. *Obstetrics & Gynecology, 115*(5), 982–988. doi:10.1097/AOG.0b013e3181da9423.

Rosenbaum, M., Hirsch, J., Gallagher, D. A., & Leibel, R. L. (2008). Long-term persistence of adaptive thermogenesis in subjects who have maintained a reduced body weight. *The American Journal of Clinical Nutrition, 88*(4), 906–912.

Schousboe, K., Visscher, P. M., Erbas, B., Kyvik, K. O., Hopper, J. L., Henriksen, J. E., Heitmann, B. L., Sørensen, T. I. A. (2004). Twin study of genetic and environmental influences on adult body size, shape, and composition. *International Journal of Obesity & Related Metabolic Disorders, 28*(1), 39–48. doi:10.1038/sj.ijo.0802524.

Singh, P. N., Haddad, E., Knutsen, S. F., & Fraser, G. E. (2001). The effect of menopause on the relation between weight gain and mortality among women. *Menopause, 8*(5), 314–320.

Soni, A. C., Conroy, M. B., Mackey, R. H., & Kuller, L. H. (2011). Ghrelin, leptin, adiponectin, and insulin levels and concurrent and future weight change in overweight, postmenopausal women. *Menopause, 18*(3), 296–301.

Sowers, M., Zheng, H., Tomey, K., Karvonen-Gutierrez, C., Jannausch, M., Li, X., Yosef, M., & Symons, J. (2007). Changes in body composition in women over six years at midlife: Ovarian and chronological aging. *Journal of Clinical Endocrinology & Metabolism, 92*(3), 895–901. doi:10.1210/jc.2006-1393.

Stevens, J., Truesdale, K. P., McClain, J. E., & Cai, J. (2006). The definition of weight maintenance. *International Journal of Obesity, 30*(3), 391–399.

Stunkard, A. J., Foch, T. T., & Hrubec, Z. (1986). A twin study of human obesity. *The Journal of the American Medical Association, 256*(1), 51–54. doi:10.1001/jama.1986.03380010055024.

Stunkard, A. J., Sørensen, T. I. A., Hanis, C., Teasdale, T. W., Chakraborty, R., Schull, W. J., & Schulsinger, F. (1986). An adoption study of human obesity. *New England Journal of Medicine, 314*(4), 193–198. doi:10.1056/NEJM198601233140401.

Swenne, I. (2008). Weight and growth requirements for menarche in teenage girls with eating disorders, weight loss and primary amenorrhea. *Hormone Research, 69*(3), 146–151. doi:10.1159/000112587.

Tam, J., Fukumura, D., & Jain, R. K. (2009). A mathematical model of murine metabolic regulation by leptin: Energy balance and defense of a stable body weight. *Cell Metabolism, 9*(1), 52–63. doi:10.1016/j.cmet.2008.11.005.

Thomas, J. J., Roberto, C. A., & Brownell, K. D. (2009). Eighty-five per cent of what? Discrepancies in the weight cut-off for anorexia nervosa substantially affect the prevalence of underweight. *Psychological Medicine, 39*(5), 833–843. doi:10.1017/S0033291708004327.

Tyson, E. P. (2010). Medical assessment of eating disorders In M. Maine, B. H. McGilley & D. W. Bunnell (Eds.), *Treatment of eating disorders: Bridging the research–practice gap* (pp. 110). Amsterdam/Boston: Academic Press/Elsevier.

Wabitsch, M., Ballauff, A., Holl, R., Blum, W. F., Heinze, E., Remschmidt, H., & Hebebrand, J. (2001). Serum leptin, gonadotropin, and testosterone concentrations in male patients with anorexia nervosa during weight gain. *Journal of Clinical Endocrinology & Metabolism, 86*(7), 2982–2988. doi:10.1210/jc.86.7.2982.

Weinsier, R. L. (2001). Etiology of obesity: Methodological examination of the set-point theory. *Journal of Parenteral and Enteral Nutrition, 25*(3), 103–110. doi:10.1177/0148607101025003103.

WHO Expert Committee on Physical Status (1995). *Physical status: The use and interpretation of anthropometry: Report of a WHO Expert Committee* (No. 854). Geneva: World Health Organization.

WHO Expert Consultation. (2004). Appropriate body-mass index for Asian populations and its implications for policy and intervention strategies. *Lancet, 363*(9403), 157–163. doi:10.1016/S0140-6736(03)15268-3.

Wildman, R. P., Muntner, P., Reynolds, K., McGinn, A. P., Rajpathak, S., Wylie-Rosett, J., & Sowers, M. R. (2008). The obese without cardiometabolic risk factor clustering and the normal weight with cardiometabolic risk factor clustering: Prevalence and correlates of 2 phenotypes among the US population (NHANES 1999–2004). *Archives of Internal Medicine, 168*(15), 1617–1624. doi:10.1001/archinte.168.15.1617.

Wing, R. R., Lang, W., Wadden, T. A., Safford, M., Knowler, W. C., Bertoni, A. G., Hill, J. O., Brancati, F. L., Peters, A., Wagenknecht, L., & Look AHEAD Research Group. (2011). Benefits of modest weight loss in improving cardiovascular risk factors in overweight and obese individuals with type 2 diabetes. *Diabetes Care, 34*(7), 1481–1486. doi:10.2337/dc10-2415.

Chapter 9: Restoring Weight

Academy of Nutrition and Dietetics. (2012). Nutrition prescription (anorexia nervosa). In *ADA nutrition care manual*. Chicago: American Dietetic Association. Available from https://nutritioncaremanual.org/content.cfm?ncm_content_id=77774 (accessed September 15, 2012).

American Psychiatric Association. (2006). Practice guideline for the treatment of patients with eating disorders. *American Psychiatric Association Practice Guidelines for the Treatment of Psychiatric Disorders Compendium 2006*. Retrieved September 15, 2012, from http://psychiatryonline.org/guidelines.aspx.

Boateng, A. A., Sriram, K., Meguid, M. M., & Crook, M. (2010). Refeeding syndrome: Treatment considerations based on collective analysis of literature case reports. *Nutrition, 26*(2), 156–167. doi:10.1016/j.nut.2009.11.017.

Boullata, J., Williams, J., Cottrell, F., Hudson, L., & Compher, C. (2007). Accurate determination of energy needs in hospitalized patients. *Journal of the American Dietetic Association, 107*(3), 393–401. doi:10.1016/j.jada.2006.12.014.

Cockfield, A., & Philpot, U. (2009). Managing anorexia from a dietitian's perspective. *Proceedings of the Nutrition Society, 68*(3), 281–288. doi:10.1017/S0029665109001281.

Copeland, P. M., Sacks, N. R., & Herzog, D. B. (1995). Longitudinal follow-up of amenorrhea in eating disorders. *Psychosomatics Medicine, 57,* 121–126.

El Ghoch, M., Alberti, M., Capelli, C., Calugi, S., & Dalle Grave, R. (2011). Resting energy expenditure in anorexia nervosa: Measured versus estimated. *Journal of Nutrition and Metabolism.* doi:10.1155/2012/652932.

Fairburn, C. G. (2008). *Cognitive behavior therapy and eating disorders.* New York: Guilford Press.

Forbes, G., Kreipe, R., Lipinski, B., & Hodgman, C. (1984). Body composition changes during recovery from anorexia nervosa: Comparison of two dietary regimes. *The American Journal of Clinical Nutrition, 40*(6), 1137–1145.

Forman-Hoffman, V. L., Ruffin, T., & Schultz, S. K. (2006). Basal metabolic rate in anorexia nervosa patients: Using appropriate predictive equations during the refeeding process. *Annals of Clinical Psychiatry, 18*(2), 123–127.

Garner, D. M., & Garfinkel, P. E. (1997). *Handbook of treatment for eating disorders.* New York: Guilford Press.

Genazzani, A. D., Riccieri, F., Lanzoni, C., Strucchi, C., & Jasonni, V. M. (2006). Diagnostic and therapeutic approach to hypothalamic amenorrhea. *Annals of the New York Academy of Sciences, 1092*(1), 103–113. doi:10.1196/annals.1365.009.

Golden, N. H., & Meyer, W. (2004). Nutritional rehabilitation of anorexia nervosa. Goals and dangers. *International Journal of Adolescent Medicine and Health, 16*(2), 131–144.

Golden, N. H., Jacobson, M. S., Sterling, W. M., & Hertz, S. (2008). Treatment Goal weight in adolescents with anorexia nervosa: Use of BMI percentiles. *International Journal of Eating Disorders, 41*(4), 301–306.

Greenblatt, J. (2010). *Answers to anorexia: A breakthrough nutritional treatment that is saving lives.* North Branch, MN: Sunrise River Press.

Hadley, S. J., & Walsh, B. T. (2003). Gastrointestinal disturbances in anorexia nervosa and bulimia nervosa. *Current Drug Targets – CNS & Neurological Disorders, 2*(1), 1–9.

Harrison, A., O'Brien, N., Lopez, C., & Treasure, J. (2010). Sensitivity to reward and punishment in eating disorders. *Psychiatry Research, 177*(1), 1–11. doi:10.1016/j.psychres.2009.06.010.

Hart, S., Williams, H., Wakefield, A., & Russell, J. (2012). The role of nutrition. In J. Alexander , & J. Treasure (Eds.), *A collaborative approach to eating disorders* (102–113). London: Routledge.

Herzog, T., Zeeck, A., Hartmann, A., & Nickel, T. (2004). Lower targets for weekly weight gain lead to better results in inpatient treatment of anorexia nervosa: A pilot study. *European Eating Disorders Review, 12*(3), 164–168.

Kaplan, A. S., & Noble, S. (2007). Management of anorexia nervosa in an ambulatory setting. In J. Yager, & P. S. Powers (Eds.), *Clinical manual of eating disorders* (pp. 127–147). Washington, D.C.: American Psychiatric Publications.

Keel, P. K., & Brown, T. A. (2010). Update on course and outcome in eating disorders. *International Journal of Eating Disorders, 43*(3), 195–204.

Keys, A., Brozek, J., Henschel, A., Mickelsen, O., & Taylor, H. L. (1950). *The biology of human starvation* (2 vols.). Minneapolis: University of Minnesota Press.

Khan, L. U. R., Ahmen, J., Khan, S., & Macfie, J. (2011). Refeeding syndrome: A literature review. *Gastroenterology Research and Practice, 2011*(410971). doi:10.1155/2011/410971.

Kohn, M. R., Madden, S., & Clarke, S. D. (2011). Refeeding in anorexia nervosa: Increased safety and efficiency through understanding the pathophysiology of protein calorie malnutrition. *Current Opinion in Pediatrics, 23*(1), 390–394.

Kreipe, R. E. & Uphoff, M. (1992). Treatment and outcome of adolescents with anorexia nervosa. *Adolescent Medicine, 3*(3), 519–540.

Lask, B., & Frampton, I. (2009). Anorexia nervosa? Irony, misnomer and paradox. *European Eating Disorders Review, 17*(3), 165–168. doi:10.1002/erv.933.

Lock, J., & Fitzpatrick, K. (2009). Anorexia nervosa. *Clinical Evidence, 3*(1011). Published online 2009 March 10. PMCID: PMC2907776.

Lund, B. C., Hernandez, E. R., Yates, W. R., Mitchell, J. R., McKee, P. A., & Johnson, C. L. (2009). Rate of inpatient weight restoration predicts outcome in anorexia nervosa. *International Journal of Eating Disorders, 42*(4), 301–305.

Mayer, L. E. S., Roberto, C. A., Glasofer, D. R., Etu, S. F., Gallagher, D., Wang, J., Heymsfield, S. B., Pierson, Jr., R. N., Attia, E., Devlin, M. J., & Walsh, B. T. (2007). Does percent body fat predict outcome in anorexia nervosa? *American Journal of Psychiatry, 164*(6), 970–972.

Mayer, L. E. S., Klein, D. A., Black, E., Attia, E., Shen, W., Mao, X., Shungu, D. C., Punyanita, M., Gallagher, D., Wang, J., Heymsfield, S. B., Hirsch, J., Ginsberg, H. N., & Walsh, B. T. (2009). Adipose tissue distribution after weight restoration and weight maintenance in women with anorexia nervosa. *The American Journal of Clinical Nutrition.* doi:10.3945/ajcn.2009.27820.

Mehler, P. S., & Andersen, A. E. (2010). *Eating disorders: A guide to medical care and complications.* Baltimore, OH: Johns Hopkins University Press.

Mehler, P. S., & MacKenzie, T. D. (2009). Treatment of osteopenia and osteoporosis in anorexia nervosa: A systematic review of the literature. *International Journal of Eating Disorders, 42*(3), 195–201.

Mehler, P. S., Winkelman, A. B., Andersen, D. M., & Gaudiani, J. L. (2010). Nutritional rehabilitation: Practical guidelines for refeeding the anorectic patient. *Journal of Nutrition and Metabolism.* doi:10.1155/2010/625782.

Miller, K. K., Grinspoon, S. K., Ciampa, J., Hier, J., Herzog, D., & Klibanski, A. (2005). Medical findings in outpatients with anorexia nervosa. *Archives of Internal Medicine, 165*(5), 561–566.

Misra, M., Soyka, L. A., Miller, K. K., Grinspoon, S., Levitsky, L. L., & Klibanski, A. (2003). Regional body composition in adolescents with anorexia nervosa and changes with weight recovery. *The American Journal of Clinical Nutrition, 77*(6), 1361–1367.

Nicholls, D., Hudson, L., & Mahomed, F. (2011). Managing anorexia nervosa. *Archives of Disease in Childhood, 96*(10), 977–982. doi:10.1136/adc.2009.177394.

Olmsted, M. P., McFarlane, T. L., Carter, J. C., Trottier, K., Woodside, D. B., & Dimitropoulos, G. (2010). Inpatient and day hospital treatment for anorexia nervosa. In C. Grilo, & J. E. Mitchell (Eds.), *The treatment of eating disorders: A clinical handbook* (pp. 211). New York: Guilford Press.

Peat, C., Mitchell, J. E., Hoek, H. W., & Wonderlich, S. A. (2009). Validity and utility of subtyping anorexia nervosa. *International Journal of Eating Disorders, 42*(7), 590–594. doi:10.1002/eat.20717.

Pike, K. M., Carter, J. C., & Olmsted, M. P. (2010). Cognitive–behavioral therapy for anorexia nervosa. In C. Grilo, & J. E. Mitchell (Eds.), *The treatment of eating disorders: A clinical handbook* (pp. 83–107). New York: Guilford Press.

Polito, A., Fabbri, A., Ferro-Luzzi, A., Cuzzolaro, M., Censi, L., Ciarapica, D., Fabbrini, E., & Giannini, D. (2000). Basal metabolic rate in anorexia nervosa: Relation to body composition and leptin concentrations. *The American Journal of Clinical Nutrition, 71*(6), 1495–1502.

Powers, P. S., & Thompson, R. A. (2007). Athletes and eating disorders. In J. Yager, & P. S. Powers (Eds.), *Clinical manual of eating disorders* (pp. 357–382). Washington, DC: American Psychiatric Publications.

Rigaud, D., Verges, B., Colas-Linhart, N., Petiet, A., Moukkaddem, M., Van Wymel-beke, V., & Brondel, L. (2007). Hormonal and psychological factors linked to the increased thermic effect of food in malnourished fasting anorexia nervosa. *Journal of Clinical Endocrinology & Metabolism, 92*(5), 1623–1629. doi:10.1210/jc.2006-1319.

Roberto, C. A., Mayer, L. E. S., Brickman, A. M., Barnes, A., Muraskin, J., Yeung, L.-K., Steffener, J., Sy, M., Hirsch, J., Stern, Y., & Walsh, B. T. (2011). Brain tissue volume changes following weight gain in adults with anorexia nervosa. *International Journal of Eating Disorders, 44*(5), 406–411. doi:10.1002/eat.20840.

Robinson, P. H. (2000). The gastrointestinal tract in eating disorders. *European Eating Disorders Review, 8*(2), 88–97.

Rock, C. L. (2010). Nutritional rehabilitation for anorexia nervosa. In C. Grilo, & J. E. Mitchell (Eds.), *The treatment of eating disorders: A clinical handbook* (pp. 187–197). New York: Guilford Press.

Royal College of Psychiatrists. (2005). *Guidelines for the nutritional management of anorexia nervosa*. London: Royal College of Psychiatrists.

Santonastaso, P., & Sala, A. (1998). Water intoxication in anorexia nervosa: A case report. *International Journal of Eating Disorders, 24*(4), 439–442.

Schebendach, J. E., Mayer, L. E., Devlin, M. J., Attia, E., Contento, I. R., Wolf, R. L., & Walsh, B. T. (2008). Dietary energy density and diet variety as predictors of outcome in anorexia nervosa. *The American Journal of Clinical Nutrition, 87*(4), 810–816.

Schulze, U., Schuler, S., Schlamp, D., Schneider, P., & Mehler-Wex, C. (2010). Bone mineral density in partially recovered early onset anorexic patients—a follow-up investigation. *Child and Adolescent Psychiatry and Mental Health, 4*(20). doi:10.1186/1753-2000-4-20.

Setnick, J. (2010). Micronutrient deficiencies and supplementation in anorexia and bulimia nervosa: A review of literature. *Nutrition in Clinical Practice, 25*(2), 137–142. doi:10.1177/0884533610361478.

Stanga, Z., Brunner, A., Leuenberger, M., Grimble, R. F., Shenkin, A., Allison, S. P., & Lobo, D. N. (2008). Nutrition in clinical practice—the refeeding syndrome: Illustrative cases and guidelines for prevention and treatment. *European Journal of Clinical Nutrition, 62*(6), 687–694. doi:10.1038/sj.ejcn.1602854.

Steffen, K. J., Mitchell, J. E., Roerig, J. L., & Lancaster, K. L. (2007). The eating disorders medicine cabinet revisited: A clinician's guide to ipecac and laxatives. *International Journal of Eating Disorders, 40*(4), 360–368. doi:10.1002/eat.20365.

Sum, M., Mayer, L., & Warren, M. P. (2011). Bone mineral density accrual determines energy expenditure with refeeding in anorexia nervosa and supersedes return of menses. *Journal of Osteoporosis, 2011*(720328). doi:10.4061/2011/720328.

Sunday, S. R., & Halmi, K. A. (2003). Energy intake and body composition in anorexia and bulimia nervosa. *Physiology & Behavior, 78*(1), 11–17. doi:10.1016/S0031-9384(02)00879-X.

Thompson, R. A., & Sherman, R. T. (2010). *Eating disorders in sport*. New York: Routledge.

Treasure, J., Schmidt, U. & Macdonald, P. (2010). *The clinician's guide to collaborative caring in eating disorders: The new Maudsley method*. New York: Routledge.

Van Wymelbeke, V., Brondel, L., Marcel Brun, J., & Rigaud, D. (2004). Factors associated with the increase in resting energy expenditure during refeeding in malnourished anorexia nervosa patients. *The American Journal of Clinical Nutrition, 80*(6), 1469–1477.

Waldholtz, B. D., & Andersen, A. E. (1990). Gastrointestinal symptoms anorexia nervosa. A prospective study. *Gastroenterology, 98*(6), 1415–1419.

Waterhous, T. & Jacob, M. A. (2011) Nutrition intervention in the treatment of eating disorders. Practice paper of the American Dietetic Association. Available from http://www.eatright.org/Members/content.aspx?id=6442464620.

Yamashita, S., Kawai, K., Yamanaka, T., Inoo, T., Yokoyama, H., Morita, C., Takii, M. & Kubo, C. (2010). BMI, body composition, and the energy requirement for body weight gain in patients with anorexia nervosa. *International Journal of Eating Disorders, 43*(4), 365–371. doi:10.1002/eat.20700.

Chapter 10: Treating Binge Eating

Alpers, G. W., & Tuschen-Caffier, B. (2004). Energy and macronutrient intake in bulimia nervosa. *Eating Behaviors, 5*(3), 241–249. doi:10.1016/j.eatbeh.2004.01.013.

American Psychiatric Association. (2006). Practice guideline for the treatment of patients with eating disorders. *American Psychiatric Association Practice Guidelines for the Treatment of Psychiatric Disorders Compendium 2006.* Retrieved September 15, 2012, from http://psychiatryonline.org/guidelines.aspx.

Ansell, E. B., Grilo, C. M., & White, M. A. (2012). Examining the interpersonal model of binge eating and loss of control over eating in women. *International Journal of Eating Disorders, 45*(1), 43–50. doi:10.1002/eat.20897.

Bacon, L., & Aphramor, L. (2011). Weight science: Evaluating the evidence for a paradigm shift. *Nutrition Journal, 10*, 9–22. doi:10.1186/1475-2891-10-9.

Bacon, L., Stern, J. S., Van Loan, M. D., & Keim, N. L. (2005). Size acceptance and intuitive eating improve health for obese, female chronic dieters. *Journal of the American Dietetic Association, 105*(6), 929–936. doi:10.1016/j.jada.2005.03.011.

Cooper, P. J. (2009). *Overcoming bulimia nervosa and binge-eating.* New York: Basic Books.

Cooper, Z., & Fairburn, C. G. (2010). Cognitive behavior therapy for bulimia nervosa. In C. Grilo, & J. E. Mitchell (Eds.), *The treatment of eating disorders: A clinical handbook* (p. 270). New York: Guilford Press.

Corsica, J. A., & Spring, B. J. (2008). Carbohydrate craving: a double-blind, placebo-controlled test of the self-medication hypothesis. *Eating Behaviors, 9*(4), 447–454.

Devlin, M. J., Walsh, B. T., Kral, J. G., Heymsfield, S. B., Pi-Sunyer, F. X., & Dantzic, S. (1990). Metabolic abnormalities in bulimia nervosa. *Archives of General Psychiatry, 47*(2), 144–148. doi:10.1001/archpsyc.1990.01810140044007.

Fairburn, C. G. (1995). *Overcoming binge eating.* New York: Guilford Press.

Fairburn, C. G. (2008). *Cognitive behavior therapy and eating disorders.* New York: Guilford Press.

Franz, M. J., VanWormer, J. J., Crain, A. L., Boucher, J. L., Histon, T., Caplan, W., Bowman, J. D., & Pronk, N. P. (2007). Weight-loss outcomes: A systematic review and meta-analysis of weight-loss clinical trials with a minimum 1-year follow-up. *Journal of the American Dietetic Association, 107*(10), 1755–1767. doi:10.1016/j.jada.2007.07.017.

Gorin, A. A., Niemeier, H. M., Hogan, P., Coday, M., Davis, C., DiLillo, V. G., Gluck, M. E., Wadden, T. A., West, D. S., Williamson, D., Yanovski, S. Z., & Look AHEAD Research Group. (2008). Binge eating and weight loss outcomes in overweight and obese individuals with type 2 diabetes: Results from the Look AHEAD trial. *Archives of General Psychiatry, 65*(12), 1447–1455. doi:10.1001/archpsyc.65.12.1447.

Hudson, J. I., Hiripi, E., Pope Jr., H. G., & Kessler, R. C. (2007). The prevalence and correlates of eating disorders in the national comorbidity survey replication. *Biological Psychiatry, 61*(3), 348–358. doi:10.1016/j.biopsych.2006.03.040.

Jain, A. (2005). Treating obesity in individuals and populations. *BMJ: British Medical Journal, 331*(7529), pp. 1387–1390.

Jönsson, T., Granfeldt, Y., Erlanson-Albertsson, C., Ahren, B., & Lindeberg, S. (2010). A paleolithic diet is more satiating per calorie than a Mediterranean-like diet in individuals with ischemic heart disease. *Nutrition & Metabolism, 7.* doi:10.1186/1743-7075-7-85.

Koenig, K. R. (2005). *The rules of "normal" eating: A commonsense approach for dieters, overeaters, undereaters, emotional eaters, and everyone in between!* Carlsbad, CA: Gurze Books.

Lowe, M. R., Thomas, J. G., Safer, D. L., & Butryn, M. L. (2007). The relationship of weight suppression and dietary restraint to binge eating in bulimia nervosa. *International Journal of Eating Disorders, 40*(7), 640–644. doi:10.1002/eat.20405.

Lowe, M. R., Berner, L. A., Swanson, S. A., Clark, V. L., Eddy, K. T., Franko, D. L., Shaw, J. A., Ross, S., & Herzog, D. B. (2011). Weight suppression predicts time to remission from bulimia nervosa. *Journal of Consulting and Clinical Psychology, 79*(6), 772–776. doi:10.1037/a0025714.

McElroy, S.L., Guerdjikova, A. I., Mori, N., & O'Melia, A.M. (2012). Pharmacological management of binge eating disorder: Current and emerging treatment options. *Therapeutics and Clinical Risk Management, 8,* 219-241.

Matz, J., & Frankel, E.,. (2006). *The diet survivor's handbook.* Naperville, IL: Sourcebooks.

Mehler, P. S., & Andersen, A. E. (2010). *Eating disorders: A guide to medical care and complications.* Baltimore: Johns Hopkins University Press.

Mitchell, J. E., Pomeroy, C., & Adson, D. E. (1997). Managing medical complications. In D. M. Garner & P. E. Garfinkel (Eds.), *Handbook of treatment for eating disorders* (2nd ed., pp. 383–393). New York: Guilford Press.

Neumark-Sztainer, D., Wall, M., Guo, J., Story, M., Haines, J., & Eisenberg, M. (2006). Obesity, disordered eating, and eating disorders in a longitudinal study of adolescents: How do dieters fare 5 years later? *Journal of the American Dietetic Association, 106*(4), 559–568. doi:10.1016/j.jada.2006.01.003.

Ozier, A. D., & Henry, B. W. (2011). Position of the American Dietetic Association: Nutrition intervention in the treatment of eating disorders. *Journal of the American Dietetic Association, 111*(8), 1236–1241. doi:10.1016/j.jada.2011.06.016.

Provencher, V., Bégin, C., Tremblay, A., Mongeau, L., Corneau, L., Dodin, S., Boivin, S., & Lemieux, S. (2009). Health-at-every-size and eating behaviors: 1-year follow-up results of a size acceptance intervention. *Journal of the American Dietetic Association, 109*(11), 1854–1861. doi:10.1016/j.jada.2009.08.017.

Rosenbaum, M., Hirsch, J., Gallagher, D. A., & Leibel, R. L. (2008). Long-term persistence of adaptive thermogenesis in subjects who have maintained a reduced body weight. *American Journal of Clinical Nutrition, 88,* 906–912.

Siegfried, N., & Mullins, E. (2009). *Shame on you: Shame-reduction exercises in treatment of eating disorders. Perspectives,* Summer, 13–15.

Stice, E., Davis, K., Miller, N. P., & Marti, C. N. (2008). Fasting increases risk for onset of binge eating and bulimic pathology: A 5-year prospective study. *Journal of Abnormal Psychology, 117*(4), 941–946. doi:10.1037/a0013644.

Tenconi, E., Lunardi, N., Zanetti, T., Santonastaso, P., & Favaro, A. (2006). Predictors of binge eating in restrictive anorexia nervosa patients in Italy. *Journal of Nervous Mental Disorders, 194*(9), 712–715.

Tribole, E., & Resch, E. (2012). *Intuitive eating: A revolutionary program that works* (3rd ed.). New York: St. Martin's Griffin.

Vanderlinden, J., Norreì, J., & Vandereycken, W. (1992). *A practical guide to the treatment of bulimia nervosa.* New York: Brunner/Mazel.

Weltzin, T. E., Fernstrom, M. H., Hansen, D., McConaha, C., & Kaye, W. H. (1991). Abnormal caloric requirements for weight maintenance in patients with anorexia and bulimia nervosa. *American Journal of Psychiatry, 148*(12), 1675–1682.

Wilson, G. T., Wilfley, D. E., Agras, W. S., & Bryson, S. W. (2010). Psychological treatments of binge eating disorder. *Archives of General Psychiatry, 67*(1), 94–101. doi:10.1001/archgenpsychiatry.2009.170.

Winocur, J. (1990). Nutrition therapy. In N. Piran & A. S. Kaplan (Eds.), *A day hospital group treatment program for anorexia nervosa and bulimia nervosa* (pp. 61–78). New York: Brunner/Mazel.

Wolfe, B. E., Baker, C. W., Smith, A. T., & Kelly-Weeder, S. (2009). Validity and utility of the current definition of binge eating. *International Journal of Eating Disorders, 42,* 674–686. doi:10.1002/eat.20728.

Zimmerli, E. J., Devlin, M. J., Kissileff, H. R., & Walsh, B. T. (2010). The development of satiation in bulimia nervosa. *Physiology & Behavior, 100*(4), 346–349. doi:10.1016/j.physbeh.2010.03.010.

Chapter 11: Managing Purging

Agras, W. S., & Apple, R. F. (1997). *Overcoming eating disorders: A cognitive–behavioral treatment for bulimia nervosa and binge-eating disorder: Therapist guide.* San Antonio, TX: Psychological Corporation/Graywind Publications.

Ainsworth, B. E., Haskell, W. L., Herrmann, S. D., Meckes, N., Bassett, D. R. J., Tudor-Locke, C., Greer, J. L., Vezina, J., Whitt-Glover, M. C., & Leon, A. S. (2011). 2011 compendium of physical activities: A second update of codes and MET values. *Medicine & Science in Sports & Exercise, 43*(8).

American Psychiatric Association. (2006). Practice guideline for the treatment of patients with eating disorders. In *American Psychiatric Association Practice Guidelines for the Treatment of Psychiatric Disorders Compendium 2006.* Retrieved September 15, 2012, from http://psychiatryonline.org/guidelines.aspx.

Bo-Linn, G. W., Santa Ana, C. A., Morawski, S. G., & Fordtran, J. S. (1983). Purging and calorie absorption in bulimic patients and normal women. *Annals of Internal Medicine, 99,* 14–17.

Bruce, K. R., Steiger, H., Israel, M., Kin, N. M. K. N. Y., Hakim, J., Schwartz, D., Richardson, J., & Mansour, S. A. (2011). Effects of acute alcohol intoxication on eating-related urges among women with bulimia nervosa. *International Journal of Eating Disorders, 44*(4), 333–339. doi:10.1002/eat.20834.

Carter, F. A., Mcintosh, V. V. W., Joyce, P. R., Gendall, K. A., Frampton, C. M. A., & Bulik, C. M. (2004). Patterns of weight change after treatment for bulimia nervosa. *International Journal of Eating Disorders, 36*(1), 12–21. doi:10.1002/eat.20021.

Celio, C. I., Luce, K. H., Bryson, S. W., Winzelberg, A. J., Cunning, D., Rockwell, R., Celio Doyle, A. A., Wilfley D. E., & Taylor, C. B. (2006). Use of diet pills and other dieting aids in a college population with high weight and shape concerns. *International Journal of Eating Disorders*, *39*(6), 492–497. doi:10.1002/eat.20254.

Cooper, Z., & Fairburn, C. G. (2010). Cognitive behavior therapy for bulimia nervosa. In C. Grilo, & J. E. Mitchell (Eds.). *The treatment of eating disorders: A clinical handbook* (p. 270). New York: Guilford Press.

Devlin, M. J., Walsh, B. T., Kral, J. G., Heymsfield, S. B., Pi-Sunyer, F. X., & Dantzic, S. (1990). Metabolic abnormalities in bulimia nervosa. *Archives of General Psychiatry*, *47*, 144–148.

de Zwaan, M, & Mitchell, J. E. (1993). Medical complications of anorexia nervosa and bulimia nervosa. In A. S. Kaplan & P. E. Garfinkel (Eds.), *Medical issues and the eating disorders: The interface* (pp. 60–100). New York: Brunner/Mazel.

Edler, C., Haedt, A. A., & Keel, P. K. (2007). The use of multiple purging methods as an indicator of eating disorder severity. *International Journal of Eating Disorders*, *40*(6), 515–520. doi:10.1002/eat.20416.

Fairburn, C. G. (2008). *Cognitive behavior therapy and eating disorders*. New York: Guilford Press.

Fairburn, C. G., Marcus, M. D., & Wilson, G. T. (1993). Cognitive–behavioral therapy for binge eating and bulimia nervosa: A comprehensive treatment manual. In C. G. Fairburn & G. T. Wilson (Eds.), *Binge eating: Nature, assessment and treatment* (pp. 361–404). New York: Guilford Press.

Fontana, L., Klein, S., Holloszy, J. O., & Premachandra, B. N. (2006). Effect of long-term calorie restriction with adequate protein and micronutrients on thyroid hormones. *Journal of Clinical Endocrinology & Metabolism*, *91*(8), 3232–3235. doi:10.1210/jc.2006-0328.

Garner, D. M., Rockert, W., Olmsted, M. P., Johnson, C., & Coscina, D. V. (1985). Psychoeducational principles in the treatment of bulimia and anorexia nervosa. In D. M. Garner & P. E. Garfinkel (Eds.), *Handbook of psychotherapy for anorexia nervosa & bulimia* (pp. 513–572). New York: Guilford Press.

Herzog, D. B., Keller, M. B., Lavori, P. W., & Sacks, N. R. (1991). The course and outcome of bulimia nervosa. *Journal of Clinical Psychiatry*, *52*(Suppl. 10), 4–8.

Kaye, W., Weltzin, T., Hsu, L., McConaha, C., & Bolton, B. (1993). Amount of calories retained after binge eating and vomiting. *American Journal of Psychiatry*, *150*(6), 969–971.

Khaylis, A., Trockel, M., & Taylor, C. B. (2009). Binge drinking in women at risk for developing eating disorders. *International Journal of Eating Disorders*, *42*(5), 409–414. doi:10.1002/eat.20644.

Kotler, L. A., Devlin, M. J., Matthews, D. E., & Walsh, B. T. (2001). Total energy expenditure as measured by doubly-labeled water in outpatients with bulimia nervosa. *International Journal of Eating Disorders*, *29*(4), 470–476.

Mayo Clinic. (2010). *Alli weight-loss pill: Does it work?*. Retrieved September 15, 2012, from http://www.mayoclinic.com/health/alli/WT00030.

Mehler, P. S. (2011). Medical complications of bulimia nervosa and their treatments. *International Journal of Eating Disorders*, *44*(2), 95–104. doi:10.1002/eat.20825.

Mitchell, J. E., Specker, S., & Edmonson, K. (1997). Management of substance abuse and dependence. In D. M. Garner & P. E. Garfinkel (Eds.), *Handbook of treatment for eating disorders* (2nd ed., pp. 415–423). New York: Guilford.

Pfister, R. L. (2010). Ipecac: A lesson in clinical guidelines. *The Internet Journal of Allied Health Sciences and Practice*, *8*(2).

Roerig, J. L., Mitchell, J. E., de Zwaan, M., Wonderlich, S. A., Kamran, S., Engbloom, S.,

Burgard, M., & Lancaster, K. (2003). The eating disorders medicine cabinet revisited: A clinician's guide to appetite suppressants and diuretics. *International Journal of Eating Disorders, 33*(4), 443–457.

Sedlet, K. L., & Ireton-Jones, C. S. (1989). Energy expenditure and the abnormal eating pattern of a bulimic: A case report. *Journal of the American Dietetic Association*, 89, 74–77.

Steffen, K. J., Mitchell, J. E., Roerig, J. L., & Lancaster, K. L. (2007). The eating disorders medicine cabinet revisited: A clinician's guide to ipecac and laxatives. *International Journal of Eating Disorders, 40*(4), 360–368. doi:10.1002/eat.20365.

U.S. Food and Drug Administration. (2010). DA Drug Safety Communication: Completed safety review of Xenical/Alli (orlistat) and severe liver injury. Page Last Updated: 08/02/2010. Retrieved September 25, 2012, http://www.fda.gov/Drugs/DrugSafety/PostmarketDrugSafetyInformationforPatientsandProviders/ucm213038.htm.

Vanderlinden, J., Norreì, J., & Vandereycken, W. (1992). *A practical guide to the treatment of bulimia nervosa.* New York: Brunner/Mazel.

Weltzin, T. E., Bulik, C. M , McConaha, C. W., & Kaye, W. H. (1995). Laxative withdrawal and anxiety in bulimia nervosa. *International Journal of Eating Disorders, 17*(2), 141–146.

Weltzin, T. E., Fernstrom, M. H., Hansen, D., McConaha, C., & Kaye, W. H. (1991). Abnormal caloric requirements for weight maintenance in patients with anorexia and bulimia nervosa. *American Journal of Psychiatry, 148*(12), 1675–1682.

Chapter 12: Managing Exercise

Adkins, E. C., & Keel, P. K. (2005). Does "excessive" or "compulsive" best describe exercise as a symptom of bulimia nervosa? *International Journal of Eating Disorders, 38*(1), 24–29. doi:10.1002/eat.20140.

American Psychiatric Association. (2006). Practice guideline for the treatment of patients with eating disorders. *American Psychiatric Association Practice Guidelines for the Treatment of Psychiatric Disorders Compendium 2006.* Retrieved September 15, 2012, from http://psychiatryonline.org/guidelines.aspx.

American Psychiatric Association. (2010). *DSM-5 development. Proposed revisions. Feeding and eating disorders.* Retrieved September 15, 2012, from http://www.dsm5.org/proposedrevision/Pages/FeedingandEatingDisorders.aspx.

American Psychiatric Association. (2000). *Diagnostic and statistical manual of mental disorders: DSM-IV-TR.* Washington, DC: American Psychiatric Association.

Becker, A. E., Grinspoon, S. K., Klibanski, A., & Herzog, D. B. (1999). Eating disorders. *New England Journal of Medicine, 340*(14), 1092–1098.

Beumont, P. J. V., Arthur, B., Russell, J. D., & Touyz, S. W. (1994). Excessive physical activity in dieting disorder patients: Proposals for a supervised exercise program. *International Journal of Eating Disorders, 15*(1), 21–36.

Beumont, P. J. V., Beumont, C. C., Touyz, S. W., & Williams, H. (1997). Nutritional counseling and supervised exercise. In D. M. Garner , & P. E. Garfinkel (Eds.), *Handbook of treatment for eating disorders* (2nd ed., pp. 178–187). New York: Guilford Press.

Biller, B. M. K., Saxe, V., Herzog, D. B., Rosenthal, D. I., Holzman, S., & Klibanski, A. (1989). Mechanisms of osteoporosis in adult and adolescent women with anorexia nervosa. *Journal of Clinical Endocrinology & Metabolism, 68*(3), 548–554. doi:10.1210/jcem-68-3-548.

Bratland-Sanda, S., Sundgot-Borgen, J., Rø, Ø., Rosenvinge, J. H., Hoffart, A., & Martinsen, E. W. (2010). Physical activity and exercise dependence during inpatient treatment of longstanding eating disorders: An exploratory study of excessive and non-excessive exercisers. *International Journal of Eating Disorders, 43*(3), 266–273.

Calogero, R. M., & Pedrotty, K. N. (2004). The practice and process of healthy exercise: An investigation of the treatment of exercise abuse in women with eating disorders. *Eating Disorders, 12*(4), 273–291. doi:10.1080/10640260490521352.

Cloud, J. (2009, Why exercise won't make you thin. *Time, 174*(6), 42–47.

Dalle Grave, R., Calugi, S., & Marchesini, G. (2008). Compulsive exercise to control shape or weight in eating disorders: Prevalence, associated features, and treatment outcome. *Comprehensive Psychiatry, 49*(4), 346–352. doi:10.1016/j.comppsych.2007.12.007.

Davis, C., Brewer, H., & Ratusny, D. (1993). Behavioral frequency and psychological commitment: Necessary concepts in the study of excessive exercising. *Journal of Behavioral Medicine, 16*(6), 611–628.

Davis, C., Katzman, D. K., Kaptein, S., Kirsh, C., Brewer, H., Kalmback, K., Olmsted, M. P., Woodside, D. B., & Kaplan, A. S. (1997). The prevalence of high-level exercise in the eating disorders: Etiological implications. *Comprehensive Psychiatry, 38*(6), 321–326.

De Young, K. P., & Anderson, D. A. (2010). Prevalence and correlates of exercise motivated by negative affect. *International Journal of Eating Disorders, 43*(1), 50–58. doi:10.1002/eat.20656.

DiVasta, A. D., Feldman, H. A., Quach, A. E., Balestrino, M., & Gordon, C. M. (2009). The effect of bed rest on bone turnover in young women hospitalized for anorexia nervosa: A pilot study. *Journal of Clinical Endocrinology & Metabolism, 94*(5), 1650–1655. doi:10.1210/jc.2008-1654.

Exner, C., Hebebrand, J., Remschmidt, H., Wewetzer, C., Ziegler, A., Herpertz, S., Schweiger, U., Blum, W. F., Preibisch, G., Heldmaier, G., & Klingenspor, M. (2000). Leptin suppresses semi-starvation induced hyperactivity in rats: Implications for anorexia nervosa. *Molecular Psychiatry, 5*(5), 476.

Fairburn, C. G. (2008). *Cognitive behavior therapy and eating disorders.* New York: Guilford Press.

Feingold, D., & Hame, S. L. (2006). Female athlete triad and stress fractures. *Orthopedic Clinics of North America, 37*(4), 575–583.

Garber, C. E., Blissmer, B., Deschenes, M. R., Franklin, B. A., Lamonte, M. J., Lee, I. M., Nieman, D. C., & Swain, D. P. (2011). Quantity and quality of exercise for developing and maintaining cardiorespiratory, musculoskeletal, and neuromotor fitness in apparently healthy adults: Guidance for prescribing exercise. *Medicine & Science in Sports & Exercise, 43*(7).

Goodwin, H., Haycraft, E., Willis, A., & Meyer, C. (2011). Compulsive exercise: The role of personality, psychological morbidity, and disordered eating. *International Journal of Eating Disorders, 44*(7), 655–660. doi:10.1002/eat.20902.

Klein, D. A., Schebendach, J. E., Gershkovich, M., Bodell, L. P., Foltin, R. W., & Walsh, B. T. (2010). Behavioral assessment of the reinforcing effect of exercise in women with anorexia nervosa: Further paradigm development and data. *International Journal of Eating Disorders, 43*(7), 611–618.

Krahn, D. D., Rock, C., Dechert, R. E., Nairn, K. K., & Hasse, S. A. (1993). Changes in resting energy expenditure and body composition in anorexia nervosa patients during refeeding. *Journal of the American Dietetic Association*, *93*(4), 434–438.

Lanser, E. M., Zach, K. N., & Hoch, A. Z. (2011). The female athlete triad and endothelial dysfunction. *Physical Medicine and Rehabilitation*, *3*(5), 458–465.

Mehler, P. S., & MacKenzie, T. D. (2009). Treatment of osteopenia and osteoporosis in anorexia nervosa: A systematic review of the literature. *International Journal of Eating Disorders*, *42*(3), 195–201.

Meili, T. (2004). *I am the Central Park Jogger: A Story of Hope and Possibility*. New York: Scribner.

Mond, J. M., Hay, P. J., Rodgers, B., & Owen, C. (2006). An update on the definition of "excessive exercise" in eating disorders research. *International Journal of Eating Disorders*, *39*(2), 147–153.

Nattiv, A., Loucks, A., Manore, M., Sanborn, C., Sundgot-Borgen, J., Warren, M., & American College of Sports Medicine (2007). American college of sports medicine position stand. the female athlete triad. *Medicine & Science in Sports & Exercise*, *39*(10), 1867–1882.

Olmsted, M. P., Carter, J. C., & Pike, K. M. (2012). Relapse prevention. In J. Alexander , & J. Treasure (Eds.), *A collaborative approach to eating disorders* (pp. 2001–2011). London: Routledge.

Pike, K. M., Carter, J. C., & Olmsted, M. P. (2010). Cognitive–behavioral therapy for anorexia nervosa. In C. Grilo, & J. E. Mitchell (Eds.), *The treatment of eating disorders: A clinical handbook* (pp. 83–107). New York: Guilford Press.

Pinheiro, A. P., Thornton, L. M., Plotonicov, K. H., Tozzi, F., Klump, K. L., Berrettini, W. H., Brandt, H., Crawford, S., Crow, S., Fichter, M. M., Goldman, D., Halmi, K. A., Johnson, C., Kaplan, A. S., Keel, P., LaVia, M., Mitchell, J., Rotondo, A., Strober, M., Treasure, J., Woodside, D. B., Von Holle, A., Hamer, R., Kaye, W. H., & Bulik, C. M. (2007). Patterns of menstrual disturbance in eating disorders. *International Journal of Eating Disorders*, *40*(5), 424–434. doi:10.1002/eat.20388.

Salisbury, J. J., Levine, A. S., Crow, S. J., & Mitchell, J. E. (1995). Refeeding, metabolic rate, and weight gain in anorexia nervosa: A review. *International Journal of Eating Disorders*, *17*(4), 337–345.

Seigel, K., & Hetta, J. (2001). Exercise and eating disorder symptoms among young females. *Eating and Weight Disorders*, *6*(1), 32–39.

Shroff, H., Reba, L., Thornton, L. M., Tozzi, F., Klump, K. L., Berrettini, W. H., Brandt, H., Crawford, S., Crow, S., Fichter, M. M., Goldman, D., Halmi, K. A., Johnson, C., Kaplan, A. S., Keel, P., LaVia, M., Mitchell, J., Rotondo, A., Strober, M., Treasure, J., Woodside, D. B., Kaye, W. H., & Bulik, C. M. (2006). Features associated with excessive exercise in women with eating disorders. *International Journal of Eating Disorders*, *39*(6), 454–461. doi:10.1002/eat.20247.

Steffen, J. J., & Brehm, B. J. (1999). The dimensions of obligatory exercise. *Eating Disorders*, *7*(3), 219.

Taranis, L., & Meyer, C. (2011). Associations between specific components of compulsive exercise and eating-disordered cognitions and behaviors among young women. *International Journal of Eating Disorders*, *44*(5), 452–458. doi:10.1002/eat.20838.

Thompson, R. A., & Sherman, R. T. (2010). *Eating disorders in sport*. New York: Routledge.

Treasure, J., Smith, G., & Crane, A. (2007). *Skills-based learning for caring for a loved one with an eating disorder: The new Maudsley method*. London: Routledge.

Waugh, E. J., Woodside, D. B., Beaton, D. E., Coté, P., & Hawker, G. A. (2011). Effects of exercise on bone mass in young women with anorexia nervosa. *Medicine & Science in Sports & Exercise, 43*(5), 755–763. doi:10.1249/MSS.0b013e3181ff3961.

Zunker, C., Mitchell, J. E., & Wonderlich, S. A. (2011). Exercise interventions for women with anorexia nervosa: A review of the literature. *International Journal of Eating Disorders, 44*(7), 579–584. doi:10.1002/eat.20862.

Chapter 13: Working with Families

Bulik, C. M., Baucom, D. H., Kirby, J. S., & Pisetsky, E. (2011). Uniting couples (in the treatment of) anorexia nervosa (UCAN). *International Journal of Eating Disorders, 44*(1), 19–28. doi:10.1002/eat.20790.

Campbell, M. & Schmidt, U. (2011). Cognitive–behavioral therapy for adolescent bulimia nervosa and binge-eating disorder. In D. Le Grange, & J. Lock (Eds.), *Eating disorders in children and adolescents: A clinical handbook* (pp. 305–318). New York: Guilford Press.

Ellison, R., Rhodes, P., Madden, S., Miskovic, J., Wallis, A., Baillie, A., Kohn, M., & Touyz, S. (2012). Do the components of manualized family-based treatment for anorexia nervosa predict weight gain? *International Journal of Eating Disorders, 45*(4), 609–614. doi:10.1002/eat.22000.

Herrin, M., & Matsumoto, N. (2007). *The parent's guide to eating disorders: Supporting self-esteem, healthy eating, & positive body image at home.* Carlsbad, CA: Gürze Books.

Hoste, R. R., Stiles-Shields, C., Labushagnee, Z, & Le Grange, D. (2012). Family-based treatment for eating disorders: where are we now?, *Perspectives*, Winter, 10–12.

Le Grange, D. (2011). Family-based treatment for bulimia nervosa. In D. Le Grange, & J. Lock (Eds.), *Eating disorders in children and adolescents: A clinical handbook* (pp. 291–304). New York: Guilford Press.

Le Grange, D., & Eisler, I. (2009). Family interventions in adolescent anorexia nervosa. *Child and Adolescent Psychiatric Clinics of North America, 18*(1), 159–173. doi:10.1016/j.chc.2008.07.004.

Le Grange, D., & Lock, J. (2007). *Treating bulimia in adolescents: a family-based approach.* New York: Guilford Press.

Le Grange, D., Crosby, R. D., Rathouz, P. J., & Leventhal, B. L. (2007). A randomized controlled comparison of family-based treatment and supportive psychotherapy for adolescent bulimia nervosa. *Archives of General Psychiatry, 64*(9), 1049–1056. doi:10.1001/archpsyc.64.9.1049.

Lock, J. (2011). Family-based treatment for anorexia nervosa. In D. Le Grange, & J. Lock (Eds.), *Eating disorders in children and adolescents: A clinical handbook* (pp. 223–242). New York: Guilford Press.

Lock, J., Le Grange, D., Agras, W. S., & Dare, C. (2001). *Treatment manual for anorexia nervosa: A family-based approach.* New York: Guilford Press.

Lock, J., Le Grange, D., Agras, W. S., Moye, A., Bryson, S. W., & Jo, B. (2010). Randomised clinical trial comparing family-based treatment with adolescent-focused individual therapy for adolescents with anorexia nervosa. *Archives of General Psychiatry, 67*(10), 1025–1032.

Strober, M. and Johnson, C. (2012). The need for complex ideas in anorexia nervosa: Why biology, environment, and psyche all matter, why therapists make mistakes, and why clinical benchmarks are needed for managing weight correction. *International Journal of Eating Disorders, 45*(2), 155–178. doi:10.1002/eat.22005.

INDEX

generalized anxiety disorder 68
genetics: and binge eating 230; and
    biologically appropriate weight 74,
    170; and eating disorders 3
goal setting 40, 49–51; *see also* weight
    goals
Golden, N. H. et al. 216
Goodman, L. J. 73
Graves, L. 45
grazing 24
Greenblat, J. 226
Greene, G. W. et al. 33
guided self-help 244
guiding 98
Guisinger, S. 134

Haas, V. K. et al. 12
hair in anorexia nervosa 13
Halmi, K. A. 55
Health at Every Size 239
Health Insurance Portability and
    Accountability Act of 1996
    (HIPPA) 35, 36; guidelines
    form 300–1
healthy activity 260–1
healthy eating obsessives 5t
healthy exercise 260, 261
Heffner, M. 99
height: measurement 189; in puberty 174
Hill, L. S. et al. 45
homework 51, 52–3, 54
hope 48
hormonal changes in anorexia nervosa 7,
    8t
hunger and fullness: in binge eating 15,
    232–3, 238; in food planning 133–5;
    in weight restoration 197–8
hydration 253, 257
hypercarotenemia 13–14
hypoglycemia 5t, 194
hypokalemia 21, 196
hypomagnesemia 196
hypophosphatemia 195

ideal body weight (IBW) 180–1
idealization 65
in-patient hospitalization 151, 153–4
initial session: beginning 35–43;
    (collaborative relationship 37–9, 44;
    confidentiality 35, 36–7; rapport 42–
    3; rolling with resistance 39–42,
    50, 61); middle 43–51; (assessing
    the problem 43–4; diagnosis 44–7;

expectations 48–9; goal setting 40,
    49–51); end 52
insurance *see* Health Insurance Portability
    and Accountability Act of 1996
    (HIPPA); third-party reimbursement
    issues
introduction packets 35–6; authorization
    for release of confidential
    information 299–300; financial
    agreement form 303; HIPPA
    guidelines form 300–1; patient
    information form 302
Intuitive Eating 239
ipecac 247
Ireton-Jones, C. S. 253

Jacob, M. A. x, 27, 195
Johnson, C. 279
Johnson, C. L. et al. 158

Kaplan, A. S. 215
Kater, K. 99
Kaye, W. et al. 252
Keel, P. K. et al. 24, 158, 263
Kellogg, M. 35, 56, 57, 64, 65
ketosis 134, 135, 233
Keys, A. et al. 12–13, 193
Kingsbury, K. B. 76
Klein, D. A. et al. 275
Koenig, K. R. 171, 176
Kratina, K. et al. 76
Kristeller, J. L. 88

lapses 156
laxative abuse 247; anorexia nervosa 23;
    bulimia nervosa 21, 22t, 23; caloric
    absorption 252; and gastrointestinal
    problems 10, 196; halting use 255,
    257; psychotherapy 259; *see also*
    purging; purging management
Le Grange, D. 277, 281, 296
levels of care 150–66; Level 1: outpatient
    care 151–2; Level 2: intensive
    outpatient program 151, 152; Level 3:
    full-day outpatient care 151, 152–3;
    Level 4: residential treatment 151, 153;
    Level 5: inpatient hospitalization 151,
    153–4; recovery 54, 57, 158;
    relapse 57, 156–8; third-party
    reimbursement issues 158–66;
    transition from inpatient to
    outpatient 154–6
listening 37, 44, 95–6